W9-ADM-660

Roots of Strategy

Book 3

0 11557 03060 0

Roots of Strategy

Book 3

3 Military Classics

von Leeb's DEFENSE
von Freytag-Loringhoven's
THE POWER OF PERSONALITY IN WAR
Erfurth's SURPRISE

Stackpole Books

Copyright © 1991 by Stackpole Books

Published by
STACKPOLE BOOKS
5067 Ritter Road
Mechanicsburg, PA 17055

Cover design by Caroline Miller

Printed in the United States of America

First Edition

10   9   8   7   6   5

Library of Congress Cataloging-in-Publication Data
(Revised for volumes 2 & 3)

Roots of strategy.

    Includes index.
    Contents: [Bk. 1]. The art of war / by Sun Tzu.
The military institutions of the Romans / by Vegetius.
My reveries on the art of war / by Maurice de Saxe.
The instruction of Frederick the Great for his
generals. The military maxims of Napoleon. — Bk. 2.
Battle studies / by Ardant du Picq. Principles of
war / by Carl von Clausewitz. Jomini's Art of war. —
Bk. 3. Von Leeb's Defense. Von Freytag-Loringhoven's
The power of personality in war. Erfurth's Surprise.
    1. Strategy.   2. Military art and science.
I. Phillips, Thomas Raphael, 1892–
U161.R66   1985   355.02   84-26685
ISBN 0-8117-2194-9 (v. 1)

CONTENTS

DEFENSE

Field Marshal General Ritter von Leeb

First translation, 1943,
by
Dr. Stefan T. Possony
and
Daniel Vilfroy

CONTENTS

Foreword

THE principles of conduct of war and conduct of combat as expounded in this book by Field Marshal General Ritter Wilhelm von Leeb were written only a few years before the present war.

Von Leeb realistically and meticulously examined and re-examined the existing conceptions of defense to analyze what of value remained from World War I. He originally published his theories in the Militarwissenschaftliche Rundschau ("The Scientific Military Review") of the German War Office. They were later issued in book form, under the title Die Abwehr, in Berlin in 1938, and appear for the first time in English translation in this work.

In his DEFENSE von Leeb, as a military thinker and scientist, comparable to any of the outstanding authorities of the old German army—Schlieffen, Falkenhayn, Groner, Seeckt, etc.—offered his government a plan for the next war in which Germany might be engaged. It is estimated by competent judges as probably "the most important piece of research in the field of strategy and tactics in modern warfare that has appeared in a decade."

The substance of von Leeb's theories was developed in parallel and simultaneously in Berlin and Moscow. Some of the ideas were included in the 1936 Soviet Field Service Regulations. However, according to Max Werner*, Hitler rejected von Leeb's plan, while the Russian army in 1941 fought under it and stopped the Germans.

Von Leeb's recommendation was that the war be opened with active defense, as a preparation for the offensive later. He wrote in DEFENSE:

**The Great Offensive,* by Max Werner. Copyright, The Viking Press, New York.

"*Since in any war to come we* [*Germany*] *cannot count on numerical superiority or superiority in war materials, the defense must help to support and prepare the attack, which can alone bring a decision. In event of the enemy's absolute superiority, his strength and power must be worn down.*"

His plan of defense was to be adjusted in accordance with the enemy's war plan, with the object of maintaining a successful defense against it, for, as he wrote:

"*We know that defense is dependent upon attack. It must be adapted to the measures of the aggressor. Its state is that of operative and tactical dependence upon the attacker in war, in an operation or in an engagement.*"

Defense is aimed at attaining a shift in favor of the defender in the balance of power.

"*More than ever before, the defense is in a position to serve its original purpose, on account of its increased power. The purpose is to break the strength of the attacker, to parry his blows, to weaken him and to bleed him white. The reversal of strength resulting from this will enable the defender himself to acquire the strength to attack.*"

In emphasizing the importance of having at all times ample reserves in readiness, von Leeb says:

"*In the final analysis the question of which side can maintain fresh reserves decides the success of the defense as well as that of the break-through.*"

Use of weapons of offense is required in the defense.

"*The defense, as well as the attack, can put aviation and speedily-moving units of all sorts to excellent use. They certainly can mitigate, even neutralize, perhaps, the advantages possessed by the offensive in tanks and planes. Weapons of the same kind must be opposed by operative defense to an attack by such arms and weapons. These are needed by the defense as well as the attack.*"

Strategy of attrition against a stronger enemy is urged by him.

"*The first aim, when the enemy has great superiority, is to reduce the disproportion by strategy of delaying combat; a strategy of attrition that has for its purpose the weakening of the enemy to a point where one is strong enough to attack.*"

Two combat forms are placed by von Leeb to the fore-front of effective modern defensive strategy, i.e.: battle in depth and systematic cooperation between different service arms.

"*Mobility in grouping, deep rear organization, are demanded by tactical defense. Also formations in deep echelon. By these one is enabled to absorb enemy surprise actions, to slow up the attack and entangle the enemy in an advanced defense network, to deprive him of his strength and, above all, to gain time for countermeasures. New weapons and means of combat, fast units, aviation, the broad use of all kinds of artificial obstacles are today in a position to make the defense more varied, more mobile, to take it away from rigid linear forms of trench warfare and to organize it in depth.*

"*Coordination of all arms and means is a basic condition for full utilization of every defense possibility. In our war experience, 1914-18, we learned the meaning of close co-operation amongst all infantry arms and between artillery and infantry. But before an enemy equipped with strong armored forces, this cooperation is no longer sufficient. It now must be augmented by a uniform plan of antitank defense; employment of all means of reconnaissance, use of artificial obstacles of all kinds, combined use of all offensive arms, the preparation and use of reserves, armored units, aviation. Not one arm alone nor one method by itself brings the decision. Cooperation amongst all of them is necessary.*"

Von Leeb, known as the "Family-Tree General" because of his authorship of the Chronicle of the von Leeb Family, is an aristocrat famed for his austerity and forbidding personality.

"*If von Leeb ever tried to smile, it would crack his face,*" *his friend, Marshal Siegmund Wilhelm List, said of him.*

Von Leeb was born in 1872 and christened Wilhelm Joseph Franz. He entered the Bavarian 4th Artillery Regiment at the age of 19, fought at Peking in 1900 during the Boxer uprising and, after special training at the War Academy, was assigned to the Prussian General Staff. At the beginning of World War I, von Leeb was a captain on the General Staff of the 2d Bavarian Army Corps and served with the 11th Bavarian Infantry Division on the Western Front. At the time of the Armistice, he was attached to the army group commanded by Crown Prince Rupert of Bavaria. He received the Max Josef Bavarian Military Order and after the revolution helped crush the red government in Bavaria.

After the war, he remained on the General Staff, where he was steadily promoted. He received two successive troop commands: those of the 7th Division in Munich and Army Group II in Cassel. He was promoted General of artillery in 1934 and, after 42 years of service, was retired at 62 with the rank of Colonel General.

World War II saw him recalled to active duty. He did not play a prominent role in the Campaign of France, because he was not assigned to a decisive sector. The laurels went to his colleague and rival, General von Kleist, who commanded the army group that broke the spine of the French resistance by winning the premier successes of all modern wars: Sedan, Montherme, Dinant. Von Leeb, the great advocate of extensive and economical defense under certain conditions, was assigned to a defensive job. His was the successful task of tying up the French forces entrenched on the Maginot Line, so as to prevent their being switched to the critical zone of operations further west. Not until the French forces were in full disintegration did General Weygand give the order to retreat.

Von Leeb chose this moment to attack and accelerate the French rout. The great strategical barrier of the Rhine on June 15th was crossed by his troops, which used smoke screens and were helped by a powerful artillery. Von Leeb exploited his success and crushed the French defense in

*Alsace-Lorraine. In July, 1940, he obtained the rank of
Field Marshal General. He was also given the Knight's
Cross of the Iron Cross.*

Field Marshal von Leeb's great contribution to the German
blitz campaigns of World War II was the brilliant action of
the northern group of armies he commanded against Russia
from June 22, 1941. He carried the initial main effort against
65 Russian divisions concentrated north of the Pinsk marshes
and defeated them in a series of swift and powerful engagements centered around Kaunas, which recall the typical
battle on the inner lines fought at Tannenberg in 1914.

The objectives of his army group were the seizure of
Lithuania, the break-through of the Stalin Line and the capture of Leningrad. The Russian northern group had pushed
too far away from its bases, in a flat country without any
serious strategical obstacles. Of its 65 divisions, 50 had
been sent west of the Niemen River, with the probable intention of starting an offensive. It was surprised by the
swift German attack, forced into disorderly retreat and split
into helpless and awkward masses which one by one became
isolated and were reduced. The situation as it developed
offered to the Germans an ideal repetition of the Tannenberg
battle. The Russian northern group could not be helped by
the southern group from which it was cut off by the Pinsk
marshes.

Von Leeb's advance was well prepared and thought out.
His enemy was paralyzed by a tremendous bludgeon blow in
the air which destroyed many planes on the ground and interrupted their communications with the rear, thus forbidding
any timely intervention from the Stalin Line. Then the
Lithuanians revolted, seized Kaunas and Vilna and destroyed
depots. They held both cities with 10,000 insurgents until
the arrival of the German panzers.

The main German thrust was delivered from the north
against the Russian concentration around Kaunas. It suc-

ceeded completely. The defenders then retreated around Minsk, where a great panzer battle took place. The Germans displayed their ability to utilize the tanks en masse. Counter-attacking with their infantry in dense waves of 10 successive firing lines, the Russians were mowed down with terrific losses.

Quick reorganization after their victories at Kaunas and Minsk allowed a renewed German advance. The Stalin Line consisted of a series of towns and centers of communication organized in strongholds of resistance, such as Dvinsk, Polotsk, Vitevsk, Mogilev and, after the Pinsk marshes, Korosten. They were insufficiently held, a good part of the troops having been sent forward. At the beginning of July, 1941, the Germans were already in contact with this defensive zone. The Russians had not destroyed the bridges, hoping to use them in saving the forces sent west. The German advance surprised the defenders in full period of installation, awaiting the arrival of reinforcements from the east. Against this insufficient preparation, the plane-gun-tank combination reduced the strongholds one by one. Von Leeb had proved that a complete defeat could be inflicted upon an enemy numerically superior, having a greater quantity of armored matériel, but allowing himself to be surprised strategically, outmaneuvered and constantly outgunned. (The Russians committed the same mistakes as the French in 1940.)

Having broken through the Stalin Line on August 21, 1941, von Leeb assembled an army of 300,000 infantrymen, four divisions of shock troops, 1000 tanks and 1000 planes at Leningrad. Two months later, Russia's second city and key stronghold of the entire northern theater of operations, was surrounded. But he failed to take it. The Russian national flag still flew over the former Czarist capital in September 1942, when the Russians broke through the first lines of German defenses in an attempt to raise the siege.

There have been reports that the Marshal offered his

resignation and had been replaced. In spite of this lack of success at the hands of the energetic Russian people, von Leeb deserves to be considered one of the outstanding strategists of World War II.

INTRODUCTION

THE attack suits the soldier better than defense. All war-like and fighting virtues such as daring, decision, courage, offensive spirit, destructive will and self-confidence are awakened by, and take their full value from, offensive action. These virtues repel influences—such as chance, incertitude, doubt, irresolution, hesitancy, the unforeseen—which affect the conduct of battle and the conduct of war. But also they make their success questionable.

"If prudence should be the particular genius of defense, audacity and confidence belong to offense," says Clausewitz.

The moral power of self-confidence, of initiative, make the offensive superior to the defensive. The attacker feels superior in power and will.

That is why the offensive is the force which, in the conduct of war and combat proper, wins the decision. It fulfills the primary aim of war; forces the enemy down, vanquishes him, compels him to give way and makes him disposed to accept peace.

[TRANSLATORS' NOTE: One has to distinguish, indeed, between conduct of war and conduct of combat. 1. Conduct of war is on the strategic level; the Germans would say operational level, because it involves not only mere disposition of forces in view of future operations, but also all problems of transportation, supply, etc. Conduct of combat is confined to the tactical level where one's forces are already facing the enemy on the terrain. 2. Both are not always in accord with each other. What may bring success on a certain sector of operations may not be useful to the success of global strategy. A general-in-chief has, as it were, a certain budget in personnel and matériel. The repartition of means and weapons at his disposal is of a decisive importance. History abounds in instances of victories rendered useless through an inadequate division of forces.]

The very essence of defense is distinctly opposed to that of offense.

Defense, to say the least, is forced waiting. It tries to

13

anticipate the intentions and activities of the attacker, so as to take the proper measures. Hence, defense depends upon the moves of the attacker. It springs from a feeling of weakness, of moral and numerical inferiority.

"Defense is mostly the necessary recourse of distress; the defenders are nearly always in a critical position." So Clausewitz sets out the defensive.

Defense vs. Offense

Clausewitz depicts defense as "the stronger form"; offense as "the weaker one." This interpretation can best be understood, from the point of view of actually conducting a combat, in the following manner: The activities of the attacker mainly are those of movement and fire. During his advance the attacker generally can make no use of his own arms. While advancing he becomes an open target for the fire of the defender, whose activity consists in fire, not in movement. The defender finds a favorable terrain, digs in, hides and protects himself from losses. These advantages of tactical defense are transferred to the strategic defense.

"The aim of the defensive is to hold; that of the offensive, to win. It is easier to hold than to win."

Since defense is thus the "stronger form," if only in a figurative sense, it is used by the weaker combatant, or the one who feels weaker or who does not believe he has sufficient superiority, so indispensable for attack. By means of this "stronger form"—the defensive—he desires to attain a compensation in forces and exhaust the attacker, until such time as he judges himself strong enough to take the offensive, which is the only form that gains the decision.

"One should make use of the defensive, which has a negative aim, only when one must resort to it because of weakness; but it must be abandoned so soon as one is strong enough to conceive the positive aim." (Clausewitz)

A decision through defense alone, is conceivable only when the attacker is so exhausted that he renounces any continuation of the war or combat, even in a defensive way. When such a case presents itself, the "strategy of exhaustion"—about which there was so much discussion both before 1914 and after 1918—has fulfilled its object. However, in the hostilities between valorous nations, one could not very well count upon such a breakdown of will-power, especially when it involves the survival or complete annihilation of a people.

A courageous foe can be forced down only through force. Warlike, fighting strength reaches its peak in the tactical and strategic attack. Only in the offensive can those previously mentioned warlike virtues be best displayed. The offensive hence corresponds better than the defensive to what constitutes the very essence of the soldier.

Defensive Cannot be Eliminated

From all this, one might infer that in the conduct both of war and combat one should utilize only the offensive as the surest means of attaining success. Unfortunately, however, this is not the case; nor is it possible, when considering the problems of the nations involved and the particular conditions of the combat. Neither in the conduct of war nor of combat can the defensive be eliminated.

Thus, the art of war depends first upon the reasons which brought it about and the aims to be fulfilled after the successful cessation of hostilities; further, on the ways and means put at the disposal of those responsible for the conduct of war or combat; and finally, on the possibilities of replacement of personnel and matériel. "The less great the political aim, the less important our efforts." (Clausewitz)

With armies numbering millions and the corresponding requirements in ammunition, it is impossible to resort to constant attack. Winter and impassable mountains can render attacking impossible.

There are other reasons which divert combatants from offensive warfare and compel them to be satisfied with a more sluggish conduct of hostilities, or a "strategy of manoeuvering." Those reasons lie in the impossibility of replacing necessaries, dependence upon reserve stores, the unreliability of mercenaries—mostly foreigners who lack a true feeling for the country on the side of which they are arrayed.

"To us Germans, defense has a particular significance, because in all the wars which had to be fought since the time of Frederick the Great, we found ourselves obviously on the defensive—politically as well as militarily—on account of our geographical position."

Frederick the Great had to defend himself, with his small band of Prussians, against the attacks of a considerably superior force. In the wars of liberation, we had to reconquer our lost political freedom. In 1870-71, the pretentions of the French had to be repelled. In World War I, we had to defend ourselves, as did Frederick the Great, against a world of enemies.

G. H. Q. Memorandum

G. H. Q. sized up the general political situation of Germany, [internationally] before World War I in a memorandum dated December 12, 1912, which was sent to the Chancellor. It was couched thus concisely: "Russia has the understandable desire to implant herself, through the downfall of Austria, as the predominant Slav power in Europe. France wants to reconquer her lost provinces and take revenge for her fall in 1870. England wishes, with the help of her allies, to free herself from the nightmare of German seapower."

All these "wishes' could be satisfied only by an attack upon Germany. But Germany had no desire either to expand her territory, or to acquire sea hegemony.

Together with political encirclement, went a military predominance of the Triple Alliance, which directed all its forces toward the exterior. France levied, before the war, an average of 83% of her enrolled men; Germany, only

54%. The German G. H. Q. counted the respective forces of both sides, thus:

    Germany and the Central Powers
        would have .... 3,547,000 men
    Our enemies would have .... 5,856,000 men

As events proved, this data corresponded closely to the truth.

To this military superiority on the enemy side was added the particularly unfavorable geographical position of Germany. Her frontiers, both in the east and west, were almost open and scarcely protected by nature. East Prussia, situated farther east, was vulnerable to attack by Russia. Access from overseas—except the Baltic Sea—was easy to bar. Our military means, already inferior in themselves, had to create fronts on five sides.

The political, military and geographical positions of Germany pointed entirely towards the defensive. Our country had to face a political and military supremacy which threatened her existence as a nation and ours, as a people.

We have thus to show which conceptions—strategic for the conduct of war and tactical for the conduct of combat proper—prevailed in this defense, and to what extent the will to carry on a decisive war was linked with these conceptions.

Then, by examples drawn from World War I it will be shown to what extent these conceptions of strategic and tactical defense were verified in the hostilities and exposed to changes and other developments.

Finally, the defense must be discussed in the light of its present day effectiveness.

[TRANSLATORS' NOTE: The Germans have always been haunted by the idea of encirclement; and since the true father of their nationalistic policy is Frederick the Great it is not to be wondered that this foremost preoccupation started with him. It has ever been present in the minds of the military caste as the *postulatum* upon which they built their operation plans. This explains why they are past-masters in the art of conducting operations on the inner lines.

There is one most curious aspect of German psychology: They consider themselves most unfortunate that nature and historical developments have put the Vaterland in the position in which it is. They sadly complain about it and seek to provoke the pity of understanding peoples throughout the world. At the same time they are more than ready, not only to take advantage of it, but to abuse it and utilize to the fullest all of the enormous strategic possibilities their geographic position procures them. It can be observed that in each war Germany assails brusquely by surprise an enemy on one side; then, having had time to cope with the first enemy, she turns around and deals with the remaining foe.

In peacetime, the German statesmen have successfully made theirs the Clausewitz axiom: War is but "the continuation of policy by means of force." Offensives cannot be undertaken on all fronts. In the conduct of war there is a full-scale and mass attack on one well-chosen front, but a general defensive elsewhere. Under "peace" conditions, we - have seen full-scale pressure and threats against one country, well chosen for the purpose, but cajoleries and *"finassieren"* elsewhere. General von Leeb explains very well why no other conduct is possible.

Let us now examine this situation of encirclement of Germany in World War II. From the very beginning, Hitler has had a war on two fronts, and there is a definite parallel in situations in 1914 and in 1939. At the outset of both hostilities, the German General Staff thought that victory could be won quickest on the western front. Germany had to temporize in the east; the non-aggression pact with Russia of August 23, 1939, gave her a free hand to liquidate Poland and to proceed immediately with the war against France and Great Britain.

But she had to purchase the time necessary to insure the

defeat of her western enemies by selling space to the enemy in the east. The Germans in 1914 were ready to give up East Prussia; in 1939 and 1940 they abandoned half of Poland, the Baltic states, and strategic positions in Finland and Bessarabia. In spite of repeated difficulties arising in settlements with Russia, Germany avoided trouble because she did not forget that her major mission was the overthrow of France and Great Britain in the west. From this end she could not afford to divert substantial strength.

The German General Staff knows that a war on two fronts or an operation on inner lines cannot be successful unless one enemy is thoroughly defeated. The Germans in 1914 failed to defeat the French at the Battle of the Marne. In 1940 the French were knocked out before the Russians could intervene, but the skill and courage of the British won the Battle of Britain. There is now no doubt whatever that in World War II the opposite number of the Battle of the Marne was the Battle of Britain; it marked the first essential turning point of the war.

The Germans have confessed to being surprised by the swift disintegration of the French armies. They had not conceived in advance the matériel and preparations needed for the invasion of England. With their systematic thoroughness they wanted to prepare for landings on the British coast. But they had not studied in time the special problems of cooperation between the navy, the task-forces of swift landing-barges and of the air force, in which the Japanese were so well versed. But after Dunkirk they tackled the training at once. Off the French coast, groups of barges loaded with shock troops underwent frequent exercises. Numbers of them even ran into trouble, having been discovered by British planes. The British took the exercises seriously, sprayed the surface of the sea with inflammable liquid and ignited it. Numerous German soldiers were burned to death.

The German General Staff thought they would be able

to knock out the English by a gigantic bludgeon blow in the air, which they had prepared. But they did not dare to launch a full-scale land and air invasion for which they had not well prepared. They did not take the risk of sacrificing perhaps 100,000 men, although they showed later that they were willing to lose more than that number to capture a stronghold like Stalingrad. When they opened their air blitz England had only 80 old tanks and 2 divisions fit for combat. But every day lost in a retarded conquest rendered the German task more difficult and hazardous. In these crucial and tense moments the Royal Air Force shot down German bombers by the hundreds, hampered their bombings and made them largely ineffective. The United States, realizing that the fight of England was waged on the second line of resistance of the American continent, supplied a considerable contribution to the British defense, the transfer of destroyers being only the most spectacular help.

Hitler felt he had to render his rear secure before concentrating all his military forces against England. Russia was by no means a reliable ally. She had considerably infringed upon the terms of the midnight agreement of the 28th of September, 1940, which delimited the territories to be taken and controlled by both nations. She had definitely made clear on the 13th of November, 1940, at the meeting of Molotov with Hitler in Berlin, that she wanted to stay neutral and not join the "unconquerable coalition against the plutocratic governments." She had even then dared to express precisely to Hitler her intention of occupying Finland, Rumania, Bulgaria, and Istanbul. The war in the east was decided then. Here is what Goering said about the Russian infringements in a speech on the 20th of May, 1942:

"Slowly the Russian columns penetrated, first in the north against Finland. In the south, they took over Rumanian positions. And they would have pushed farther and farther to the north and to the south, on the Balkans,

over Scandinavia, in order in these pincers then to give the
final blow to Germany which was involved in a hard struggle
against the other powers."

This is indeed the true reason for the war in the east.
The alleged need for supplies was of no decisive importance.
If the supply situation deteriorated more and more, it was the
result of the terrific drain upon Germany of the war in
Russia, in reserves, resources and men. Without the Russian
war on her hands, Germany could have waged war indefinitely,
with the pooled resources of the European continent. The
war in Russia was not an economic necessity. It was imposed by the strategic imperatives of "encirclement," as Hitler explained it to his compatriots when he warned them
against the dreaded Bolsheviks, on the morning of the invasion's beginning, the 22d of June, 1941!

"While our soldiers from May, 1940, had been breaking
Franco-British power in the west, Russian military developments on our frontier were being continued to a more and
more menacing extent. From August, 1940, I therefore
considered it to be in the interest of the Reich no longer to
permit our eastern provinces, which moreover had been already laid waste so often, to remain unprotected in the face
of this tremendous concentration of Bolshevik divisions.
Thus there resulted British-Soviet Russian cooperation, intended mainly to tie up such powerful forces in the east
that radical conclusion of the war in the west, particularly
as regards aircraft, could no longer be vouched for by the
German High Command."

Winston Churchill the same day threw the entire weight
of the British Empire on the side of Russia: ". . . I said
there was one deeper motive behind Hitler's outrage. He
wishes to destroy the Russian power because he hopes that
if he succeeds in this, he will be able to bring back the main
strength of his army and air force from the east and hurl
it upon this island, which he knows he must conquer or
suffer the penalty of his crimes.

"His invasion of Russia is no more than a prelude to an attempted invasion of the British Isles. He hopes, no doubt, that all this may be accomplished before winter comes, and that he can overwhelm Great Britain before the fleets and air power of the United States will intervene; he hopes that he may once again repeat upon a greater scale than ever before that process of destroying his enemies one by one, by which he has so long thrived and prospered, and that then the scene will be clear for the final act without which all his conquests would be in vain—namely the subjugation of the western hemisphere to his will and to his system."

A war against Russia has never inspired any enthusiasm in the attacking armies. Napoleon's *grognards* were never very eager and the German soldiers have known also that a Russian campaign cannot be a jolly and gay war. Hitler could not avoid thinking of his predecessor. But he thought, and rightly, that he had considerable advantage over him. Napoleon's army comprised a large number of foreigners. The nationalistic sense of these reluctant soldiers was given birth by the very man who wanted to draw them into a vast European undertaking and was used against him.

Hitler's foreign contingents in 1941 did not contribute much either in quantity or in quality to the success of his campaigns. His veteran army of Germans had gone from victory to victory, without any serious crippling of its fighting power.

Napoleon's *Grande Armee* had become weary after twenty years of uninterrupted wars.

But Hitler's great advantage over Napoleon resided in the superior organization of a modern army that can be supplied quickly and effectively without resorting to local resources. Napoleon drew his supplies from France, two thousand miles away, at a cost of how many weeks of marching in the days of wagon and horse! The modern German army concentrates supplies and resources in huge strongholds and bases;

they are brought up by truck and train and delivered relatively close to the fighting outfits.

Finally, the Napoleonic campaign was but a narrow push towards Moscow which became an attempt to close with an elusive enemy. The German army made swift and vast thrusts on the whole length of the front, not against an indefinite space, but against an awkward and reachable mass.]

PART ONE

Defense In the First World War

• • •

SECTION ONE

Operative Defense In A War of Movement

Inner Line Operations
General War Plan

CONCERNING the diversity of wars, Clausewitz says: "The greater and stronger the motives of war, the more they absorb the whole of a people, the greater the tension which leads to war, and the more closely does war approach its abstract form. It becomes more a question of striking down the enemy; the war aims and political issues become more closely associated; the war appears more warlike and less political." In World War I our enemies intended to carry on such a war in an abstract form, or, as Clausewitz puts it elsewhere, in "absolute form."

Not only did they muster up great armies; but behind these armies these enemy nations placed their total resources—spiritual, material and economic—so as to crush completely our military and economic power. Such was the aspect of this "abstract war" imposed upon us. It involved "the whole being" of our people.

This must be kept in mind before even considering the war plan and the military cause of hostilities.

Our enemies at the beginning of World War I were: France, England and Belgium, in the west; Russia, in the east; Serbia and Montenegro, in the southeast. On our side, after the spring of 1914, Rumania could not be counted upon as an ally. Despite the very definite assurances of the Italian Chief of the General Staff, General Pollio, during the winter of 1913-14, the help of the Italians—their 3rd Army, with 5 Army corps and two cavalry divisions—was out of the question. Germany and Austria-Hungary had no recourse other than to depend entirely on themselves. They had no political war aims and wanted merely to preserve the *status quo*. Politically, they carried on only a defensive war against an adversary whose war aim was that of extermination.

Relative Strength

Concerning the proportions of relative strength, the General Staff conceived the following general picture:

The estimated enemy strength in active divisions, discounting the formations corresponding to our *landwehr* [Territorials] comprised:

In the west: about 92 French, English and Belgian infantry divisions and 12 cavalry divisions.

In the east: about 101 Russian infantry divisions and $34\frac{1}{2}$ cavalry and Cossack divisions.

In the southeast: about 11 Serb infantry divisions and 1 cavalry division.

Total: 204 infantry divisions and $47\frac{1}{2}$ cavalry divisions.

To these figures may be added 18 Russian infantry divisions which could be brought from Asia after a month of hostilities. Our enemies thus, could count on a total of 222 infantry divisions and $47\frac{1}{2}$ cavalry divisions.

Against these forces, we could oppose:

The German army—$87\frac{1}{2}$ infantry and 11 cavalry divisions
The Austro-Hungarian army—$49\frac{1}{2}$ infantry and 11 cavalry divisions

Total: 137 infantry divisions and 22 cavalry divisions.

The estimate of the German High Command corresponded in its essentials to reality; i.e., the enemy had a superiority of about 65 infantry and 25 cavalry divisions, or about 1,832,000 men. As a result, we had to wage a defensive war—not only politically, but militarily as well—against a much greater force and on three fronts: in the west, in the east and also against Serbia; or on four fronts, if one considers East Prussia and Galicia a separate front.

Moreover, the enemies' armies were drafted from the entire manpower of their peoples, whereas, on our side, the fighting will of Austria-Hungary could not be based on a people well-unified and well-decided. Thus, the defensive capacity of Austria-Hungary was hindered, especially as concerns military equipment.

Since we stood between our enemies and were surrounded by them, a large-scale operation in the grand manner, with an army of a million men, had to be on inner lines. We have seen that in such an operation it is essential to come to grips with, and strike at, part of the enemies' forces, holding off the remainder in the meanwhile and keeping them away from the field of decisive battle. This task accomplished, the remaining enemy forces could then be tackled.

Plan of Campaign

The German campaign plan foresaw the attack of the immediate foes in the west—France, England, Belgium—with the main bodies of their armies, 77 infantry and 10 cavalry divisions. These would be beaten decisively and, immediately afterward, the main German forces would turn against Russia. General von Moltke stated in a meeting with the Austro-Hungarian Chief of Staff, Marshal von Conrad, on May 12, 1914, at Carlsbad, that he could turn his troops against Russia six weeks after the beginning of hostilities, or around the middle of September. During this time, the 8th army in East Prussia ($10\frac{1}{2}$ infantry divisions and 1 cavalry division) had to protect our eastern provinces against a Russian intervention. In case the Russians did not intervene, the 8th army would then have to penetrate into

Russia in such a direction as to bring about the greatest
easing of the burden of the Austro-Hungarian armies.

Austria-Hungary wanted to lead a campaign of destruction
against Serbia with the 5th and 6th armies.

The 1st, 2nd and 3rd armies and the Köves Army group—
$30\frac{1}{2}$ infantry and 9 cavalry divisions in all—planned to
march into Galicia to the Dniester-San line and "resort to
the offensive as early as possible, pushing back the Russian
armies on the southeastern front towards the east and southeast." Besides, on the basis of his conversation with General von Moltke on the 2nd of August, Marshal von Conrad
counted absolutely upon the 8th army attacking "in the
direction of Sjedlce, thus at the back of Warsaw," so as to
constitute "one jaw of the Polish pincers into which Marshal
von Conrad wanted to take the Russian army."

The absence of the 2nd Austro-Hungarian army from the
opening operations of the war, was severely felt; at that
time, it was being transported towards Galicia from the
Serbian front.

Relative Strength

The complete repartition of forces among the four theaters of operation at the beginning of the war, was as follows:

In the west: 92 infantry and 12 cavalry divisions on the
enemy side, against $77\frac{1}{2}$ infantry and 10 cavalry divisions
on the German side.

In East Prussia and Galicia: 119 infantry and $34\frac{1}{2}$ cavalry
divisions on the Russian side, against 41 infantry and 10
cavalry divisions on the German and Austro-Hungarian side.

In Serbia: 11 Serb infantry and one cavalry divisions,
against 12 Austrian infantry divisions.

In accordance with this reparation of forces, offensive
operations had to be launched on three fronts—and on a
fourth, as well, to include the Austrian assumption in East
Prussia—with the handicap against the Germans on the
western front, against the Austro-Hungarians on the Russian
front.

Two nations aimed at the annihilation of the enemy, the French and the Serbs. Germany wanted merely to hold Russia; Austria hoped to obtain a decisive victory over her.

Clearly enough, these aims were not in keeping with the forces available. Thus, all of these plans—except those concerning German intentions in East Prussia—were ill-fated.

The attacking German armies in the west, despite an astonishing offensive power and an incomparable fighting spirit, did not succeed in breaking through. They did not destroy the enemy, but had to resort to a long war of position. In East Prussia German troops fulfilled their mission brilliantly. Seen from the Austrian point of view, the failure of their own offensive in Galicia was partly attributable to the fact that the German attack and advance past the Narev, in the direction of Sjedlce, did not take place. The Austro-Hungarian armies suffered severe setbacks in both theaters of operation, Galicia and Serbia.

Hopes Were Blasted

How was it that these plans did not succeed? In the west, the head of the German General Staff hoped that "the fighting power of an entire nation, the warlike qualities—courage, self-denial, discipline, excellent leadership—ought to be appraised higher than mere superiority in men." This hope was not fulfilled. It has often been pointed out that the reason for the defeat was a weak army wing and the withdrawal of the 11th Army corps and the 8th cavalry division from that wing. One might also take a pencil and trace figures to prove that it would have been better to divert this or that division from East Prussia and use it in the west. But are these reasons sufficient to explain why no battle of destruction took place in the west, a battle wherein 77 infantry divisions were supposed to win the decision against the 92 of the enemy within six weeks? Or, does it not appear clearly—more clearly than in the previous Russo-Japanese and Balkan wars—that the fire-power of automatic weapons, particularly machine guns and rapid-fire guns, favored the defense? The general reasons why the war finally came to a stalemate will be explained later.

From the failures of the offense and the evident strengthening of the defense by the use of automatic weapons, it follows that the defensive, rather than the offensive, was in the better position to gain preeminence. It would have been more advantageous to initiate the war with a tactical defense; allow the enemy to attack on all fronts, thus bringing about an equality in forces through the enemy's self-expending efforts; and only then adopt the strategical offensive ourselves.

But in starting the war in this manner, full initiative would have been left to the enemy and full advantage would not have been taken of an operation on the inner lines. Consequently, this fundamental law of defense—to hold oneself on the defensive first of all—should be applied only when the relation between the forces is such that it does not allow an operation on the inner lines.

Offensive Losses and Resources

Such an unfavorable relation· between the opposing forces was by no means the case at the beginning of the war. Moreover, from the failure of the offensives at the beginning, another thing follows: In face of the material strengthening of the defensive, the offensive, too, needed strengthening if one wished to force a quick decision, and this required a concentration of elements of attack, personnel and matériel, on one front. Offense had to suffer greater losses. The relation of defense, "the stronger form", to attack, "the weaker one," had become more detrimental to attack.

In order to compensate for this inferiority, the offensive required greater resources. If the relation between the opposing forces makes it necessary, the place or front where the decisive victory has to be won must be favored at the expense of all other fronts. Since the western front had been decided upon as the decisive point, a sufficient attacking force there was imperative, because here the bulk of the German forces had to wage a frontal attack and annihilate within six weeks the French, English and Belgians. There was also the possibility, if we were not sure of having superior attacking forces on the entire front, of providing the right wing of the armies with such superior and deeply-articulated forces that this wing alone could follow through to win the decision. Then one avoided a premature exhaustion, such as must soon take place in the linear disposition of all armies without great depth.

There was another thing, too, about this absolute war, the object of which, for our enemies, was our destruction.

Austro-Hungary's Fate

In this war, was France an affair of concern to Germany alone? Was Serbia of concern only to the Danube monarchy? Was it only against Russia that the interests were common to us and our allies? The answer to this was given by Field Marshal Count von Schlieffen who, only a short time before his death, declared that the fate of Austria-Hungary was to be finally decided not on the Bug, but on the Seine. In itself, this interpretation infers the necessity of disposing all the available forces of both states in the west, to assure victory on the Seine, and only later to be content with defense on all other fronts. The reprisal against Serbia could have been carried on with greater efficiency afterward than at the beginning of the war. Russian pressure in the east had to be held off only sufficiently to secure the rear of the western front while in no way endangering the outcome of the struggle in the west. If such delaying conduct of the war could be combined with isolated offensive operations, which was what actually happened, it would be all for the best.

Against such a scheme of war, based upon a conception of political and military unity, many obstacles and objections would assuredly arise; they are bound to, in a war of coalition and in the political, military and combat realms. The chief

of the Austro-Hungarian General Staff considered the war
against Serbia as an operation against a "secondary foe."
However, it was conducted as a prime operation because the
whole military and political set-up was aimed at punishing
Serbia.   After the complete failure of the first attack on
August 24, Field Marshal von Conrad decided to leave only
a minimum force on the Serbian front and direct everything
that could be spared from there against Russia.   However,
the Austrian Minister of Foreign Affairs and the Hungarian
Prime Minister meddled here, caused a resumption of the
attack against Serbia with undiminished force, contrary to
the judgment of the responsible military leader of the war.
They hoped that success against Serbia would induce both
Bulgaria and Rumania to consent to being annexed to their
country.   A victory of politics over the generals on the field,
in an absolute war!   Militarily, a defense on the Danube,
Drina and Save rivers would have been possible with very
limited forces, especially since the Serbs lacked sufficient
bridge engineering talent.   In addition, if the launching of
a full-fledged offensive in Galicia had been renounced, it
would certainly have relieved the western front.   At least
the Austro-Hungarian army would not have suffered a decisive defeat, and it would even have permitted the withdrawal
of a goodly number of troops.

Public Sentiment

With this conception of the conduct of "absolute war" one
would have had to create a unified command.   One could
not have been satisfied with settling merely military matters.
The whole of the people had to be deeply convinced that
the decision concerning the fate of the Danube monarchy
did not lie in Serbia.

But is it possible for a great power to inject itself so
completely into an over-all military aim, as to forget its own
particular military and political problems?   I return to the
already mentioned phrase of Clausewitz.   It was a war of

defense for the "very existence of our people," an absolute war. In such a war, one has to strive as a soldier to give to the whole war scheme the absolute form corresponding to such a war of defense, and oppose everything which threatens to crush this ideal form, which undermines it and brings on crumbling and destruction.

At the beginning of the Seven Years' War, Frederick the Great had assigned more than 30,000 out of his 150,000 men to East Prussia, as security against Russia. Nevertheless, in Article 2 of his General Principles of War, he writes, from his experience, that one must also understand how to sacrifice a province to an enemy, in proper time. This does not mean that it would have been better, or even necessary, to abandon East Prussia or a large part of the Danubian monarchy, during World War I. It means merely that it is very difficult, in the actual realities of war, to hold firmly to that supremely simple law of defense, the operation on the inner lines, which Count von Schlieffen had worked out so vigorously; to throw oneself against one side with overwhelming superiority, annihilate it, and at the same time prevent all other enemies from interferring.

Operation on Interior Lines, East Prussia, 1914.

THIS simple law of war so difficult to carry through and which found no solution in the general war conceptions of Germany and Austria, was applied in a brilliant manner on the defensive front in East Prussia. Let us discuss it here.

The 8th Army was in charge of the defense in the east. On the first day of the Tannenberg battle, August 26, 1914, it comprised 9 infantry and reserve divisions, 4 territorial and replacement divisions with very weak artillery, and nearly no heavy machine guns, and the First Cavalry Division. Its mission was to assure the "security of our eastern provinces against a Russian aggression," as well as the "support of the offensive projected by the Austrians." This offensive would

Situation in East Prussia Before the Tannenberg Battle

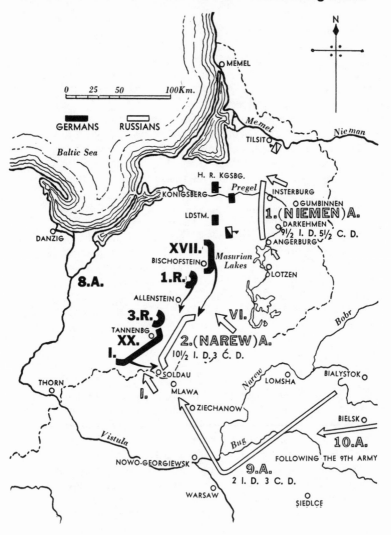

be supported with the greatest efficiency when the 8th Army tied up as many enemy forces as possible and attracted them away from the Austrian army. If the Russians did not proceed towards East Prussia, this mission would be accomplished through an offensive into Russia. If the situation permitted, a southeastern route, east of Warsaw, would be recommended. "If Russia sends particularly strong forces against the 8th Army, this situation would not be disadvantageous. In case of extreme danger, Prussia would be abandoned east of the Vistula, until the army could be reenforced." Besides, the commanding general "can conduct the operations in the east according to his own appreciation." He also had complete initiative in their execution.

It happened as the German General Staff had expected: Russia sent very strong forces against East Prussia.

Russia's Task

The Russian command had a triple aim. It wanted to push deeply into German territory. The prerequisite to launching such an attack was to free both flanks. On the northwestern front, the action on the right flank was left to the 1st and 2d Armies; to conquer East Prussia and take possession of the Vistula line from Dantzig to Thorn. On the southwestern front, the four armies on the left flank— the 3d, 4th, 5th and 8th—were to break down the Austro-Hungarian army. As for the third aim, the push into Germany, it was to be accomplished by two armies, the 9th and 10th. These were to be transported behind the 1st and 2d Armies, in the direction of Warsaw. When the weakness of the German forces in East Prussia was recognized, the Russian command decided, as early as the 7th of August, to launch its push into Germany. It sent the 9th Army in the direction of Thorn-Posen and the 10th in the direction of Posen-Breslau.

The conquest of East Prussia, as expected on the German side, was to be completely accomplished by the 1st

Army of General von Rennenkampf, the Niemen Army,
marching from the east to just north of the Masurian Lakes,
and the 2d Army of General Samsonov, the Narev Army,
marching from the south to just west of the Masurian Lakes,
On the 26th of August, 1914, the eve of the Battle of
Tannenberg, the Russians had the following forces:

    1st Army: 9½ infantry divisions, 5½ cavalry divisions.

    2d Army: 10½ infantry divisions, 3 cavalry divisions.

    9th Army: 2 infantry divisions, 3 cavalry divisions.

    Total: 22 infantry divisions, 11½ cavalry divisions.

These forces opposed only 9 infantry and reserve divisions,
4 territorial and replacement divisions and 1 cavalry division,
which comprised the 8th German Army. At that time, there
was no contact with the 10th Russian division.

Despite its numerical inferiority, the 8th Army performed
its mission of defense by attacking. The separation of the
1st and 2d Russian Armies by the Masurian Lakes, permitted
the possibility of an operation on interior lines, similar to
that already worked out in peacetime manoeuvers by Count
von Schlieffen. The German 8th Army first attacked the
Russian Niemen Army, but broke off the battle at Gumbinnen before it could culminate in a German victory, because it was concerned about the peril to its rear from the
Russian Narev Army. It then intended to withdraw behind
the line of the Vistula, between Thorn and Dantzig, but
decided instead to attack the Army of the Narev. Under
the leadership of General von Hindenburg, as Commander-
in-chief, and General Ludendorff, as Chief of the General
Staff, the Narev Army was enveloped on both flanks and
annihilated, in the Battle of Tannenberg. The Niemen
Army was completely encircled and annihilated at Tannenberg. The six divisions of the Russian south wing withdrew and thus avoided capture. The Russian 1st Army also
escaped, but it was nevertheless greatly shaken.

Bold Leadership Won

Such were the events of this brilliantly conducted defensive operation. The reasons for its success lay in effective and bold leadership which, while facing the whole Russian 1st Army, left fronting it only a cavalry division, a few battalions of Landsturm and the main reserve of the Koenigsberg fortress—11 battalions and 9 batteries—and sent all the rest, to the last man and last cannon, to the decisive battlefield, where they effected a double envelopment and won, despite numerical inferiority and a thin center. Regardless of the threat of envelopment from the south by the two Russian wings of the 1st and 6th Army Corps, the many severe crises arising from the 6-day battle, and the arrival of the forward elements of the Russian Niemen Army to within about 40 kms. of the battlefield, with its menace to the rear of the hard-fighting troops—notwithstanding all these difficulties, the 8th German Army held its own and, immediately after the battle, threw itself against the Army of the Niemen and enveloped it, in spite of its own inferiority.

Another reason was the incomparable performance of the troops and their cadres, their offensive power—result of their formations in peacetime—their feeling of superiority, their marching feats, their resistance during almost inhuman tests. "The energy of forced marches, the boldness of quick attacks, the great activity, which win great souls in moments of danger," such according to Clausewitz are the reasons for similiar victories.

Underrated Germans

The third reason was the efficiency of enemy leadership. Neither the leaders on the northwest front, nor those of the Russian 1st and 2d Armies, realized that their enemy, which was far inferior to them, was leading a defensive operation on interior lines. They underrated us and the danger lying in the separation of their armies which, as they pushed forth into East Prussia, should have presented itself as a warning. They thought too far ahead, on the farther aim, the Vistula. The 2d Army, separated from the 1st, allowed itself to be entangled in a fatal fight and the 1st Army left the 25 in the lurch. For eight days, from the 22d to the 29th of August, while the 2d Army bled to death, with its left wing withdrawing from Darkehmen to Bischofstein it marched 80 kilometers or an average of only 10 kilometers a day.

Numerically, the results of the defensive operation in East Prussia were: 37,000 losses on the German side; 250,000 on the Russian. More will be said about the strategic results, later.

This brilliant defensive puts in the shadow all previous campaigns of a similar nature. Napoleon led the fall campaign of 1813 from Dresden on the interior lines. He marched his main forces aganst Blucher. The latter, however, skillfully evaded him with the Silesian Army. When Napoleon then turned toward the Bohemian Army, Blucher threw himself against General MacDonald, who had been left behind, and beat him on the Kathbach, on August 26th. Napoleon won a battle at Dresden over the Bohemian Army, but his main lieutenants were beaten at Kulm and Gropsbeeren. Despite Napoleon's genius and the endurance of his army, this operation on interior lines failed because of the skill of his enemies and the inefficiency of his own lieutenants.

As a classical example of a defensive operation on interior lines, one can indicate the attacks of Napoleon on the Blucher Army marching against Paris, which unrolled between the 10th and 14th of February, 1814; an "imperishable" operation, as it is depicted on the French side. Napoleon shattered the Russian Olsufiev Corps on the 10th of February, at Champaubert; struck against the Sacken Corps at Montmirail, the next day; York at Chateau-Thierry on the 12th; and on the 14th, at Etoges, struck against the Kleist Corps and the Kapzewitsch Corps under Blucher himself.

But although Napoleon had dealt Blucher's Army heavy blows, it had not been annihilated. "That old devil," Napoleon said later about Blucher, "attacked me a second time with the same fury as at first. I had hardly finished beating him, when he again confronted me, ready to fight all over again!"

Napoleon's accomplishments in the campaign of 1796 in Italy also pale in comparison with the achievements won in East Prussia in 1914.

Strategic Influence On Defense

Let us return to the latter operations and consider their strategic influence on the general defensive task in the east. The Russians, as we have already seen, had three aims: the conquest of East Prussia, a deeper push into Germany, and victory over the Austro-Hungarian Army. The first two failed from the beginning, nor could they be pursued during the entire later course of the war with the same force and violence. Thus, so far as the German forces were concerned, the defense in the east was completely resolved; the Russian advance was stopped and its influence on the operations· in the west was suppressed. When, in the middle of September, it seemed imminent that France would launch an attack upon Germany, the Russian High Command insisted that France must at all costs prevent the shifting of German troops from the west to the east. Furthermore, in the hands of the Germans, East Prussia would stand as a threat to the flank of any Russian advance through Poland towards the west. This advance required, at least, that any such menace be suppressed. Moreover, the additional mission of the German 8th Army, which was to sustain the intended Austrian offensive in Galicia, was performed to an unhoped for extent.

While, on the 26th of August, the first day of the Tannenberg battle, there were 22 Russian infantry and 11½ cavalry divisions in position against East Prussia, this number of effectives was raised by the 10th of September, the second day of the Battle of the Masurian Lakes, to $34\frac{1}{2}$ infantry and $11\frac{1}{2}$ cavalry divisions. In addition $4\frac{1}{2}$ infantry divisions came up on the following days. Besides the 1st and 2d Armies, the entire 10th and part of the 9th Armies were also sent against East Prussia, at that time. Overwhelmed by the crushing defeats of Tannenberg and the Masurian Lakes, General Russki, Commander-in-chief of the northwest front, abandoned the line of the Narev, on September 22d, retreating to the Lomsha-Malkin line with his left wing, despite advice to the contrary from the High Command which was sending up two Siberian Army Corps to strengthen the left wing. He feared, nevertheless, a German attack towards the south and decided upon a further retreat in the direction of Bjelostok-Bjelsk.

Retreat Instead of Advance

An attack from the east by the 1st and 10th Armies could have checked the dreaded German offensive from East Prussia towards the south. Instead of an advance into Germany, retreat! For the Germans, the roads to Warsaw and Sjedlce were free! These events also had their effect on the Russian southwestern front. General Ivanov, the Commander there, assigned to his 4th Army, on the right wing, the primary mission of covering the flanks and rear of the southwest front from the northern Lomsha-Zjechanow direction. The Tsar himself, on the 23d of September, expressed his intention of continuing the war to the last extreme, "If necessary, I will retreat to the Volga!" Consequently, there was given both directly and indirectly important support to the armies of the Danube monarchy.

These strategic results were not recognized on our side. Moreover, the position of the Austro-Hungarian Army, which had in the meantime been badly beaten, now seemed to be threatened so that it appeared indispensable immediately to bolster its left wing with strong German forces. For these reasons, the envisaged Austrian offensive on Sjedlce could not take place and no troops could be shifted from the east to the hard-fighting west, which would have greatly facilitated the war plans. It must not be overlooked, also, that only one out of ten Russian armies was destroyed and that new troops were continually flowing toward the theater of operations from the interior of the Empire.

There was also a third effect: On the Russian side, a feeling of inferiority to German leadership and the offensive spirit of the German troops; on the German side, a confidence in German superiority which constantly worked out to compensate for numerical inferiority.

It is clear that an absolutely defensive solution of the defensive task in East Prussia—a withdrawal to the Vistula before the Russian pressure, as it was envisaged—would have weakened the whole defensive in the east. The Russians would have had a free hand, either to turn against the Austrians or to push into Germany. The absolute defensive solution would have been advantageous, in connection with the entire strategic situation, had it allowed the shifting of strong German forces to the western front. If the Russians were to pursue the withdrawing Germans with the mass of their four armies on the northwestern front, such a mission would have been impossible. If they turned against the Austrians, the question might perhaps have been answered in the affirmative, had the Austro-Hungarian Army in Galicia been in a position to check the Russians. But such was not the case, as we will see.

Austria-Hungarian Campaign
Against the Russians.

THE German and Austro-Hungarian High Commands were in accord concerning the general conduct of the war: "The main thrust must be first that of Germany against France, while Austria-Hungary led the fight against Russia alone (outside of some weak German forces in East Prussia) until the decision against France could be rapidly won, after which German forces would be sent en masse to the east, to join with those of Austria-Hungary in winning the decision against Russia."

During the last consultation between General von Moltke and Marshal von Conrad, which was held in Karlsbad on May 12, 1914, the question was put to Moltke as to when a decision over France could be hoped for. The answer was, "We hope to have finished within six weeks after the beginning of operations against France, or at least to the extent that we shall be able to shift our main forces to the east." The reply of Conrad was, "Then, during at least six weeks we shall have to hold our backs to Russia."

This meant that the campaign of Austria-Hungary against Russia would assume principally a defensive character. The Russians had to be prevented from exerting even an indirect influence on the German campaign against France.

In order to avoid sudden defeat by the superior Russian forces, the Austrian campaign could not be conducted purely on the defensive. Furthermore, the defensive task had to be lightened by isolated, yet effective, strokes at the enemy, before the complete concentration of the Russian Army, thus gaining needed time prior to the arrival of support from the German troops. "If, as it could be foreseen, important Russian forces would march into Poland, east of the Vistula, with the intention of delivering a mass attack on Breslau and Posen and proceeding on to Berlin, then such forces would have to be stopped by our own offensive between the Bug and the Vistula." The "attack in force" was to come only after the arrival of the Germans.

This attack, designed to ease the defensive mission, was soon enlarged in scale, when the 1st Army won over the Russian 4th Army at Krasnik. On the basis of these successes, Marshal von Conrad decided, on the 25th of August, to launch "a decisive offensive by the 1st and 4th Armies, between the Bug and the Vistula." The 3rd Army was to strike simultaneously against the weakened enemy between

Tarnopol and Brody. It would then, also, resort to the offensive. This plan of campaign, tending towards a decision, was further elaborated, on the 1st of September, when, after its success against the Russian 5th Army, the 4th Army had to take part in the combats of the 3rd Army in the north. A telegram sent to the German Kaiser by Duke Friedrich, Commanding General of the Austro-Hungarian Army, on the 3rd of September, speaks of the "great aim to defeat Russia and the effort of strong forces of the 8th Army from East Prussia towards Sjedlce is deemed to be of pressing necessity." The plans went even further. In case the individual blows succeeded, "attempts could be made to push the bulk of the Russian South Army against the Black Sea or back to Kiev, and it would then be of utmost importance to cut off at the earliest opportunity Russian communications through the marshy region of Polesia."

Thus, this campaign actually loses its defensive character, and falls outside the framework of these considerations on defense. Since it must, nevertheless, remain a defensive campaign, from the viewpoint involving the effective situation, it may be particularly instructive to compare desires with achievements.

Von Conrad's Moves

Following are the intentions and events as they occurred: General von Conrad hoped to have the initial advantage in the operations of concentration and preparation. Profiting by this advantage, both the 4th and 1st Armies on the left, were to attack the Russian 4th and 5th Armies toward the north. In a bitter frontal attack at Krasnik lasting three days, from the 23d through the 25th of August, the Austrian 1st Army forced the Russian 4th Army back towards the north. During fierce engagements at Tomaszov and Komarow, the Austro-Hungarian 4th Army enveloped both wings of the Russian 5th Army, forcing the latter to withdraw with heavy losses. In the meanwhile, to protect itself against the ap-

proaching Russian 3d and 8th Armies, the Austro-Hungarian
3d Army had attacked with ten divisions in an easterly
direction. It was, however, outflanked by 20 Russian divisions on both sides, especially in the south, and had to retreat past Lemberg with heavy losses. The victory achieved
by the 1st and 4th Armies made von Conrad confident that
the situation at Lemberg could be reestablished. According
to his intentions, the 4th Army had now to leave only part
of its forces to confront the weakening Russian 5th Army.
Its main forces could thus cooperate with the 3d Army in
its fight, by striking decisively from the north at the same
time that the newly arriving elements of the 2d Army would
be pushing their attacks against the south wing of the defending forces. The German High Command had full confidence in the past and future intentions of Marshal von
Conrad.

These intentions, however, were not to materialize. Against
the Austro-Hungarian 1st Army, the Russians opposed three
new corps (two of the 9th Army and one of the 3d). On
the 9th of September, the Austro-Hungarians were rapidly
forced back; but the Russians had to give up the offensive
because of their heavy losses. Despite these difficulties,
Marshal von Conrad held to his intentions with unswerving
tenacity. He hoped a sudden turn in fortune would be
hastened by the arrival from Serbia of the fresh troops of
the 2d Army, to bolster the south wing of the 3d Army.
However, the 4th Army had not been able, in the meantime,
to launch its expected flank attack from north to south, but,
instead had to face towards the east; it was fighting frontally in a prolongation of the lines of the 3d Army.

Following its retreat towards the south, a gap of 60 kilo-
meters was opened in the lines of the 1st Army, between
Rawa Ruska and Bilgoraj. Through this gap pushed the
Russians' 5th and 17th Army Corps and the Dragomirow
Cavalry Corps of the 5th Army, which had been recently
freed, to attack the flanks and rear of the Austro-Hungarian

4th Army. After seventeen days of bitter fighting, at noon on the 11th of September, Marshal von Conrad decided to retreat behind the San; on precisely the same day, the 8th Army in East Prussia was winning the Battle of the Masurian Lakes.

Such, essentially, were the principal events. General von Conrad commands our admiration. With an inflexible will, he stuck to the offensive, never let the initiative get out of his hands, and persisted with new and surprising expedients when his intentions exceeded the power of his means and the enemy thwarted his plans. He pressed repeatedly against the Russians, beat them seriously at different places, and believed in victory until the end. But finally, and only as a last resort, because of his heavy losses, he was compelled to order the retreat of the entire Austro-Hungarian Army.

Intentions and events on both opposing sides are today well-known, and, since we need not shoulder the heavy burden of responsibility, we must try to understand why this campaign failed, instead of ending as did the campaign in East Prussia. Such a study is particularly fruitful, because of the complete strategic idea it embodies.

Odds Favored Austria

Merely with pencil in hand, it is impossible to trace a satisfactory answer. The General Staff believed that Russia would be able, within 20 days of mobilization (by the 20th of August) to concentrate against Galicia 35 infantry and 13 cavalry divisions; within 30 days (by the end of August) 60 infantry divisions. Against this, meanwhile, Austria could hold in immediate readiness, $38\frac{1}{2}$ infantry and 10 cavalry divisions. Actually, the situation presented itself even more favorably for Austria. On the 20th of August, $30\frac{1}{2}$ Austrian infantry divisions were available, as against no more than 32 Russian. On the 3d of September, according to Russian indications, only $38\frac{1}{2}$ and not 60 of their infantry divisions—as anticipated by the Austro-Hungarian

General Staff—were available. By the 11th of September, the first day of actual combat, 48 Austro-Hungarian divisions (including two of the German Landwehr) were engaged against a maximum of 51 Russian Divisions. This was a favorable situation, as compared with the status on the front in East Prussia. The difference in cavalry forces was greater: 11 Austrian against 21 Russian cavalry divisions. The Russians had a considerable superiority in artillery; 3,060 cannons against 2,140 of the Austrians.

The fact that the Russian 3d and 8th Armies, upon the insistence of the French government, had crossed the frontier of Galicia before concentration of forces was complete and earlier than the expectations of the Austro-Hungarian High Command, is not sufficient to explain the failure of the Austrian offensive plans.

The positions won by both armies at the end of their marches of concentration, had a much greater influence upon the evolution of the campaign. The four Russian armies of the southwestern front marched in a continuous and strategic curve around Galicia, which province projects far out to the northeast from the Austro-Hungarian territory. Encircled within this advanced bend, the Austro-Hungarian army was concentrated. With united forces, together with the 3d Army, which had to be on the defensive, it attacked in three different directions without any definite center of gravity. Everywhere, it had to meet the enemy frontally. The 4th Army alone succeeded in a double envelopment; but the Russian 5th Army was able to fight its way out. Hence, this army could win success against a superior enemy only through difficult frontal attacks.

Moreover, when one tries to comprehend the development of this campaign, particularly the defeat of the 4th Army it becomes obvious that provision for the success of this operation on interior lines was insufficient. The Austro-Hungarian northern group, the 1st and 4th Armies, could not beat the Russian 4th and 5th Armies, but could only push them back frontally. When the Austro-Hungarian 4th Army turned aside from its first foe, the Russian 5th Army, to attack the northern flank of the Russian 3d Army, time and space were insufficient to win a victory there, since the Russian 5th Army could resume the attack, strike at the flanks of the Austrian 4th Army and render its victory against the 3d Army impossible.

Furthermore, the superiority that prevailed on the side of the 2d and 3d Austro-Hungarian Armies fighting against the 8th Russian Army on the south wing, (20½ Austro-Hungarian infantry divisions against 12 Russian) neither was nor could be utilized at the end of the battle.

Reasons for Austria's Failure

These strategic reasons, together with certain intrinsic reasons that had even a stronger bearing, made it impossible to fulfill Austro-Hungarian hopes for victory. Any attack which is not followed up by fresh troops is bound to stand still. Its force decreases all the quicker when the defender brings up fresh reinforcements. First, there arises a situation of equilibrium, a "point of culmination," according to Clausewitz's word; then a superiority of the defender takes place which compels the attacker to defend himself. This is particularly inevitable when, as here, the defensive position becomes almost an offensive one. "Everything depends upon a fine sense of appreciation of this culmination point," says Clausewitz. In East Prussia, the culmination point was chosen too soon when the Battle of Gumbinnen started on the 20th of August; on the contrary, the General Staff of the Austro-Hungarian army chose it too late. Its offensive power, particularly that of the 3d and 1st Armies, was exhausted by the prolonged frontal engagements against the Russian positions, superior in automatic fire and artillery fire. Its casualties were so high that the driving force could not be sufficient in many places even for defensive missions. Hence, we have to admit that our own offensive power was overrated, while the enemy defensive capacity was under-estimated. The entire Austro-Hungarian army was almost exclusively educated and built towards offensive. "My definite dislike for any procrastination and my conviction of the value of initiative prompt me to adopt the offensive as early as I can," wrote General von Conrad on the 25th of February, 1915, to General von Moltke when they considered the plans of the Russian campaign.

This explains also that the 3d Army, which had to cover the attack of the 4th and of the 1st Armies towards the east against the Russian 8th and 3d Armies, had to fulfill its mission in a frontal attack against a double superiority. But on the other hand, defense was favored by considerable river obstacles. Possibly also the sword which had to strike this blow did not have the sharpness which General von Conrad considered necessary to his bold plans. From the German Imperial manoeuvers of 1913, he had acquired the impression that the German Army was "an armed force animated by a unified spirit, educated to take the initiative, extraordinarily fit," but he appreciated even more the education and the formation of the Austro-Hungarian army on many points. Perhaps there was here an over-estimation which was made more acute by the fact that the Russian leaders in Galicia faced the Austro-Hungarian armies with much less precaution and passivity than in East Prussia. "Perhaps the Chief of the General Staff expected too much of himself and of his army for such a task," as it is written in the official Austro-Hungarian history of the war.

General von Conrad attributed to a considerable extent the responsibility of the grave defeat in Galicia to the fact that the Germans had failed to attack in the direction of Sjedlce. This reproach is closely related to the transformation of the defensive campaign into a definite offensive campaign. For a defensive campaign, the easing of pressure on the front in Galicia obtained by the victories in East Prussia was sufficient. But looking at the situation as a decisive campaign—which on the German side was not wanted nor striven for—a German offensive in the direction of Sjedlce would have had to follow immediately after the Tannenberg battle, had it been designed to exert a timely influence upon the operations in Galicia. The object of such an offensive, which would have been the weakening of the Russians on the Lomsha-Malkin line was feasible, but it would have lacked necessary power since the German troops disposed in East Prussia were weak and considerable forces had to stay in position to tie up the unbeaten 1st Russian Army of the Niémen. Also the position in Galicia required an immediate attack of the Austro-Hungarian troops. Despite the courage and abnegation of the Austro-Hungarian army, the offensive was broken.

Russia Thwarted

But while the campaign did not succeed in bringing the desired decision, nevertheless one must acknowledge that the Russian intentions were thwarted and that the Austro-Hungarian Army fulfilled its mission—if limited in time. The planned annihilation of the Austro-Hungarian Armies in Galicia by the Russians failed, but the Austro-Hungarian armies succeeded, on the contrary, in checking the Russian advance, though with heavy casualties which bore heavily on the ulterior conduct of the war in the East. The hard blow suffered, the loss of cohesion, of self-confidence and of trust in victory diminished the power of the army to a considerable extent. "The best army which old Austria in the many centuries of its existence had ever sent against an enemy [and this was indeed true of the army of 1914, despite its weaknesses] disintegrated prematurely. The flower of its officers and of its soldiers fell." (Judgment of the Archives in Vienna.)

According to Russian sources, about 250,000 Austrians were killed or wounded, about 100,000 were taken prisoners, more than 400 cannons captured. And this marked only the beginning of the Russian power at the outset of the war.

The Austro-Hungarian Army deployed too early, it strove to obtain a decision by taking the offensive when according to the general situation, the defensive could have reaped better results. Here is the tragic side of the so highly praised offensive spirit. Missions which could have been successfully performed by a cautious and thrifty defensive were accomplished by a man-consuming offensive. The immediate result for the German High Command was that German forces had to be brought up from East Prussia to reinforce the Austrian left wing, and later again other German forces were sent East "in small quantities," according to the bitter expression of Marshal von Conrad. At the same time, everything required keeping strong forces in the west and even to reinforce them with troops brought from the east.

As we see the situation now, the conduct of the operation in a defensive manner might have fully succeeded. The temporary advantage realized by the Austro-Hungarian army was sufficient to insure the success of the partial offensives of the 4th and 1st Armies against the Russian 4th and 5th Armies in the frame of a defensive operation, despite the early engagement of the Russian 8th and 3d Armies. Violent attacks to block the Russians, to attract and lure them away from an advance into German territory were, as we know already, utterly unnecessary. Indeed, the Russians could not with the mass of their forces penetrate into Germany nor was it their intention to do so, because such an enterprise would have been threatened on both flanks by the German 8th Army in East Prussia and the Austro-Hungarian army in Galicia. The Russian armies had first to get rid of these threats on their flanks by sending their main forces against Austria-Hungary. In this essentially defensive position, it was important not only to avoid defeat, but to maintain one's forces intact so as to be able to exert a permanent threat on the flanks of the Russians, had they intended to push west. For such a defensive mission Galicia, with its river obstacles and the wall of the Carpathian mountains standing behind, would have been particularly fit. A delaying combat, for instance, could have effected the indispensable compensation of forces; considering the general strategy, it might even have been possible to shift forces to the west.

The very essence of defense consists in allowing the attacker, who must suffer heavier losses than the defender, to exhaust himself until the latter becomes by this process strong enough to resort to the offensive and take the initiative. Furthermore, the purely offensive decision is absolutely opposite to the mission of the Austro-Hungarian army in the general war plan, since its casualties and its loss in intrinsic power must be appraised much higher than those of the enemy.

For the favorable development of the general situation, for the success of the decision in the west, the most useful course would have been for the Austrian army to consider its task a defensive mission, while also being ready to deliver offensive blows, provided the result to be expected from such blows had fitted the general purpose.

Defense of the 9th Army in Poland, Fall, 1914.

HERE is an example of how one should envisage such a form of defense. It is according to its principles that the Germans operated in the east after the defeat of the Austro-Hungarian army in Galicia.

This retreat had impaired the strength of one of both pillars; one of both flank positions, that of Galicia, which threatened the Russian advance towards Germany in the direction of Posen-Breslau. The inner force of the Austro-Hungarian Army to launch a powerful attack from this flank position was no longer sufficient. The Russians could

Campaign in South Poland, Situation at the End of September

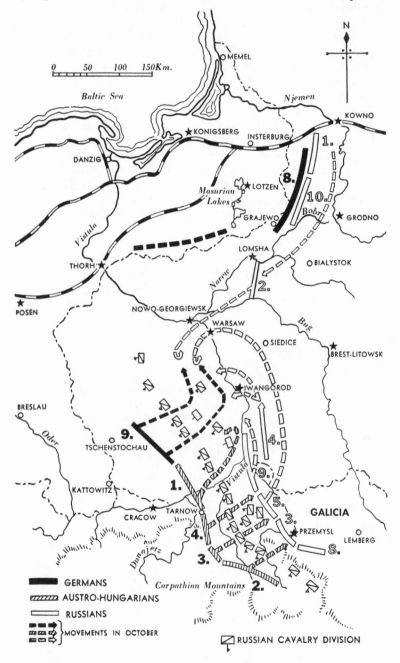

GERMANS
AUSTRO-HUNGARIANS
RUSSIANS
MOVEMENTS IN OCTOBER

RUSSIAN CAVALRY DIVISION

cover themselves with small forces against this weakened Austro-Hungarian army. The road through Poland between the lower and the upper Vistula was open to their masses.

Thus the weak German forces were confronted with a most ticklish problem of defense. "We cannot envisage with a peaceful mind the Russians marching across the Vistula, the Oder and the Elbe. It is absolutely impossible to continue the war against France," had declared Count von Schlieffen in a kriegspiel in 1905. The situation would still be aggravated if the German High Command had not its liberty of action in this operation, but were compelled to bolster without delay the Austro-Hungarian army. All the more so if the Russian army could be reinforced daily by the arrival of the units not yet concentrated and those army corps which were hurrying from Asia—four Siberian, one Turkestan, one Caucasian. Thus General von Hindenburg had to face a superior and active enemy with weak forces on a front of 1400 kilometers.

First, in such a plight, from his objectives we shall see that his intentions fitted exactly his available forces. On the contrary, the Austro-Hungarian campaign is an example of excessive intentions. The processes of defense adopted by General von Hindenburg show us in an exemplary manner the way in which an offensive campaign should be led with an astonishing success with due consideration for what is only possible. This campaign is a combination of surprise attacks with superior forces in well chosen directions and of a defensive practiced with weak forces on the whole front. This essential law of defense seems to be very simple and understandable. However, how great courage, ability, tension are required, to hold out in face of repeated critical situations!

The first surprise attack was in south Poland. After the defeat of the Russian First Army in the Battle of the Masurian Lakes, in the middle of September important forces of the German 8th Army had been freed. An attack

with those forces through the Narev in the direction of
Sjedlce had lost purpose and efficiency because of the Austro-
Hungarian retreat on the Dunajetz. Too, the Austro-
Hungarians needed immediate help. For this reason, the
German forces could not be sent in the direction of Iwan-
gorod-Warsaw. They were concentrated under General von
Hindenburg; they formed the 9th Army and comprised
eleven infantry divisions and one cavalry division. The
mission of the 9th Army was to "act in an autonomous
manner, though in agreement with the Austrian High Command against the flanks and in the rear of the Russian
army group which followed up the retreating Austrians."
During this time, the 8th Army was to "protect Eastern and
Western Prussia against a renewed Russian attack." Marshal
von Conrad intended to act in concordance with the operations of the 9th Army.

Basis of Flank Attack

The intended flank attack was based upon the presumption that the Russians would press the Austro-Hungarian
armies then becoming weakened behind the Dunajetz.
Furthermore, the Russian forces in the southwest under the
leadership of General Ivanov had followed the Austro-
Hungarian armies only as far as the San; there they halted,
reorganized their concentration and only 12 cavalry divisions were sent south of the Vistula against the new Austrian
front. When the Commander-in-Chief of the Russian
armies, Grand Duke Nikolai Nikolajewitsch realized that
important German forces were concentrated in South Poland
he thought that they would intervene against the middle
Vistula.

He then decided to annihilate them and "to push with a
group of from 10 to 12 army corps in the direction of
Posen-Breslau." For that operation against the Austrian army
only the 3d and 8th Army, and against East Prussia only
parts of the 1st and the 10th Army, were left. Behind the

middle Vistula, 4 armies—the 2d, 5th, 4th and 9th were concentrated, with the gravity point near Warsaw. To protect the whole concentration, 9 cavalry divisions and some infantry elements had been sent forward.

First, the German 9th Army and with it the Austro-Hungarian 1st Army engaged only the Russian artillery sent ahead and the left wing of the whole Russian group of attack. Later they encountered parts of the Russian 9th and 4th Armies which during this time had passed the Vistula in the region of Ivangorod, and finally repelled all these forces behind the Vistula. The German 9th Army had then immediately to turn north against the bulk of the Russian forces pushing ahead towards Warsaw. It engaged them and despite its marked inferiority succeeded in repelling them in the direction of Warsaw.

But the Russians were reinforced constantly and finally 8 German infantry divisions—half of the Landwehr—and 2 German cavalry divisions struggled against $18\frac{1}{2}$ Russian infantry divisions and $6\frac{1}{4}$ cavalry divisions. The 9th Army had to break out of the battle to avoid encirclement. Furthermore, the Austro-Hungarian 1st Army comprising $2\frac{1}{2}$ German and 7 Austro-Hungarian infantry divisions (weak in artillery) had to retreat from the 26th of October on near Ivangorod in front of the great superiority of $17\frac{3}{4}$ Russian infantry divisions. South of the Vistula, the Austro-Hungarian forces could not pass the San despite their strong numerical superiority.

For these reasons General von Hindenburg on the 27th of October ordered the retreat in the direction of upper Silesia with complete destruction of all railroads and passage points. The Russians who followed were soon outrun. On the 2d of November they abandoned the pursuit, partly because they were concerned by flank threats, partly because they had to prepare a new action. During these struggles in south Poland, the 8th German Army with $9\frac{1}{2}$ infantry and 1 cavalry division protected East Prussia against the

attack of 20 infantry and 8 cavalry Russian divisions which
had not yet been engaged.

War of Position Avoided

Thus the first partial attack of the German 9th Army
thwarted the Russian plan. The 9th Army had felt "with
a fine judgment the culmination point" of its offensive operation; it did not give to the more numerous Russians the
opportunity to realize their mission of destruction; it stopped
their intended march towards the west in the direction of
Posen-Breslau, at least for the time being, thus securing
liberty of action in the west for the German High Command.
By thus averting the danger, the 9th Army had avoided a
war of position and had preserved its liberty of movement.
This withdrawal of the bulk of the Russian forces in the
direction of the southwest left their right wing no longer
protected by the Vistula. This wing uncovered itself; it
was attacked on its flank by the 9th Army; a gap opened
between it and the Russian armies in East Prussia.

In this manner new and more favorable manoeuvering
possibilities opened. This development of the situation, and
also the firm stand in East Prussia and the favorable railroad
communiciations with the west, allowed the High Command
to transfer the center of gravity of the entire war in the
east, since in the west a favorable and quick decision could
no longer be expected.

Through the successful defensive operations in East
Prussia, strong Russian forces, at the end of October still
numbering 21 infantry divisions and 8 cavalry divisions,
were checked. The 8th Army stood in a threatening position
on their flanks and now in their rear after the push of the
Russians across the Vistula towards the southwest. The
Russian High Command felt constantly the heavy pressure
of this threat on its flanks and in the rear. At the request
of the German 8th Army, a new reserve army corps was
sent to it.

Finally the attack of the 9th Army compelled the Russians to shift important forces away from the Austro-Hungarian front and prevented further deterioration of the withdrawal in Galicia. This lightening of the Austrian burden was so marked that at the end of October against the Austro-Hungarian army, south of the upper Vistula, comprising $41\frac{1}{2}$ infantry divisions, only 26 Russian infantry divisions were opposed. Whereas north of the upper Vistula, $12\frac{1}{2}$ German infantry divisions faced 30 Russian and $11\frac{1}{2}$ Austro-Hungarian divisions faced 17 Russian divisions. The roles of defense and attack between the 9th Army and the Austro-Hungarian armies had then been interchanged; but the latter were no longer able to resume successfully the role of the attacker.

It has been often asserted by some writers that the campaigns in south Poland failed. Yes, if one speaks of an absolutely offensive campaign. But in reality it was a defensive campaign and as such, despite the unfavorable direction of the engagements at the outset, it formed an important part of the defensive disposition in the east.

The chain of these defensive operations was not closed with the campaign in south Poland; the Russian offensive spirit was not broken. Only a temporary check to their moves had been realized. Another link had to be added to the chain.

We shall now see what were the intentions of the Russians, so as to measure the effect on them of the German counter-dispositions. Grand Duke Nikolai Nikolajewitsch had by no means abandoned his intention of breaking into Germany. Four armies in front, the 2d, 5th, 4th, 9th, were to carry their attack deep into German territory. The first objective, which was to be the launching basis of the offensive, was the Jarotschin-Kattowitz-Auschwitz railroad line. The 1st Army had to cover the right flank against the German fortified Thorn-Posen lines. Then the 10th Army was to cover the right flank of the 1st Army against any attack on

the lower Vistula. The armies which fought south of the
upper Vistula—4 divisions of the 9th Army, the 3d, the
11th, the 8th armies and the army group of the Dniester—
had to take the Carpathian passes and break into Hungary,
immediately afterwards, with their 12 cavalry divisions.

Russian Morale Intact

We can see by these intentions that the Russians had an
unbroken offensive spirit despite their heavy losses and their
incipient lack of arms, ammunition and equipment. The
troops inside the Vistula bend, which were animated by
a high offensive spirit, comprised, first, 2 army corps of
the 1st Army (6th Russian and 6th Siberian) on the right
bank of the Vistula behind Warsaw. They had been already
engaged in the combats south of the Vistula. It also comprised 19 army corps with 41 infantry divisions and $10\frac{1}{2}$
cavalry divisions. The German 9th Army was installed on
the Wielun-Novo-Radomsk line, facing south. The advance was to begin on the 14th day of November in the
direction of the southwest. On the 10th of November, the
day on which the German 9th Army was reinforced for its
new attack, there were on the Russian side 102 infantry and
31 cavalry divisions in front and 9 infantry divisions held in
reserve.

General von Hindenburg writes in his memoirs: "In the
present situation, if we had tried to repel frontally the
attack of the enemy, the combat would have developed as
in Warsaw. It is not in this manner that Silesia can be
saved from the enemy. It can be done only by attacking.
A frontal attack led against a far superior foe would be
completely crushed. We must try to direct our attacks
against the weakly protected flanks of the enemy."

The mass of the 9th Army under General von Mackensen
was to strike south of Thorn. The great value of this decision stems from the absolute subordination of all missions
to this particular one. The 8th Army in East Prussia received

the mission of retreating as far as the Augerapp, while fighting against superior Russian forces. Only 6½ infantry
divisions—later only 5½—and mostly of the Landwehr—
and 1½ cavalry divisions were left to this 8th Army against
23 Russian infantry and 8 cavalry divisions of the 10th
Army. On the previous front in Poland, only the parts
of the 1st Austro-Hungarian army north of the Vistula (10th,
1st Army Corps, Cavalry Corps of Hauer), plus the German
Guard Reserve Corps and the Landwehr Corps stayed to
face the 14 Russian army corps remaining on the front.
Some formations of the Landwehr and Landsturm were constituted as "corps," to deceive the Russians. They were
thrown into the wide gaps opened between the attacking
army, the 9th, and both defensive formations in south
Poland and in East Prussia. The attacking army could then
be brought to a strength of 11 infantry and 5 cavalry divisions, including an Austro-Hungarian. It was possible to
uncover to such an extent both defensive fronts in Silesia
and in East Prussia only in dependence on the belief that
the attacking army would be quickly ready to operate, and
also that the Russian command would procrastinate and the
Russian troop movements would be slow. If the Russian
command had trusted the power of its troops and had
understood how to fend off an unexpected stroke by a
counter-stroke, they would have been easily able to meet
with sufficient force the German attacking formation of
5½ army corps with their available 19 army corps and to
keep their offensive dispositions.

Advance To Germany Checked

General von Hindenburg and General Ludendorff expressed their opinions of the enemy during the course of
the campaign in north Poland. A few days after the decision was made, the 9th Army under General von Mackensen
was concentrated without attracting the Russians' attention.
On the 11th of November in the battle of Wlozlaweck

it engaged the enemy and beat the 5th Serbian Corps of the 1st Russian Army between the 11th and the 13th of November. It beat three Russian army corps in the three-day battle of Kutno, between the 14th and 16th of November.

General Russki, commander of the Russian northwestern front, to which the 2d, 5th and 4th Armies belonged, recognized the extent of the threatening danger on the morning of the 15th of November. The German 9th Army had thrown itself behind his 1st and 2d Armies and was now threatening the right flank of the whole Russian advance. This realization of the danger had immediate effects. The 2d and 5th Armies were ordered to stop their march towards the west which they had begun seven days before; they withdrew northward, to take part in the fights of the 1st Army. The 4th Army had to stop. The whole advance towards Germany was at once checked. Fifteen Russian army corps withdrew in front of $5\frac{1}{2}$ German army corps.

In the battle of Lodz, which lasted seven days between the 19th and 25th of November, the 9th Army could almost have emerged victor. On the 22d of November at two in the afternoon, General Russki gave to the 1st, 2d and 5th armies the order to retreat on the 24th of November. This retreat did not take place because the 9th Army with its 11 infantry divisions could not hold in front of the $26\frac{1}{2}$ German infantry divisions and had to withdraw from encirclement at Bshesiny.

At the battle of Lodz, the "culmination point" of the German defensive operations in North Poland was reached and recognized. A Russian attack on the German defensive group in south Poland could not succeed on account of the Russian withdrawal towards the north, which proves that it was right to tie them up only with weak forces. The 8th Army in east Prussia could fulfill its mission in spite of its weak effectives. The active operations of the campaign finally came to a stop at the end of December and it reached a situation of equilibrium on the Nida-Rawkalower course of the Bsura line. Only on the Carpathian front before the Austro-Hungarian army, did the offensive continue, although feebly. The hopes which from time to time had been formulated on the German side to deal renewed and decisive blows were not fulfilled, because the reinforcements from the west necessary to launch an offensive arrived late or only in insufficient quantities. The opportunity to bring to a final decision the war in the east remained unused.

Russian Offensive Power Spent

The aim of all these battles, however, was attained. The chain of defense was closed, the advance was brought to a standstill.

The offensive power of the Russians had been exhausted throughout the entire succession of these battles; at the beginning, the battles in east Prussia, the engagements with the Austro-Hungarian army, the German attacks in south and north Poland and finally the battle of Limanowa, successfully led by the Austrians. The essential purpose of these defensive operations had been to break the enemy will to attack.

The Russian High Command had to bow to German will, despite their strong numerical superiority. All their plans were disrupted. They could not fend off the German flank threats in East Prussia. When they wanted to push through Poland into Germany, the masses of their troops had to retreat towards the southwest in front of the weak 9th Army. Then, when they endeavored to execute their advance in this direction towards Germany, they were attacked in the flank by the 9th Army. They had to withdraw and finally renounced their purpose. The Russian High Command was made dependent upon the German will to such an extent that at the northwestern front a retreat was deemed to be unavoidable. On the 27th of November they learned of the arrival of three new German army corps from the west. The Russian High Command then believed for a time that this retreat would have to extend as far as beyond the Vistula. All these results of imposing one's will upon the opponent would never have been reached by a mere frontal defense. They should be attributed to a High Command imbued with a strong offensive spirit. German initiative triumphed over a far superior enemy.

The Serbian Defense, Late Fall, 1914

HERE is an example where the defender is unable to attack even locally with some elements, but tries to create the opportunity to attack, through the exhaustion of the attacker. This is the case of the defense of the Serbs against the Austro-Hungarians in the late fall of 1914.

The Serb army—6 infantry divisions of first reserve (conscripts), 5 infantry divisions, second reserve (conscripts) and 1 cavalry division, under the command of the chief of the General Staff, Voivode Putnik, was "unified with a common national sentiment, rendered fanatic by 10 years of war against Austria-Hungary, and high-spirited by its success in both Balkan wars; it was rich in war experience."

This army was articulated in three units in the Uzice army group. It had successfully repelled the first Austrian attack on the Drina and the Save in violent battles between the 12th and 24th of August. The Serbs attacked on the Save, towards Syrmien, after a frontal struggle of one week, but had to withdraw to their initial positions. The Uzice army group attacked towards Bosnia. Other local offensives did not break through. During October there was a pause until the end of the month when the Austrians resumed attacking. General Potiorek, fanatical advocate of attack, commanded the Austro-Hungarian 6th and 5th Armies (12 infantry divisions, among which were 17 mountain brigades and numerous second reserve formations). These armies were numerically superior to the Serb army and he intended to beat down Serbia in a new offensive campaign. At the same time on his own initiative and under pressure of the political power, he wanted to revive the charter of August.

Early in November, after lengthy frontal attacks, the wings of both armies started from the north and the southwest to resort to envelopment tactics. The Serb army which, according to the Austrians, had already lost 15,000 prisoners and 60 guns, suffered a lack of ammunition because they had not received the quantities promised by France. The supplies had to be sent from the rear in mountainous country over a few bad roads or paths. The Serb troops gradually became demoralized. Voivode Putnik, unable to attack, saw that in such a situation even the defense was in great danger. On the evening of the 7th of November he decided to withdraw behind the Ub and the heights west of Valjevo. He did not proceed with this withdrawal without interruption, but he fought a delaying action, giving ground only in face of the enemy's superiority. In the course of this retreat all roads and bridges were destroyed, and cattle and other means of subsistence were either destroyed or taken to the rear.

Putnik's Waiting Game

On the 12th of November, the Serb army reached its new position. The supply situation improved with the shortened communications, while the Austrian army had to face increasing difficulties—destroyed roads, mud, no railroad of supply, chalky high plateaus, lack of water, great differences in level (Drina Valley 17 meters, plateaus up to 700 meters), snow, heavy losses in horses. When the attacks were about to ripen into a decision, the Serb withdrew in good time, using his knowledge of a roadless country. Also on the frontiers of the Ub and west of Valjevo, Voivode Putnik did not allow his intended counter-attack of the 2d Army to materialize. He did not deem the situation ready for that counter-attack. He withheld from the enemy the opportunity the latter expected to profit by and on the evening of the 14th of November he ordered his troops to withdraw, while fighting a delaying action, to the position of the Kolubara, which was reached on the 17th. The enemy followed as

Serbian Campaign, November and December, 1914

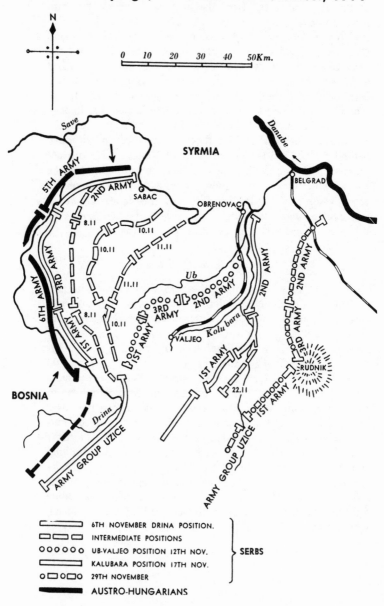

anticipated. His difficulties increased. Casualties mounted, ammunition and artillery were left behind; physical trials became greater and greater. For the Serb army also this retreat of 9 days was exhausting. The Austro-Hungarian General Staff claimed a booty of 8000 prisoners and 42 guns. The offensive flame of the Serb army diminished; many formations gave up the fight, refused to obey orders. Voivode Putnik took most drastic measures; death penalties, confiscation of property and fortunes of the deserters, heavy penalties against all those who gave help to them were enforced.

On the Kolubara position, new intense battles took place. General Misic, who commanded the 3rd Army, counterattacked. Voivode Putnik did not yet deem that his moment had arrived. He wanted to wait until "the enemy was faced with bigger difficulties, so that he could crush even more of the enemy forces, and assume the offensive himself at the propitious instant." This is why he abandoned the position on the Kolubara, from which he had withdrawn slowly while still fighting. Voivode Putnik repelled a repeated pressure to force him to retreat further. The enemy had to fight foot by foot in strenuous struggle. Melting snow and high waters destroyed the Kolubara bridges. The attacker suffered more and more physical exhaustion, the sanitary situation grew worse, supply service became more difficult, rations were cut to a third.

Serbian Defensive Tactics

In order to improve the Austro-Hungarian supply situation, General Potiorek wanted to take possession as early as possible of the only railroad existing—the narrow gauge line of the Kolubara valley. He believed the enemy to be exhausted. Hence he ordered a pause of a few days, during which he planned that advanced troops would press back the Serbs. But these advance engagements did not let the bulk of the troops rest. The Serb positions were attacked. The Serbs brought their defense further back into the mountains, east of the Kolubara. They withdrew the 2nd Army to the southeast, abandoning the capital to the Austrians. But in the Austrian army, the ammunition supply and available artillery decreased progressively. One of the divisions reported that it had only 4 guns, because the others had been left behind due to lack of ammunition. The heights in front of the Austrians reached 1170 meters; the strength of the army had diminished terribly and the limit of its ability to fight was reached.

Nevertheless, Potiorek did not lose confidence; he hoped that with a last effort, the Serbs finally would be beaten. But French ammunition had reached the Serbs from Salonika; the troops had rested during pauses. Discipline was reinforced, reserves were drawn to the left wing. At last, the aim of this continuous retreating combat—to exhaust the forces of the attacker—was attained. On the 1st of December, General Misic announced: "The difficult and sad plight of the enemy must be exploited now. He must be attacked everywhere; he must not be given any rest, neither any pause, until he is destroyed and chased from our soil."

On the 3rd of December, the Serb counter-attack was unleashed with a strong left wing, "at the most favorable moment for this counter-offensive" as it was admitted by the Austro-Hungarian staff. The next day, the Austrians could have taken the Kolubara railroad, by which they could have insured the supply of the 6th Army and the 5th Army. But the defeat of both Austro-Hungarian armies was complete. Early on the 13th of December, the 6th Army had crossed back over the bridge on the Save at Sabac. Two days later, the 5th Army had left Serbia, through Belgrade. The Austro-Hungarian General Staff indicated the number of their killed, prisoners, missing and wounded at 226,000. The Serbs set their casualties at 132,000.

The Austrian General, Krauss, who commanded corps of the 5th Army, feels that the Serb armies could have been beaten if they had been attacked from the north on both sides of Belgrade, by making use of the railroad through Belgrade and of the Kolubara railroad. It would have been even better

to utilize the mass of the Austro-Hungarian armies on the
western theater of operations or in Galicia. The memorandum
of the Austro-Hungarian Staff observes with resignation: "If
Russia had won, the whole war would have been decided, and
it would have been of no avail whether or not the Serbs had
been beaten."

The defensive measures of the Serbs consisted in attracting
the enemy in combat from the frontier into the interior
of the country, so as to deplete his forces, to exhaust and
wear him out, in order to be able to bring a decision by a
counter offensive. As they said:

"We have voluntarily withdrawn into the interior of our
country as an indirect manner of resistance, during which time
the foe might be beaten not so much by the force of the sword
as by his own efforts . . ." To quote Clausewitz's "Vom
Krieg":

". . . . This weakening of the attacker is still increased
when the defender through his constant, well-measured resistance, compels the attacker to buy every inch of soil with his
blood." This manner of conducting operations is opposed to
the "strategy of annihilation" of Clausewitz; it might be
termed a "strategy of attrition." It should not be interpreted
as conduct lacking in force and *élan,* but as one which purports to "exhaust a foe by blows and damages of all kinds in
such a manner that he finally prefers to accept the conditions
of the victor," as Hans Delbrück says in his "History of the
Art of War." But an energetic enemy, who fights for his
existence, will only accept these conditions if his fighting
means are so depleted that a continued struggle appears to
him entirely out of question.

One cannot succeed in breaking down the will of the enemy
by mere exhaustion, but only through a victorious battle.
There exist also cases—such as Napoleon's campaign against
Russia in 1812—where "the reversal of the tide succeeds
without a decision being obtained at the culmination point
after a victorious battle." (Clausewitz). Such cases are however dependent upon particular circumstances.

SECTION TWO

Tactical Defense, War of Movement

A LL the preceding examples of operative defense are taken from operations of movement. They show how permanent are the few great laws pointed out. They show also that their application is based on many varied foundations. Warfare is similar to a chess game. It is limited to the moves of particular figures. The art resides in choosing and carrying out such and such moves.

In contrast to this permanence in the operative field, the tactical forms of defense are subject to constant change; this is also true of the tactical devices corresponding to the modifications and ameliorations brought by the use of existing weapons and in the introduction of new ones. The necessity and the extent of these changes cannot be recognized entirely in peace time. This comes with war itself. The full value of tactical defense was recognized only during World War I.

The war on all fronts had been started by an offensive, in accordance with our peace-time education, even where a defensive attitude would have been possible, such as in Serbia, in Galicia, in the west on the left wing of the army, in Lorraine and in Alsace. At the beginning of the war, the entire German army attacked, and learned the material strength of defense, due mainly to machine guns and the invisibility of artillery. Our attacks at the beginning of the war succeeded even against superior and well organized defenses, because of our insurpassable moral cast and the systematic emphasis on offensive, but the casualties were high. Above all, in the west, the German army became exhausted by its continuous attacks. General von Falkenhayn on taking his post as Chief of General Staff of the army expressed the hope in an order of the day dated September 15, 1914, that the "unsurpassable offensive spirit will steadily enable our army to accomplish the highest feats, to meet all war hazards, and to bend the enemy to our will." But this very army was weakened to a great extent by the abundant bleeding of weeks of battle. Its attacks did not break through; the army could no longer overthrow the enemy defense. With a given proportion in forces, the defensive had proved to be stronger than the offensive tactics learned in peace time. Before the offensive could force an operative decision, it had been tactically exhausted.

The power of defense was a material one, above all in the increased fire power of machine guns. At the beginning of the war, the French infantry regiment—as the German—had only one company of machine gunners. Then, heavy machine guns were used with great ability and artillery was used from camouflaged emplacements. At the beginning of the war, outside of captive balloons and very limited air reconnaissance, there was yet no means of detecting camouflaged artillery; there was neither optical nor radio transmission, nor possibility of overcoming atmospheric influences, nor sufficient planning. Hence it was not possible to neutralize artillery according to a plan. Attacks had to be led against an intact artillery.

We now proceed to consider two examples where we shall see the strength of tactical defense during a war of movement.

Tactical Defense, 4th Reserve Corps, Marne Battle, 1914

IN THE battle of the Marne, the 4th Reserve Corps, which by that time comprised only 15 battalions, under General von Gronau, received orders to cover the right flank of the 1st Army north of the Marne against Paris. General von Gronau attacked between Saint Couplet and Meaux; he realized that the enemy had strong superiority and on the night of the 6th of September he withdrew to a defensive position on both sides of Etrepilly. During three days, this corps

waged an ardent defensive battle, supported by some parts of
the 1st Army just arriving.

On the morning of the fighting day, the 6th of September,
the 36th Reserve Infantry Regiment was on the right wing,
southwest of Acy-en-Multien. The 7th Reserve Division was
installed on the ridge west of Vincy-Manoeuvre, and extended
as far north as Etrepilly. Farther, at Etrepilly, there was the
22nd Reserve Division, and finally, on the ridge west of
Varreddes, the 3rd Infantry Division of the 2nd Army Corps
had arrived during the 26th of September.

The infantry began to dig trenches at daybreak; the artillery was emplaced close behind, a few batteries in open
emplacements. The front was extended over 14 kilometers;
15 battalions were in first-line, with weak tactical reserves.
There were some gaps in the front; it was in such articulation that the 4th Reserve Corps awaited the attack on the
morning of the 6th of September.

General Maunoury, who was in command of the enemy,
was well aware of the role which his army, the 6th, had to
play. He had to deal a blow on the flanks and in the rear of
the German army's wing. He ordered his troops to "pass the
Ourcq river on the 6th of September and to push on tire-
lessly with all forces towards Chateau-Thierry." On the 6th
of September, between the Marne and the Gergogne,—a
rivulet—4½ French infantry divisions and 1⅓ French cavalry
divisions, comprising 55 battalions, and some 38 light batteries attacked 3 German infantry divisions comprising 30
battalions and 26 batteries, among which were 4 heavy batteries. An ardent battle took place. The German batteries and
machine guns from quite a distance away opened up on the
attacking French infantry. But since most of the camouflaged
French batteries could not be detected, the German lines
suffered greatly from strong French artillery fire.

On the right wing of the 7th Reserve Division, a grave
crisis developed. The German battalions in position retreated
east of Vincy-Manoeuvre; the situation was reestablished by a

counter-attack of the reserve of division, the 11th Jager Battalion, supported by 2 batteries, taking position at 200 meters of the enemy. They opened fire on the storming French riflemen. The 22d Reserve Division recaptured Etrepilly. In front of the 3d Infantry Division, all assaults were repelled "with heavy enemy losses," according to the French themselves. In the French 55th Infantry Division, three colonels fell. On the right wing of the German front, north of the Gergogne, the arriving 4th Infantry Division attacked, repelled a threatening envelopment and threw back the enemy. The day of the 6th of September ended with a complete defensive success on the entire front; but there had been heavy losses and the troops were tired.

In the evening of the 6th of September, the offensive will of the enemy remained unbroken. General Maunoury ordered that the attack be resumed on the morning of the 7th; its purpose was to take the heights east of the Ourcq river. That day again hard battles developed, creating many changes. The 7th Reserve division suffered particularly; 6 batteries took position immediately behind the first line, protected it and permitted the infantrymen to hold out. All enemy attacks had failed by noon.

At 12 o'clock, the General commanding the 2nd Army Corps, General von Linsingen, who by that time had taken command of the entire front, ordered the 2nd Army Corps to attack north of the Gergogne, and the right wing of the 6th Reserve Corps to attack south of the Gergogne. Half of the 8th Infantry division was assigned to this sector. It gained ground in front of Vincy-Manoeuvre, but could not reach the Nogeon Farm. At 11 o'clock, the French 56th Infantry division broke into Etrepilly; but it had to evacuate the village under the counter-attack of the 22nd Reserve division. The 7th of September marked a complete defensive success of 33 German battalions and 41 batteries against 63 French battalions and 57 batteries in the front between the Gergogne and the Marne. But the troops, particularly the 4th Reserve Corps, suffered new heavy losses and were quite exhausted.

French and German Problems

Hence, on the 8th of September, it was a problem for the Germans to dig in and resist. The 3rd Infantry division, at a given order, could withdraw to the heights northeast of Varreddes.

On the 7th of September, the French also were confronted by a grave crisis. The 63rd Infantry division retreated before the German 8th Infantry division. Its infantrymen could consolidate their positions only because parts of the artillery (under General Nivelle, General Joffre's successor) fired from among the weakening lines. However, General Maunoury maintained his intention to attack. He ordered for the 8th a continuation of the attacks against the German "flank protection" which had to cover the retreat of the German armies.

He ordered for the 8th of September a break-through of the German front on the Ourcq in the direction of Ocquerre-Vernelle, the center of gravity of the danger zone being north of Marcilly at the position of the 56th Infantry Division, which was reinforced by the entire artillery of the 55th Infantry Division and 4 heavy batteries of fortification. Behind the 56th Infantry Division the infantry of the 55th Division was installed.

The defensive battle reached its climax on that day, the 8th of September. The German front had to undergo all the punishment of a defensive until the end.

Defensive Will Unabated

The 7th Reserve Division, which had suffered particularly in the two preceding days of the battle and felt unable to stand renewed attacks on the same positions, withdrew on the height north of Trocy during the night. The 22nd Reserve Division also during the night evacuated the village of Etrepilly, which was a shambles, and withdrew towards the east, in front of Trocy, to a defensive position. The 3rd Infantry Division dug in on a shortened front, northeast of

Varreddes. A good part of the artillery took position in a deep formation behind the thin infantry lines. To reinforce still more the defense against the expected attempt at breaking through, the 4th Cavalry Division and the reserve of the 4th Reserve Corps—two battalions—were emplaced west of May-en-Multien, and the 5th Infantry Division installed itself south of Le Plessis-Placy.

We can see that there is on the German side a completely unabated defensive will. The front was withdrawn only 1 or 2 kilometers during the night, so as to give a breathing spell to the hard-fighting infantry and to reorganize the forward elements. The new attempt at breaking through, on the 9th of September, did not succeed; a real barrier of fire checked it. Around noon, the struggle became stagnant, the climax of the battle was passed; the defense of 48 German battalions and 51 batteries south of the Gergogne had won over the offensive of 67 French battalions and 54 batteries.

At 8 P.M., General Maunoury gave the following secret order to his commanding generals: "After 3 days of uninterrupted combats, the 6th Army can no longer hope to pierce the German flank protection. But it can attempt to hold its ground." He completed this opinion by a report to General Joffre that his "thinned out and exhausted troops do not seem able to resume the battle." The German troops had suffered heavily, but they held their own which permitted an envelopment attack by the right wing of the army, the 4th and 9th Army Corps.

There is a real tragedy for us Germans in the fact that the full significance of this defensive victory was not recognized. The French offensive failed and had been completely exhausted by the German defense. But also the exploitation of the attack by the German right wing, which was to outflank the shattered French front and should have brought victory, did not take place. The sacrifices of defense were useless.

During these 3 days, both sides had abundant fighting will and displayed a spirit of high sacrifice. Hence, if one considers that the moral forces were equal on both sides, but one conclusion can be drawn: Not that the defensive should be preferred to offensive, but that the numerical superiority of the attacker both in personnel and matériel must be greater than it was in the examined case, in order to win over the material strength of defensive.

The tactical features of this defensive battle in a war of movement still show linear trenches, shoulder-to-shoulder disposition, heavy machine guns which are not disposed in depth, but often are even installed in the infantry trenches; an artillery brought close together, partly in open terrain; a distaste for fortified works. These formations rendered camouflage more difficult, lacked depth, and caused heavy casualties; also, the artillery on both sides, so far as they were not used against enemy batteries emplaced in open terrain, directed their fire power against the enemy infantry.

Defensive Battle on the Aisne,
September 13th-14th, 1914

IN THE preceding example, a strong defensive front withstood successfully an offensive. We shall see on the Aisne the formation of a defensive front.

After the battle on the Marne, the German 1st and 2nd Armies withdrew in diverging directions, so that between them a gap opened which enlarged still more during the retreat. On the 12th of September in the evening, the 1st Army was behind the Aisne, its left wing west of Vailly, the 2nd Army behind the Vesle, its right wing east of Rheims. Between both a gap of 40 kilometers had opened, in which there were only a few cavalry divisions and 3 Landwehr battalions near Bourg, and the 13th Division in front of the Aisne at Roucy. The latter division was sent during the night of the 13th of September to the right wing of the 2nd Army, where it seemed to be particularly needed against the threat of an outflanking movement of the enemy. General von Bulow, who commanded the 2nd Army, and had received also the command of the 1st Army and of the 7th Army which was being formed near Saint Quentin, intended to hold the position of the 1st and of the 2nd Armies; he wanted also to close the gap with the available 7th Reserve Corps of the 7th Army. This corps was to reach Laon during the night of the 13th of September.

On the left wing of the French army, on the 12th of September, there were the 5th Army, the B. E. F. and the 6th Army. General Franchet d'Esperay, who commanded the 5th Army, wanted to cross the Aisne near Neufchatel with his right wing and his center—the 10th, 1st, and 3rd Army Corps and the Valabrègue group; at the same time, the left wing of the Army—the 18th Army Corps and the Cavalry Corps Conneau—had to establish liaison with the English in the north. With the 1st Army Corps, General d'Esperay thought he could triumphantly enter Rheims. The English were to push towards Laon with their right wing, the French 6th Army was to march in the northwestern direction and cross the Oise, in order to pursue the German 1st Army and outflank it on the left.

On the 13th of September the frontal attacks of the French 6th Army against the German 1st Army were checked. The English found the bridges over the Aisne destroyed and climbed the slopes of the Chemin des Dames with hesitation. They met the elongated left wing of the 1st Army and the 7th Reserve Corps, which during the night had passed only through Laon. The 7th Reserve Corps made a forced march of 60 kilometers on the morning of the 13th of September, reached the height of the Chemin des Dames, dug in and effected liaison with the 1st Army. The English did not take the offensive on the 13th, but prepared it for the 14th of September. The attacks of the French 18th Army Corps against the left wing of the 7th Reserve Corps and against the 28th Infantry Brigade in Craonne did not succeed. At the end of the day the French had taken possession only of the Craonne-Corbeny heights. The Conneau cavalry corps and the

Aisne Battle, September, 1914

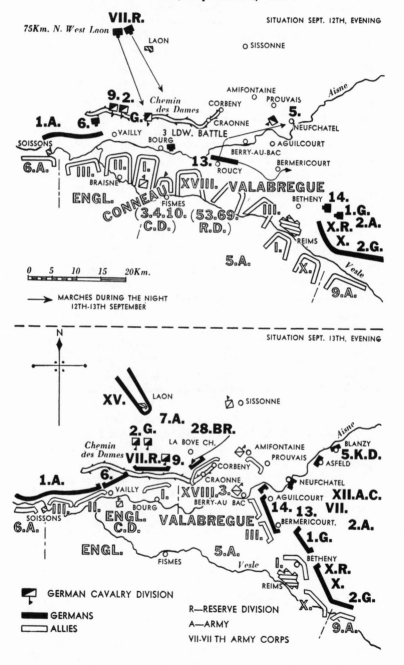

SITUATION SEPT. 12TH, EVENING

VII.R.

75 Km. N. West Laon

LAON

○ SISSONNE

AMIFONTAINE

9.2.

Chemin
des Dames

CORBENY

PROUVAIS

5.

Aisne

1.A.

6.

G.

CRAONNE

NEUFCHATEL

3 LDW. BATTLE

VAILLY

BOURG

SOISSONS

BERRY-AU-BAC

○ AGUILCOURT

6.A.

13.

ROUCY

BERMERICOURT

BRAISNE

III.   I.

ENGL.   CONNEAU   XVIII.   VALABREGUE

14.

BETHENY

1.G.

FISMES   (3.4.10.   (53.69.
(C.D.)   R.D.)

III.

X.R.

2.A.

REIMS

X.

2.G.

5.A.

X.

Vesle

9.A.

0   5   10   15   20 Km.

MARCHES DURING THE NIGHT
12TH-13TH SEPTEMBER

SITUATION SEPT. 13TH, EVENING

N

XV.

LAON

○ SISSONNE

7.A.

2. G.

28. BR.

Chemin
des Dames

LA BOVE CH.

AMIFONTAINE

Aisne

BLANZY

VII.R. 9.

CORBENY

PROUVAIS

5.K.D.

ASFELD

1.A.

6.

CRAONNE

NEUFCHATEL

VAILLY

XVIII. 3.

BOURG

BERRY-AU-BAC

AGUILCOURT

XII.A.C.

6.A.

SOISSONS

III.   II.   I.

ENGL.
C.D.

VALABREGUE

14. 13.

VII.

BERMERICOURT.

2.A.

III.

1.G.

ENGL.

5.A.

FISMES

Vesle

BETHENY

X.R.

I.

X.

GERMAN CAVALRY DIVISION

REIMS

X.

2.G.

GERMANS

ALLIES

R—RESERVE DIVISION

A—ARMY

VII-VII TH ARMY CORPS

9.A.

Valabrègue group met only a weak opponent; they pushed deep into the gap opened between the 1st and the 2nd German Armies; General Conneau reached Sissonne with his 10th Cavalry Division. Amifontaine with the 4th, Berry au Bac with the 3rd, and the Valabrègue group reached Prouvais and Amifontaine. The German 2nd Army prolonged its right wing with the 13th and 14th Divisions and the 1st Guard infantry division. It repelled all frontal attacks of the French 5th and 9th Armies, counter-attacked and reached the Aguilcourt-Bermericourt line. It also commanded the bridges on the upper Aisne on its right flank with the 5th Cavalry Division and small detachments of the 14th Infantry Division. The French 1st Army Corps, which already had to engage 2 brigades in the morning, entered Rheims at noon. It then learned of the counter-attack of the German 2nd Army. In the evening it could only take possession of Betheny. Valabrègue had to withdraw with its right wing.

General von Bulow saw that the situation on the evening of the 13th was notably more favorable than the day before. Both 1st and 2nd Armies had repelled all enemy attacks, the 2nd Army had extended its right wing as far as the Aisne. However, there were still 2 gaps in the 7th Reserve Corps, one of 4 kilometers and one of 14 kilometers, between this corps and the 7th Army Corps, all facing the stronger forces of the enemy. The 7th Army was to push the 15th Army Corps, just arriving, into the gaps and the Guard Division as well as the 2d Cavalry Division. This being done, the enemy had to be thrown back behind the Aisne. The 2nd Army was to carry out the attack. Besides, the 1st and the 2nd Armies had to defend themselves.

Joffre's Urge to the English

The enemy hoped to be able to break in a decisive manner the unexpected German resistance put up on the 14th of September with a more energetic attack. Particularly, General Joffre invited the English to make a more energetic exploitation of the success. He thought the Germans were still in complete rout.

On the 2nd day of the battle, the 15th of September, bitter fighting took place. The German 1st Army repelled all assaults and, counter-attacking, forced parts of the English 2nd Army Corps to cross back over the Aisne. The 7th Reserve Corps waged a fluctuating defensive battle against the English 1st Army Corps.

On the whole, it could hold its own. The 28th Infantry Brigade had to withdraw upon La Bove Chateau. The arriving 15th Army Corps relieved it, took Corbeny and compelled the French Conneau Cavalry Corps and parts of the Valabrègue group to withdraw behind the Aisne. The 14th Division had to give way and was bolstered by an infantry regiment of the arriving 15th Army Corps. All attacks of the French 2nd, 1st and 10th Army Corps were repelled.

The result of this German defensive, which lasted 2 days, was that the attacks of a superior enemy did not succeed, the break-through did not take place. Marshal French, who commanded the B.E.F., ordered his force to dig in on the 14th of September in the evening. On the night of the 14th to the 15th General Joffre ordered in a general order-of-the-day the launching of "a methodical attack with all means at our disposal, and in which any position, once it is taken from the enemy, must be immediately consolidated."

This constituted the swan song of the war of movement and marked the advent of the war of position.

Here again in this Aisne battle, the attacking means and the attacking will of the troops had proved too weak to break through the defensive, though this defensive was handicapped since it had to be built up and since there were large gaps to be closed by the arrival of reinforcements. Defensive was successful particularly on account of a suitable training in peace-time, which taught leaders and men alike to resort to counter-blows and counter-attacks whenever possible, according to the local situation. A good part of the success in this Aisne battle should be ascribed to this offensive element in the defensive against a superior offensive. But the defense suffered also heavily, especially because it fought, according to the principles learned and practiced in peace time, in linear formations without the necessary articulation in depth, which rendered camouflage more difficult and exposed the troops to the full enemy fire.

SECTION THREE

Defense In A War of Position

Why Did a War of Position Take Place?

ON neither side did the result of the Aisne battle diminish the will to carry on the struggle to a decisive finish. Both enemies tried for this decision in offensive; both wanted to outflank their opponent and beat him in attacking the uncovered flank. The intentions of both failed. Nowhere did the offensive bring a decision. Everywhere the opponents promptly resorted to defense. Neither did the new French 2nd Army under General de Castelnau, comprising 5 army corps and 2 cavalry corps—which was called often the "armée de poursuite"—nor the Army de Maud'huy, nor the B.E.F. in Flanders advance. In a similar manner, on the German side, all efforts failed, particularly the engagement of 4 new reserve corps of the 4th Army in the ardent battle of the Yser and of Ypres at the end of October, despite demonstration of the greatest spirit of sacrifice. The will of both sides to hold out was often close to breaking. Under the pressure of the violent German attacks on both sides of the Somme, particularly at Roye, on the 5th of October General de Castelnau had decided to break battle and retreat; but the chief of the newly constituted group of northern armies, General Foch, entered into the headquarters of the 2d Army in Breteuil, at 4 o'clock in the morning of the 5th. He suspended the order of retreat and gave orders to hold out at all cost. The same incident repeated itself a few hours later with the army of General de Maud'huy, adjacent to the 2d Army in the north; the General believed his front was enveloped, and he had even prepared the order to evacuate Arras. Marshal French also, at the end of October, had envisaged a withdrawal of the English troops from the salient of Ypres. General Foch was able to induce him to resist.

In this manner, neither the Germans nor the Allies could break through. As in the east, a war of position began in the west.

The advocates of the defensive remark with satisfaction that this form of warfare proved it to be the stronger form, and that it could win over the offensive. Both opponents, French and German, started the war with a strategic offensive. Both had a strong offensive will, which displayed itself particularly in the outflanking battles, but both were compelled to adopt the defensive, and this led to a war of position.

It would not be right to draw from this general conclusions and principles applicable to the conduct of war. It would be wrong to prefer the "detour to success" (the expression is from Marshal von Moltke), namely, the exploitation of the material advantages of defensive, so as to block the offensive which would devour itself, to the direct road to success—the decision-seeking offensive.

Furthermore it is our duty to try to discover the reasons why the decisive form of warfare—offensive—did not bring success. Why did a stalemate in all operations, a war of position, a general defensive take place? Why did the German war plan, based upon a quick decision in the west, fail as completely as the French plan, which had also sought to win a decision in a great offensive battle?

These questions must concern us all the more, since the danger in future of a war of position is no less than in the past, especially owing to the increase of material forces. The answer to this question depends largely upon whether or not fundamental changes take place in the respective efficiencies of offensive and defensive on the tactical as well as on the operative level.

Seasoned Troops Needed

To explain the failure of our outflanking movements, particular circumstances which proved unfavorable to us can be brought forth, such as the opening of the drainage ditch locks at Nieuport during the night of the 29th-30th of October, 1914. The resulting inundations rendered progress of the offensive on the right wing impossible. Furthermore, it is said that decisive results could have been obtained by the attack of the 4th Army Corps in Flanders if instead of young, unhardened corps, seasoned troops had been utilized. The energetic character of General Foch on the enemy side was also responsible for the ill fate of the fighting on our side. Assuredly, all these considerations diminished our chances of success. However, a success of capital importance likely to influence decisively our situation on the entire front would not have happened even if these chances had been favorable to us. In order to see why such a decisive result was denied us as well as our enemy, why both sides adopted the defensive, we must examine deeper, more general causes, not those connected with such and such local situation. These causes are moral as well as material, tactical as well as strategic.

At the beginning of the war, the German Army was animated by an incomparable offensive will. This moral élan had been impaired, however, by uninterrupted marches without rest, by fierce fighting at the beginning of the war and by heavy casualties. Against the increasing fire power, this strong morale was not sufficient compensation. Troop losses, which until the middle of September were as high as 50% in certain formations, had to be replaced.

Extreme efforts and prolonged and heavy battles had left deep marks in the structure of the French army. Grave signs of this stress required the personal intervention of the high military chiefs and provided lasting worry for the French High Command.

Purely material reasons also compelled abandonment of the offensive. The increased fire power required increased ammunition; the multiplication of automatic weapons, the growth in size of the armies by millions led very soon to a lack of ammunition on both sides. The Germans used their last peace time supplies in the battles of Flanders. Fresh ammunition could never be turned out in sufficient quantities. Other difficulties involving raw material came up. With the French, the lack of artillery ammunition also was great. The offensive could no longer be supplied with the necessary quantities of additional ammunition, while the existing ammunition required by defensive was sufficient. Herewith, we have an essential reason for stabilization of the fronts, and for resorting to a war of defense and position.

Each pause in movement was a benefit to the defensive. Defense forces could find time to dig in and brace themselves against heavy attacks.

Enemy Fire Power

The strong offensive spirit and a sufficient material equipment, particularly ammunition, did not allow at the beginning of the war full recognition of the material strength of the defensive and the difficulty of conducting an offensive. "The moral élan of the German infantry had been so great in the engagements at the beginning that the force of its advance dominated all obstacles of the enemy fire power and remained intact in spite of terrific blood sacrifices."

When this moral élan ceased, enemy fire power could be fully displayed.

We already said that the defensive had been notably reinforced by the introduction of machine guns, of quick-firing guns, by the use of emplacements for indirect firing, by the prolongation of ranges and through the impossibility of neutralizing masked defence artillery. Each infantry attack had to be launched against an intact enemy artillery and each defense could be protected by that intact artillery. This reinforcement of fire power favored the tactical defense, and hence contributed to strengthen the operative defense. But it had another consequence, to the benefit of both the operative and the tactical defense. In preceding wars, a battle and with it the fate of an entire country could be, and usually was, decided in a few hours. In World War I the fronts were often engaged fiercely for days before a decision could be reached. Formerly the defender found hardly any time to take counter-measures, to be reinforced, to camouflage, to bring up reserves, to shift forces, to provide the front with munitions and other supplies in order to be able to hold against his opponent. On the contrary, in the battle of the Aisne the German defender succeeded in building up a sufficient defensive front in only two days. Then during World War I, defense did not have the formations, rigid and particularly sensitive to surprise, which it had, for instance, in the time of Frederick the Great; but instead it became adapted to the terrain. This is why surprise lost much of its effect against a defender.

There are equally strong reasons to explain why offensives did not succeed on the operative field. In the outflanking attempt after the battle of the Aisne, the engaged troops on both sides were too insufficient to win over the opposing fire-power. Even the engagement of the 4th Reserve Corps in Flanders at the end of October could not break through the uninterrupted front of machine guns established by the English.

Outflanking operations were blocked by the sea. This situation contributed to reinforcement of the defensive. There was no longer any flank. The entire territory between the sea and the Swiss frontier was occupied by armies. As Clausewitz said: "When the defensive line extends from sea to sea or from neutral country to neutral country, then offensive cannot be concentrated." An outflanking movement, a "concentration of attack" was no longer possible, excepting locally. The enemy front had first to be broken

in frontal attacks. Hence, the main danger of any defense—
of being encircled or outflanked—disappeared. "The weakness of defense is in the flanks" the official infantry regulation book of 1906 had already laid down.

The Chief of General Staff at that time, General von
Falkenhayn, advocated that no position that had just been
captured should be abandoned. "Keep what you have, and
do not give up an inch of what you won," he wrote on the
16th of November, 1914, to General von der Goltz. Such
an operative process was bound to lead necessarily to a war
of position, which is a particularly strong form of defensive.

What von Falkenhayn Wanted

There is an opinion according to which a dynamic operative conduct of the war in the west would have preserved us
from a war of position and could have brought a favorable
decision. General von Falkenhayn wanted also to retreat
still further with the German right wing and thus win time
and space for an outflanking attack. Since this was not done,
we cannot see whether this daring proposition would have
led to a decisive or only to a local success.

One should not pay particular attention to the fact that
the French fought on their own territory, could make use
of all means of subsistence, had the benefit of an intact and
thick network of railroads and hence could take suitable
counter-measures, owing to numerical superiority—97 infantry divisions against 77—and also manage a favorable
concentration of forces. In the east, during the campaigns in
East Prussia, in south and north Poland, we have seen an example of ideal operative manoeuverability, a defensive strategy
conducted according to offensive lines. Despite these characteristics, a war of position took place finally, although imposed by powerful Russian superiority.

In the west, both enemies attacked. Neither had indispensable superiority, either on the whole front or at the

main points of gravity, against increased fire-power. Both attackers became worn out and were brought to a situation of equilibrium due to their physical, moral and material exhaustion.

The attacking strength mustered, the concentrated gravity were nowhere sufficient, either in the east or in the west, to break the force of the defensive. The last effort of the war of movement was the attack of the French 10th Army in Artois on the 17th of December and of the French 6th Army in Champagne on the 20th of December. They failed at the very beginning. The order of the day of the Commander-in-chief proclaimed that the soil of France must finally be freed from the foe and that the nation counted more than ever on everyone's will to win. But this exertion had no better effect than previously. The offensive power had passed its climax and needed new concentration, new efforts and new strength.

The relation of forces at the beginning of the war by 15 infantry divisions was in favor of the opponent who the Germans sought to beat decisively in six weeks. Hence, one would be tempted to try to gain a compensation of force first and then a superiority of force through the defensive. But such a process would mean giving up entirely one's initiative and make one entirely dependent upon the enemy and his actions. This attitude is to be adopted only when one is nowhere strong enough to resort to local offensives. [The infantry divisions mentioned above were composed of between 15 and 16 thousand men.]

We have seen that attack—in itself the "weaker form"—was more costly than defense, and that defense—the "stronger form"—increased in strength. Against this increasing superiority of defense in general, a compensation can be obtained, both tactically and operatively, only by an increase of offensive strength in the gravity zone of the attack. Thus, offensive can win superiority over defensive on one chosen place by a concentration of power.

Pre-1914 Thought

Nowadays, we know all the steps necessary to carry out a tactical attack in face of increased defensive strength. That is, reinforced personnel and matériel at decisive places, systematic and thorough preparation for attack against a strong, reconsolidated defensive; strict cooperation of all arms and weapons and constitution in due time of localized points of fire concentration. Hasty and insufficiently prepared attacks lead only to heavy losses.

But this increased defensive strength requires on operatively decisive places, as well as on the tactical plane, a concentration, a gravity and a deep articulation of the attack. Unwillingly does one allow the impression to assert itself that tactics and operations before the war were influenced by identical thoughts. On the tactical plane, we saw linear trenches; on the operative side, armies marching in parallel formation and without particular depth. Contrary to the French, who displayed a strong inclination for operative articulation in depth, we tried to align our forces and engage them on the front at the same time, so as to give the greatest possible strength to the first blow and also to outflank the enemy with an extended front and thereby win the decision.

The indispensable constitution of a zone of gravity— operative as well as tactical—is rendered possible by increased fire power. It allows also the holding of one's positions at no decisive places with a minimum of personnel and matériel. We know also today how to carry out an efficient resistance by massing strength at decisive places.

We know today that this increased fire power would have allowed, at the beginning of the war in the west, the formation of a much weaker left wing—the 6th and the 7th Armies—so as to favor the right wing, where the decision was sought. We would thus have followed Schlieffen's advice to reinforce the right wing. This reinforcement would have been all the more suitable inasmuch as we know now that the French operations plan called for an attack of its right wing against Lorraine. This French right wing would have been exposed to the full efficiency of the German defense and to the strength of our fortifications in Lorraine. In this manner, it is possible that the attack by the reinforced right wing could have prevailed against the French defence, before reaching premature exhaustion. Instead, the German troops were too weak to win the decision that they expected to gain in six weeks by the operations plan.

One could have even made a better use of the efficiency of defense and of the space won in the west, and this indeed is often recognized by present military reviewers. Early in November, at the beginning of the campaign in north Poland, the gravity point of the war could have been shifted to the eastern front, since the depth of the terrain conquered in the west and the power of automatic weapons could have liberated a great part of the western army. Instead, both enemies struggled against each other in the west in useless encounters with insufficient offensive means. Both wanted a decision; they did not want to give up, but they could not break through. Hence, a war of position was unavoidable. "Any attack, which does not lead directly to peace, must end by a defensive" (Clausewitz), so soon as the offensive power has reached its peak and is worn out.

All these reasons explain the consolidation of the fronts. The attack in the west, which sought to reach a decision, failed. The tragic side of this failure for us Germans is that it rendered a long war unavoidable, and that time favored the enemy who had at his disposition the resources of the entire world to enable him to complete and increase his troops and his fighting elements. It is true that an absolute consolidation of the enemy fronts did not take place, that a series of brilliant and successful offensive campaigns were carried on, as in 1915 and 1916 against Russia, in 1915 against Serbia, in 1916 against Roumania, in 1917 against Italy. But it was not possible to break our chains in the west, which after all was the decisive theater of operations.

Once the war had entered into a stabilized phase, all efforts to reconquer operative movement could have succeeded only by breaking away from this stabilization, either by a withdrawal or by a break-through.

Operative and Tactical Defense, War of Position

THE operative possibilities in a war of position resemble those in a war of movement, when the defender, instead of holding firmly to his positions, and to the entire static system in all places, is willing to abandon some parts of the front, so as to withdraw while fighting and thus afford to himself new bases of operations. The principles are similar to those directing a war of movement.

The operative possibilities of defense are, however, limited when one aims to remain on the same positions. The defender opposes his continuous and locked front to the continuous and locked front of the attacker. The operative defense must essentially prevent the enemy from breaking through. Its aim must be the same as in a war of movement: it should not be satisfied with this first act of withdrawal, but, immediately after the start of the enemy attempt at breaking through, resort to an operative counter-attack, either on the same place or on other places, utilizing the element of surprise, so as to force a decision.

The tactical defense in a war of position is quite different from the tactical defense in a war of movement.

According to Clausewitz, defense is the stronger tactical form and superior to attack. The defender can deliver a well directed and well prepared fire from his secure position, but the attacker must fire while advancing. Each progression of attacking riflemen is attended by weakness, inferiority. But this inferiority does not exist in a war of position, since the attacker does not need to get closer; he is installed in a protected position in front of the defender, at a suitable distance of irruption. The attacker, in a few seconds, throws himself against the defender with all his forces. The latter would be overpowered if he fought in linear entrenched positions, according to the manner prescribed before World War I, *i.e.,* without depth. This is why the defender was compelled to give deep articulation to his system. Instead of the long approach of the attacker, which devoured forces and caused heavy casualties, we saw penetration by the attacker through deep defensive zones, which gave chance and time to the defender to wear him out.

Another important reason compelled the breaking up of rigid lines into their particular defense elements and to articulation in depth: constant increase of offensive fire and of offensive means, which finally led to the "war of matériel". In the first defensive battles in the west, the fighting was still on the first-line trenches. Most of the time, these trenches were lost to the enemy with heavy casualties. This is why one came to resort to a division of forces emplaced in trenches one behind the other. Later, one came to articulate particular combat elements in depth. The rigid, visible line of trenches, which cost so many lives, disappeared more and more. The intense enemy fire could no longer concentrate on the linear trenches, but had to be spread over the defensive positions in their entire depth, and thus was weakened.

Another result appeared with this new disposition in depth: It facilitated camouflaging from land and air observers. The individual and dispersed defensive elements could hardly be detected by observation, especially in cut-up and shelled terrain. Thus, they could be spared from punishment by enemy fire, as the result of observation. This disposition compelled the artillery to adopt less effective emplacements in open terrain.

The entire development of defensive tactics was oriented towards economizing fighting capacity as much as possible until the moment of the enemy assault, so as to insure victory in this short, but decisive instant of a break-through battle. In this effort new conceptions appeared; a rear position was organized, which was kept from direct enemy observation and direct enemy fire. A system of outposts was calculated to leave the enemy in ignorance of the real emplacement of the main battlefield. In this manner, the attack was exposed in open terrain—its main weakness—and the defender was protected from surprise. The position became more and more elaborated; barbed wire entanglements were disposed in great width and according to irregular designs, in front of the trenches. Instead of one defensive position occupied by strong forces, there were several, each one comprising a deep and strong fighting field.

Trenches, Dispersion, Camouflage

However, the trench did not disappear. It remained as a permanent position, allowing a cut in the terrain to be occupied with a minimum of troops. But so far as defensive battle itself was concerned, dispersion and camouflage of personnel and matériel remained primary preoccupations.

The defender, as well as the attacker, increased the number of his weapons and introduced new ones: grenades, mortars, flame-throwers, light machine guns, planes, tanks. The machine gun became the main weapon of infantry. The number of batteries grew enormously. Finally, in break-through battles, on each 100 meter battlefront a battery could be counted, outside of the other batteries entrusted with other missions and disposed in depth. The masked artillery emplacements were detected by observation planes, or by light and sound observation; they were attacked by gas. Hence, the masked emplacement could no longer offer satisfactory protection. Defense and attack suffered this disadvantage in equal measure.

The manner in which war was waged had also to take into account this increased importance of matériel, and the extraordinary growth of the material offensive power. How could infantry hold out for days and weeks during enemy preparation fire? In the front zone, which was particularly exposed to violent enemy fire, only weak forces were pushed; the attacker was thus left guessing where the main battle-field emplacements and those of the main line of resistance might be. Local withdrawal of the small forward elements corresponded to the idea of "mobile defense". Powerful reserves were held close to the front, although just out of range of enemy fire. They were held in readiness to be engaged immediately and without receiving orders from higher echelons, since communications might be cut off. These reserves would be important enough to be divisions. All these features characterized the infantry defensive combat in a war of position.

The artillery defensive combat in a war of position was characterized by the unified command of important artillery masses, by the concentration of its fire in space and time in decisive moments, by great disposition in depth, so as to diminish the effect of enemy fire, and also to enable fighting to continue in case the position should be penetrated by the enemy. Above all, artillery strove to pound the attacker so soon as the fighting started.

It was impossible that the defense be ready to receive a break-through assault on the entire front at the same time. In this long war of position, it was important for the defender to recognize the intention of his attacker, so as to check him by proper counter-measures, and to break up the offensive even before it was unleashed. The enemy intentions had to be known in due course of time by a constant observation of the enemy terrain, either from the air, or on the ground, through listening posts, as well as by shock-troop undertakings. The detection of the enemy's offensive intentions was rendered considerably more difficult when his artillery ceased firing, but it was rendered easier when the offensive preparations were important and long. All these efforts purported to keep up the defensive strength of the infantry, on which rested the main burden of the battle.

We can see that the main forms of the tactical defensive in a war of position differed on essential points from those of the tactical defensive in a war of movement. There had to be taken into account the material power and the numerical increase of fire weapons.

Examples, Operative and Tactical Defensive

W E shall now see by a few examples drawn from the war of position the effect of operative and tactical defensive. At the same time we shall study the reasons why defense did or did not work.

During the fall of 1914, all outflanking attempts of both opponents in the west failed. The German High Command in 1915 began to shift the gravity of its effort towards the east; in the west, it stayed on the defensive until March, 1918, except for the big-scale attack on Verdun and for a few partial offensives, which could not give many results. Hence, in the west, a material and moral struggle took place for 3 years, in opposition to the German defensive and the operative and tactical efforts of the French and the English at breaking through. This only shows that we Germans acquired a very wide experience which we were able constantly to add to for 3 years.

In this struggle, which ever assumed more gigantic proportions, defensive won, although time was in favor of our enemies who steadily increased their forces. We shall see why defensive won, and also why the attacks of the French and of the English failed. Finally, we shall see that the attack—which is the decisive form of the conduct of war—can win over the power of defensive.

General Joffre, the French generalissimo, was forced to realize that his numerous local attacks in the winter of 1914-1915 could not come through, and even that in certain places, he had to face serious setbacks. This lack of success led him to recognize that the German defensive could be broken only by engaging strong matériel and personnel in coordinated attacks and in mass.

The series of these attacks began with the winter battle of Champagne, between the 16th of February and the 20th of March, 1915. According to peace-time methods, the German positions were weak and did not have the necessary depth. The chalky terrain had been transformed by steady rains into glue. However, the 8th Army Corps and the 8th Reserve Corps held firmly, despite the heavy casualties in the front lines. The attack of the French 4th Army on a 12 kilometer line was unleashed on a much too small front, the forces engaged were not big enough, the preparations too conspicuous. The element of surprise lacked completely.

The German artillery succeeded at different times in bringing the enemy lines under strong fire and breaking the offensive will of the assault troops even before they started their offensive. The long pauses between the large-scale offensives left time for the defensive to reorganize. Tactically as well as operatively, the break-through was a failure.

The same fate was met by another break-through attempted by the French 10th Army of General d'Urbal and the British 1st Army of General Haig in Artois from the 9th of May until the end of June 1915, against the German 6th Army of Crown Prince Rupprecht of Bavaria. The power of 33 French and British divisions, engaged during all those weeks, was not sufficient to break the defense of 20 German divisions. From these battles it should not be concluded that the numerical superiority of offensive should be much larger than this to break defensive. The original superiority of the attacker in artillery of 2 to 1 came down to 3 to 2, since the defender had time to bring up reinforcements.

The French 10th Army fired 2,156,000 shots between the 3d of May and the 18th of June; the German 6th Army 2,176,000. Matériel was opposed to matériel. The moral forces themselves on the side of the attacker were not superior. Indeed, General d'Urbal had exalted his troops to an exceptional effort. "As soon as the infantry is engaged, its offensive will be pursued with the greatest activity and élan, night and day." Later on he said, "We shall attack constantly and everywhere, so long as one enemy stands in front of us." But the infantry of the German 6th Army opposed just as strong a defensive power and repelled the danger of a break-through.

Break-through Possibilities

General Joffre came to think that a break-through was only possible if "the operation had a sufficiently broad base. The hour has come when we must concentrate all forces to be engaged." Thus, the efforts of the enemies increased again in 1916, in the Somme battle.

Nineteen French divisions in the front-line attacked the German 2d Army on a front of 40 kilometers, after an artillery preparation of 7 days by 3000 guns. The 2d Army, commanded by General von Bulow, comprised 7 divisions in front and 488 guns. The German front was broken on a width of 20 kilometers, but the French were not active enough to exploit this initial success. Then during 2 months, a struggle followed which opposed 106 enemy divisions to 57½ German; there were 270,000 enemy and 200,000 German casualties. In spite of a uselessly strong occupation of the front lines and an insufficient depth, the defensive still emerged victor. No break-through occurred; there was only a local gain of terrain 25 kilometers broad and 8 kilometers deep, result of a battle which lasted 2 months. The initial success of the first day of battle was not exploited. The defensive was not beaten, but it exhausted the attacker, thus fulfilling its ultimate aim.

From the battle of the Somme, France drew the conclusion that the offensive power had not been sufficient to break the defensive, hence that it should be increased. The Nivelle offensive in the spring of 1917 was then organized on a front of 100 kilometers, from Soisson as far as to the east of Rheims; 1½ million soldiers, 3300 guns and 200 tanks were kept in readiness, 33 million shells were stored for the artillery. On the 6th of April the artillery fire began, and pounded the German positions for 10 days without interruption, until the 16th of April. General Nivelle launched an order-of-the-day in the evening of the 15th to inspire his assault troops "L'heure est venue! Confiance! Courage! Vive la France!" On the 16th of April, at 6 o'clock in the morning, the attacking infantry launched its assaults by hundreds of thousands on the entire front of 100 kilometers. It broke up completely with heavy losses under the German defensive fire. The following local offensives could not change this defeat.

Why did the German front hold in front of so heavy attacks? It cannot indeed be said that the French infantry lacked in offensive will. The French riflemen knew that the entire country hoped that this attack would mark a decisive turning point of the war. However, the offensive failed.

On the German side, thanks to the activity of reconnaissance and combat aviation, the preparations made for this attack were known; the defense accordingly could be bolstered. There was no surprise. Between the 7th Army of General von Böhn and the 3d Army of General von Einem, both of them in a threatened situation, the 1st Army Corps of General von Bulow was engaged. The entire artillery available on the western front was sent there; sufficient ammunition was ready and behind the front 14 divisions were held prepared to intervene immediately. The disposition was deep; the front lines not too heavily occupied, so as to be protected from enemy fire; artillery fire was delivered early against the enemy offensive preparations. The German infantry was animated by a complete confidence in the outcome of the ultimate moment of assault.

Attack Which Was Bound to Fail

In a war of movement, the attack has a good chance to succeed when it has superiority in matériel and in personnel over the defensive in the front zones; and success is certain when these front zones are taken. Here, the attacker must build up a superiority over the defender. In a war of position, the defensive power is increased by the defensive organizations and the possibilities of camouflage. The superiority of the attacker must be greater. In the Nivelle offensive, this was not the case. It surprised the defender neither operatively—since he knew in advance of the offensive preparations—nor tactically because of the long artillery preparation. The defender could reinforce his defense in time. The power of the defensive was nearly as great as that of the offensive. The attack was bound to fail.

Here is another example of successful defensive—on the part of our enemies. After the great German offensive in the spring of 1918, following the battles of Armentieres in April, of Soissons, Rheims and Noyon in May and June, another German attack of diversion was to take place on both sides of Rheims, before the main thrust against the English in Flanders was to be dealt. This attack of the German 1st and 3d Armies, east of Rheims on the 15th of July, 1918, failed for reasons similar to those which defeated the Nivelle offensive. The enemy—the French 4th Army under General Gouraud—was surprised neither tactically nor operatively. Since the beginning of July, the French believed this offensive was coming. Sufficient reserves were brought up, the defense was bolstered. On the 16th of July, in the region of Mourmelon-le-Grand, German prisoners were captured by the French, who learned from them of the day and hour of the attack. General Gouraud left his ad-

vanced positions weakly occupied, and shifted his main resistance to his second position. The German offensive overpowered the weak advanced resistance, but was blocked by
the second position.

The defensive also stopped other heavy break-through attacks in other theaters of operations. At Isonzo, on the
Italian front, the Austrians repelled 12 attempts by the
Italians. Despite their considerable material superiority, the
Italians could not win the Austrian positions. On the other
hand, in the middle of May, 1916, the Austro-Hungarians
did not succeed in their attack in south Tyrol. The Austro-
Hungarian 11th Army under General Dankl, with 9 divisions, was to press forward on the plateaus of Vielgereuth
and Lafraun, and force back the enemy into the plain. The
attacker took the defensive positions and captured 40,000
Italians and 300 guns. But after this great initial success
the offensive power slackened. This offensive did not surprise the opposing Italian 1st Army; the defense was
strengthened, although it lacked artillery. Reinforcements
were brought up by rail and by road more rapidly than was
possible on the Austrian side; advance was slow in difficult
mountainous country. The climax of the offensive power
was reached too early; the tactical initial success could not be
enlarged into an operative break-through.

But, the defense in a war of position has not been always successful. In many instances, it could not hold. Let
us examine the reasons.

Tarnow-Gorlice Break-through

The break-through battle of Tarnow-Gorlice on the 2d
of May, 1915, had far-reaching consequences. Six German
and 2 Austro-Hungarian divisions of the German 11th Army
under Marshal von Mackensen opened an artillery preparation with 352 light and 144 heavy guns against 2 active and
1 reserve division of the 3d Russian Army. They attacked

on a front of 35 kilometers and took the first Russian position. The Russians, since the middle of April, had noticed "signs of a probable German attack." But, aside from calling up the 3d Caucasian Corps, already ordered, the threatened front was not reinforced. Its defensive power proved insufficient. The local reserves—1½ division— were kept 15 to 20 kilometers behind the front, too far to be engaged during the short German preparation. They could no more prevent capture of other Russian positions on the 3d and 4th of May. Since insufficient rail and road communications did not allow the Russians to bring up further reserves in due time, the gap could not be closed. The tactical break-through was enlarged and became an operative break-through. The reasons for this failing defensive were surprise, owing to the short time devoted to offensive preparations, lack of sufficient reserves and inadequacy of communications.

In June, 1916, the Brussilov offensive overpowered the Austrian defensive front in Volhynia and in east Galicia. This Russian success cannot be ascribed to surprise or superiority. The artillery preparation was not exceptional and lasted only during the 4th and 5th of June. The main offensive of the 5th of June was launched by the Russian 8th Army with only 6 divisions in front and 5 in second line against 4 Austro-Hungarian divisions in front and 2 in second line, comprising the 4th Army of Archduke Joseph Ferdinand. The front of the latter army broke up just as thoroughly as did the 7th Army of General von Planzer-Baltin on the 10th and 11th of June on both sides of the Dniestr, despite that, according to the judgment of German and Austrian leaders, there was nothing to fear. The Russians already claimed on the 11th of June to have taken 106,000 prisoners. The break of this defensive front was due essentially to the carelessness of the army command and to the mediocre resistance of the defending troops, among whom confusion due to varied national origins worked as a con-

stant handicap. This break happened in spite of the fact
that 5 infantry divisions had been shifted there from the
eastern front. While the fronts of the 7th and 4th Armies
broke up, the German Southern Army, installed between
both, held firmly, thanks to the active and strong leadership
of General Bothmer, who disposed then had at his disposition only 1 division.

However, in spite of its great tactical initial successes,
the Brussilov offensive did not ripen into a wide break-
through of any operative significance. The attack had succeeded on the 5th of June. On the 8th of June General
Brussilov, who was concerned about his flanks, gave the
8th Army the order to stop. On the 12th of June, the advance was resumed, but by then General von Linsingen was
ready to counter-attack from the direction of Kowel with his
"assault group of the Marwitz."

Operations on the Isonzo

The break-up of the Italian defensive front on the Isonzo
in the fall of 1917 is similar to that of the Austro-Hungarian
front. The attack of the German 14th Army of General
von Bulow did not surprise the Italians either. The mass
of the Italian army was in position. "The great hour has
come, the important, maybe the decisive one! Let them
come, these little descendents of Arminus, they will no
longer find the legions of Varus!" proclaimed the General
of the Italian 4th Army Corps, General Gavaciochi, in an
order-of-the-day of the 23d of October. The next day, on
the 24th of October, "the little descendents of Arminius"
answered this order-of-the-day. The defender could not
hold his excellent positions in front of the attacker. Careful
offensive preparation, superior artillery fire, the effect of gas,
and above all, the dynamic élan of the attacking infantry
triumphed over the defender, despite the difficulties offered
by the high mountains confronting the attacker. The Italian
Marshal, Count Cadorna, in a letter addressed to the Chief

of General Staff of the 14th Army, General von Dellmensingen, on the 30th September 1926, said: "Doubtless the operation of the German 14th Army would not have succeeded, if the spirit of the Italian army had been the same as two months before, when it conquered the Austrian position on the heights of Bainsizza on a depth of 12 kilometers. This proves to me that success or failure depends to a great extent upon the morale of the combatants." In the investigation to which he was subjected, he explained; "It would have been sufficient had each man fired a clip of cartridges, each machine gun a belt, each gun a shot."

It is only on the Piave that the Italians succeeded in consolidating a defensive front, with the help of 6 French and 5 English divisions. The German offensive had passed its climax.

In the battle of Cambrai on the 20th of November, 1917, the English obtained a tactical success against the German defensive front through the use of a new weapon, the tank. After a short artillery preparation of about half an hour, they laid smoke screens on a front of about 10 kilometers between Havincourt and Gonnelieu. Six infantry divisions, 3 cavalry divisions and more than 300 tanks were engaged. The particularly strong Siegfried position was overpowered and in a few hours the entire German defensive system was broken. Tanks and surprise caused this offensive success. Fortunately for the German defensive, the attack was launched on too short a front. It was possible to fill the gap with reserves in a short time, as that the crisis was overcome and the operative exploitation of the tactical success checked.

France, Spring of 1918

The German offensive in the spring of 1918 was a well-exploited surprise; the great battle of France. A well-coordinated plan had organized transportation, storage of ammunition, the arrival of artillery and of the attacking divisions. All activities were conducted only by night. On the 21st of March, 3 armies, the 17th, the 2nd and the 18th, a total of 62 divisions were held in readiness on a front of 75 kilometers between Arras and La Fere. The opposing artillery was attacked by gas. During 3 hours, artillery and mortars neutralized the enemy positions by their intensive fire. The attacking infantry rushed to the assault at the same time, 9:40 o'clock, on the entire front. The English 5th Army, under General Gough, was stretched out widely on a front of 67 kilometers with its 11 divisions in front lines and 2 divisions in reserve. It was shattered by the 42 divisions of the German 2nd and 18th armies. The English 3rd Army, under General Byng, which had 8 divisions on a front of 43 kilometers, with 8 divisions in reserve, was pushed back by the 17 divisions of the 17th Army.

The tactical defensive of the English was surprised and destroyed by the German attack, which was pushed deeply. It overpowered all enemy defensive organizations, but it could not accomplish the operative break-through. It proved to be too weak. Its force was consumed too early, no reserve army followed, no diversion or confusion attack was carried out in order to tie up enemy reserves elsewhere. Until the 5th of April, the Allies were able to bring up 45 infantry and 6 cavalry divisions by road and rail to fill up the gap, and opposed a consolidated defensive front to the exhausted offensive, which was not nourished by fresh forces.

The successes of the French flank attack of the 18th of July, 1918, from the woods of Villers-Cotterets against the flank of the German 7th Army should be ascribed to the element of surprise and to the use of the tank. The same causes explain their success on the 8th of August east of Amiens against the salient of the German 2nd and 18th Armies. On the 18th of July, after a very short artillery preparation, the French attacked with a great number of tanks, which advanced under the screen of high wheat fields, against a weak German front unsupported by any armored vehicle. On the 8th of August the surprise attack, under cover of thick smoke screens, was successful. In both cases, success remained local and new defensive fronts could be consolidated in due course of time. The scope of the attacks was not sufficient to warrant a great operative exploitation.

The battle of Verdun, the great Flanders battle in 1917 and the eleven Isonzo battles have a particularly important place in the record of the war of position. In all of these operations, the attacker renounced the element of surprise and strove to beat down the defenses by sheer force, in struggles lasting months and always in the same positions. The attacker sought to wear out the defender and to use up his forces by prolonged attacks. He assumed the role which belongs to the defensive, which, as the "stronger form", designs to create an equalization of forces. The chief of the German General Staff, General von Falkenhayn, assumed that the German attacks at Verdun would force the French High Command to engage little by little all its available reserves so that the rest of the front would· be weakened and thus allow a decisive blow. The Italians, by their attacks of June, 1915, until August, 1917, hoped to wear out the defensive front of the Austrians, in such a way that. they could advance into the Austrian grain lands.

The English believed they would be able to weaken the defender, push him back and occupy the German U-boat bases on the Flanders coast.

All these three operations had this in common: the defender had to fight and could not withdraw. General von Falkenhayn in 1915 said in his Christmas proclamation: "There are aims for which the French High Command is compelled to engage its very last man. But, while doing so, is has to bleed France's troops, because there can be no retreat." The French Prime Minister, Briand, confirmed this when he brusquely said to General Joffre: "If you withdraw,

all Frenchmen would spit in your face!" A complete break-up
of the Austrian front on the Isonzo would have been followed by immense consequences to the structure of Austria.
Germany could not retreat in Flanders, since she could not
give up the U-boat bases, upon which depended her success
in the U-boat war, which at that time constituted such a
grave menace to the English. In all these three cases, the defender had to stand firm before the attacker. He was compelled to submit himself to the attacker's intentions, to wear
him out.

Theory of Exhaustion

This theory of exhaustion finds a justification when
the defender can be surprised and is not yet prepared to
meet a big-scale attack. Then, the casualties, the weakening
of the defender must be greater than with the attacker, as is
shown by numerous examples in the first World War. But
if the defender establishes a strong defensive front, he is
not the only one to face heavy losses and exhaustion. He is
not the only one to wear out his strength. This also is the
position of the attacker, and at least to an equal extent.

In the Verdun battle, between the end of February, 1916,
and the 11th of July, 1916, the day when the attacks ceased,
the German losses amounted to 282,000 men, the French
to 317,000. The attacker, intent upon paralyzing the defender, became almost as weak as the latter. What does a
surplus loss of 35,000 men for the defender mean, when the
superiority of the Entente in the west consisted of 1,135,000
men, at the beginning of February? On the German side,
47 divisions had to bear the brunt of the fighting with
average casualties of 6,000 men per division of only 3 infantry regiments. For weeks, these divisions waged an exhausting struggle, and they had to spend months in the rear
before they could again be fit for combat. But the trials
of French divisions, which were supposed to be worn out,
were much less exacting. Eighty-seven divisions, with

an average of four infantry regiments per division, were engaged and frequently relieved, and lost an average of 4,500 men per division.

"A good proportion of the best forces of the German army remained at Verdun," says a German sanitation report. The aim, to wear out the French army by "softening" its other fronts and then launching a decisive battle at a well-chosen place, was not attained. Not only did the French hold firm in front of the German offensive, but they still had the strength during the same summer to attack on the Somme, with the English. The initiative, which General von Falken-hayn wanted to secure for a following decisive battle, passed to the enemy.

In Flanders, the Germans wanted to hold all their positions against English large-scale attacks, which began with the reduction of the salient of Wytschaete on the 7th of June, 1917, and were followed by other engagements of particular violence on the 31st of July, the 16th of August, the 20th of September and the 22nd of October. These attacks ceased only towards the end of November. The Germans had to bar the road to the U-boat bases. The intention of the English was to wear out the German front. Between the 20th of May and the 30th of November they lost 264,000 men, prisoners, wounded and missing, against 231,469 on the German side.

On the Isonzo after two years, the Austrian defender had almost reached the limits of his force. He had to turn to the German High Command for support. But the attacker had not succeeded in breaking through the defensive and reaching his aim. The defender lost 386,971 men, the attacker 625,525.

From these experiences, the German High Command drew its conclusions for the plan of operations in 1918. In a war of position, the defensive could not be crushed, unless the element of surprise could be brought into play and unless it could be attacked at different places. The bludgeon blows had to be applied in various places and also to surprise the defender. The defender did not need to be prepared with the same efficiency on the entire defensive front, since the troops and the matériel of our enemies could not be sufficient for the latter's purpose.

In March, 1918, the Germans attacked in the direction of Amiens against the juncture of the Franco-English armies. It was the great battle of France. Then they attacked the French on both sides of Rheims. The English were again to be attacked in Flanders. But this intention was not realized, since the attacker could not follow through with the necessary reserves, which had been absorbed. The defender remained the victor, not because of the fact that defense is the stronger form, but because the superiority in strength of the attacker was too weak to beat down the defender.

The German High Command then was compelled to resort to the defensive on the 18th of July, 1918. The Entente steadily received new forces from the Americans; its superiority became so great that the weaker form of defensive, the combat of resistance, had to be chosen. Without even considering the undermining influences inside Germany, there is no doubt that the defensive could not have succeeded in wearing out the attacker, realizing an equalization of forces and then resorting to an all-out defensive on the prepared position between Antwerp and the Meuse: the complete rupture of the Bulgarian front of Salonik took the sword out of the hands of the German High Command.

Success of Tactical Defense

Let us point out in conclusion that the success of tactical defensive in a war of position depends upon certain presumptions. Defensive in a war of position had increased considerably in power. Its positions were organized through years of effort; they were fronted with deep barbed-wire entanglements; its fire power had become much greater. Hence, offensive could break through defensive only by displaying sufficiently great superiority, making use of the surprise element, while leaving the defender no time to be reinforced. Hence the offensive must have strong superiority in men and material. We reached the most extreme form of this characteristic in the "battles of matériel." These, however, did not take into account the element of surprise. For this very reason, they did not yield results.

Since the defense could not be held in readiness against a break-through attack on the entire front, it had to detect in due time offensive intentions, in order to block surprise attacks and assemble a certain weight of force in face of a foreseen offensive. Furthermore, during the enemy preparation fire, the defender had to maintain his fighting strength. He must then disperse his forces, articulate them in depth, camouflage his disposition, and keep reserves in readiness for an immediate counter-blow. Finally, only combatants of high warlike virtues could resist the severe tests of a break-through battle. The successes of the Brussilov offensive and of the German offensive in Italy are examples of these virtues.

On the operative level, in a war of movement, the defensive succeeded always in blocking a tactical break-through, before it could be enlarged into a definitive victory, when the attacker in the course of his offensive had not utilized the element of success. Military writers have frequently considered this superiority of defense as a victory of the operative defense in the operative attack. It is now suitable to examine the reasons which helped the defense check the operative completion of a tactical break-through. Indeed, neither the sentence of Clausewitz about the "stronger form," nor the increased fire power can be sufficient to explain this.

Possibilities of Defense

In every case where the defender could dispose of reserves, of a sufficient railroad network, of trucks and motorized troops, he was able to patch up the gaps opened in his front, and this in a short time, sometimes in a few hours. He thus could build up a new front with fresh forces. This happened as well for our enemies as for ourselves on the western theater. of operations. An operative break-through has a chance to succeed when the enemy reserves are tied up elsewhere by some diversion or confusing operation, or when his needed reinforcements cannot be brought up through lack of communications or of transportation, or again when they are utilized elsewhere. Finally, the success of defensive, or of break-through offensive, depends upon whether the fresh troops can hold out or not. Before the time of the railroad and of the truck, victory rewarded an army on one field. The victor then could turn towards a new mission. Nowadays a hard-pressed defender can summon reinforcements from hundreds of kilometers away. There is a solidarity in space. The present defensive battle, then, has an impact on all available forces and matériel. Defense has to bow to attack only after all these forces have been used up. In the fall of 1918 the German High Command was forced to resort to that attitude. It had to give up defensive and resort to a mere delaying resistance.

The operative defensive power has been also increased by the play of military alliances. The particular states did not fight for themselves alone, they did not depend only on their own forces and matériel; they could exchange help. None of the German break-through victories against the Serbs, the Rumanians, the Italians led to complete victory against these peoples. Furthermore, the Rumanians received protection and support from the Russians and they were able to re-consolidate a new defensive front on the Sereth. In Serbia, the English and the French established a new front north of Salonika, as well as in Italy on the Piave. Thus, the beaten Allies prevented a military and political exploitation of victory.

Russia alone had to count on herself. Since she did not

have sufficient transportation and communications, she could not patch up the gap opened on the 2nd of May, 1915, at the battle of Gorlice. But these immense spaces which had already saved her once, in 1812, came to her aid. At the cost of great casualties and of wide territory, the Russians could finally succeed after months in blocking our pressure and reforming a continuous front.

Conclusion

When we look back upon the entire development of World War I, we are struck by the fact that in this great war which involved many fronts and countries, a predominant part of the operations fell upon defensive. Before the war, we hoped to be able to defeat France in a quick offensive, so as to turn towards Russia afterwards. Operative conceptions, training and education before the war were almost exclusively oriented towards the decisive offensive. But the plan of operations failed, because the superiority of the attacker was not sufficient to win over the defender. The increased fire power brought a reinforcement of defensive; before the war this had not been fully recognized.

The increase of the tactical strength of defensive led to an increase of its operative strength. But the plan of operations had not taken this into consideration, so that it did not engage a sufficient superiority; it could bring nowhere a quick decision, but failed everywhere.

Before the war, defensive had fallen into a secondary position. During the war, it became an essential part of the operations. The more remote the decision of the war appeared to be the more troops and matériel were thrown in, the less easy it was to surprise on a definite spot with a superior force, and the more was the defensive bound to gain in influence and in importance. It is not possible to launch constantly armies of several million men in offensive battles. Offensive had to give way to defensive. At the beginning of the war, the entire German army attacked on all fronts; later most of it had to be on the defensive the year around.

The relation between attack and defense kept changing all the time; but the few fundamentals of operative defense were not modified. The law according to which defensive alone does not lead to a decision in face of a determined attack; the conduct of an operation on interior lines, which can be successful only when it beats one of the enemies; the necessity of forming a superior gravity where the decision is sought; the efforts towards an equalization of forces, through delaying conduct of operations when one does not feel strong enough to resort to offensive—all these few fundamental laws found their confirmation in the first World War and their operative application.

The increased fire-power also rendered the operative defense more efficient. It allowed to engage in the more decisive places much less important forces than was thought necessary before the war, for the benefit of the decisive theater of operations. It also allowed forces to be equalized quicker and more thoroughly, if one was satisfied with a delaying operation. For these reasons, the importance of a delaying procedure grew, as in the Serb campaign for instance.

Hence, defense should not be considered as a tactic of inferior rank. The operative possibilities have been considerably enlarged by the experience of the first World War; they since have become much more powerful, much more efficient.

The influence of growing fire-power on tactical defense is evident. Defensive was bound to be favored by the improvement of weapons. It could realize its mission more easily; block the enemy attacks by its fire. The increase of tactical defensive strength was bound also to influence the concentration of forces; weak forces could be disposed on the defensive front, and strong forces massed to counter-attack.

Towards the end of the war, it is well known that we Germans were no longer able to lead a true defensive action, because the forces of our enemy—especially after the arrival of American divisions in the summer of 1918—increased all the time, and we could not hope to effect a sufficient equalization of forces. We had to resort to a delaying conduct of operations.

Changes In Tactical Form

The war has shown that the systematic preference given to tactical attack can lead to premature and unnecessary misuse of the moral and material offensive power, instead of reaching the same results, sometimes even with more certitude, through defensive. Clausewitz on this point expresses himself in a forceful manner, when he says, "We do not give any consideration to the exclamations of those who expect everything from offensive and from movement and think they discover the true image of war in the hussar who storms forward with his saber swinging above his head."

Furthermore, we have to point to a complete change in the tactical form of defensive. The linear trenches, thickly occupied, have disappeared. Dispersion, camouflage, disposition in depth were the fundamentals which permitted the defender to be hidden from the observation of the enemy and to keep his forces intact from enemy fire power.

The war of position brought particular characteristics and forms. The defensive power was increased by organizing positions and by bringing up strong reserves to threatened points. Then, the attacker had to overpower the defender by concentrating swiftly a superior offensive force.

The previous World War also confirmed the first law to have been expressed in this study: Defense by itself is not able to compel an enemy animated by a strong will to accept peace. But the defensive is able more than before to carry out its original mission, which is to break the strength of the attacker, to parry his blows, to weaken him, to bleed him, so as to reverse the relation of forces and lead finally to the offensive, which is the only decisive form of warfare.

PART TWO

Defensive Conceptions, German School, Between Wars

● ● ●

Present Defensive Tactics;
New Weapons and Means

WAR is the infallible testing field where the teachings and interpretations of the principles of the conduct of war and of combat which have been elaborated in peace time are tested and where the entire formation of leadership and troops can prove whether or not it has been established on a basis of reality.

World War I submitted the German army, its leadership and its troops to this hardest of all tests. It proved again the intangibility of the few fundamental laws of defensive in the conduct of war and of combat; it has also shown which kind of defensive must be given up. It is not possible in such a war to attack everywhere constantly, but, in order to be sufficiently strong to attack decisive points, one of the forms of defense must be used.

Above all, the war brought considerable modifications to tactical defensive. We will later deal with these experiences and consequences.

Since the end of the war, 18 years have passed. [von Leeb wrote in 1936.] Are the experiences of this war of four and a half years still valid? Are the fundamentals of defense, as confirmed in World War I, to be revised or not?

Napoleon once said that any army must change its tactics

113

every 10 years, in order to surprise the enemy with new tactics, and thus counteract and overcome his customary attacking methods. This does not seem absolutely sound, but these modifications should spring from the improvement of existing weapons and war means and from the use of new weapons. And now, does operative and tactical defensive rest on the same bases now as at the end of the first World War? There is nothing more fatal for a soldier than to consider as right the ideas once accepted, without proving whether what was once recognized is still valid or is merely endorsed by habit.

In the realm of operative and tactical defensive we Germans have all reason to base our principles of action on reality, because the defensive situation in which we have found ourselves for centuries, has become still worse since the war. Politically, after as well as before the war, we have been on defensive; militarily, all other states are ahead of us in the development of those weapons, which have been denied us since the end of the war. We are confronted by highly-equipped neighbors, more so than before the former conflict. Geographically, our position is always the same. In the very heart of Europe, almost without natural frontiers, even part of our territory, East Prussia, separated from the main area; the necessity forced upon us of facing more than one front; access from the ocean easy to bar. Hence it is sheer necessity for us to clarify all possibilities offered by operative and tactical defensive.

The first World War, the bitterest of all wars ever fought "for the existence of our people" has called for the moral force of all. The existing weapons and tools were improved, rendered more efficient. The introduction of the internal combustion motor was the most important of the innovations. It was utilized

    (a) for armored troops
    (b) for aircraft
    (c) as a means of transportation

[TRANSLATOR'S NOTE. Here follow a number of general remarks on modern armies. They are, of course, considerably cancelled by the developments of World War II. Only what appeared to the translators to be of interest has been used, not because these remarks offer anything new, but because they show that German military thought on the whole was well oriented before this war. General von Leeb first considers the extreme advocates of the tank; according to them, the brave, staunch marching infantry division belongs to a past era. He continues:]

It is argued that infantry is rendered operatively obsolete because of its slowness. That on the field, also, it would be beaten by the tank. Furthermore, that on the battlefield, the decision would no longer rest with infantry, but the tank. The advocates of such opinions go so far in their enthusiasm as to describe advocates of previous methods as backward imbeciles.

Planes vs. Land Armies

The enthusiasts of the air force also claim that the decisive weapon of war is the plane. This is the interpretation of the Italian General, Douhet, who considers the land army fit enough for defensive, because of the difficulties of offensive. But since defensive alone cannot bring a decision, the decision would rest with the air force and in air fighting. Others contend that the air force would also play a decisive role in land operations by creating the basis for infantry success.

Others again trust to fortifications of frontiers, like the French. They consider that an attack against these fortifications with the existing means is inconceivable, so that they, like Douhet, conclude that the decision cannot be brought about on land. [But they did not try to achieve a decision in the air. TRANSLATORS.]

This very variety of opinion proves how difficult it is to recognize in peacetime the extent of the influence of im-

proved or new weapons on the conduct of war and of combat; and also to conceive a picture of a future war, and
consequently to see what is reality and what is not reality.
The first World War has also shown that in the past we did
not recognize the full power of automatic weapons and the
importance of defensive.

We do not now wish to fix our opinions according to
such or such a school, but, supported by past experiences, to
see what influence the new improvements and weapons had on
the operative and tactical defensive.

All motorized weapons enlarge considerably the value of
two of the laws of the conduct of war, namely: rapidity of
movements and length of engagements. . . . These two
characteristics alone make of the air force, of armored troops
and of trucks operative means of primary importance. They
allow the building up of a strong gravity where decision is
sought, be it a break-through attack, an operative outflanking movement, a counter-attack, or a shifting of forces
from one front to another. This swiftness of concentration and of engagement allows operative and tactical surprise, one of the essential elements of decisive success. Furthermore, the tremendous power of tanks and planes can
be unleashed in a decisive manner, when they are used in
mass.

Tanks and planes have this in common, that they can
be used only in attack. They simply do not know defensive,
except in the form of a counter-attack. During the previous
war, as we have seen, the defensive had in reality a much
greater force than was before generally recognized. The
new weapons may be able to re-establish the superiority of
offensive and its strength. Let us hope that they will allow
such strengthening of attack as to be in position to overcome even the strongest form of defense—defense in a war
of position.

Anyhow, it is possible to state that all qualities such as
rapidity and surprise will contribute to avert static opera-

tions in a future war, and allow us to hope for a freer, more mobile conduct of war.

This movement will also be favored by another means, the radio. It makes the High Command independent of the wire telephone, permits quicker transmission of orders, and helps overcome the danger of slowness in the conduct of war and of combat. In this way, leadership will be able to take fullest advantage of favorable operative and tactical situations.

We knew that defensive is dependent upon offensive. It has to be organized to function in step with the attacker. But it does not always need to wait until the actions of the attacker are launched. It can anticipate them. In any case, the defender is in a situation of dependence upon the attacker, both on the tactical and on the operative level. When one wants to know the influence of all these new weapons upon the defensive, it is suitable first to see what influence they have on offensive, so as to infer from this the necessary counter measures that should be taken by the defensive.

Operative Attack
Depends on Surprise

R APIDITY and surprise have a reciprocal effect. Rapidity is an essential condition for surprise. If one does not act promptly, usually the enemy is not surprised. He has time to take counter measures.

Hence we must expect that a country which would attack Germany, would exercise extreme secrecy in putting its army or parts of it on a war footing and would begin the war by surprise. Success is assured the one who makes use of quick-firing weapons of the air force and of all motorized land arms.

The same is valid for an operative attack. An offensive can succeed in the form of an operative envelopment or in the form of a break-through. The more such an operation is realized, by surprise, the less time the defender finds to take counter-measures, and the more likely success appears. Hence, the quickest, motorized parts of the army will be utilized for the decisive part of an offensive operation, either envelopment or break-through.

Concerning the use of such rapid storm-troops, and the conduct of such decisive offensive operations, a great deal has been written. In particular, many French military writers have taken an active part in this new utilization of mobile troops. All interpretations have a certain number of points in common. One needs:

Quick air reconnaissance. It corresponds to the reconnaissance of the old foot armies, which was insured by cavalrymen. One needs now quicker means of reconnaissance.

Light armored reconnaissance. It is sent forward to occupy important strategic points in advance of the main troops, and also to insure security of the open flanks.

Quick pioneer detachments, charged with the mission of removing obstacles.

Armored elements to eliminate all oppositions to the advancing troops and to open a gap into any enemy disposition that tries to form a continuous front.

Motorized detachments of all arms which relentlessly exploit the results gained temporarily by tanks.

Air forces to take part in land operations with surprise; prevent any counter-measures, and particularly the arrival of reserves, to destroy railroad installations used in the concentration of enemy forces and also to neutralize enemy aviation.

Such an offensive operation has to be enlarged; the first rapid offensive wave is followed by reinforcements brought up by rail or by truck or even afoot.

However, not all troops can be motorized. In the previous wars, cavalry was quicker than infantry; nevertheless, the bulk of the armies was composed of foot soldiers.

A great advantage of motorization is that any motor truck can be utilized by motorized armies.

Any attacker will make best use of his quick weapons by utilizing surprise, if he can. He will do everything to avoid disclosing prematurely his operative intentions. He will concentrate his quick forces in large spaces, far from the territory of the proposed engagement. He will camouflage and disperse formations so that they can not be detected by air reconnaissance. In general, he will avoid taking any steps likely to point to the presence of great troops concentrations; false information will be released; all movements will take place under the protection of obscurity.

Mobile forces allow also prompt formation of an operative gravity concentrated either in view of obtaining an envelopment or a break-through. Such troops facilitate attack against the flanks of the enemy or in his rear; at the same time, they diminish the danger of a counter-attack on an elongated front.

Operative Defense
Guards Against Surprise

THE characteristic qualities of the new weapons give a better chance to surprise the enemy—namely, to attack him off his guard with superior forces on a decisive place. Against such danger operative defense must recognize the intentions and the actions of the foe, so as to take the proper counter-measures and be protected from surprise.

Operative defense must provide protection against such swift attack, and find time to take necessary decisions.

First of all, air reconnaissance must detect promptly the intentions of the enemy. The air force is the quickest arm. Since it is more difficult for land reconnaissance, even motorized, to press through advanced enemy elements, air reconnaissance has great importance in operative defense. The results of this air reconnaissance, of course, are obtained much quicker than by any land reconnaissance.

The enemy seeks to protect the secrecy of his disposition by camouflage and that of his movements by advancing at night. This is why sufficient results can be obtained only by intensifying air reconnaissance on the entire terrain to be observed. It has also to be constantly exercised, since the enemy can advance far in a few hours and thus surprise his opponent. To the present, military leaders felt safe when they knew the terrain in front of their armies to be free from enemy troops for one or two marching days. The operative reconnaissance now must extend to one or two days' march of mobile forces and hence have a depth of several hundred kilometers. This is why any operative defense absolutely requires air reconnaissance well coordinated with land operations.

Air reconnaissance is additionally indispensable since land reconnaissance has become more difficult. Operative land reconnaissance can depend only on motorized forces. These, however, are not always certain of finding a necessary network of roads. The enemy himself can oppose them by similar motorized elements. These motorized reconnaissances can yield satisfactory results only when they are strong enough to repel, at least in a few places, enemy reconnaissance and to fetter enemy advanced forces.

An active operative defense organizes and brings into play such services as listening posts, air warnings and protection radio.

The second characteristic of all motorized formations lies in the rapidity of their movements. Hence, it pertains to a good operative defense to hamper the quick advance of the attacker, when this is necessary to gain time.

The air force, which is the most speedy arm, here also comes in first place. It can attack and hamper the operative offensive movements of the enemy. Hence, the necessity of holding air fighting forces in reserve, ready to intervene immediately. This is an essential part of operative defense.

Obstacles are another means of slowing up offensive moves

of the enemy. When one has to deal with an enemy who can throw rapid mobile forces into an operative attack, all available time should be used in building up wide and numerous obstacles to prevent his progression by surprise or any movement aimed at a break-through or at an envelopment. If the defender can dispose troops in these prepared territories by sowing it with obstacles and mines, the effect is multiplied.

Defense Motorization

If the obstacles cannot be erected preventively, but only when the enemy troops are already threatening, then it is a condition indispensible to success that the troops charged with the mission of placing the obstacles be as mobile as the attacker's, and hence also be motorized. If one succeeds in slowing up the advance of the attacker, time has been gained to erect in depth further obstacles behind the first ones. The leader of such an operation of operative defense must have quick formations, principally motorized pioneers and armored protection, that should be able to engage the enemy in the direction from which threat proceeds, be it in front or on the flanks. The more numerous are such formations in charge of a delaying mission, the easier this mission will be accomplished. All these counter-measures of operative defense can be applied with equal effectiveness to prevent an enemy break-through or in a delaying operation of retreat.

If there is no contact yet realized between the opponents, there is a greater liberty of movement both for the attacker and the defendant. Then defensive should not place the bulk of its forces in static positions; instead it should manage an articulation in depth, all rapid formations being held in readiness for prompt intervention. Rapidity and maneuverability in defense must correspond to rapidity and maneuverability in attack.

But, if contact is realized, operative defense must oppose enemy attempts at breaking through or at envelopment. Since the attacker is quicker and more apt to surprise than in the past, operative defense to resort to a counter attack should dispose quick reserves drawn up to the threatened point. These reserves are composed of motorized infantry, armored elements, air bombing formations. The technical condition of a successful engagement of defensive are, then: camouflaged preparations, swift liaison, sufficient transportation means.

The air force is a particularly ideal reserve for operative defense. Its rapid mobility allows it to arrive on time. Its intervention is all the more efficient and decisive because it is in a position to take part in decisive land battles. The air force is the only arm which can hinder the bringing up of reserves behind the front of the enemy, particularly in a break-through operation. This makes it an essential element of defensive.

Operative defense can also utilize other means in order to create for itself favorable conditions in face of a superior enemy. In peace time it can create wide fronts, organize deep zones of obstacles, make use of natural obstacles or cuts in the terrain, so as to wage combat with weak forces and thus economize strong forces ready for counter-measures. Such fronts, such obstacles, such cuts in the terrain hinder the progression of mobile formations and render operative defense considerably lighter.

We have seen how operative attack had been favored by the modern use of swift formations of all kinds, by air reconnaissance, combat and bombing elements. Operative defense must meet the threat of offensive by using the same weapons and the same means. The stronger and the more mobile are its land and air formations, the better it can face a mobile enemy utilizing the element of surprise.

We now have to see what influence these new weapons did have upon defense.

Essentials of
Operative Defense

WE have already seen that in absolute war, defense alone does not lead to the final decision. Conduct of war which is based on exhaustion of the enemy is not sufficient to compel a strong foe to yield and accept peace. Indeed, the history of war presents exceptions to that rule, such as Napoleon's campaigns in Spain in 1808 and against Russia in 1812. But these exceptions are due to particular conditions and should not be accepted as a rule.

The forces, which because of a numerical inferiority or other reasons are on the defensive, prepare themselves to resort to offensive. This preparation is obtained by a passive defense, when one is not strong enough or by a delaying combat when, for instance, the enemy has gained an advantage in war preparations.

The new weapons and devices, the mobile land formations, the air force, the extensive use of obstacles, the utilization of chemical means do not modify this principle. But they multiply the efficiency of defense, they make it more mobile and get rid of the linear and rigid forms of war of position. Thus, defense can be articulated in depth and it is made less apprehensive of the danger on its flanks. These new means diminish also the need for direct flank protection and support; they lessen the risks of operative gaps, since the defender can quickly resort to counter-measures and counter-attacks. He enjoys greater liberty of decision and greater initiative in use of his reserves.

If the commander of an operative defense can make use of mobile land formations and powerful air forces in front of his disposition and on his flanks, while at the same time erecting operative obstacles, he finds himself able to look forward with more confidence to a battle waged against a superior enemy. Had such principles been applied in the east during the fall of 1914, the German reinforcements which were deemed to be necessary by Marshal von Conrad to bolster his left wing, would not have been engaged there. In the west, during the outflanking movements of September and October, 1914, instead of lightly engaging army corps brought up by rail and then by road after long marches, an important shock-corps should have been formed and engaged in one robust blow, with corresponding economy of time.

Operation On Inner Lines

This possibility of a more mobile, more resistant conduct of defensive finds particular application in the second fundamental law of defensive, the operation on the inner lines. We recognize here immediately the great operative meaning of the air forces which can be shifted from one theater of operations to the other, from one front to the other, in a short time, even in a few hours. They can be concentrated on the decisive front and contribute considerable aid. They can hinder enemy progression on nearby fronts, thus gaining time and add a definite contribution to the main front. All mobile land formations can carry out operations on the inner lines with surprise, strength and rapidity. These operations are all the easier when the movements take place in one's own country and are thus hampered by enemy obstacles or other delaying means.

Let us think a moment of the 8th Army in East Prussia in August, 1914, had it comprised quick land formations and strong air forces! It could have engaged its forces against the Russian 2d Army, the Narev Army, much quicker. The battle of Tannenberg would have been fought more decisively. Above all, the Russian 1st Army, the Niemen Army, would have been beaten at the Masurian Lakes worse than it was. This army's escape should have been prevented.

The operation on the inner lines is made easier by the fact that it is possible to dispose only light bodies of troops on the non-decisive fronts. The increased fire-power, the multiplication of automatic weapons, the installation of guns in masked emplacements, the use of obstacles, of chemicals, the practice of delaying tactics, the blocking effects of air attacks against enemy troops and their rear communications—all these strengthen defensive and allow time for the decisive battle to develop. They likewise provide more security to the operation on the inner lines.

The third principle of operative defense is the engagement of small forces on non-decisive places of the front. Thus a gravity can be created on a certain part of the front, as has been shown in an ideal way by the campaign in south Poland and in north Poland.

What Might Have Happened

First, it is possible to hold out on non-decisive places with limited forces. This is all the more easy when the general situation does not allow a resistance on the same position, but delaying tactics. Then, on decisive places, the mobile land formations and the air forces allow swift reinforcement of the gravity. Let us see what could have happened on the western front at the beginning of the first World War had modern means been employed. The left wing of the German army could have carried out a delaying battle against the 1st and 2d French Armies by using the defensive fortified zone of Metz and of Strasbourg, by establishing big-scale obstacles, by using gas in defensive areas. A considerable gravity could have been built up with swift land formations and powerful air forces.

When one thinks of the extensive fronts in the west at the beginning of the last war, the superiority of modern formations over the quickest formations of that time (which were the cavalry divisions) is evident, since the rapidity of the horse cavalry was not sufficient to accomplish the quick and extensive shiftings which were necessary. The operative importance of the mobile formations and of the air forces is also displayed when defense is confronted with a dangerous situation in a certain sector.

The determination of the decisive sectors and of the non-decisive ones does not depend only on the defender, but also on the attacker, at least to the extent that the defender must take his opponent's actions into account. Each attacker knows that against an organized defensive front, be it in a war of movement or in a war of position, only an attack led with force and articulated in depth has any prospect of breaking through with its entire gravity. Strong and mobile reserves spare many worries to the commander of an operative defense. But he needs also increased, constant and far-reaching reconnaissance and observation.

The fourth fundamental law, in case of strong enemy superiority, is to carry on a delaying battle, to practice the "strategy of exhaustion," in order to weaken the enemy in such a way as to be able to resort later to offensive. The retreat of the Serbs is a typical example of such a campaign, a "manoeuvre en retraite." This law is also reinforced by the utilization of modern weapons and devices.

The final aim of such an operation should never be lost sight of. It is the exhaustion of the enemy! With the exception of the Russian campaign in 1812, a retreat without putting up successive fights does not attain this purpose. However, the mobile formations should not be used up in local and partial operations, which lead to a premature consumption of one's own forces, thus jeopardizing the final aim. The Austro-Hungarian campaign in Galicia at the beginning of the last war constitutes a warning against this!

In general, it should be noticed that the fundamental laws of operative defensive remain unchanged. Development of land weapons, motorization, air forces, organization of obstacles, have reinforced these principles. Consequently we have more than before the hope that we shall rid ourselves of the fixed forms of the war of position, of the false dangers of open wing and unprotected flanks, of the fear of operative gaps, since the defender can protect himself by using these new weapons and devices. But the defender must also heed the fact that the attacker also draws advantages from the same elements, since they allow him to threaten the flanks, the rear, the gaps of the defender more dangerously than before.

Stopping-power In
Tactical Defense

WHAT is the influence of the new weapons and devices upon defensive? Especially on its two principal forms—resistance in the same positions, delaying tactics.

Any tactical defense must make use of its stopping power from as great a distance as possible. On the other hand, it must hide from the observation of the enemy and thus escape the effect of his fire. Then, it must repel the final attack.

If the enemy disposes of mobile shock troops, it is a prime necessity that the defender organize a far-flung reconnaissance, so as to protect himself against surprise and occupy his positions in due course of time. But the tactical land reconnaissance encounters the same difficulties as the operative one; it cannot quickly pierce through the enemy advanced guards and discover the direction of effort of the main forces. This is why a strong air reconnaissance is indispensible to defensive.

In order at an early stage to engage these mobile enemy forces, once they are detected by reconnaissance and also in order to slow up their progression and weaken their strength, a certain number of extensive measures should be taken in liaison with the entire operative set-up so as to complete it. These measures are:

Strong air forces, engaged early.

Motorized formations, with anti-tank equipment, pushed far ahead.

Tactical obstacles of all kinds erected in the front, or on the flanks, in the gaps, in the rear.

Strategically important spots and cuts in the terrain gassed.

Artillery fire organized with the help of O. P. and artillery plane observers.

Tactical defense against mobile formations requires a strong articulation in the front, so as to engage the surprise advance of the enemy, to slow him up and compel him to abandon his means of quick transportation. He will thus be deprived of his characterized strength at an early stage, and the defender will have time to take counter-measures.

The swiftness of mobile formations, their possibility of effecting surprise in unexpected directions, their ability to feel out enemy positions and to offer the necessary gravity only at the last minute, without losing time—all these qualities of attack require great mobility of concentration and a deep articulation. If the defender were to install the mass of his forces too early against a mobile enemy, he would then offer to the latter the opportunity to attack in a favorable direction in the front, or in the rear or against a flank.

The more mobility this articulation in depth can preserve, the better can defense promptly meet surprise.

At a later stage, when the intentions of the enemy begin to clarify themselves, when it is possible to detect here and there signs of where his gravity is being built up, the fluid disposition becomes thicker; forces from the rear are pushed to the front to bolster it up.

Defensive's Dependence On Offensive

We can here again see how much defensive depends upon offensive, and also how difficult its task is since, generally, it disposes of limited forces. It has to push forces ahead, articulated in depth; the front has to be consolidated at the right time; the intentions of the enemy have to be recognized at an early stage. Besides, the attacker has the initiative, the independence which give him an initial advantage. Truly, such a situation requires all of a leader's calmness, cold decision, not to let the propitious moment pass and not to take counter-measures too late.

In the stage of the attacker's installation on his base of departure, the prime preoccupation of the· defender should be to avoid enemy observations and hence the violence of his precise fire. The attacker will try to destroy the defensive weapons. Hence, the defensive anti-tank guns especially will have to remain silent and camouflaged. All weapons for checking the enemy should fire from masked positions or from shifting emplacements. The fluidity and the mobility of enemy movements require that they be as numerous as possible. All weapons which do not serve such a neutralizing purpose should remain silent. The enemy will remain undecided; he must be brought to feel that he has arrived at the main line of resistance without being able to detect its essential organization. If defensive succeeds in deceiving the enemy, it has realized the ideal condition for facing assault.

The commander of mobile shock troops leads his attack according to the general tactical principles. Such an attack is characterized by the quickness with which a gravity is concentrated, by the engagement of strong armored forces, to which the main part of the attack will accrue, rather than by an effort against the flank and in the rear. The attacker can launch local attacks of diversion and entice the defender into splitting up his forces or engaging them too early and in a false direction. Strong air forces support the attack. Other useful aids can be used, such as smoke or gas. The attack will be unified and led deeply into the enemy disposition. With ardor.and rapidity, the gap in the defensive system is prolonged in depth, or enlarged towards the flanks; the defensive disposition is rolled up towards the rear.

Against such an attack, violent and surprising, defense must be equipped with all necessary neutralizing weapons and means. To that effect, it must erect obstacles against armored attacks on the front, in the flanks, in the gaps, and utilize mine fields. It must have a deep system of anti-tank defense offering security against envelopment and men ace in the rear; and engage strong air forces at the decisive time and at the decisive spot.

Essentials of Defense

If one wants to be sure to get the necessary weapons at the crucial moment, appeal to the higher echelons for orders should not be the rule. Instead there should be direct collaboration between all fighting elements. Defensive must be in a position to:

Use gas and smoke if useful to the purpose.

Send reserves and armored formations to an immediate counter-attack. Hence, they should not be maintained too far away to prevent them from intervening promptly, although kept out of front activity.

Insure normal communications of command.

Be prepared to receive orders and fight.

All mobile weapons, masked utilization of machine guns and smoke allow a quick disengagement of the defender and his reconsolidation on new lines of resistance. Obstacles, gas, smoke clouds hinder the pressure of the enemy.

Hence, operative defense can draw great advantages from the newly developed weapons and means of war, without the fundamental tactical laws being modified by such changes. But the cooperation of all these means and weapons is a prerequisite to the best use of all defense possibilities. War experience has taught us the vital importance of close cooperation of all weapons of infantry collectively and also with artillery.

We are accustomed to organize a common and complementary fire-schedule for artillery and infantry. But such preparations are no longer sufficient to face a mobile enemy endowed with armored equipment. Aside from the fire schedule, there should be provisions for reconnaissance missions, antitank defense plan, interdiction of the zones of obstacles, concentration of reserves, missions of the air forces and of the armored elements. Not one weapon, not one means, gives the decision. The cooperation and collaboration of all of them is necessary. There is no fear that this variety of weapons has made defensive too cumbersome. But there is one thing essential: Unified orders delivered by the higher echelons and perfect understanding and cooperation in all details in the lower echelons.

Conclusion

Before the first World War, the entire formation of the general staff, of the cadres and of the troops was oriented towards offensive, in practice as well as in theory. It was the same also in France. However, after the war of 1870-1871, France clung a long time to defensive, for all questions involved by defense of the national territory. It is possible that defense, which gives precedence to fire-power, corresponds better to the French temperament than attack, which requires strength and daring. This French school was characterized by clever manoeuvering with deep articulation. It is only a few years before the last war that a complete change took place in France, and this change appears clearly in the works of numerous French military writers. The French plan of operations called for a strategic attack at the beginning of hostilities. In Russia, the conceptions were rather similar to the Germans. The Austro-Hungarian army was exclusively oriented towards the offensive and gave even greater emphasis to it than other nations.

On the basis of such an education, the first World War began with offensive employed by all belligerents. But our enemies, just as we did, had to recognize that attack, in spite of swiftly conducted hostilities, nowhere led to any decisive victory. The reasons are now clear. In the sectors where a strategic or tactical defensive, economizing forces, would have been possible, a costly offensive was used. But where an operative decision was sought, the material strength of the front was not great enough to break through the defensive; or the concentration of forces on this front did not provide the operative weight with such strong and deeply articulated reserves as to be able to exploit a success and enlarge it into a complete decision against a reinforced defense.

But there is an exception to that insufficiency of concentration in defensive strength. In the east, in 1914, the Russians, with their superiority in numbers and in disposition of forces, should have been able to reach a favorable decision. But their poor leadership did not take advantage of it, so that we could see the nearly grotesque result of a small German army checking the advance of 4 Russian armies in south Poland and in north Poland, compelling them to a war of position.

Finally, a war of attrition took place in the west first and then on all other theaters of operations, leading to an exhaustion of the fighting lines, which allowed later only a disappointing form of strategic and operative activity. Several times, indeed, there were operative breaks-through; in Galicia in May, 1915, in Serbia in the fall of 1915, in Rumania in 1916, in Italy in 1917, but the gaps were closed up again.

Decision By Movement Possible

In a future war, the war of position can be avoided and the decision can be reached by movement. The French have a word for it: *"manoeuvre"* and they distinguish the *"manoeuvre de couverture,"* the *"manoeuvre en retraite,"* the *"manoeuvre d'aile"* and still others. All efforts tending toward a resumption of movement in war will be helped by mobile land weapons and air forces. This increased mobility, the variety of war means and weapons allow leadership greater combinations of forces and liberty of action. They will tend to repel the danger of paralysis of the front.

However, in this renewed movement, there is another danger. It is possible that it will not lead to maneuvering tactics and strategy, particularly in operative defense. We know that in an absolute war the decision can be reached only when the will of the enemy can be broken, and this result is attained through the destruction of his fighting means. It accrues to operative and tactical defensive to exhaust the enemy, so as to be able either to resort to offensive, or to prevent him from attacking where he strives for a decision. If defensive is not strong enough to resist on the spot, it will by movement and use of favorable cuts in the terrain, of fortifications, of propitious local counter-attacks, then wear out the enemy until it has enough strength to resort to a general offensive.

We Germans have to look to defensive as an important, essential method of conduct of war and conduct of combat, since we are in a central position, surrounded by highly equipped nations. Defensive should not be kept in the background, as before the last war. It must be given its deserved place in the education, the formation of the cadres and troops. Since in a tentative future war, we cannot depend upon numerical superiority in personnel and matériel being on our side, defensive will have to support offensive and contribute to its preparation. The role of this defensive, in case of an absolute superiority of the enemy, is to wear out his strength. In case of an operation on the inner lines, it is to keep all enemy forces out of the front where a decision is sought. In case of fighting on our front, it is to build up a gravity which will win the decision.

In order to achieve such difficult results against superior forces, no weapon, no means of war should be neglected. All of them have their utility, when they are engaged by one will, according to a unified plan. They will then guarantee the success of defense by their interior and exterior harmony.

PART THREE*

Strategic and Tactical Defense, World War II

• • •

The "Culminating Point" of World War II in Europe

AFTER the beginning of the German-Russian war in June, 1941, until the winter of 1942-43, terrible losses had been inflicted upon the Russian armies. Great errors had been committed in concentrating the main body of troops imprudently close to the German disposition. Here it appears that the Russian High Command committed the same fundamental errors as the French in 1940. Their concentration was not deep enough, no manoeuvering mass was properly held in reserve to intervene in an appropriate direction. Consequently, large bodies of men and matériel—the best—were encircled and captured just as the French troops sent into Belgium had been cut off from the south by the panzer divisions after their break-through on the Meuse. Fortunately for the Russians, they still had vast reserves, and that greatest of all allies, space, previously their savior in 1812!

The Stalin Line was found largely unprepared to receive the German shock. The last time Russian matériel had been in contact with German matériel was in Spain, in 1936. The Russian tank had proved the best. Since then, much had been done to the German war machine. It had accumulated experience upon experience. Each campaign had meant the development of an improved type of tank, a perfected

---

* Part Three was written by the translators.

utilization of all arms. The Russians had made a great effort, indeed. They have turned out an enormous quantity of matériel, even more than the Germans. But during the entire campaign, they suffered much from the effects of their late start in actual war experience. Particularly, they failed to achieve the well coordinated team work between the air force, artillery and armored divisions which provides the true secret of German performances in modern warfare.

This cooperation between all ground and air forces allowed the Germans to penetrate at will into the stunned and disabled Russian masses, to disarticulate their dispositions, partly paralyse their military nervous centers and prevent arrivals of reserves. The same procedure was repeated over and over again, at Kerch, at Vyazma, at Izyum, etc., and each time the Germans captured great numbers of men, and a considerable booty in tanks and guns. Such an inappropriate and awkward defense resulted in making defensive much more costly than offensive.

Germans at Stalingrad

The German armies in September 1942, had reached the Volga. Most of Stalingrad, an elongated urban industrial agglomeration on the western bank of that river, was in their hands. The defenders retained only a small bridgehead in the city. But they never lost it! It was under these conditions that Hitler made his rashly boastful Stalingrad speech in the Berlin Sport Palace, in which he promulgated his new policy:

"First we must under all circumstances hold whatever must be held. That is to say, we must let the others attack as much as they wish, wherever we have no intention to advance. We must hold everything and wait and see who tires the soonest.

"Second, we must attack under all circumstances where attack is necessary."

Of Stalingrad he had this to say: "No human being will push us away from that spot . . ." Then came an enumeration of all the territories gained, of all points of strategic preeminence captured, with the exclamatory comment that Germany had won the war with Russia, but that it was impossible to understand why the enemy with all this concrete evidence of defeat before him, did not realize he was beaten. In this picture of an autocrat arrived at the peak of his destinies there was something tragic and ludicrous.

A little more than a century before, Napoleon after he had reached Moscow, had sent emissary after emissary including even a mere captain to the Tsar. The Tsar and his armies were unreachable, remote, but ever present! In 1942 we see Hitler ostensibly amazed by the conduct of an enemy who refuses to see that he is vanquished, in the way a judge might be affected by a criminal caught in the act and refusing to confess.

Hitler, for all the truthful evidence of his achievements, was wrong. He spoke at the zenith of his power. Soon he would be forced to give way at Stalingrad, retreat, face new gaps in his lines in Russia, close new breaches in Africa. Having been unable to liquidate one of his two fronts in 1940 and 1941, the steel ring of his enemies would close upon him, imposing upon him the necessity of sacrificing all fronts in favor of the most dangerous, the Russian.

However, the reinstatement of his war policy on September 30th, was sound. Hitler everywhere adopted the strategical defensive, the stronger form, together with the tactical offensive. Experience had proved that any major change in battle lines initiated in winter had entailed great losses of men and matériel. In the preceding winter, motor transportation had been frozen into relative immobility. With this new attitude, the Germans could hold their lines economically with a thin curtain of troops, while sending many divisions to the rear for rest and reorganization. At the same time, large air forces would be held in reserve, ready to intervene at once when their aid might be needed. The center of gravity of the German forces would be shifted elsewhere. There was to be only one offensive, the reduction of the small Russian bridgehead at Stalingrad.

Value of Initiative

One factor of importance in modern warfare lies in the immutable fact that initiative provides a considerable superiority. A proper concentration of tanks and planes used unexpectedly in a well-chosen theatre of operations is almost sure to bring success. There is great danger in leaving to the enemy's selection the areas and dates for starting campaigns. Until now, the Russians had never had that opportunity, even during the preceding winter which had seen merely operations involving the straightening of lines and use of harassing forces, moves possessing no great strategical importance. They were glad to accept the chance. Hitler himself seemed to be content and confident in giving it to them.

The morale of the Russian troops was good. The modern matériel received from the United States and Great Britain had allowed reequipment of the combatants. They decided to launch a certain number of offensives.

Two attacks were made, converging towards Smolensk, east and west of Rzhev. They were powerful, but the Germans were well organized and expected this offensive. The losses incurred seem to have been out of proportion to the gains realized.

The other attacks, on the contrary, succeeded very well. They relieved Stalingrad, encircled the German army entrenched in the Don loop, and forced its capitulation. They gained momentum all along the line in the south and forced the Germans to a general and definite retreat.

The Russians knew that the Germans G. H. Q. desired to reach the Volga under all circumstances and to consolidate definite defensive positions on this line. This would have cut off communications between the Russian southern and northern fronts, and prevented any regular supply by the United Nations. Beyond the Volga, the network of Russian communications is extremely thin; the transportation problems would have been vastly increased. The absence of any cover on immense expanses of steppes would have made concentration of troops noticeable; hence the element of surprise would never have been in favor of the Russians. The enemy had to be stopped at Stalingrad.

Towards the middle of December, 1942, the German 6th Army had been cut off from the main forces. It occupied around Stalingrad an area extending between the Volga and the Don 150 kilometers long from north to south. The German army, attenuated by long battles, comprised 200,000 men. This force was insufficient adequately to garrison such an extended area. General Hoth, the commander of the 6th Army, reduced the area by drawing the north and south boundaries closer.

To relieve besieged Stalingrad, two German efforts had to be made: sorties from the inside and relief expeditions from the outside. None of these succeeded. The sorties could not muster enough strength to batter through the encirclement, and the Russians maintained generally a tactical defensive.

The nearest German expedition to the aid of the Germans in the city started, December 12th, 300 kilometers to the south near Kotelnikovski under General von Mannstein with about 120,000 men. The terrain is a flat steppe, where the German armored troops had the advantage of easy manoeuvering, but where, on the contrary their preparations could not be concealed. Their concentrations were easily discovered. In the area of Millerovo, two Russian armies pressed on large German forces farther to the west and kept them away from the Stalingrad battle.

Russians on the Don

Around Kotelnikovski, Mannstein started his offensive by a frontal attack which was checked by the powerful artillery barrage of the Russians. He then resorted to flanking movement on the Russians' right along the Don river. The Russians had the same idea and sent two columns on both banks of the Don. They checked the German flanking movement. Mannstein resorted to a new frontal attack in the steppes, forcing the defenders to fall back slightly. On the 24th, the Russians, feeling that the enemy had reached his "culmination point," counter-attacked and succeeded in stopping definitely the frontal attempt at relieving Stalingrad.

Having tied up the front, the Russians resumed their flanking advance in the west in the Don Valley. Their artillery fire was so severe that they destroyed a good part of the German panzers. Mannstein completely failed in his expedition.

In the Millerovo area the Russians attacked 12 Axis divisions well-entrenched behind a net-work of barbed wire, mine fields and anti-tank obstacles. A tremendous artillery preparation allowed the Russian infantry to occupy the enemy front zone. The armored troops passed in their wake and completely disrupted the German defensive. Kantemirovka was recaptured by the Russians.

All through December and January, the situation of the 6th Army inside Stalingrad steadily deteriorated. The opposing armies occupied positions very close to each other, and the Germans were unable to support their front lines by adequate air and artillery neutralizations. During the entire assault at the Volga line, the Russian infantrymen displayed an admirable stoicism. His mission was to fight and die where he stood. He carried it out in a way which will forever embalm Stalingrad in history, with Verdun, as symbols of dogged faith in the destiny of one's country and willingness to defend it at all individual or collective cost.

Principle of the Offensive and General Defensive, World War II

THE German armies have applied this principle in all their campaigns. The development of existing weapons, the cooperation between all arms, have been intensified. A greater homogeneity characterizes modern armies. Nevertheless these same great strategical principles are more than ever valid.

In Poland the defending armies were disposed in thin and linear formation all along the border. The Germans concentrated their armored attacks in converging directions. When the tanks of different columns met, large bodies of Polish combatants and civilians were helplessly exposed to annihilation.

In France, the Germans had chosen the very center of the French disposition to launch a big offensive that was to develop into an immense strategical break-through. The attack was unleashed through the rough and difficult wooded region of the Ardenne, against the weak pivot of the French armies entrenched behind the barrier of the Meuse. Napoleon said that the enemy must be attacked where he expects it least. More than ever the German military chiefs understood that the use of modern and adequate weapons allowed them to realize the two essential elements of success: speed and surprise. The lessons of their 1914 failure had not been lost.

So this is what happened in 1940: Rupture of the French lines at Sedan and Montherme and encirclement of the Allied forces in Belgium. It was a well known tactic, simple as are all great military tactics, and it was executed to perfection. The final blow was sufficient almost to consummate a victory. It did, in the end, insure defeat to a still powerful enemy and neutralize his intact reserves, which were maintained far in the east, and thus render them incapable of extending assistance.

The defensive of the Germans consisted in a general and constant pressure in the east from Stenay to Lanterbourg applied against the forces of the Maginot Line, so as to tie them up and prevent them from being shifted; but in order to protect their rear it was also part of their plan to repel frontally the modern and efficient troops sent in Belgium, and push them into the pocket created by von Kleist's army.

Defensive Conceptions Compared

In Russia, let us consider now how the Germans have dealt with the vast expanses of Russia and the immense Russian armies. They certainly had to limit the number of their offensives and to choose adequately the directions of their efforts to force, as they did, huge masses of Russians to fall or surrender like inert and unsupported units. Outside of these expanses they had to carry an efficient and economical defensive.

It will be interesting also to see how the Russians have led their defense, and to compare the values of both defensive conceptions. By now, a certain number of conclusions can be reached, imposed by the use of modern weapons and devices, that could not be forseen in 1937 when General von Leeb wrote his book. But, as he points out himself, the battlefield is the actual test of tactical conceptions; we may add, also the only ground on which to check the specifications of modern weapons and consequently the all important orientation of war production.

The great notion of concentrating forces on one well chosen sector or theatre of operations, and organizing a deep defensive — Clausewitz's stronger form — on the rest of the front, has been largely verified in the Russian campaign.

Here is a prime example wherein the *gravity of offensive* —as von Leeb would put it—*need not be considerably superior to defense in modern warfare.* A case wherein a very dynamic and well coordinated attack triumphs over a static and hasty defense. Namely the reduction of the Kerch Peninsula in May, 1942, by the Germans.

The Kerch Peninsula is linked to Crimea by the narrow Parpach bottleneck of 13 miles. Its length is 50 miles. At the beginning of May, more than 200,000 Russian troops had been pushed back into this peninsula, while the Axis troops occupied the rest of the Crimea, except

Sevastopol which they had besieged. This important Russian force threatened the rear of the siege forces. The Germans decided to wipe it out. They would attack the enemy's left, push through the gap and outflank the entire Parpach position from the south. Then, an expedition would be sent by sea to land in the enemy's rear, disorganize his resistance and smooth out the advance of the armored forces once they had pierced the Parpach position.

Attack on Kerch

The attack opened unexpectedly on the 8th of May. An artillery preparation was launched. Pioneer detachments were detailed to clear the enemy's foreground of mines and thus allow free passage to the tanks. (This procedure is normal whenever an offensive is launched against an organized front; a very curious similarity is that offered by the piercing of the Alamein bottleneck position by General Montgomery in November, 1942). On the 9th, an armored division closely supported by planes and artillery, attacked the Russian left. Motorized infantry divisions followed the tanks, turned north and proceeded to roll up the Parpach line. They then consolidated their positions to the west and to the east, building up two solid dykes to resist the Russians counterattacks. Other motorized elements proceeded further towards the rear where they were helped considerably by the landing expedition. The operations against the Parpach corridor, and those in the Russian rear were constantly supported by two powerful air forces.

On the evening of the 9th the Sea of Azov was reached and the Parpach position encircled. By the 10th the Russian forces were cut in two, leaving in the west, the Parpach troops, in the east the troops based at Kerch.

As for the Germans, the western wall of their corridor remained on the tactical defensive against the Parpach troops; but the eastern wall took the offensive and reduced progressively the entire Kerch peninsula. The Parpach contingent, feeling that they were abandoned, gave up the resistance on the 13th of May.   Three days afterwards all the Russians were overcome.   They had suffered many casualties, especially from air bombings of their confined masses; part of them only could flee to the Caucasus.

The Russians were numerous and had both artillery and air force.   But they were surprised by the unexpected attack on May 8th; their resistance was disrupted by the landings in their rear.   Above all, they had shown neither the necessary cooperation of arms nor unity of command.   The local commanders utilized any troops at hand.

Nevertheless, these shortcomings of defense should not conceal the efficient handling of the German offensive.   Nowadays, the armored division is a powerful and supple drilling machine that pierces through the hard, but superficial, crust of an inadequate defense, and labors inside the enemy disposition to pinch off, isolate and destroy large sections of it.   But here we feel, nevertheless, that von Leeb's orthodox recommendations are far from matching the numerous potentialities offered by the swiftness and the power of modern machines of war.   In spite of his emphasis on deep formations, he remains on the whole attached to the idea of one single front against an enemy.   Modern means allow an enemy to be tackled simultaneously in the rear, from the west, from the east, from the north, as in the Kerch peninsula during a few days of May, 1942.

Finally, it should be noticed that an attacker has to consolidate his gains at once by digging in and emplacing anti-tank guns.   This is what the Germans did in the Parpach peninsula in building up two walls orientated towards the sides from which the Russians would counter-attack to reassemble their severed forces.

The Crimea and Kerch

During the spring campaign of 1942 the German offensive was concentrated upon reduction of the Crimea and of the

Kerch peninsula. Strategically, they were on the, defensive everywhere else.

The Kharkov counter-offensive of the Russians is a case wherein *a mobile manoeuvering retreat succeeds in wearing out an attacker;* it presents an example of what Clausawitz termed the *"culmination point."* In taking the initiative east of Kharkov, on the 12th of May, 1942, the Russians hoped to relieve the southern front, obtain an important tactical success, by capturing Kharkov, push on to Dniepropetrovsk and recover the entire Ukraine. For that purpose, Timoschenko had massed 35 divisions on the front between Kharkov and Izyum, a bridgehead on the Donets 100 miles to the southeast, the gravity of his concentration being around Izyum. Bock's army was considerably inferior at the beginning of hostilities, particularly around Kharkov; but the Germans had built new roads and regauged the railroad lines in the rear areas during the winter. They could thus effect prompt concentrations of troops.

The Russian attack east of Kharkov broke through the first defensive zone of the Germans and progressed from the 12th until the 16th of May. On the 16th, the progression became very difficult; the impetus of the attacker had dulled. Bock judged his enemy to be practically exhausted; he consolidated his lines and decided to resort to counter-offensive against the Izyum salient. By that time the Kerch campaign was almost settled, and strong air forces could be shifted from there to join in the reduction of the Izyum hedgehog. As usual, the offensive was preceded on the 17th by an intense artillery and air preparation. The armored divisions were sent first to drive their wedges through the front zone, then around both flanks of the position. In spite of their fierce resistance, the cooperation of the German air and ground forces proved largely superior to that of the Russian troops. The contours of the hedgehog were progressively compressed; the German reconnaissance kept the ground forces posted on the Russian moves while bombers and artillery wrought destruction and disorder. The hedgehog split up into numerous smaller sections, between which the tanks moved and aggravated the dissolution process. Large scores of defenders surrendered. The Russian commanding general committed suicide.

Panzers at Voronezh

An example of the power at the disposal of panzer divisions to enlarge a tactical success into an immense strategical break-through is offered by the German offensive against Voronezh, between June 28 and July 7.

On the first day of the offensive, the fighting zone was in the Kursk area. On July 7th the Germans had captured Voronezh and advanced 150 miles, breaking the Russian positions on a front of 100 miles.

Surprise seems to have played a considerable part at the start of the attack. In the rear zones panzer divisions had been secretly massed. Just before the attack, waves of strong air squadrons reconnoitered and bombed the Russian ground forces. Most important of all, the fighter planes kept the Russian air force from the fighting zones and assured air superiority for the attacker. Whenever resistance was reported by the ground forces dive-bombers intervened together with the artillery and neutralized the enemy position. At the same time, observation planes kept the ground commanders informed of the degrees of resistance offered by the enemy dispositions.

On the ground, the now classical scheme was applied: each of the three columns launched in the attack was preceded by one or several panzer divisions. With such a terrific and well coordinated concentration of fire, the Russian front was broken and quickly swarms of enemy armored troops dashed around rear areas disrupting command and communications and dispersing any consolidated defense. The Oskol River, a tributary of the Donets, was reached on July 2nd. Behind it, motorized units, preceded by armored outfits, followed through the gaps and fanned out, attacking in flank or from the rear the strongpoints of the defending lines. As usual, in this amazing team-work between plane-gun-tank the first weapons neutralized the strongpoints, the tank pushing deeply to prevent any reconstructed defense. Armored forces ignored the resisting elements of the former enemy disposition. The infantry behind was assigned the task of mopping up the battlefield by encircling isolated commands which, deprived of any basis of resistance, were progressively eliminated. In some sectors the Germans used parachutists in the Russian rear areas to destroy key points which would interfere with transportation.

The Russian front could be reformed only on the Don from Voronezh toward the south. The defenders tried to recapture Voronezh; they made enormous efforts, but could not succeed. The German forces had been regrouped after considerable advance and they held firmly.

Air and Ground Coordination

This offensive is an illustration of the successes obtained by a perfect coordination of the ground and air forces. It shows the predominant influence of air action against an enemy driven from his positions. As for the defensive, it shows that a deep zone bolstered by well-organized hedgehogs is necessary; however a defensive front can generally be reformed by bringing up reserves from other sectors behind a deep cut in the terrain, such as a river. The zone of concentration should be chosen far enough from the enemy's bases, forcing him to stop and regroup his forces, dispersed by pursuit.

It seems that with the multiplied drilling power of modern armies, the rapidity of "mobile forces," offensive has been favored in modern warfare over defensive. It has become increasingly able to concentrate forces and to launch a surprise attack that breaks into the enemy disposition before he can take any measures. Three years before the war, Leeb expressed the official optimism of the German High Command in believing that the coordinated use of "mobile forces" would be at the origin of a rehabilitated offensive.

The German campaigns of 1942 will probably remain as the best illustrations of perfect team-work between all offensive air and ground elements. Their most outstanding feature was the utilization of great air fleets not only as had been seen in France, in close and continuous cooperation with the troops in battles, but also acting as a general reserve rushed rapidly from a secondary or already liquidated theatre of operations towards a new and important one. Finally, these vast squadrons harassed a disbanding enemy, in waves operating 24 hours a day. Thus the Germans achieved a much greater concentration of bombing on the one theatre of operations estimated as the most important at a given time. In France, instead, they had assigned a certain number of missions to their planes. From their English blitz they had understood that it did not pay well enough to bomb cities.

The most concentrated type of modern tactical offensive confronted with the most concentrated type of modern tactical defensive has almost always been resolved in favor of the former. The case is similar to that involved in the reduction by the tank, plane and gun of a strong bridgehead formed in hedgehog.

For instance, at the end of July, 1942, the German spearhead directed towards Stalingrad had reached the Don and wedged in between the large Russian forces anchored on this river at Kalatsch and at Kletskaya. These two centers of resistance had to be reduced before pushing on to the Volga. The German army under General Paulus attacked successively the first, then the second concentration of forces.

Paulus had at his disposal the large air fleet of General von Richthofen. The Russians were fighting with the Don at their backs. The process of reduction is always the same. Concentric attacks from all sides by tanks and bombs reduce progressively the size of the bridgehead. Since in such an isolated situation supplies either do not reach the besieged garrison at all or in insufficient quantities, the energy of the defending fire decreases, while the constant hail of enemy shells and bombs becomes deadlier. At some places, the defenders give way and the weakness, immediately discovered by air reconnaissance, is reported by radio. At once, armored troops rush to the softening spots and enlarge them. Tanks push onward, followed by motorized infantry and artillery. A wedge is formed in the enemy disposition. Under such conditions, the exercise of command in defensive is extremely difficult. The Russians often lacked unity of command. Certain units tried to cut off the wedge by counter-attacking on its flanks. Others remained on their positions while others tried to reform farther in the rear.

Limited Value of Fortifications

THIS war has disproved completely the impregnability of fortresses. The most formidable barrier, be it a natural one such as a river, or an artificial fortification, can always be coped with by troops of firm resolve, well-trained and well-supported by a precise and continuous fire-power. Such troops can be checked by a defense so disposed as to be able to see all and to cover everything by defensive fire. The defender must therefore be well entrenched within his fortification, and at the same time be in position to rely upon outside aids. One who contents himself with being shut up in a fort or standing on the other side of a great river, without closely surveying its approaches, pursues the policy of the ostrich.

In a fortification, there are always weaknesses possible of detection by detailed reconnaissance. They can be exploited by a troop armed with suitable weapons and imbued with *élan* and a burning spirit of action. In a line of fortifications as well, there is also a soft spot. On June 15th, 1940, when France's defeat was practically achieved, in the very center of the Maginot Line, at Sarralbe, a German regiment dented the fortifications on a front of 20 kilometers.

Indeed, troops which rest on concrete blocks, present a fixed front, in which the attacker may pick a weak point at will.   He establishes contact when he chooses and the contact may become a break-through.   On the contrary, the defender who is imprisoned and has no mobile detachments outside, does not make contact with the attacker.   As a rule, he does not know what the latter is doing, whether he moves, whether he switches forces elsewhere, or whether he grows stronger.   Briefly, he does not enlist on his side the modern element of success: surprise.

Results From Concentration

On the 11th of May, 1940, the fort of Eben-Emael controlling the Albert Canal, one of the most formidable fortresses in Europe, armed with numerous and up-to-date cannon, A. T. guns and machine guns, was taken by a force twice less important than its garrison.   The conquerors were a single battalion of pioneers who were known to be close to the fort, but who surreptitiously approached it without any exterior force appearing to sweep them away.

On the 14th of June, 1943, the formidable and modern Fort Stalin, in the center of a strong fortified ridge, barring access to Sevastopol on the north, was taken in a day.   It was attacked by dive bombers, using the heaviest caliber bombs, and by artillery.   After this preparation, which opened cracks in the structure of the fort, pioneers attacked and captured it.

Then the German advance progressed against Sevastopol in a narrow channel, hammering out successively all obstacles standing in their way.   We find here again the principle of concentration used by the panzer divisions against an organized disposition.   The Germans reached the interior of Sevastopol at the beginning of July.   Most of the pounding was done not by air, but by artillery, because of the greater precision of its fire.   Here also the Russians showed great passivity in their defense, under all blows dealt by an assaulter full of initiative. The latter advanced from the north and the south. Both advances finally met, because the defender did not try to counter-attack on the left flank of the northern progression, as he could have done.

Strategical Initiative
By the Germans

UNTIL Hitler's Stalingrad speech in September, 1942, announced and decided a contrary attitude, the German armies always assumed the strategical initiative.

Particularly in the first phases of the hostilities, the Germans were continuously on the offensive, both strategically and tactically. On the contrary, the Russians were continuously on the strategic defensive, and resumed only occasionally the tactical offensive. The result is that they lost all the western area of their country on a depth of more than 500 kilometers.

Tactically, the Russians sometimes assembled forces to counter-attack savagely; they even won successes, which they could not, however, transform into strategical victories. Some of their successes, as at Smolensk, played into the hands of the enemy by bringing up troops to places where they could be surrounded by the more mobile German troops.

At the beginning of hostilities the Russians had large armored forces. Tanks were used tactically inside their dented lines to counter-attack and repel a pressing enemy, as at Minsk and Smolensk. This was the classical conception of the tank as a weapon of direct support or counter-attack. To check the German incursions they merely planned to close in behind hostile armored forces and cut them to pieces. They failed. It was only later that they began to push their armored elements forward. After a suitable artillery preparation, they sometimes succeeded in piercing the German lines and in operating in rear areas. Whenever they could break through the crust of the German front, they won great successes, as around Millerovo and Kantemirovska in December, 1942.

One of the most brilliant campaigns of the war in the east was certainly comprised in the operations in the Vyasma-Bryansk area in October, 1943. It was not essentially different from the preceding Bialystok-Smolensk-Uman-Priluki campaigns, but the execution was more perfect, the results more complete.

Moscow was covered in September, 1941, by a large force, estimated at some 70 divisions and commanded by Timoschenko. After the extensive encirclements and eliminations of the first weeks of the war, these were the best equipped troops Russia yet had in the field.

The manoeuvering idea was to wipe out this big concentration of well above a million men by piercing its center and cutting its mass into two groups. At the same time, both flanks would be encircled by panzer armies. As usual, infantry divisions were to follow the panzers and eliminate separately the split sections.

Greatest Recorded Offensive

The campaign was started by a gigantic artillery and air preparation. Reconnaissance had indicated in advance the softer spots that received particular attention from the guns. The Germans assured us that on this single day of October 2nd they delivered the greatest offensive ever unleashed.

Four great panzer armies dashed on a front of five miles each and storming through the front lines reached the rear areas. The surprise was complete. There were no Russian reserves in the rear.

The panzers found but weak resistance. They all reached their objectives Vyasma, Bryank, Orel. They then began rounding up the Russians toward the Russian front.

At H plus 12 hours, after renewed artillery preparation, German infantry divisions rushed into the gap opened by the panzers. They were supported constantly by a strong artillery and air force. They began to establish siege lines 20 to 40 miles behind the front. Each division was to leapfrog the preceding one. Once emplaced, the divisions constructed field fortifications facing west and prepared to hold a defensive position. ["H" is the hour of an attack's start.]

As did the French in 1940, the Russians thought the panzers in their rear soon would run out of gas and that they then could be easily exterminated. But the advance was so rapid that it surprised and captured supply depots, off which it could subsist. Furthermore, no elastic defense was enacted. Instead, the defenders remained on their old lines, as the Germans wanted them to do.

Two days after the start of the attack, the enemy was completely separated in two main groups, one toward Vyasma, the other toward Bryansk. They then adopted a hedgehog formation and tried to find out weak spots upon which to make sorties. Very severe fighting took place. But the Russians attacks were not coordinated, while the German air force informed the panzers where they could wedge through and split up the hedgehogs into smaller ones.

The German infantry divisions, realizing that the enemy was disorganized and short of supplies, attacked everywhere. Their pressure increased. Encircling lines shortened. The reduction of the hedgehogs was continued by attacking from different sides. Finally, both sections surrendered. More than 500.000 prisoners were captured. The siege of Moscow was to begin shortly.

Phases In
Evolution of Tanks

(In the below discussion the writers present what may be called the Continental Theory, since they do not enter in detail into the developments in England.)

The history of war weapons proves that the best innovations and the most revolutionary ones were derived from tools of civilian use. The tank is evidently a military application of the agricultural tractor. Hence the immense ramifications and possibilities inherent in some modern tools, and also the present evident fact that war implies absolute mastery over production.

Several phases can be distinguished in the evolution of tanks.

First phase, 1914-16. In France particularly, the military had been hypnotized by the idea that the newly devised weapon should be conceived so as to pierce an organized and linear front. The problem consisted in getting the infantry past the enemy trenches. After the infantry, the cavalry would follow, in order to exploit the gaps opened. All infantrymen in 1914 knew that what stopped them was essentially the machine gun; every time an infantry company was checked in its advance, it was due to a machine gun nest that had not been cleared. Then the commanding officer of the company effected contact with the next artillery officer. Guns would be sent up during the night and in the morning they would liquidate the machine guns with explosive shells.

Instead of depending upon artillery alone, one thought of building a tank, which was merely the same piece mounted on a tracked tractor. The tank was only capable of throwing explosive shells against personnel; the armament was the 75. Such was the Schneider tank in France.

Second phase, 1916. After a series of experiments, it was found that it was not necessary to mount 75 mm guns to confront personnel or machine guns. Particularly it was discovered that when the tank was used alone, it was extremely vulnerable. The first requirement of any tactical success for tanks was to use them en masse. This sort of tank became the typical tank of infantry support, and in France the FT type, a Renault tank of six tons which mounted a 37 gun and was protected against infantry fire only. This tank corresponded to an absolute defensive formula and on the whole the French army still depended on it in 1940.

Certain successes were obtained, especially when the effect

of mass and the secrecy of preparations allowed a decisive surprise. But in piercing organized line of resistance, one had merely a tactical success which could not ripen into a strategical break-through, and everything had to be started over again.

Third phase, 1917. General Estienne and General Foch conceived the idea of a heavy tank, with rather high speed, reasonably well protected, strongly armed, and capable of breaking through a defensive system up to and including artillery positions. They conceived not only the tool itself, but also the tactical entire set-up in which the tank was to be used. Heavy tanks were to be sent forward to destroy artillery. Light tanks would follow and destroy machine guns behind artillery. The new heavy tank type 2C mounted a 75 field gun in turret, had a 30 mm armor and great capacity for crossing obstacles.

Ideas of Foch and Estienne

This organization was to be applied to the attacks in 1919. But the Germans were already worn out. Attacks by the FT tanks were better organized in 1918 than they had been in the past. Surprise could be obtained tactically (for instance at Villers-Cotterets by General Mangin). In the organization envisaged by General Estienne and General Foch, the cooperation of the air force was even considered. In the spring of 1918, when the French front had been broken at Chateau Thierry, General Foch sent all the available air force to close the gap. It can even be said that in 1918 Foch and Estienne had conceived the essential use of the modern armored division; they had understood that the heavy tank was to be the basis of the whole disposition, including:

Medium Somua tanks, quick, strongly protected, mounting 47 mm antitank guns: weight 20 tons. The Germans use them still. They were particularly utilized in the Greece campaign.

Heavy tanks Model B, Renault, weight 30 tons; mounting

a 47 mm antitank gun in turret and 75 howitzer in casemate.
The basis of the French armament was still the light tank.
It was the only one to be constructed on the assembly line.

On the German side there was a combination of light
tanks and armored cars having an antitank power almost
double that of the French 37 mm gun. But the basis of
their armored strength was the Panzer KW4, mounting a
75 mm gun in turret. They also had antitank guns placed on
self-propelled chassis or drawn on six wheels. The same
guns in France were towed by light trucks or tractors.
Generally speaking, the technical developments of the German
matériel were quite inferior to those of the French. The
French had really found remarkable technical solutions.

After the Armistice of 1918 the conception of the tank
stagnated. The scheme involving its use remained unchanged. This comprehended a tank of direct support, used
to help infantry pass lines of resistance. The essential role
of the heavy tank, as it had been envisaged so clearly by
General Foch and General Estienne, was passed over. Between 1919 and 1939, in all countries, three ideas have been
widely discussed in technical circles: The orthodox tank of
infantry support; the tank as incorporated in motorized and
armored outfits, but limited to reconnaissance missions; and
the tank as integrated in autonomous entirely armored and
mechanized divisions, able to exploit the break-through of a
defense and to demolish all nerve centers.

The first advocate and the true originator of the modern
panzer division is doubtless Generel Estienne. In a serious
of striking lectures delivered at Brussels in the presence of
the late King Albert I, he developed in a graphic manner
the scheme which gave the Germans their blitz victories. He
said: "As the industrialist, the modern soldier must always
conceive something new, and not remain hypnotized by the
lessons of the last campaign, which does not mean however
that they should not be mediated."

DeGaulle as a Critic

Having painted in vivid colors the spectacles that ten years later were to unroll themselves on the ground where he was talking, he concluded: "One will certainly find a parry against these dispositions, but too late and the tardy discoverer will be destroyed, just as happened at the battle of Cannae." This idea was defended by a certain number of officers in France, among whom now the best known is General de Gaulle. During peace-time manoeuvers, de Gaulle always presented bitter criticisms against the imposed official schematic use of the tank as a mere weapon of infantry support. He strove also to interest politicians in his project of creating a professional, but limited, army of mechanized units, as part of the regular national army.

In Great Britain also some persons became converted to the idea of an armored division; but as is often the case of this vast empire, they had more particularly in view army police activities, etc.

In Germany, Colonel Gudérian, the future commander at Sedan in May, 1940, was the chief advocate of the heavy tank. His book "Achtung Panzer" is very interesting. He was considerably influenced by Estienne and to a lesser degree by de Gaulle. What is less known is that he, too, had plenty of opposition from a powerfull source that was still under the impression that France's obstacles and resistance were too tough to be broken by a tank outfit. But at least he won, in the end.

Tanks and Guns

Such were the ideas. It is easily conceivable that the *specifications of the armored matériel* different widely, according to the general scheme adopted by the general staff. For instance, a matériel destined to direct support of infantry, as in 1918, was planned to be strongly armored, to shoot explosive shells, because the weapon of the tank is not the gun, but the shell. Antitank obstacles, mines, were too numerous.

Since it is a matter of firing through organized and fixed lines, the guns to be brought up by road; they would not need to be self-propelled or tracked.

On the contrary, if the matériel is not intended to be used against concrete fortifications, but against enemy tanks or clusters of resistance, the tanks will be rapid, less protected, but powerfully armed. Their shells will be armor-piercing. Artillery should be able to follow close behind. For that purpose, it must be entirely treaded and self-propelled, allowing quick changes of position. On the other hand, antitank defense will be insured by special self-propelled guns that should have qualities both of great piercing capacity and of aiming quickly all around, since the tank menace can come from any direction.

Of course, the advantage belongs to the tank or the antitank weapon that mounts the gun able to attack efficiently its opponent from the farthest possible distance. This problem is the same as in the navy. The Germans have understood this situation very well; from the beginning of World War II, they have outgunned successively all their opponents; the French Somua, mounting a 47 mm gun, with their PZKW4 mounting a 75 mm; the British 2-pounder in Libya with the new 75 with improved muzzle velocity and with their 88 mm; the Russians 45 mm, especially in the beginning of hostilities, with the same weapons. They have really begun to be about matched with the new American 3-inch gun—the weapon that made its surprise appearance at El Alamein in November, 1942.

Of course, if the scheme conceived by the General Staff is false, the matériels conceived to function with it are condemned to sure destruction, and this without regard to the technical value of the construction.

The Spanish civil war has not shown the relative values of the methods of utilization of the tanks, because they were used in too small quantity. Each school, in France, in Germany, remained firm in its postulations. However, certain data were made available; they proved useful to the Germans, but ill-fated to the French.

The very few tanks utilized in Spain were easy targets for the antitank guns. If the gunners remain calm, any antitank gun is sure to put a few tanks out of action. But if 50 tanks attack, they quickly overcome antitank defense. During the Spanish civil war the very light German tanks, and the still lighter Italian "tankettes" could do nothing against the opposing antitank guns, particularly the Russian 45 mm, the same gun that has been so inefficient in Russia against the German 75.

Lessons of Spain

From this Spanish experience, the German Staff deducted that they had to increase the protection of their matériel; but they did not estimate that the conception was altogether erroneous.

On the contrary, in France the school of direct support which advocated stronger armors, was supported by the Spanish war.

Nothing is more imprudent than to draw general conclusions from limited experiences.

However, in France there were more and more doubts creeping into the minds of responsible persons. There was really a great crisis in military art. Never had an army or a command known or suspected the covert and demoralizing uneasiness and worry that prevailed. It was no longer a matter, as before 1914, of knowing whether one should, under certain circumstances, attack or defend, and what were the best methods appropriate to either course. Above all, it was a question of knowing whether what one decided to do should be done, could be done. Everything was on precarious ground. One did not know what to believe or was in flux, variable, or whom to believe; what to modify, what to plan or what to create, in order to attack or to defend.

Doctrine was completely disrupted; men's minds were in full aberration.

There was a firmer tendency in 1939, to favor the autonomous armored outfits; it is probable that in 1942, excellent mechanized divisions would have been ready. But when the war started, the matériels were not at all conceived in that line, except in the medium Somua and the armored Panhard car. Just as had been foreseen by General Estienne, the surprise was total and the Germans exploited their success to the limit.

Since the French staff did not have any fixed doctrine, they had ordered types of matériel belonging to both schemes. The most important models were the following:

Wheeled armored cars; rapid; slightly armored; mounting 25 mm antitank guns, rather efficient.

Light and slow tanks to act in direct support of infantry; they mounted 37 mm guns model 1918, intended to fire at very short range.

The French utilized their excellent mechanized divisions in Belgium. These elite units prevented the entire northern group from being encircled by the panzer divisions and from being compelled to capitulate in open country. After having made possible the embarkation at Dunkerque, they had to abandon their modern matériel in Flanders. As for the heavy armored divisions, they were not conceived for large-scale action, but to take part in limited engagements.

Debacle Unavoidable in 1940

After the break-through on the Meuse, the military disaster could hardly be avoided, since all of the armored matériel was bound to be destroyed. As for the suggestions that vagrant bands, with no tank or plane support, could have taken to the hills and defended themselves in either the "Brittany redoubt" or the "Massif Central redoubt", these pertain to mere fancy.

If hostilities in 1940 had lasted two weeks longer, not two million combatants would have been captured, but two additional millions of non-combatant troops, an appreciable consideration for a country which had lost a substantial part of the flower of its youth only 20 years before when 27% of the men in the field, between the ages of 20 and 45, did not return.

Very limited forces only could have escaped from France since the German panzers were already at the Pyrenees border when the bulk of the French forces were still wandering miserably between the Cher and the Dordogne on June 22nd. With their absolute control of the air, the Germans could have easily penetrated into North Africa from both Spain and Sicily. A swift occupation of strategic points by air-borne troops would have paved the way for the occupation of the North Africa coast, a country which had no sizable supply of modern matériel and without industrial production.

This was not as in 1914. The Germans then had won the battle of the frontier in Charleroi, but the slow march of the armies of that time, the simplicity of the armament, which was of the same general nature for both attacker and defender, allowed a consolidation of the defending positions.

The tank battles in 1940 have amply proved the essential rules to observe in the conception of armored matériel. Here are the main lessons to draw from World War II:

In France, the Somua tank was well conceived. Its realization was perfect. However, this tank was handicapped by its 47 caliber in comparison with the Panzer K. The K 4 mounted a 75 gun, firing efficiently at 1800 meters as against the Somua's range of 1200 meters. The heavy Renault 30 T, model B 1 bis, had a 50 millimeter armor. In spite of this thick protection it could intervene against the German tanks only with its 47 gun in turret, because its 75 howitzer was in a casemate and hence required too long to aim. Finally, many antitank guns became lost because they were not self-propelled and could not be disengaged quickly enough to avoid capture or destruction.

Results in France Repeated

In Russia, from the very beginning, we witnessed a war of movement. The same story as in France repeated itself. The good 45 mm Russian guns of the Spanish civil war had become inefficient against the German 75. In spite of their numerical superiority in personnel and even in tanks, the Russians were trapped, encircled, and captured or annihilated. Each tank battle left an immense junk pile of Russian armored vehicles. Fortunately, the Russians still had immense reserves of personnel, particularly in the Moscow region, and, behind the lost terrain still vaster stretches of land and still greater natural obstacles. But the strategical set-backs they suffered in the first weeks of hostilities were as great as those of the French.

In Libya, the 75 gun of the German K 4 triumphed easily over its less powerful opponents. Then, the new 75 gun with a higher muzzle velocity caused even more trouble to the British. Finally, the 88 gun mounted either on the Mark VI or towed as an antitank gun, wrought as much damage as it had already done in Russia.

The evolution and adaptation of tank and antitank weapons since the beginning of this war has been one of the most vital questions. The tendency is to devote more and more attention to the formula of the antitank gun, particularly in the United States. The antitank gun increasingly resembles the regular tank. The new and effective 3-inch gun mounted on an M-3 chassis is a considerable improvement over what was in use only two years ago. In both weapons, the tendency is towards larger calibers. With smaller guns too many hits are required to immobilize a tank. The heavier gun does a bang-up job in one good shot. Basically, the antitank gun must ambush the tank. It is safe so long as its position remains undiscovered. Mass and homogeneity give success to the tank; surprise brings it to the silencing of the antitank. Hence the conditions of service cannot be the same. The concealment of the antitank gun is a difficult problem; the Germans often succeeded in solving it by placing them behind trucks.

Is Defensive Still
The "Stronger Form"?

WHILE the triumph of the attacker seems so far to repeat itself during the World War II, a certain number of conclusions can be reached, which do not at all disprove that defensive is still the "stronger form".

In the cases cited herein offensive had always the *initiative;* defensive quailed under converging hail of fire. In other words, offensive took profit of all choices offered by the strategical level of its operations, while defensive remained on the tactical level. This of course was made possible to the Germans by their supple and mobile handling of the situation through command and means. An illustration of this confined and fettered defensive unable to use all the means at its command, is offered by the fact that for instance the Germans claimed to have captured 1000 tanks and 750 guns on August 11, 1942, at Katatsch.

The *German defensive was very efficient* in spite of repeated Russian attacks through 1942. Its principles of organization are: A deep and strong structure of strongholds, protected by mine-fields against surprise tank attack. Since the mine-fields and obstacles have to be blasted away first by a powerful artillery preparation, it leaves time for the defending command to concentrate quickly mobile forces in the axis where an enemy effort is feared. Thus a network of obstacles largely covered by fire dulls the bite of the attack. This entire static organization is combed by a mobile reserve of machine weapons which are kept under control of the High Command in the theatre of operations.

Once reconnaissance detects a danger, the machines are placed at the disposal of the threatened local commander who uses them *en masse*. When the defender knows that should the situation deteriorate he can also receive the support of large air squadrons, he is imbued with great confidence. With such a set-up, it is more than ever true that an attacker needs an overwhelming superiority in tanks, planes and guns to overcome a deep defensive zone.

German Strategical Defensive

In the spring and summer of 1942 the Germans lavishly expended forces in a strategical defensive on an immense front of 600 miles between Orel and Leningrad. Mobile force and modern fire play just as well into the hands of an expert by managed defensive as they do in favor of offensive.

The same cannot be said of the Russian defense of the Don and Donets valleys in July and August, 1942. After having been defeated early in July in the Kharkov sector, which decidedly will have been the scene of most of the battles of the Russian front, Timoschenko did not reinforce on the lower Donets and the Don where the major campaigns were to take place, as a normal continuation of the push toward the Volga. Instead he weakened this front and left the road to the Don bend open to the German panzers.

The Russians had anticipated the *advance of the armored columns,* just as did the French after the campaign of Poland. Both had noted the effects of armored columns harassing the rear areas. The French thought that the Germans could try the same thing again; but they did not take the armored threat seriously enough, the official presumption being that once the tanks had been "imprudently advanced", they could be cut off from the following masses and reduced progressively; or that, isolated from their bases of supply, they would be canalized into narrow zones where they could be disposed of. The Russians also thought that the best counter-plan was to allow the armored columns to advance and, having protected depots and other similar soft points against sudden attack, to close in on the rear of the invaders and cut them off.

Shortcoming on Russian Side

The counter-offensive methods to which the Russians often resorted have not displayed a taste on their part for manoeuvering and disrupting a surprised enemy. The Russian campaigns have offered many examples where preference has been given by the defenders to classical assaults of infantry in force. They deployed their infantrymen in great depth and launched them in successive waves which in certain sectors ran as high as 15. Leading waves advanced as far and as fast as possible; any stopped wave was leap-frogged by the next, and the attack thus was supposed to be kept rolling forward.

But under the terrific concentration of modern fire and its fatal efficiency against untrenched personnel, this wild process resulted in extraordinarily crowded masses becoming bogged down, with terrific losses. Since enemy dive-bombers, artillery and machine guns simultaneously participated in the slaughter, there was hardly any chance to break through an encirclement or a solid disposition.

The lack of manoeuvering ability and of initiative displayed on the Russian side is sometimes amazing. They fought often with equal numerical odds, and if they allowed themselves to be so regularly outflanked, or pounded through or encircled, it is certainly not due to lack of valor of the Russian soldier, who has been the real savior of his country. The Russian High Command has been obsessed with obsolete defensive conceptions which the Germans regularly out-witted. They have given predominance to moral forces and thought that when the soldier is firmly entrenched, he can fend off the strongest attacks. Absolute confidence was given to defensive as "the stronger form", but this defensive was conceived statically, not only on the tactical level, but and still more grave, on the strategical level.

For instance, in the fall of 1941, in order to save Moscow, they concentrated an enormous quantity of troops around the capital and did not dare send some of them to the rescue of the great armies about Vyasma and Bryansk which were abandonded to their own resources and sacrificed. In the south, the same attitude dictated the abandonment of Odessa and the loss of vast armies in the southern Ukraine in order to save the Caucasus. There are two methods to play checkers: one is to keep the men close to the rear line as long as possible; the other is to form combinations from the very start of the game, so as to surprise the opponent and trap him. His entire game is then disorganized.

The first method is purely defensive and aims to cover materially the positions to be saved. It never wins and rarely succeeds in fending off an enterprising opponent. The second purports to tackle him as early as possible, win favorable positions and disrupt his arrangements. It conceives offensive as serving the double purpose of winning and defending oneself. The game then is won by clever manoeuvering, not by a rigid occupation of the terrain. The latter method is the German one. It can be applied even in a strict defense .

Mobility Essence of Defensive

Von Leeb cites the Serb campaign in World War I as a remarkable example of a *"manoeuvre en retraite"*, tiring out an enemy until our men resume a propitious counter-offensive. In World War II, the Kharkov campaigns of May, 1942, and March, 1943, are good examples of a defensive which inflicts heavy losses to the enemy, until he has become weak enough to be fully attacked. The Germans have often called "elastic defense" the defensive which seeks to deal with a foe on a deep zone and without necessarily retaining ground, already held. It should be noticed that in order to succeed, such a supple form must be determined by a well-established doctrine as to give to mobility its real rank, which is first. But since long before the war the Russian official doctrine, in spite of certain definite tokens indicative of progress, such as paratroops, has been very similar to that of the French.

Mobility, the essence of modern warfare has given to defensive an aspect which von Leeb did not foresee, in spite of his optimism and his confidence in a rehabilitated offensive Defensive has gone a long way from the orthodox form embodied in fixed trenches.

The most common aspect of modern defense is the *defense in depth.* It is the normal counterpart of mechanized warfare with its daring incursions into the enemy disposition. In World War I an organized front consisted of some outposts, placed before the position to be defended. These were not meant to resist, but to act as alarm devices and withdraw as soon as their mission was performed. Behind, there were two or three lines of trenches designed to include the most favorable points and to allow as extensive fire-cover of the terrain ahead as possible. These lines were separated by the distance of some kilometers. The men were stationed in the trenches, side by side.

Such an installation appears to contemporaneous commanders as a waste of personnel and inadequate to meet the tremendous and constant pressure of a mechanized force which, wave after wave, pushes against the whole opposing front, finds a weak spot and drives a wedge into it. Once the line is broken, there is no manpower to fill up the gap, since the defenders are spread out in length and immobilized instead of being concentrated in deep echelons, which the armored enemy forces would have to tackle successively, thus dislocating the homogeneity of their assaulting effort.

Communications Control Vital

The linear disposition was proper and useful in 1917 and 1918, when the tank did not have its present drive and endurance. But in 1942, one should not even use the term

"line," but "front" and "zone," which are more consistent
with realities. The control of all communications is as vital
as the control of all points tactically important, such as
heights or cuts in the terrain. The communications lead
inside; the commanding points stretch out the defending
forces in length. Hence, the combination of the whole
defense disposition assumes the aspect of a checker board.
In striking against the strongpoints of this checks defense,
the armored push of the enemy must zigzag; its lines of communication thus becoming divided and canalized. The
force of the push becomes more and more dulled. The tanks
finally are absorbed and annihilated or cut off from the
bulk of the forces.

In fact, under existing conditions of warfare, the linear
disposition proceeds from the erroneous conception that a
terrain is defended when it is physically occupied, instead
of recognizing that it is really defended only when it is covered
by fire. Not necessarily by fire opened at the same time and on
a straight line, but by fire the installation of which in depth
may proceed from any angle and in any direction.

Thus if one of these fire-radiating clusters, which are now
known as "strongpoints" or strongholds, is by-passed by
an enemy force, the whole defense organization does not fall,
since its fate is not dependent upon that of any one sector.
It does not mean, even, that this particular sector has fallen
or that its effort has been neutralized, since the by-passed
stronghold can continue in its role against any subsequent
waves of attacking units.

The entire set-up economizes forces in utilizing them
where danger manifests itself, i.e. not in length, but in
depth, and its works as an immense and supple shock-absorber.
It is really the only manner in which to check a mechanized
incursion.

Success, of course, depends on troops whose mental serenity is equal to their dogged resistance and possession of an adequate number of antitank weapons.

Weygand and Defense in Depth

The first important example of defense in depth is offered by the "three days of Weygand" on the Somme between the 5th and the 8th of June, 1940. In a general order of the day, he said: ".........To the notion of continuous line must be substituted that of complete mastery of all communications. Every commander of larger units must take command of all communications in his own zone by establishing a complete net of strongholds. These strongholds will be made up of antitank guns and 75 mm guns, and such zones must have sufficient depth; better an exaggerated depth than an insufficient one.

"If a unit finds that it is not in liaison on one of its flanks, because the neighboring unit is shaken, it must not withdraw at any cost. It must seek to reestablish the situation and, if it is unable to do so, draw up into the shape of a hedgehog and form a stronghold of resistance. The rear of the main line of resistance, beginning with the front, and proceeding to the greatest possible depth must be organized in a net of strongholds, particularly near the main highways."

When terrain is organized for a relatively short period of time, we find the type of zone such as the one hastily prepared by Weygand on the Somme sector in the first days of June, 1940, or the type of zone in which the Germans prepared to hibernate between December, 1941, and March, 1942, so as to resist harassing enterprises of the Russian cavalry and infantrymen. When the terrain is organized as a permanent fortified sector, we have the Siegfried Line. This fortified organization is not really a line, but a zone, since it is made up of numerous small concrete works, rarely big enough to shelter more than a section of 30 men. Technically, they cannot be compared with the very fine installations of the Maginot Line which included absolutely everything to enable the garrisons to stand a long siege. But strategically, the Siegfried Line is far superior to what was the Maginot Line.

Concrete Not Enough

The Maginot stretched out on two main lines of resistance, and was conceived as a static shield. On the contrary, the Siegfried comprises a maze of works, which in themselves do not present the fine elaborate features of the Maginot Line and possess nothing of secrecy. In certain sectors its depth reaches 40 miles. What is more remarkable, the Germans were not satisfied with defending the approaches to their country solely by pouring concrete. The Siegfried strategical set-up comprises as well an entire system of mobile forces able to manoeuver in the whole region. Concrete by itself is not sufficient. It serves only to support by the fire it shelters a complete defense organization.

On the Eastern front, the Germans now have three important and deep defensive lines in rear of the Russian front. These are:

The old Stalin Line which was the main Russian line of resistance. It faced to the west along the course of the Dnieper. The fortifications comprise great concrete works around important communication centers, highways and railroads. These are woven together by numerous minor works in between.

The Bug River Line completed early in 1942, and the Oder Line.

The second aspect of modern defense is seen where absolutely no fixed position is held, because there is no protection offered by nature, such as cuts in the terrain, masks, marshes, etc. This was the case in the Russian steppes; it was particularly the case in the *desert*. The most ideal form of that kind of defensive has been evident in the war in Libya. It is a *pure war of space*. The occupation of a stretch of barren and flat land is of no avail. On such terrain there is no type of land warfare more similar to naval engagements, where the two conditions of success are mobility and superior range of fire. In the steppe and in the desert the Germans long dominated their enemies, not so much on account of better maneuvering as on their ability to dispose of the enemy from a greater distance than that from whence he could effectively use his weapons. The defender has no reason to cling to valueless terrain. He is out in the open, as is the attacker. Hence, defensive is no longer the recognized "stronger form"; moreover, the laws differentiating offensive from defensive do not operate any longer. Both words have hardly any sense. A feasible defensive, that considered by Clausewitz and von Leeb, must resort to offensive, precisely as the attacker does.

Washington, May, 1943.

THE POWER OF
PERSONALITY IN WAR
(Die Macht der Persoenlichkeit im Kriege)

Major General Baron Hugo von Freytag-Loringhoven

Translated from the German
by the Historical Section, Army War College,
September 1938,
under the Direction of
Brigadier General Oliver L. Spaulding

CONTENTS

Publisher's Foreword

The Author:

ALTHOUGH 31 YEARS have passed since his death, Major General Hugo Baron von Freytag-Loringhoven is still considered one of Germany's foremost military writers. He wrote 15 books on various military subjects, numerous pamphlets for German Army use, and was a steady and widely read contributor to the German Army's quarterly military review.

The scope of his writing included such titles as: *Clausewitz's Observations On the Military Lessons of the Campaigns of 1813 and 1814; Infantry Drill Regulations Explained in the Light of Military History; Studies of the Conduct of Operations, Based On the North American War of Secession in Virginia; Modern War and Diplomacy; The Essential Elements of Military Success; The Exercise of Command in Recent Wars.*

As he indicates in his preface, he undertook the development of this book largely in response to numerous requests from German officers for more information on military psychology, especially Clausewitz's observations in this field.

He was born in Copenhagen, Denmark, in 1855, served for a few years in the Russian Army, and in German Army (Prussian Guards) from 1878 until his death.

At the time he wrote the second edition of this book [1911], he was serving as Assistant Chief of Staff for Special Studies on the German Army General Staff.

During World War I, he served first as Deputy Chief of Staff of the German Army General Staff's Field Echelon, and was responsible for the administration of occupied territories. When von Moltke died in 1916, he succeeded him as Chief of the Army General Staff's Rear Echelon.

The Book:

This book is an enlightened, penetrating analysis of Clausewitz's more important theories and observations on the psychological aspects of leadership, especially the effect on battles of the personalities of the leaders involved. The author points up the pertinency of these dictums to all ages and strengthens their validity with actual incidents taken from military events from the period of Frederick the Great to the close of the Russo-Japanese War, which to him was recent military history.

The author supplements these observations and illustrates them further with extracts from the works of other great writers of that period, and with his own provocative views on military character and personalities. The net result is a book that not only gives us a novel and fascinating insight into the causes of many of the battle successes and failures of the mid-18th and 19th centuries, but one which automatically prompts recall of numerous instances since the author's time (especially in World Wars I and II and in Korea) which reaffirm the truth of the views the author includes. One cannot discuss any facet of this subject, for example, without at once wanting to include expressions and actions of such colorful contemporary personalities as those of Pershing, Foch, Patton, MacArthur, Eisenhower, Montgomery, Rommel, and others of perhaps lesser fame, whose characters and accomplishments paralleled those of Washington, Lee, Grant, Sherman, Sheridan, and other older military leaders discussed in this book.

The reader undoubtedly will find the author's views on universal military training especially interesting in the light of current efforts to improve the military posture of the United States. General Freytag-Loringhoven points out that Prussia was forced to adopt universal military service (including training) simply *to survive,* and through it, later on, transformed itself from a weak east German state into a great military power. The reader will also find the author's views on coalition warfare (getting along with allies) equally interesting.

While no one expects a modern military student to accept

all of any military writer's views, much less those of a typical Prussian Junker, still the sincerity and forcefulness with which the author argues his case, and his standing as a writer and student of military psychology compels us to give more than passing thought to his arguments, even including such an eyebrow raiser as . . . "the real foundation of the doctrine of eternal peace is nothing more than selfishness and love of comfort, hidden under a vague idealism . . ."

The scope of the ideas presented in this book is extremely broad, and since the majority of the comments contained in it are timeless, a passage or two from this book could add depth and perspective to most any military problem. The book for this reason can be re-read profitably many times.

Additional footnotes have been added to the many included by the author to help students who are just beginning their study of military history.

Acknowledgments:

Expressions of gratitude are due the following for their help and encouragement in the preparation of this book:

The Office of the Chief of Military History, which reviewed the manuscript and has shown a keen interest in the project throughout.

The library of the National War College, which loaned valuable reference material.

Brigadier General Oliver L. Spaulding, without whose discerning translation this book would not have been possible.

Author's Preface

THERE IS NO PROFESSION in which personality training is more important than the military. Yet in this field our accomplishments are limited by the fact that the best opportunities for this training arise only in war. In a long period of peace, the mental and moral qualities which are all-important in war are often relegated to the background; and, as Scharnhorst says, "mechanical thinking triumphs over the qualities of the heart and soul." This must be prevented if the spirit of an army is to remain strong and if that army is to prove itself in war. Fortunately, more and more voices have been raised of late, urging greater attention to personality development.

Marshal von der Goltz points out in the preface to his "Conduct of War" ["Krieg-und Heerfuehrung"] that all the elements necessary for a thorough study of the psychological aspects of the art of war are to be found scattered throughout Clausewitz's immortal works; and he urges that these scattered teachings be collected and logically arranged, and their practical value brought out in military instruction. This suggestion gave the writer a definite direction for his studies on Clausewitz. The result was this book, which originally appeared [1st edition] in the "Vierteljahreshefte fuer Truppenfuehrung und Heereskunde," and whose first edition appeared in 1905.

The writer does not expect to do complete justice to his title in all respects, for the power of personality in war is immeasurable and the material for discussion inexhaustible. His only effort in this book has been to extract, connect, and illustrate Clausewitz's fruitful thoughts on this subject. In doing this it seemed best to use examples from fairly recent military history, and, considering the point of view from which Clausewitz wrote, restrict discussion to general principles and large unit actions. Even though fate may not

make us great captains ourselves, we must take the great
captains as our models, for as Clausewitz says, "what genius
does is the highest rule."

In this second edition many additions and corrections
have been made; and numerous references have been made
to the Russo-Japanese War. The events of that war have
not yet [1911] become known with sufficient clearness; but
two things seem beyond question. First, man is still the
most important element in war in spite of all improvements
in armament; and secondly, what Clausewitz wrote of war
nearly a century ago is still valid.

In these studies no detailed discussion is undertaken of
many other valuable works which deal with the psychological
element in war. The intention has been to follow Clausewitz
closely, and thus limit the vast amount of material available on this subject. The writer can only hope that these
pages, like those of the previous edition, may have some
influence in spreading more widely in the German Army
the doctrines of the master to whom we [Germans] owe
all our intellectual conceptions of the art of war.

CHAPTER 1

War Is the Domain of Danger

> "ALTHOUGH OUR INTELLECT always calls for clarity and certainty, our spirit is often attracted by uncertainty. The intellect leads us by the narrow path of philosophical inquiry, seeking logical conclusions. Almost unconsciously we come into a realm where we feel ourselves strangers, where all familiar things seem to leave us. Our spirit, however, prefers to remain in imagination, in the realm of uncertainty. Instead of dealing with the stern reality of fact, it takes wings and revels in the riches of the possible. Danger and daring are the element into which it throws itself, like a bold swimmer plunging into the stream."
>
> —Clausewitz, *On War*, book I, chapter 1

To LIVE IN this "element of danger and daring," courage is necessary—the prime requisite of a warrior. According to Clausewitz, courage in the face of personal danger is of two kinds.

"First, it may be an indifference to danger resulting from the nature of the individual, from a disregard for life, or from habit. In any of these cases it may be regarded as a permanent characteristic. The second type of courage results from positive motives, such as ambition, patriotism, or inspiration. In these latter cases, courage is not a characteristic, but a feeling or an emotion.

"These two kinds of courage are different in their effect. The first type is more certain, and may become second nature. The second type has a more positive effect. The first type is steadfastness, the second boldness. The first leaves the mind cold, the second excites it, sometimes dazzles it. The most complete courage is a combination of the two."

The physical courage growing out of the nature of the individual, out of disregard for life, or out of habit, is to be found most commonly among primitive, warlike peoples. Clausewitz says:

"If we consider a primitive, warlike people, we find the warrior spirit in many more individuals than among peoples of a higher culture. Among the former, almost every warrior possesses it, while among a highly cultured people the great mass is carried along by necessity, and not by any inner urge. Among uncultured peoples, however, we shall never find a really great general, and very rarely a military genius; for such talent calls for a developed intellect which an uncultured people cannot possess."[1]

Intellectual power makes up a large part of what we term "great military genius," and for this reason the officer who is training for high position in war should endeavor to develop his reasoning powers. But he must do this through constant, critical examination of the past and present, rather than through forms of metaphysical speculation. As Clausewitz has said: "While life's rich experiences can never produce a Newton or an Euler, it may help develop a Conde or a Frederick."[2]

Two Types of Courage Difficult to Separate in Great Leaders

In analyzing great leaders it is generally impossible to decide which of their actions in the face of danger bore the mark of boldness and which that of steadfastness. Both types of courage are characteristic of the truly great. In addition to his unequalled boldness, Frederick the Great displayed an unshakable steadfastness in misfortune. Napoleon says of him: "He was at his greatest in his most critical moments. This is the highest praise that can be given his character." His defiance of a world in arms during seven years of war shows his steadfastness; yet this quality appears just as prominently within the narrower limits of the battlefield. At Torgau[3] (fig. 6) he proved his

[1] Clausewitz, *On War*, bk. I, ch. 3.
[2] *On War*, bk. I, ch. 2.
[3] Fought in 1760 during the Seven Years War. Frederick defeated a greatly superior Austrian army under Marshal Daun in this battle. It was fought near Leipzig, in southeastern Germany.

boldness when he divided his force to strike the enemy from both flanks. At the same time, his words to his staff under the immediate influence of the useless and costly attacks illustrated his steadfastness. Even before he had received news of the night attack and capture of the heights of Siptitz, he predicted confidently that the enemy would abandon the field. The enemy, he said, had suffered at least as heavy loss as himself, and Ziethen's Corps was in his rear. The enemy, therefore, had no alternative but to withdraw across the Elbe.

Napoleon showed the same stability at Preussisch Eylau.[4] His repeated attacks had been beaten off with heavy loss along the entire Russian front. Toward evening, Davout's III Corps on the French left had suffered a severe defeat in an attack by L'Estocq's Prussian Corps. Yet the Emperor remained in position in the face of the enemy. He intended to resume the action the next day, his left reinforced by Ney's Corps which had arrived during the evening; but the enemy abandoned the field and admitted defeat. Both Torgau and Eylau proved the truth of Suvorov's[5] epigram, "a lost battle is a battle which we believe lost." Or in the words of General von Blume: "Military history shows us that after a battle the victor seldom knows the full extent of the enemy's defeat. Often he considers a battle as indecisive, or even lost, when as a matter of fact his enemy is in flight."

Effect of the Nature of the Leader's Army

Whether a general's actions show greater steadfastness or boldness often depends on the nature of his army as well as on his own characteristics. In 1757, for example, Daun[6] was ordered to relieve the army of Prince Charles of Lorraine besieged in Prague; and although he was superior to Frederick by 20,000 men he did not venture to attack, but preferred to take a position in which Frederick must at-

[4] Usually called the Battle of Eylau. This engagement took place in February 1807 in East Prussia between Napoleon's army and a combined force of Prussians and Russians.
[5] A Russian commander in the early Napoleonic wars.
[6] Austrian marshal in Seven Years War.

tack him. He did this not only because he hesitated to meet the King and his undefeated army, but also because his army, the last Austrian force remaining in the field, had been hastily thrown together and had little cohesion or mobility. Since Frederick was compelled to attack at Kolin, Daun was able to relieve Prague by a defensive battle. Later on, when the objective was not so limited, and it was necessary to strike the Prussian power a staggering blow, Daun's half measures failed. That war's great objective could be gained only by offensive battle, not by the selection of impregnable positions, in which the Austrian leader's skill was extraordinary, or by tricks of maneuver.

Daun's defensive preoccupation is partly explained by the fact that in coalition warfare each power is inclined to leave the heaviest burden to the others. It must be remembered also that throughout the Seven Years War the Austrians were inferior to the Prussians in maneuver. The Austrian battle lines, in particular, lacked depth, which handicapped them badly in making decisive attacks. Only the Prussian Army under Frederick overcame this tactical defect of the period.

Daun's over-cautious attitude also had its effect. He, like most of the other higher commanders in the Imperial Austrian Army, was definitely inclined to the defensive. To change the whole spirit of an army, once ingrained, requires not only a general of genius, but a king. A man like Daun could distinguish himself by skill, foresight, personal bravery, and steadfastness, but never by boldness.

During the Seven Years War and even down to the time of Napoleon, the Russian commanders were limited to the simplest of maneuvers by the unwieldiness of their battle formations. Yet the steadiness of their troops in defense, particularly at Zorndorf and Kunersdorf[7] (figs. 4 and 5), was worthy of the highest praise. The lack of skill of Russian troops at the beginning of the summer campaign of 1807

[7] Battles of the Seven Years War. At Zorndorf, northeast of Berlin, Frederick defeated the Russians (1758), and at Kunersdorf, southeast of Berlin (1759), he lost heavily in an attack against a combined Russian-Austrian force.

made it impossible for Bennigsen[8] to maneuver with separated columns. Yet in February of that same year, the courage of these troops had repulsed Napoleon's attacks at Eylau with great firmness.

General Kuropatkin[9] had many of the same characteristics and problems as Daun. He too had to take into account weaknesses in his army arising from its spirit and the way it was organized. He, too, fell into the habit of retreat and defensive tactics which further reduced the morale of the Russian army, and led him to neglect good opportunities.

Wellington's[10] character was marked by cool prudence, but his conduct of operations was also greatly influenced by circumstances. The nature of his professional army, its linear tactical system, and the characteristics of the British soldier all had their effect. On the Iberian Peninsula, he had only a very small British army, which formed a nucleus for Spanish and Portuguese levies. He very rightly avoided engaging his British troops in costly battles, especially since he was cut off by the sea from the resources of his home country. For this reason he did not make an offensive movement in 1809 from Portugal to Madrid, but with his 60,000 men (including only 20,000 good British troops) took a strong position at Talavera, upon which Joseph Bonaparte's[11] 45,000 men made no impression in a two days' battle.

Again in 1810 and 1811 in Portugal, Wellington always chose strong positions to meet Marshal Massena.[12] At the same time, however, he did not hesitate to incur losses where the situation made this necessary. In 1812, for example, he ordered the storming of the fortresses of Ciudad Rodrigo and Badajoz because their capture would open the road to Spain. Yet even when the general collapse of Napoleon's empire made it possible for him to undertake the offensive which finally brought him across the Pyrenees,

---

[8] A Russian commander in Napoleonic wars.
[9] Russian commander in chief, Russo-Japanese War, 1904-05.
[10] British commander in Napoleonic wars. Famous for his victory at Waterloo.
[11] Napoleon's brother, a French commander in Spain in 1809, later made King of Spain.
[12] French marshal who directed the operations against Wellington during Napoleon's all-out effort to subdue Spain in 1810-11.

his method of conducting operations did not change materially. He still moved with great caution—which, indeed, was what the situation often demanded. The same overall prudence was apparent in the 1815 campaign in Belgium.

FIGURE 1. Iberian Peninsula, 1809-11.

Effect of Circumstances

Pressure of circumstances and the character of his army may at times compel a commander to forego bold operations and restrict himself to an active defense. General Lee's Army of Northern Virginia in the American Civil War was more efficient than those of the Northern generals who faced him, but it was generally much inferior in numbers. Moreover, the Confederate troops, although they improved.

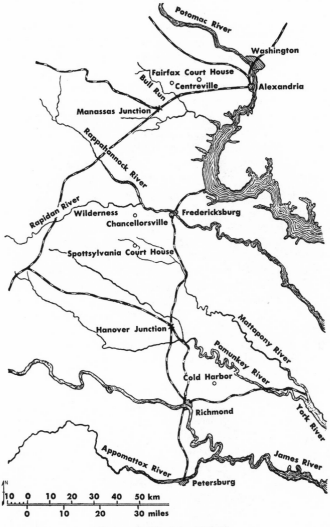

Potomac River

Washington

Fairfax Court House
○ Centreville
Bull Run
Alexandria

Manassas Junction

Rappahannock River

Rapidan River

Wilderness ○
Chancellorsville
Fredericksburg

Spottsylvania Court House

Mattapony River

Hanover Junction

Pamunkey River

Cold Harbor
○

Richmond

York River

Appomattox River

James River

Petersburg

N

10 0   10 20 30 40 50 km

0   10   20   30 miles

FIGURE 2. Virginia, 1861-65.

steadily during the war, remained essentially militia troops.[13] Like any other militia army, they were best in defensive operations in their own country and were not equal to serious offensive undertakings. Lee thus found himself restricted to the defensive. Two efforts to invade the enemy's territory failed, proving that his army was not prepared for an offensive campaign. This was, of course, due not only to the militia nature of Lee's army, but to the whole purpose of the war for the Southern States. With limited resources and population, the Confederacy could not hope to decisively defeat the Union, but could only seek independence from it. Its primary objective was to defeat the Union attempt to hold the Southern States by force.

This defensive purpose determined Lee's course of action. His purpose was to keep his army in the field, and his success here was remarkable during 1864 and even down to the final defeat of the Confederacy in the spring of 1865. With 62,000 men, he maintained his defense in the face of Grant's 120,000. When Grant attempted to turn Lee's position south of the Rapidan, moving by way of Chancellorsville, Lee struck the right flank of Grant's moving columns. This led to the fierce two days' battle in the Wilderness. Grant next attempted to push on by way of Spottsylvania. Anticipating this move, Lee occupied an entrenched position in his front which the Northern assaults could not carry. When the Northern army moved again upon Richmond, the Southern capital, its way was blocked at Hanover Junction, and again at Cold Harbor; and after several assaults had been repulsed with heavy loss, Grant gave up attempts to reach Richmond from the north.

Lee's defense during this early summer was so energetic that trenches soon covered almost the whole of Virginia from the Rapidan to the James. Even at the end of this long series of battles behind works, the spirit of the Army of Northern Virginia was still high. In the North, on the contrary, discouragement was widespread as a result of

[13] European views of the American Civil War were for the most part long-distance views and may vary at times from actual facts.

Grant's costly and unsuccessful attacks. Grant's plans seemed to have failed completely. From the beginning of May to the middle of June, he lost nearly 50,000 men.

With the help of the Navy, Grant finally changed his base of operations to the south bank of the James. The Confederate army, reduced to 50,000 men, then held out behind the Richmond-Petersburg entrenched lines until April 1865, against a constantly reinforced Union army. It finally yielded, not to force of arms, but to the breaking of its communications with the far south by General Sherman. Lee then had to retreat and finally surrender in the open field. In the last campaigns of the war, Lee and his troops showed the greatest steadfastness in the face of a desperate situation.

Long Defensive Wars Test a People's Character

The character of a people is tested in a long defensive war just as much as in an offensive one. Without the Russian soldier's heroic sense of duty, even Totleben[14] with all his skill could not have defended Sebastopol for 11 months.

The Russian with his simple passive Christian faith, which accepts whatever may come as God's will, in many ways resembles his ancient enemy the fatalistic Turk. Once a conqueror and a menace to Europe, the Turks in recent years have proved themselves extremely able in defense. They lost their opportunities for an annihilating blow against the Russians in August 1877[15] only through faulty leadership. Their degenerate government was unable to make adequate preparation for war and their generals commanded only improvised armies. The material was excellent, but the higher troop units were not fitted for offensive operations. This limited Osman Pasha at Plevna to the defensive. For five whole months he held out, checking greatly superior

[14] Russian officer who designed and commanded the defenses of Sebastopol in the Crimean War, 1854-56.
[15] Russo-Turkish War, 1877-78. Fought largely in what is now Bulgaria. Plevna, which was finally captured by the Russians after several disastrous assaults, was its principal battle. Many of the Turks in this battle were equipped with the then new Winchester repeating rifle.

hostile forces. His improvised fortress was honored by a regular siege; but he and his brave companions were denied a reward for their devotion. After an unsuccessful attempt to break through, their heroic stand ended in surrender.

Muktar Pasha in Armenia was similarly handicapped by the general political and military defects of the Turkish Empire and by the limited mobility of the armies entrusted to him. He succeeded in checking the Russian invasion and relieving the fortress of Kars; but he then had to halt on the Caucasian frontier and occupy an entrenched position based upon Kars, where he was finally defeated.

These generals, limited as they were to the defensive, could gain no real victory. All they could do was to hold out for a time. Great successes are gained, therefore, only where genuine boldness has free reign.

Frederick the Great and the Seven Years War

Seldom if ever has an army borne the stamp of its commander as thoroughly as the Army of Frederick the Great at the beginning of the Seven Years War. Availing himself of the experience of two Silesian Wars, he trained this army personally during 11 years of peace[16]—a true constable and king. His army was an instrument which justified the boldest operations, the type required in a conflict with greatly superior forces.

His opening of hostilities, which thwarted action against him by his enemies,[17] was a bold stroke; but in a strictly military sense even this daring was surpassed by his plan for the campaign of 1757, when he invaded Bohemia[18] in four widely separated columns. This plan, it is true, was not the King's alone; Winterfeldt[19] proposed it also, and Schwerin[19] assented. On 16 March 1757, Winterfeldt wrote to the King: "Under the present conditions, your Majesty

[16] 1745-56.
[17] Learning of a plan to partition Prussia, arranged by Austria, France, Sweden, Russia, and Saxony, then an independent east German kingdom, Frederick with a British subsidy took the field and captured and annexed Saxony, and added its army to his own.
[18] Now a part of Czechoslovakia. In Frederick's day, Bohemia was an Austrian province and a source of much of Austria's strength
[19] Prussian commanders under Frederick.

is in greater danger than ever before; but bold and prompt action may save this situation." On 30 March, Winterfeldt and Schwerin expressed themselves as follows on the Bohemian situation: "All the operations will be under difficulties, but these may be disregarded and overcome by good dispositions and vigorous execution. This is the only way we can rid ourselves of this crowd of enemies and weaken the Austrians before the French can arrive. The watchword must be 'Fortune favors the brave.' "[20]

Consistent with their habits of thought, training, and station, these two generals considered only an attack against the Austrians while separated, to seize their depots and forestall their offensive. The King, however, developed their views still further, into the greatest military operation of the century—an operation aimed at the destruction of the Austrian forces. He insisted that each battle must mark a long step forward toward the destruction of the enemy. Shortly before the Battle of Prague[21] he outlined his idea of annihilation in a letter to Schwerin: "By attacking at once all the concentrated forces of the House of Austria, we may destroy them all at once."[22]

The advance into Bohemia was made with two columns on each side of the Elbe River. Anticipating that the enemy's main position would be behind the Eger River at Budin, the King planned to concentrate his forces at Lobositz and Leitmeritz. The column of Prince Maurice of Anhalt-Dessau accordingly made its junction with the King on the Eger, while the Duke of Bevern forced a passage through the mountains. The corps of Count Koenigsegg, opposing Bevern, was threatened on its right flank by Schwerin's advance and fell back across the Elbe at Brandeis. Serbelloni, with the Austrian corps on the Silesian border, remained inactive at Koeniggraetz, and did nothing to delay Schwerin's march or his junction with Bevern. The column

[20] Winterfeldt, *Official Account, Wars of Frederick the Great; Seven Years War.*
[21] Frederick in this battle (1757) defeated the Austrians outside Prague, but was later defeated in the Battle of Kolin (fig. 7) and forced to abandon his effort to take Prague, itself.
[22] Frederick the Great, *Correspondence.*

under the personal command of Marshal Browne gave up the Eger line without fighting and fell back to Prague. Koenigsegg was brought back to join it. This permitted the Prussian forces to concentrate before Prague instead of on the Elbe at Lobositz. Here the campaign ended, with the main Austrian army shut up in the fortress.

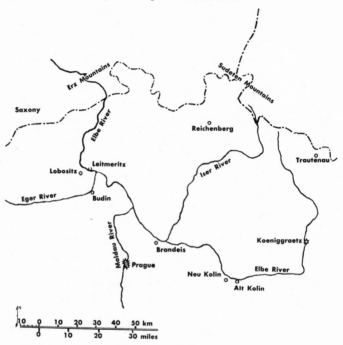

FIGURE 3. Bohemia, Area of Frederick the Great's Operations, 1757.

Was the King's plan for an invasion in separated columns more than boldness? Was it rashness—that infatuation to which, as Clausewitz says, "boldness often leads, while firmness leads to moderation"?[23] In his youth Frederick might have been open to such a charge, but not as the experienced general of 1757. Even in 1745, he was able to resist the

[23] *On War*, bk. I, ch. 3.

temptation to follow the example of Charles XII; and in the Peace of Dresden, at the height of his success, he showed remarkable moderation.

In his invasion of Bohemia, he counted upon the indecision of the enemy; and his calculations were justified, for it is one of the talents of a great general to know in each case what risks he may take with the enemy. Frederick's separated columns supported one another—the advance of one aided the others. Winterfeldt's keen military mind appreciated the situation. He wrote to the King on 22 March: "As the situation now stands, the enemy cannot choose advantageous positions. He must fight, whatever the nature of the ground."[24] These words give us an excellent evaluation of the importance of initiative, which promotes success in tactical operations.

While the invasion of Bohemia was based upon cold, rigorous calculations, they were the calculations of a bold man.

Moltke Copies Frederick's Boldness

Moltke was faced with much the same situation in 1866.[25] The war plan again was based on the idea that if the Second Army from Silesia encountered a superior enemy, it could be supported by the advance of the First Army and the Army of the Elbe from Lusatia.[26]

Here, as in 1757, the boldness of the leader inspired the subordinates, multiplied the strength of each individual, and contributed to the success of the whole campaign. Because of bold leadership, Bevern won his victory at Reichenberg;[27] and in 1866 the Second Army forced the passage of the mountains in spite of the reverse of the I Army Corps at Trautenau.

This was not the only case where Moltke adopted the

---

[24] *Seven Years War.*
[25] Seven Weeks War. Prussia won this war against Austria by means of a decisive engagement at Koeniggraetz, or Sadowa, in Bohemia (now Czechoslovakia).
[26] German province in southeast Germany, between Saxony and Upper Silesia.
[27] Bohemian campaign, Seven Years War, 1757.

ideas of Frederick and followed Frederick's bold example. In a memorandum in 1862 which discussed a possible Prussian war against Austria, Bavaria, and France, we find these words: "At the outset, Prussia will be without an ally, but may gain some from Germany itself by fighting. It would be to Prussia's advantage to take the initiative, since we can dispose our troops more rapidly than any of our German opponents. Success depends upon the immediate and unlimited use of our forces . . . Germany must be united by violence against France."[28] This memorandum is one of the most important legacies left by Moltke. "Frederick's spirit speaks from it—'enemies on every side'; no hesitation, no fears, no difficulties simply a daring attack—we must and we will go through."[29]

Optimism Marks a Great General

The invasion of 1866 led to Koeniggraetz. Critics who lacked an understanding of morale and other psychological aspects of war later picked flaws in Moltke's action, as they did in those of Frederick in 1757. Their criticism perhaps is more justified in the latter case, for Kolin[30] (fig. 7) followed the Battle of Prague, and the King found it necessary to withdraw from Bohemia. No war plan, however, can go beyond the first decisive battle; and the fact that Frederick was defeated at Kolin, fundamentally had nothing to do with the soundness of Frederick's decision to invade Bohemia. Moreover, Kolin came close to being a victory and ending the war. The King in spite of his defeat retained moral superiority. He was able to continue to stand firmly against a superior enemy and reject an unfavorable peace.

> "It is a prominent characteristic of great generals to yield as little as possible to misfortune; to trust to themselves and to fortune, and to hope that better times will come without too great a loss in the

[28] Von Moltke, *Military Correspondence*, 1866.
[29] Clausewitz, *Studies on Warfare*.
[30] Battle of Kolin, Seven Years War, 1758, in which Frederick was defeated by the Austrians and forced to abandon the siege of Prague (see footnote 21).

meantime. When good fortune returns to the side of these great leaders, however, we are always inclined to attribute the renewal of success to accurate calculations and clear insight, rather than to another turn in the wheel of fortune."[31]

In September 1813, after the defeats of his marshals, Napoleon tried to hold the line of the Elbe as long as possible. Doubtless in time he yielded more or less to a fatal self-deception, which led him to see things as he would have them. But it was not entirely self-deception at work when he hesitated to draw conclusions from a bad situation. It was in part optimism—that hope for a favorable turn which never entirely leaves a true general.

The prevailing attitude at the Russian headquarters at the Battle of Plevna in 1877, after the failure of the third assault, stands in marked contrast to this optimism that marks great generalship. Osman Pasha's force inside Plevna did not contain more than 35,000 men and 70 field pieces; and while it was only natural that the Turkish force should be greatly overestimated by the Russians after their failure to take the Turkish field entrenchments, there was still no valid reason for weak and hasty decisions. The Russians had, excluding their losses in three days' fighting, over 80,000 men with 400 field guns. The Turks, moreover, had ceased replying to the Russian artillery fire and had made no counterattacks. The Russian commanding general, Grand Duke Nicholas, under the immediate influence of his failure, nevertheless considered it impossible to remain in his Plevna positions, even though evacuation meant an early retreat behind the Danube. Czar Alexander II was also deeply impressed by the losses which the unsuccessful assaults had cost his army, but fortunately, at a council of war held on 13 September, concurred in the opinion of the principal assistant to the chief of staff, General Lewitzki, who insisted upon holding the position before Plevna. It seems to be the nature of the Russian that when

[31] Clausewitz, *Campaign of 1814.*

over-optimistic hopes are not fulfilled, he goes to the other extreme, complete pessimism.

When Frederick found his army reduced by a half, he adopted greater economies of force, and when he accepted battle he weighed chances more carefully. His force was never equal to the brilliant effort of 1757, but his conduct of operations continued to be marked by the utmost boldness, inspired in turn by the high aim for which he fought. Clausewitz expressed this idea strikingly when he advised the Crown Prince of Prussia, later King Frederick William IV, "to accustom himself to the possibility of an honorable defeat."[32] He urged his royal pupil "to think of the worst possible results and accustom himself to them," since this would furnish a foundation for heroic yet logical decisions. Clausewitz then went on to say it was because Frederick the Great was familiar with the idea of an honorable defeat that he made that memorable decision to attack at Leuthen[33] on 5 December, not because he felt his oblique order would defeat the Austrians. In those years of deep humiliation which preceded the War of Liberation,[34] when any day might have been Prussia's last, Clausewitz called up the spirit of the hero king before the eyes of the heir to the Prussian throne, saying that "some great motive must animate the strength of the general, whether it be ambition, as with Caesar, hatred of the enemy as with Hannibal, or pride in a glorious defeat as with Frederick the Great."

In the later years of the war, the King could not hope to defeat the concentrated forces of the House of Austria "all at once," but in his offensive battles he always aimed at a complete victory, the annihilation of the enemy. At Zorndorf and Kunersdorf he fought with a completely reversed front. At Torgau he divided his small army and moved with his main body to attack from two directions.

[32] *On War*, appendix.
[33] Frederick at Leuthen defeated 80,000 Austrians with 30,000 Prussians. The battle is considered one of his greatest successes.
[34] Following its defeat at Jena by Napoleon, Prussia was made a vassal state of the French Empire. When it joined the other European powers against Napoleon in 1813, its efforts were in the nature of a revolt and termed a war of liberation.

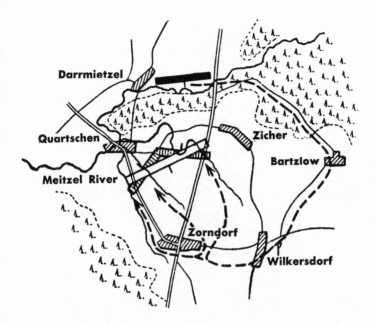

Darrmietzel

Quartschen

Zicher

Bartzlow

Meitzel River

Zorndorf

Wilkersdorf

Prussian:

■ Position, evening 24 August

- - -→ Advance, 25 August

Russian:

▥ Position, evening 24 August

▢ Position, evening 25 August

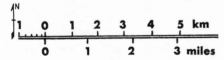

↑N

| 1 | 0 | 1 | 2 | 3 | 4 | 5 km |

| 0 | 1 | 2 | 3 miles |

FIGURE 4. Battle of Zorndorf, 1758.

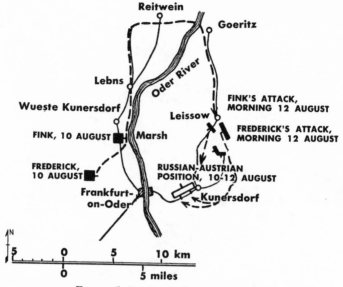

FIGURE 5. Battle of Kunersdorf, 1759.

In 1761 he avoided on principle the losses of an offensive battle in order to have a powerful force still in the field when peace was made. As Clausewitz explains:

"The King was especially careful to keep up the strength of his army, for he realized more and more every year that fear of his many battalions was a greater advantage to him than the blows which he could strike with them.

"He who would benefit by gaining time and saving his forces must not of his own motion increase the tempo of the war. The weaker one is in war, the more he must seek to profit from the mistakes of the enemy. Hence we see Frederick concentrating all further maneuvers about an entrenched position."[35]

Although perhaps in a negative fashion, Frederick's inherent boldness was still evident in his occupation of the

[35] Clausewitz, *Frederick the Great*.

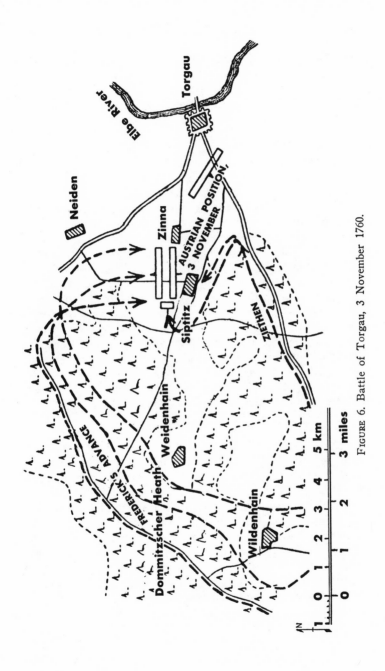

FIGURE 6. Battle of Torgau, 3 November 1760.

entrenched camp of Bunzelwitz. Deliberately cutting himself off from communication with his own country was a bold act. Yet he accepted the risk, relying upon the dissension and unreadiness of such opponents as Laudon and Buturlin,[36] and his calculations did not deceive him.

Napoleon and Frederick

Modern strategy begins with Napoleon. We have more to learn directly from him than from Frederick, for his situation and means of action were more like those of our own day. Napoleon's genius, too, was more creative than that of any other strategist or organizer in the world's history, and he will doubtless always continue to be a model. In boldness, however, he was inferior to Frederick. This is evident from Napoleon's own writings; for although he expresses the greatest admiration for the King, he criticizes him at times, especially for the battles of Kolin and Torgau. In doing so, however, the dethroned emperor, writing in captivity at St. Helena, disclosed his failure to grasp the true relation of events, and to understand the King's motives. The son of the Revolution could not appreciate Frederick's feeling of responsibility for the State, which controlled his actions. Napoleon also did not possess Frederick's "pride in a glorious defeat."

Frederick's Influence on His Soldiers

Characteristic relationships grow up in the course of a war between every great leader and his troops. Many traditions have come down to we Germans which are products of the relationships between Frederick and his soldiers. Even the private soldier in Frederick's army felt a personal acquaintanceship with the King through hardships and dangers shared together. The sternness with which the King continually demanded more and more sacrifices was feared; but every man knew that Frederick was even more stern with himself—that he did his own duty in spite of the torments of fever and gout, and that he exposed him-

[36] Austrian commanders.

self unhesitatingly to the enemy's bullets, whose whistling never caused the slightest change in his countenance. This fearless "countenance" under hostile fire also became a characteristic of his officers.

The influence of great military personalities appears most clearly and most strongly when some great idea motivates the actions of these great leaders. Although in the Silesian Army, even the Russian soldiers were inspired with enthusiasm by "Marshal Forward," their nickname for General Blucher, the Prussians saw in the tireless energy of the fiery old man something more. They saw the very embodiment of their war of retribution.

In the years of the Revolution in 1848-49, it was said with a great deal of truth that Austria existed only in Radetzky's [37] camp. Rarely has there been a finer example of esteem of troops for their commander than the loyalty of the Austrian soldiers for "Father Radetzky."

Suvorov demanded exertions from his troops which would have been considered impossible under any other commander. Skobeleff [38] also knew how to raise the spirits of the Russian soldier to the highest degree. Unfortunately for the Russians, no leader of his stamp was found in the Russian army in Manchuria. [39]

Troop Relations — Professional Army Versus One Raised by Universal Service

The relations between troops and commander are not the same in a professional army as in one raised by universal military service. Even with all the care and time Frederick lavished on his army, he still took it for granted that the private soldier could not be imbued with enthusiasm for a cause. He said: "All that can be done is to develop in him *esprit de corps,* that is, to make him believe that his regiment is the best in the world; and, since his officers must sometimes lead him through the greatest of dangers,

[37] Considered one of Austria's greatest commanders. He served in the Napoleonic wars, and in the Battle of Novara, 1849, defeated Italian efforts to win independence. He was 83 at the time of this battle.
[38] Russian field commander in Russo-Turkish war, 1877.
[39] Russo-Japanese War, 1904-05.

he must fear his officers more than the enemy."[40] In the King's mind only the officer was the depositary of the spirit of the army.

It is very different in an army formed from a "nation in arms." In it every man makes his contribution to the spirit which animates it, and leaders may properly assume that the forces motivating the people will move the troops to as great, if not a greater degree. Enthusiasm alone, it is true, will not win battles, as is attested by the bitter experiences of republican France with her improvised forces in 1870-71.[41] Still, the spirit which inspired the Prussian Army in 1813, and the whole German Army in 1870, will always exert a powerful influence toward victory.

By the time Napoleon appeared, the soldiers of the First French Republic had developed, through the experiences of several years of war, from the volunteers of 1793 into professional soldiers. The army which Napoleon led in 1805 from the Channel to southern Germany [42] was a pretorian guard. What the German historian Mommsen says of the army of Hamilcar Barca was equally true about Napoleon's army: "A great general is able to substitute his own personality in the eyes of his soldiers for their home country. . . . In the long years of war the soldier finds a second home in the camp; and as a substitute for patriotism he has his *esprit de corps* and his enthusiastic loyalty for his great leader."[43]

The army of the First Empire, continually reinforced by conscription, had a thoroughly national foundation. It was the embodiment of a national aspiration for glory and conquest. The influence of a genius like Napoleon therefore acted magically upon the easily influenced French people. His first proclamation, upon assuming command of the Army of Italy, filled his soldiers with martial ambi-

[40] Frederick the Great, *Military Testament.*
[41] After the defeat of the regular French forces in the Franco-Prussian War, 1870-71, several improvised armies were raised by the French to continue the war and in particular to raise the German siege of Paris. These improvised armies were for the most part disastrously defeated.
[42] Napoleon's campaign against the Russians and Austrians which culminated in his great victories at Ulm and Austerlitz.
[43] Mommsen, *History of Rome.*

tion. He promised to lead them out of the difficult places in which they were fighting, where the sun of glory would never shine upon their achievements, into the Lombard plain, where they would find honor, glory, and riches.

Marshal Marmont wrongly criticizes Napoleon's custom of visiting the troops and holding reviews during operations. The Emperor knew the influence which his presence had upon officers and men. He once said that a high commander must be a trifle theatrical in this respect. On this principle he addressed his troops on the battlefield at Belle Alliance before leading them to the assault upon Wellington's position.[44] The charm of his personality was so great that even in the midst of the disasters of the late autumn of 1813, the Young Guard shouted their enthusiastic "vive l'empereur" whenever he appeared.

Development of Esprit de Corps

Under a leader who gave war an entirely new character, who led the French forces from victory to victory, and extended their power to an undreamed of degree, the French Army couldn't help but develop a "noble *esprit de corps*." Limitless admiration for the Emperor and absolute confidence in success permeated all grades of the army. This was summed up by Marshal Lannes when he wrote to his wife 10 October 1805, just before the triumph at Ulm: "What a man is this Emperor! The enemy's army is more closely hemmed in than at Marengo; we hope that it will be entirely at our mercy within the week."

As a consequence of Napoleon's great victories, remarkable generals with great tactical skill were developed. Although the overwhelming prestige of their lord and master and the extreme centralization upon which he insisted, both in the State and Army, prevented them from developing into independent army commanders, they were outstanding in their narrow spheres. The men looked up to these tried and experienced soldiers, in whom the glory of the Empire seemed to be incarnated, and who furnished

[44] Battle of Waterloo.

living truth of the saying that every soldier carried a
marshal's baton in his knapsack.

Character and Influence of Marshal Ney

Of all these great subordinate French leaders, Marshal
Ney, the "Bravest of the Brave," had the greatest influence
upon the French soldier. Ney was of humble origin. He
lacked the spiritual and intellectual characteristics essential
for independent action, and for this reason typifies the
fighting generals of the Napoleonic era. He had all the
bravery of Murat, but he had more. His heroic stoicism
led him not only to despise danger, but to regard it as
a thing perfectly normal in war. A modern leader thrown
suddenly into danger after a long period of peace would
hardly have this feeling unless it were ingrained by habits
of self-discipline. Long years of war generated in Ney an
infallible equanimity, which enabled him to say to a wounded
soldier who begged for help during the retreat from Russia
in 1812, "How can I help you? You are a part of the
wreckage of war." In these quietly spoken words there
was no cruelty; there was only the expression of an old
truth—the soldier in war is doomed to destruction; a
truth almost forgotten in our peace-loving age.

The extreme bravery of the Japanese in the Manchurian
war grew out of a religious belief that no earthly reward
was comparable to an opportunity to die for the fatherland,
since this raised the soldier to the rank of a deified ancestor.
It was this alone which made it possible for General Nogi [45]
at Port Arthur to call for sacrifices which would have cost
a European general his command. The heroic words of
General Umesawa at the Battle of Liao-Yang (fig. 14),[46]
however, may hold a lesson for us. When the commander
of a battalion going into action expressed doubts of his
ability to carry out his orders in the face of a superior
enemy, the general answered, "then die."

[45] Japanese commander at the siege of Port Arthur, Russo-Japanese
War, 1904-05.
[46] Fought May-September 1904, a decisive engagement in the Russo-
Japanese War.

Leader Must Be Ready to Sacrifice Himself and His Men

The real secret of leadership in battle is the domination of the mass by a single personality. Influence over subordinates is a matter of suggestion. Discipline acquired during peace and the power of personal example are both used to exact great sacrifices.

At Koeniggraetz, the Prussian First Army had to withstand the effects of a powerful and costly frontal attack before the effect of the advance of the Second Army against the enemy's flank and rear became evident. Under effective artillery fire, individuals and even small groups began to abandon the Hola Wood and fall back seeking better cover. King William rebuked the commander of a regiment who with considerable force was retiring from the wood toward the point where he himself was standing. The King commanded him to order "guides out," and dress up his lines under shell fire, and then said, "I am sending you forward again; see that you fight like true Prussians."

At Lovtscha [47] in 1877, General Skobeleff put a wavering battalion through the manual of arms under hostile fire, and restored order in the same way. At Nachod, [48] a critical situation in the V Corps' advance guard was restored by the personal intervention of General von Steinmetz, whose sternness was universally feared in the Corps.

> "Because an ordinary man is never his natural self in battle, it should be recognized that ordinary means will accomplish nothing in battle. This becomes even more evident as the field of action broadens. Enthusiastic and stoical bravery, overpowering ambition, and long familiarity with danger, must all be employed fully by the leader to prevent results under difficult actual conditions from falling far behind theoretical calculations." [49]

[47] Minor engagement in the Russo-Turkish War, 1877. Fought near Plevna in Bulgaria.
[48] Town in northeast Bohemia, scene of a minor engagement in the Seven Weeks War, 1866.
[49] *On War*, bk. I, ch. 4.

Leader Must Be Sensitive to the Pulse of the Battle

General Kuropatkin, the Russian commander in chief in eastern Asia, who was formerly chief of staff to Skobeleff, tells of the latter's ability to feel the pulse of battle accurately—now rapid, now slow—and how Skobeleff would shape his own conduct in action accordingly, sometimes holding back, checking his own impulses by the power of his will, sometimes giving them free rein. On the afternoon of 11 September at Plevna, he sent his last reserve battalions into action on his left to carry forward his skirmish lines. At this moment a Turkish counterattack struck his advancing troops on their right flank. The Russian advance was checked, and the check seemed likely to extend itself along the line. The general had no reserve left, except himself. Spurring his horse, he dashed across a little valley to his front, and with a shout of "forward, my children," carried the line forward and entered the enemy's works.

Effect of Exhaustion and Strain

Even the influence of so energetic and popular a leader as Skobeleff, however, has its limits in action. The degree of mastery which a leader has over his troops depends upon the extent of the physical exhaustion and nervous strain to which they have been subjected.

In January 1878, two-and-a-half companies, the leading elements of Skobeleff's advance guard, were attacked just as they came down from the Balkan passes and began to enter the plain. The rest of the advance guard was still moving through the deep snows in the mountains. These leading companies held their ground with difficulty in the face of a superior enemy and under fire from the front, both flanks, and the rear. As ammunition ran short and losses became excessive, the men, exhausted by the hardships of crossing the mountains in winter, became more and more discouraged. Kuropatkin describes the impression

Skobeleff made upon this group when he joined them:

> "One glance at the brave defenders of our most advanced post was enough to show the desperate situation. The overstrain of their nerves during the several hours of fighting had had its effect. Even the appearance of their beloved leader had no effect. Their faces were indifferent, pale, and without expression; many had completely lost their heads. The general spoke to them but received few answers. He spoke to them sharply, repeated his greeting, and received more satisfactory answers; then he began to feel that he could still count upon these men for service."

Two days later the general undertook an attack upon the Turkish entrenched camp of Scheinovo, at the southern end of the Shipka Pass. The attack was checked, and for a moment even Skobeleff lost his self-control. In deep distress, he said to his staff, "It's Plevna all over again." When the first line of Turkish entrenchments had been taken, the skirmish lines came up against a second line. The reserves came forward, the drums beat, the regimental bands played, the skirmishers cheered—but they remained in place, and all the efforts of the officers could not get them forward. Under a hail of bullets, at close range, they would not even raise their heads. But the scene at Plevna was not to be reenacted. A bold drummer finally rushed forward, beating his drum; his regimental commander followed, waving the colors, and the line moved forward again.

Influence of Leaders More Limited Today

While the duties of leaders of all grades today [1911] are more difficult than they were in the Napoleonic times, the influence which an infantry officer can exercise upon a skirmish line through his personal influence and example is less immediate and more limited. In the South African War, the British infantry officers were not up to the standards necessary. As a rule they looked upon their duties from the old point of view and found difficulty in fitting themselves into warfare's new form. They were courageous—their losses, in proportion to those of their men, were proof of that; but most of them looked upon war as a sporting event. One who is accustomed to take risks in games will not flinch in the face of the enemy; but it is a long step from this kind of courage to an ability to demand victory at any cost, and a force of will which makes it possible for a man to communicate this need for victory to his subordinates. This calls for unique soldierly qualities which cannot be developed in sports, but only by long fulfillment of duty.

Although the crisis was successfully passed in the battles of the Russo-Turkish war mentioned above, it should be evident that a fortunate turn of events will not always occur. Furthermore, unaccountable instincts may at any moment take possession of a mass of men, and suddenly turn brave, successful troops into a panic-stricken mob. The South African War shows us many examples of such failures among the British troops. This fact, however, should not lead us to look pessimistically upon the difficulties of modern war. Such failures are not confined to this age alone, but have always occurred, even in the best armies of the past and during periods of their greatest success.

In Frederick's victorious Battle of Prague, his left at first was checked and gave ground, even though Schwerin himself intervened at the risk of his life, and although the Prussians in this part of the battle area were led by no lesser general than Winterfeldt. This reverse was the cumulative effect of hunger, of fatigue due to the preceding night's march, and of an exhausting approach march over marshy ground where the artillery could not follow. The battalions were nearly exhausted before they met the enemy.

In some ways the requirements of that time upon the rank and file were less than they are at present. Closed mass formations gave the soldier more of a feeling of mutual aid. He was also always under the eye of his superior and had to go forward whether he would or no. In addition, although the Frederician and Napoleonic battles were bloodier than ours, and to advance against batteries firing canister was never a joke, lack of effective long-range weapons in those days made the moments of maximum danger shorter.

In our time [1911], the fire fight may last for hours at long range. This makes great demands upon the nerves, and the failing strength of the skirmish line can be restored only by reinforcement from the rear, by the entry into action of elements on the flanks, or by some other appropriate measure taken by the commander.

Success of an Infantry Attack is Always Possible

The Prussian infantry at one time took the Frederician maxim of marching boldly upon the enemy too literally, and insisted that skirmishing is the mark of a coward. It learned better in 1806,[50] and has since shown, countless times, that even in a skirmish line there is place for the true soldierly spirit, notably at Spicheren, Thionville, and St. Privat.[51] It will show the same thing many times in the future, even though conditions may change. Despite heavier casualties and longer periods of exposure, successful infantry attacks will continue to be made, and whoever denies this should take off his uniform, for he is like one who professes religion without really possessing it.

In a country where military service is universal, the finest opportunities are open to an officer. Because the average intelligence of the mass of soldiers is much higher than formerly, it is possible for him to develop competent [enlisted] assistants for moments of need. Even as far back as 1794, Scharnhorst wrote of the action of the Hanoverian troops in cutting their way out of the little fortress of Menin: "Necessity itself leads to great deeds in war . . . In the confusion of the night attack, parties of troops

[50] Year of Prussia's decisive defeat by Napoleon at Jena.
[51] German victories in the Franco-Prussian War, 1870-71.

were noticed commanded by private soldiers. The men were obeying them as if they were officers." The German Army's regulations [1911] also speak of the examples set by courageous individuals who can, in case of need, take the place of officers.

The following words of Clausewitz's apply to the army whose sole purpose is preparation for war:

> "From wagoner and drummer up to the general, boldness is the highest attainment—the steel which gives weapons their edge and polish. . . . In large forces, boldness is a quality whose development can never operate to the disadvantage of any other quality. . . . Boldness is the tension of a spring. . . . The higher we go in the military hierarchy, however, the more necessary it becomes for this quality of boldness to be accompanied by careful thought to prevent purposeless acts of passion; for boldness on a high level becomes less and less a matter of mere self-sacrifice and more one of providing for the success and well-being of the whole army." [52]

The higher placed a leader may be, therefore, the more boldness must work in cooperation with caution. "Even in audacity there is a certain prudence and foresight, although calculated in different terms." [53]

Audacity Sometimes Prudence

Military history shows us that audacity can be the height of prudence at times. Friedjung said of Baron John, who in 1866 was chief of staff to Archduke Albert, and to whom belongs a large share of the credit for the victory of Custozza: "John was not a brilliant genius; on the contrary he was, like Gneisenau, characterized by clear vision, calmness, and firmness. The audacity of his military decisions was the outgrowth of his appreciation of the fact

[52] *On War*, bk. III, ch. 6.
[53] *On War*, bk. I, ch. 1.

that in war boldness can also be the height of prudence." [54]

Conversely, there are also cases as Clausewitz says where "the greatest caution lies in the greatest audacity." [55] In this connection he goes on to state,

> "Audacity in war has its prerogatives. When calculations of space, time, and strength have been completed, a certain allowance must always be made for the weakness of the enemy. This can readily be demonstrated philosophically. Other factors being equal, whenever boldness meets faintheartedness, boldness should win, for faintheartedness is always handicapped by a loss of equilibrium. It is only when audacity encounters calculated prudence—just as bold, and at least as strong and powerful as itself, that it will be inferior. Such cases are rare. Among the prudent, there will always be many who are so from pure timidity." [56]

Effect of Leader's Audacity and Reputation on Enemy

Audacity of itself has a powerful psychological effect on the enemy. This fact explains many of the brilliant successes Frederick the Great and Napoleon achieved, even in cases where cold calculations would predict only a minor success, or even a failure. The invasion of Bohemia in 1757 was for the Austrians, as Winterfeldt predicted, a most unexpected blow, throwing everything into confusion and terror.

At Marengo, Ulm, and Jena, Napoleon's plan of campaign laid the foundation for his victories. While he realized that his great turning movements were dangerous, he calculated their risks and took them into account. In the Ratisbon[57]

[54] Friedjung, *The Struggle For the Hegemony of Germany*. In the Seven Weeks War (footnote 25), the Austrians were forced to fight the Prussians on one side and the Italians on the other. At Custozza, in northern Italy, 80,000 Austrians defeated 120,000 Italians, but their presence here was enough to give the Prussians victory at Koeniggraetz. Gneisenau was chief of staff to Prussia's Marshal Blucher in the Napoleonic wars.

[55] Clausewitz, *Campaign of 1815*.

[56] *On War*, bk. III, ch. 6.

[57] Town in southern Germany, now called Regensburg, scene of Napoleon's initial operations against Austria in 1809.

operations of 1809, the Archduke Charles, confused by the speed with which Napoleon completely reversed a situation which seemed greatly to his disadvantage, allowed the initiative to pass out of his hands. The successes at Ratisbon, however, turned Napoleon's boldness to rashness, and led to his defeat at Aspern. His attempt to cross the Danube in the presence of the concentrated Austrian armies naturally failed; but was it surprising that the undefeated conqueror of the world should think that he might take even this risk with his opponent? In retrospect, many things appear rash simply because they failed, when actually they would seem proper and feasible to most commanders making a similar estimate.

"Immediate risks always exert a powerful influence on any man. A course of action can appear to be extremely rash until it is also seen as the only method of escape. Then it becomes a highly conservative course. Pure reason seldom causes a man to adopt an audacious course to save his command. Generally, this action is the result of an instinctive, inherent boldness that prompts one to reject surrender and seek a method of escape." [58]

In 1658, Charles X (Gustavus) of Sweden crossed from Jutland on the ice, first to Funen and then to Zealand.[59] Although he appeared before Copenhagen with only five thousand men, all Denmark was so dazed by his sudden arrival that he dictated peace on his own terms. Diebitsch accomplished much the same results in Turkey in 1829.[60] According to Moltke, "He appeared at Adrianople, south of the Balkans, with only a shadow of an army, but with a reputation for invincibility. Russia owed her success in this campaign solely to the cautious but bold reputation of General Diebitsch."

The astonishing facts that the land troops of the King of Sweden, without the assistance of a fleet, could appear

[58] Clausewitz, *Campaign of 1812*.
[59] Danish islands. Copenhagen, the Danish capital, is located on Zealand.
[60] In 1828-29 Russia intervened on the side of Greece in the latter's struggle for independence from Turkey.

before the island capital of the Danish kingdom; and that
the Russians could break through the Balkans, the outer
wall of Constantinople, broke the spirit of the defense.

Audacity on the Battlefield

Similar effects may be produced even without such
spectacular actions. The spirit of the defense may be broken
on the battlefield by a well-planned and audacious maneuver,
as was the case in the August battles of 1870.

On 6 August, General von Kameke crossed the Saar
River at Saarbrucken [61] with his German 14th Division
expecting only to delay hostile French troops withdrawing
from the heights of Spicheren. Unexpectedly, he became
involved in a hot fight with Frossard's French II Corps.
At 1600 the division was fully engaged, and only at the
expense of heavy losses could it hold the ground it had
gained with such difficulty. A determined counterattack by
the French who still had nearly half their Corps in reserve,
would have thrown the Germans back across the Saar.
But as early as 1325, when the 14th Division had employed
only its leading brigade and its artillery, Frossard had reported to Marshal Bazaine, his army commander, that he
was under heavy attack on his whole front and needed
reinforcements urgently. When, at 1600, the attack of the
isolated German division had been stopped, and its whole
force exhausted, Frossard reported only that he hoped to
be able to hold his position. At the same time, he again
asked for reinforcements, stating that the battle might break
out again at any moment. The arrival of the first German
reinforcements, parts of the 16th and 5th Infantry Divisions, caused him to telegraph again to Bazaine, "The
Prussians are bringing in considerable reinforcements, and
I am attacked from all directions. Hasten the movement
of your troops as much as possible."

For so small a German force, this was truly an outstanding success for a bold attack. Actually it was the first
sign of the "Prussian nightmare," which remained continu-

[61] Opening stages of the Franco-Prussian War, 1870-71.

ally before the eyes of the French Army, and at the time of the III Corps' vigorous attack at Thionville [62] (fig. 22) deprived Bazaine of all power of decision. On the French right in this action at Thionville, Ladmirault's IV French Corps had gained an undisputed success. But the success was not exploited because the boldness of the German attack had made the French estimate the German strength much too high.

Audacity, Even in Error, Meritorious

Combat is always dependent upon the material of the time, and hence methods used by the German Army leaders in 1870 would be inapplicable today [1911]. The policy of allowing maximum initiative to subordinates which they established, however, should always be kept in mind.

> "In a leader, audacity may in a particular case prove to be an error, but it is a meritorious error, and should be so treated. The army is fortunate in which untimely boldness often appears. It is a rank growth, perhaps, but is evidence of good soil. Even rashness or boldness without reason, is not without some merit, since it is evidence of the basic disposition of a successful soldier. Only where audacity culminates in disobedience, where the expressed will of a superior is disregarded and his plans jeopardized, is it to be treated as a dangerous evil—and then not for itself, but for insubordination, a cardinal sin in war. Other things being equal, undue timidity is a thousand times worse than undue audacity." [63]

These words of Clausewitz, like German Army training regulations [1911], emphasize that failure to act is worse than an error of judgment in selecting a course of action. Commanders in time of peace should therefore make it their duty to encourage initiative in their subordinates, in-

[62] 16 August 1870.
[63] *On War*, bk. III, ch. 6.

stead of checking it, as is the case too often. Subordinates should be taken to task only where their action was taken thoughtlessly—without a good reason.

How Audacity Becomes Insubordination

The action of General von Manstein at the Battle of Kolin illustrates the "dangerous evil" of disregarding the expressed will of a superior. Before the turning movement of the Prussian Army around the Austrian front was com-

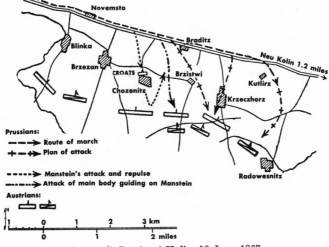

FIGURE 7. Battle of Kolin, 18 June 1857.

pleted, he left his place in the marching column with a single battalion and moved upon Chozenitz to drive out a party of Croats whose flanking fire was annoying him. He then allowed his impetuous bravery to lead him to move with five battalions beyond Chozenitz and attack the Austrian main position, against which his weak force was shattered. Such self-willed action by a subordinate is always reprehensible, but at that time of close-order linear tactics it was doubly so, for it broke the unity of the Prussian infantry attack. Manstein must bear the largest share of the responsibility for the Prussian defeat on that day.

Possibly such thoughtless action in the heat of a single battle by a leader of Manstein's temperament may be understood, if not justified. Actions contrary to the intentions of a superior must be judged more severely when they interfere with the orderly development of a whole campaign.

Boldness in the Higher Grades

The type of boldness required in the higher grades is of course different from that in the lower.

"The higher we go in the chain of command, the more that reason, intellect, and insight must be exercised constantly, and the opportunity for the development of an emotional type of boldness shrinks correspondingly. For this reason, this latter quality is seldom found in the highest grades. Yet when it is, it is to be most admired. Boldness controlled by reason makes great soldiers. This boldness does not consist in taking risks beyond the nature of things, nor in complete disregard of the laws of probability, but in vigorous support of those profound calculations which genius makes with lightning speed, half consciously, in reaching a decision. The stronger reason and insight are supported by boldness, the more they will extend one's horizons and widen one's views. This leads to more reliable results.

"As scopes widen, however, dangers increase. The average man can withdraw into a private room and there, insulated from danger and responsibility, estimate a situation and come to a reasonable decision. But under the influence of danger and responsibility, he usually loses his broad view; and even if he can keep his hold upon this broad view through the assistance of others, he normally still loses his power of decision, for in this no one else can help him." [64]

In the same vein, America's General Sherman writes— "I would define true courage to be a perfect sensibility to

[64] *On War,* bk. III, ch. 6.

the measure of danger, and a mental willingness to incur it, rather than that insensibility to danger of which I have heard far more than I have seen." [65]

Boldness Necessary Away From the Battlefield

The mark of the genuine hero is found on almost every battlefield hero. Murat was unquestionably such a man. Napoleon, his brother-in-law, praises his incomparable *elan* and his brilliant bravery. He goes on to say that Murat's whole life was spent in war, and that he was a hero, but nevertheless had his limitations. To his sister, the Queen of Naples, the Emperor wrote, "Your husband is a very brave man on the battlefield, but is weaker than a woman or a monk when he cannot see the enemy. He has no mental courage." Marshal Marmont's estimate of Ney is much the same; he says, quite justly, that Ney had no clear operative view, because wherever he could see only with his mind's eye his vision was colored. "With him everything is the result of the sensation of the moment, determined, so to speak, by his blood pressure. He may retreat with thirty thousand men before twenty thousand; or he may attack fifty men with twenty." Jomini says, very significantly, "A general should be as calm and as firm on the battlefield as before a map in his study. But if we have to choose, we should prefer the latter characteristic for a general rather than the former. Critical decisions are always made far from the heat of action, after deliberate meditation. It is here that we find the true value of a great general."

General Must Not Be Stranger to His Troops

Today, even on the battlefield, the influence of a higher commander is felt chiefly in the area of morale. The higher the position of the commander, the more this is true. While this influence is not readily apparent to the troops, and is not so immediate as in Napoleon's time, the power of the leader's personality remains a potent force. The gen-

[65] Sherman, General William T., *Memoirs.*

eral's strength of character, his decisiveness, his steadfastness, his boldness, may even be more severely tried than
in former times. Even if the troops seldom see their general on the modern battlefield, he must not be a stranger
to them. He must not fail to see and speak occasionally
to such soldiers as he can, on the march or in quarters,
especially since the motor car [and airplane] makes it easy
for him to cover ground. His influence may manifest itself
in different forms, but the substance is unchanged.

"Courage is always the outstanding characteristic of the
warrior; but it can accomplish nothing in the higher grades
under great responsibility, unless it is supported by strong
intellect. That's why we see so many brave soldiers, and
so few bold and energetic generals." [66] This "strong intellect" which the general must have, does not imply that he
must be what is commonly called an "intellectual man."
On this point Napoleon wrote very pertinently—"Your
letter is too brilliant. Brilliancy is not needed in war, only
accuracy, character, and simplicity." The spirit needed to
inspire boldness in a general, and which places upon him
the mark of the hero, is not often found. We do find it,
however, in men like Scharnhorst, Gneisenau, Lee, Moltke,
all of whom have grown greater with the passage of time.
We find it also in Marshal Turenne, whom Napoleon calls
the greatest general of old France. Turenne, Napoleon says,
unlike other men, grew bolder with advancing age.

When the liberation for which he had fought was an
accomplished fact, Scharnhorst in this spirit said he would
give all of his seven decorations and his life to hold supreme
command for a single day. Moltke felt the same way. When
he began to grow old, he said, "If it can be granted me
to lead our armies in such a war, the devil may take my
old carcass."

More fortunate than Scharnhorst, Moltke realized his
great wish. Although the most complete success was granted
him, he always ascribed this to the troops, knowing that

---

[66] Clausewitz, *Campaigns of 1799 in Italy and Switzerland.*

the boldest general is powerless if his army does not have the same spirit. As Clausewitz says, "An army may be imbued with a bold spirit, either because the whole people possess it, or because it has developed in the course of a successful war under a bold general.

"In our times there seems to be no way to inculcate this spirit in a people except through war and bold leadership. This alone can counteract that softness, that longing for comfort and pleasure, which may bring ruin to a people." [67]

[67] *On War,* bk. II, ch. 6.

CHAPTER 2

War is the Domain of Physical Exertion and Suffering

> "War is the domain of physical exertion and suffering. If one is not to be overcome by these features, he must possess a certain physical and mental strength, native or acquired, which makes him indifferent to them."
> —Clausewitz, *On War*, book I, chapter 3

"WITH those qualities, and guided simply by sound common sense, man becomes an effective instrument of war. These qualities are inherent in savage and semi-civilized peoples, but in civilized nations they must be developed by military training." [1]

Clausewitz then goes on to say: "Physical exertions must be undertaken not so much to train the body as the mind. In war the recruit often feels that any unusual physical demand placed on him is the result of some gross error committed by the commander, and is unduly influenced by these demands. This will not happen, if he has been properly prepared for them by peacetime training." [2]

Inadequate training for war's hardships and lack of discipline to overcome them are the chief reasons for the failure of improvised armies. While military history shows many instances where new levies and undisciplined militia have been able to overcome trained troops, the general and local conditions which contributed to their success must not be overlooked.

Public Always Ready to Believe Extensive Training Unnecessary

When hastily trained or untrained troops achieve success, public opinion is quick to assume that long, hard military training is unnecessary. It drew such conclusions from the North American Revolutionary War, which were as false

[1] *On War*, bk. I, ch. 3.
[2] *On War*, bk. I, ch. 8.

as those which it has drawn more recently from the Boer War.

The wars of the First French Republic at first seemed to justify the conclusion that long military training is superfluous. Recently [1847], however, Camille Rousset destroyed the legend of the volunteers of the First Republic.[3] He has shown that they were an undisciplined horde without a trace of military value. The better elements among them gradually became soldiers, and were amalgamated with the old troops of the line to form demi-brigades.

Chuquet rightly says [4] that Gambetta [5] with his improvised armies, sought to repeat the legendary miracles of 1792 and 1793; but forgot that the Revolutionary volunteers through their lack of discipline and courage had brought nothing but misfortune to their country. During the Revolution, the Republic was saved, not through the devotion and skill of its new troops, but by lack of unity in the coalition. In 1793 the Germans were weak and irresolute, and were relatively far away; in 1870 they were strong and united, and were operating not on the Sauer and the Scheldt, but in the heart of France on the Seine and the Loire.

Defeats Become Disasters With Insufficient Training

After the disaster of 1812, Napoleon's new and untried armies met many defeats. One of the worst was in the battle on the Katzbach River, 26 August 1813.[6] The defeat itself was not as serious as the disorder of the troops of Macdonald's Army of the Bober during the retreat, when it nearly went to pieces. Rousset writes:

"For trained soldiers the battle on the Katzbach might not have been a

[3] Rousset, *Les Volontaires,* 1791-94.
[4] Chuquet, *War of 1870-71.*
[5] After the defeat of the regular French forces and their entrapment at Metz and Sedan, several improvised armies were raised by the French people to continue the war and raise the German siege of Paris. These efforts for the most part failed. Leon Gambetta, a Paris lawyer, organized and led one of these improvised armies.
[6] A river in eastern Germany. A part of Napoleon's army was defeated there by the allies.

defeat. At worst, it would have been a check, easily reparable. But with mere boys, soldiers overnight, it was the beginning of a disaster. One will never see a better illustration, by contrast, of the value of physical and moral energy; of the need for bodily endurance to withstand the stress of weather, hunger, thirst, and all the other hardships of war—summed up in a word of the need for that *stoicism* which comes, not suddenly, but gradually from military training, and which, after all, is simply the ingrained spirit of honor and duty."

Few Soldiers Remain Unaffected by Hardships of War

Only a few unusual soldiers, inspired by the highest spirit of duty, can remain indifferent to the hardships of war. Von der Goltz's comment on the spirit of the Second Army on the Loire River [7] about the middle of December is very illuminating: "It is easy to see the moral effect of this latest epoch of the war. Except for a few indefatigables, everyone was tired of even victorious battles. The fire of war was flickering. The longing for rest was universal."

The warlike spirit fades even sooner when there is no inspiring object to fight for and so help soldiers over the hardships of the moment. Cases were known in which British officers captured in the South African War yielded to their fate without resistance. They felt that the cause for which they fought was not, after all, of great national importance, and this thought may have largely produced this lassitude. Nelson expressed this same idea when he wrote to the Admiralty in 1805, "If our West Indian colonies should fall into the hands of the French, the demand for peace would be so strong in England that we would have to yield." [8] The great admiral knew his people. He realized what such injury to trade would mean to a parliamentary government in a "nation of shop-keepers."

[7] Final stages of the Franco-Prussian War, 1870-71. The Germans here were operating in central France against improvised French armies attempting to relieve Paris.
[8] Mahan, *Influence of Sea Power Upon History*.

The endurance of veteran troops contrasts sharply with the weaknesses of untrained masses. On 16 and 17 December, during the withdrawl of the IX Corps from the Loire to Orleans, [9] many of the units made 75 to 85 kilometers in 33 to 36 hours under unfavorable conditions. Von der Goltz writes of these feats: "It is in this type of action that the word 'veteran' has its real significance, rather than in bravery and devotion in action. Familiarity with danger does not as a rule make one despise it. The body grows stronger and better able to bear hardships; but the heart and spirit become worn down, and begin to long for an end to their troubles."

The Napoleonic armies had veterans in this sense of the word, and had them in great numbers as long as Napoleon's series of victories remained unbroken. This made it possible after Jena and Auerstaedt to organize pursuits characterized in Napoleon's language as—"no rest, as long as there remains one man in that army." In one of these pursuit actions, the advance guard of Lannes' Corps, seeking to cut off Hohenlohe at Prenzlau, [10] made over 100 kilometers in 50 hours over sandy roads, while the main body of the Corps made this same march in 60 hours. Writing about the capabilities of this troops the Marshal boasted: "When the Prussians march 25 or 30 kilometers, they think they have done enough; they will not believe that we make 50 or 55 kilometers a day." The Prussian Army had evidently forgotten the days when King Frederick and his brother Prince Henry in the Seven Years War had often called for marches of 30 or 40 kilometers on several days in succession.

In evaluating these marches properly we need to remember that in the armies of that time the march order was the order of battle.

> "The second line had to march across country, picking its way as best it could, for in those days one rarely found two graded roads paralleling one another

---

[9] Franco-Prussian War, 1870-71 (see footnote 7).
[10] City in north central Germany, north of Berlin, where Prince Hohenlohe, one of the Prussian commanders at Jena, surrendered to the French.

a mile apart. The situation was the same for the cavalry on the flanks in a march directly toward the enemy. The artillery presented still greater problems. It had to have its own road covered by infantry. To be effective, infantry lines in those days had to be unbroken. To have marched artillery with them would not only have broken their lines but would have made the clumsy artillery columns even more clumsy and thrown everything into confusion." [11]

Heat Great Problem in War

Heat is one of the greatest hardships which the soldier must endure in war. When water is scarce, heat becomes a torture, making troops unfit for further marching or for battle. In fact, in the South African War the mobility of the British forces was greatly reduced by lack of water.

In hot weather, a commander should regard water supply as one of his primary responsibilities. The importance of water to troops is indicated by the instinctive rush they normally make for wells after storming a village. The nearness of the enemy is usually completely forgotten in satisfying physical needs for water. What troops can endure was illustrated at Gravelotte and St. Privat, where on 18 August 1870 the German regiments fought for hours in the burning heat. Equally striking was the march of the Second Army Corps, which reached this field after a march of 45 to 55 kilometers in the same heat.

Instinct of Self-Preservation Produces Astonishing Feats of Endurance

Actually, however, the real test of what human beings can endure is found in the astonishing march of defeated armies. The remarkable pursuit conducted by Gneisenau at the close of the Battle of Waterloo, whose 7 squadrons and 1¼ battalions made 17 kilometers from the battlefield that night, should be compared with the withdrawal of the French army which made 15 kilometers more, a total of 32 kilometers, to

[11] *On War*, bk. V, ch. 10.

get behind the Sambre. Seldom had a night pursuit been as well conducted as by Gneisenau in this case, and seldom has an army been so inspired with patriotic enthusiasm and hatred for the enemy as was the Prussian army that day. But fear and the instinct of self-preservation in the French army were stronger. On the morning of the second day,

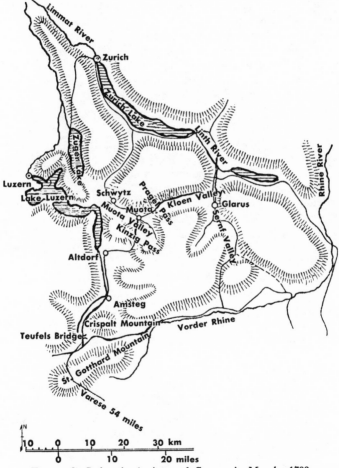

FIGURE 8. Switzerland, Area of Suvorov's March, 1799.

the French succeeded in assembling troops, fit for battle, 75 kilometers from the battlefield.

It is not flattering that the instinct of self-preservation should get better results than exalted inspiration and the energies of a clearsighted leader, who was further stimulated by a great victory. But it proves that under exceptional conditions, troops can accomplish much more than is ordinarily considered possible. In fact, "the more a general habitually demands from his troops, the more likely he is to get what he calls for. Soldiers take pride in the difficulties they have overcome and dangers they have faced." [12] This pride may sometimes make even a failure seem a success because of the tremendous difficulties overcome.

In the autumn of 1799, Suvorov with 20,000 Russians and an Austrian brigade moved from Upper Italy into Switzerland to join 40,000 allied troops who were then on the Upper Rhine and the Linth, opposing 50,000 French troops under Massena. Suvorov forced the crossing of the St. Gotthard Mountain, which was defended by a French division, and pushed on as far as Altdorf. Here he discovered that there was no road along the shores of Lake Lucerne to Schwytz, and was forced to take the difficult trail over the Kinzig Pass into the Muota Valley. After he completed this move, he learned that the allied forces in Switzerland had been completely defeated and scattered.

Despite terrible hardships, he crossed the Pragel Mountains to Glarus, his rear guard repulsing a French attack, and reached the Vorder Rhine by way of the Sernf Valley. Clausewitz describes this march this way.

"The march across the high Alps lasted three weeks, from 21 September to 10 October, with continual fighting and severe hardships. The army lost a third of its men, most of its horses, and all of its guns. While these losses were those of a lost battle; the morale effect of the operation was quite the opposite. When Suvorov and his

[12] *On War*, bk. III, ch. 5.

army later looked back upon this march through a country so strange to them, their impression of their actions must have been altogether different from what they actually were. They must have seen themselves as a rushing torrent, breaking through all the dams the enemy erected—the Gotthard, the Crispalt, Amsteg, Altdorf, and in the Kloen Valley. Each break-through was a victory over the opposing army. They must have recalled with pride that they had crossed difficult mountains on paths which had never before felt the tread of an army, and probably will never feel it again. And when actually, like hunted animals, they had taken refuge in the Muota Valley, and the enemy's general moved down expecting an easy victory, they remembered only that they had thrown themselves upon him like a bear from his den and driven him back in terror and confusion.

"If Suvorov looked upon this episode as a series of victories, we must not look upon this as ordinary boasting, intended to conceal a reverse. While Suvorov's campaign was a military failure, morally it was a success." [13]

The Russian soldier of that time bore up under hardships as perhaps no other soldier has ever done. In February 1807, General von Bennigsen avoided battle with Napoleon on the upper Alle and accepted battle at Preussisch Eylau. To get into an effective position at the later place, the Russian Army marched four nights in succession over bad roads and in snow. A German officer in the Russian Army said of this—"No army could suffer more than ours suffered during those days. Only the Russian strength and endurance got us through." [14]

The pursuit of the fragments of the French Army in 1812 was just as remarkable.

"Never was there so energetic a pursuit on so large a scale as in this campaign. While

[13] Clausewitz, *Campaign of 1799.*
[14] Lettow-Vorbeck, *The War of 1806-7.*

the Russian generals, it is true, were frequently cautious in attacking the fugitives, the pursuit itself was extraordinary. It was November and December in Russian ice and snow. The troops had just ended a most exhausting campaign. The pursuit lasted 50 days and covered 600 miles over a broken-down highway and side trails, and was pushed vigorously despite almost insurmountable supply difficulties.

"To recapitulate the action in a few words: The Russian main army moved out from Tarutino 110,000 strong, and reached Wilna with only 40,000 men. All the rest were killed, wounded, sick or worn out. Prince Kutuzov, the Russian commander, deserves great credit for obtaining such an amazing effort from his men. To prove this, one needs only to picture the wintry weather, the men's lowered physical and moral energies, and at the same time see this army moving from bivouac to bivouac, suffering from privation and sickness, its route marked by dead, dying, and worn out men. It should be evident to all that this pursuit was accomplished with only the utmost difficulty, and that only a great leader's greatest energies could have overcome the natural torpor of the mass." [15]

Modern Armies Are Not Militia Armies

Doubtless we cannot expect as much of men in these days [1911], as was accomplished by those Russians in 1799, 1807, and 1812. The old armies did not concentrate by rail, and were thoroughly trained in marching by the time they came in contact with the enemy. There was also a much greater proportion of professional soldiers in their ranks than in those of our conscript armies. But at the same time, we must not accept pessimistic suggestions about the militia character of our mobilized armies. The uprising of 1813, which was unquestionably the work of the Prussian population itself, would have been impossible without the help

[15] Clausewitz, *Campaign of 1812*.

of the officers of the old Prussian Army. Let us remember, too, the Belgian campaign of 1815. When Napoleon landed in France, there were only three Prussian corps on the lower Rhine, 30,000 men in all. From these units, a new force of 120,000 men in four corps was built almost overnight. This force, which met the French invasion on the Sambre in the middle of June, was certainly more of a "militia" army than our present day field organizations. Yet after losing Ligny it won Waterloo. Seldom has there been a more noteworthy achievement in war. It is true, its commanders were men like Blucher, Gneisenau, and Grolman; but to judge properly what our modern armies will be able to do, we should assume they will be led by men like these, and not by flat mediocrity.

Farm Versus Factory as Source of Soldiers

As a result of the extensive development of industry, a much larger proportion of men will in the future come from industrial communities. Naturally, this raises the question whether an industrial population, working in unsanitary factories and at nerve-racking tasks, can remain as fit for war as an agricultural people. While there is some justice in the views of those who feel it can't, it must be remembered that modern war makes demands upon the intellectual development of man which an agricultural people cannot satisfy to the same extent as city-dwellers. Then, too, an industrial population in general may be better fed. Though our higher standard of living has developed additional necessities of life, our improved transportation systems make it possible to satisfy demands for them. In any case, we must accept the situation as it is, including the transformation of our society and the increasing democratization of the world, even though because of it, it becomes more and more difficult to maintain discipline. Actually, there is no reason for pessimism as to the changes in the times, for things are no better with our possible future enemies. Pessimism causes weakness, and is to be avoided by soldiers even more than by other men.

Realistic Reserve Training Necessary

To keep an army fit for war, it is essential that men of the furloughed classes [16] be given an opportunity occasionally to practice military duties. The most important things for them to learn during their short period of service with the colors are the exertions and privations required of soldiers. While our peacetime training is actually giving our men that physical and moral strength which will prevent them from giving way under the strain of war, we must guard against overdoing realistic training. Too much such training is the opposite of a proper training for war. It overburdens our officers and noncommissioned officers and wears them out too fast. Excessive tension also disturbs moral equilibrium. We must, therefore, be careful not to intensify the nervousness characteristic of our age by the manner in which we regulate our service—especially our inspections. We must not upset or nullify instruction in determining progress being made. We must remember that even in war, timely rest and relaxation are of the greatest benefit to troops and leaders. Since peacetime training is preparation for war, we must take care not to blunt the tool which we are shaping in the process of finishing it.

Prince Hohenlohe in his military letters very rightly treats the expression "skilled in war" as meaning not merely accustomed to hardships, but of knowing how to get the necessities and comforts which are needed. This is particularly important where considerable intellectual as well as physical effort is necessary, as is the case in the higher headquarters. For some staff officers the heavy burdens of war cannot be avoided by a division of work—as, for example, in the case of chiefs of staff and their immediate associates.

Value of Personal Example

The commander in chief, of course, when it is possible, must visit the troops frequently and share their hardships, since his example will be of the utmost value. It is common

[16] German Army category, similar in some respects to U. S. Army Reserve.

knowledge that Napoleon did this in Egypt and Syria, and that Lee, in the long years of the American Civil War, used no shelter but his tent, thus following the example of King Frederick, who spent many nights lying among his troops beside the camp fire. The general, of course, must also keep himself fresh for emergencies.

Napoleon's later life in the field is a good example of this balance a commander must strike between the needs of his troops and his personal needs. He generally went to sleep very early, and then was ready very early in the morning when the reports of distant troop units had come in to give his final orders. He made great demands, too, upon his immediate entourage. He described the life in the field of his principal assistant, Berthier, as being "all day in the saddle, all night at his desk." It was said also of Gneisenau that he might be seen at any hour, day or night; that even when roused from the deepest sleep his mind was always clear and receptive.

To be equal to such long-continued exertions, an officer must strengthen his body through a temperate life, and accustom himself to continuous mental labor. This personal conditioning must not be neglected in peacetime, for one who is constantly overloaded with work is not preparing himself for the duties which will fall to him in war. His exhausted nerves will not have the elasticity required in emergencies.

Importance of Physical Training, Especially Sports

We should congratulate ourselves that we are today giving more attention to the physical training of children than formerly, and are no longer confining our efforts to academic instruction. Unquestionably, the present day popularity of sports benefits a large number of people and improves their fitness for war. The German of today [1911] is more of an out-of-doors man than in former generations. General world conditions also lead him to think beyond narrow domestic affairs. Today, he is beginning to realize he can learn much not only from the arts and sciences, but from everyday affairs of private life. From a military point of view, this broadening of our national thought is most welcome, since it tends to counteract the Philistine tendency of the German mind. In this, however, there is always a danger of promoting superficiality. The officer must therefore hold close to the dictum of Emerson, who said the only wisdom of life is in concentration, the only evil in looseness of thought. [17] Concentration need not lead to one-sidedness, and the better and broader an officer's education, the less will he be in danger of this. Men like Scharnhorst, Gneisenau, Moltke, and their collaborators, are brilliant examples of efficient soldiers who were at the same time extremely well-educated men.

The increased personal security, which men enjoy in our present civilized society, and the increased value attached by public opinion to life, leave few opportunities in daily peacetime activities to put our courage to the test. In general, our times [1911] do not favor the development of strong personalities. Industry offers great numbers of men the opportunity to use their abilities as organizers and leaders in peacetime, and thus develop qualities that formerly could be developed only in war. Nevertheless, the crowding of masses into our great cities overshadows personality, and leaves us mostly "sealed pattern" men.

War's Chief Demand Is Endurance Under Hardship

Sports gives us the best opportunity to develop in civilized communities in time of peace those qualities required in war which are so highly developed in savage and half-civilized peoples. One need only consider the influence that hunts and horseracing had upon the efficiency of cavalry to appreciate the value of suitable sports, but it must not be forgotten that sports are not the most important part of a soldier's training. Sports must be kept within proper bounds, or they will lead to a waste of energy.

Sports alone can only serve as one phase of war training. While they help develop physical strength and courage,

[17] Emerson, *Conduct of Life.*

they need the applause of spectators as a motivating force. They also create only short periods of excitement on the part of the participants. War, on the other hand, demands long, continuous endurance under hardships, without expectation of applause. Even the most successful wars exact considerable physical suffering, while catastrophies, such as the destruction of Napoleon's army in Russia in 1812, and Bourbaki's army in January 1871[18] demand stolid endurance beyond anything man is usually thought capable of. While the nervous strain of war lasts, and the body continues active, men who are naturally energetic can keep going for a considerable time. But during long, relatively inactive periods of privation and suffering, this becomes much more difficult.

During the investment of Metz[19] in 1870, the German troops suffered greatly from inclement weather, especially since only a part of them could be sheltered in buildings, and the rest had to be content with bivouacs and huts. The monotony of the siege work, which contrasted sharply with the hard marches and great battles that preceded the siege, depressed the men's spirits. At the beginning of September, the Germans had 10 percent sick. By the middle of the month 12 percent more were added—although this number remained at this relatively high figure for only a short time.

The Russians had a similar experience during the blockade of Plevna. Here again the cold wet autumn caused much sickness, and, as at Metz, the reaction from the preceding battles was felt seriously. The effect was even worse in this case, for the Germans had been successful, while the Russians had to bear the feeling of failure also. More than this, the Russian line of communications worked so badly that the troops were inadequately fed. It was rarely possible to issue fresh bread; and long, continued use of hard bread reduced the men's resistance to disease.

[18] Later stages of Franco-Prussian War, 1870-71. Bourbaki led one of the improvised French armies that attempted to lift the siege of Paris.
[19] Franco-Prussian War, 1870-71.

The Turks shut up in Plevna meanwhile endured almost incredible privations. Osman Pasha, for example, made 14 days' supplies last 6 weeks. In previous wars, there were cases also where western European troops endured as much under energetic leadership. In 1800, Massena during the last six weeks of the siege of Genoa[20] reduced the daily bread ration from $\frac{3}{4}$ pound to $\frac{1}{2}$ pound, and fed little else. At the very end, substitutes were used in place of even this half pound of bread which under other conditions would have been considered quite inedible.

For besieged troops, hunger is the greatest privation; but for troops in the open field, except during desert operations, winter weather causes the greatest hardships. This appears most conspicuously where it is necessary to hold positions for a long time in close contact with the enemy, as was the case with the Russians at Shipka Pass [21] in the winter of 1877-78.

"Conditions were almost unbearable with the advent of extreme cold and strong winds. As early as the end of November sentinels were blown from their posts over the precipice, and a battalion designated to relieve the outposts was unable to climb the pass. Clothing froze stiff. By the middle of December, out of twenty battalions at Shipka Pass, 81 officers and 5,214 men were sick. By 19 December, the 24th Infantry Division had lost 77 men by freezing; on the 22d. it had 788 men sick, 266 of them from frostbite. Seven men died at their posts. On 23 December, 903 men were reported sick, so that the division in frontline had to be relieved by the 14th Battalion. This battalion would have suffered the same fate if the general offensive across the Balkans had not released the Shipka troops from their untenable position." [22]

[20] During Napoleon's absence in Egypt 1799, the Austrians recaptured most of northern Italy. Marshal Massena with a small French force was shut up in Genoa, and after a long siege was forced to surrender.
[21] Russo-Turkish War, 1877-78.
[22] Kuropatkin, *The Crossing of the Balkans and the Engagement at Scheinovo.*

Such catastrophies did not occur in the Russo-Japanese War. On both sides the troops were adequately supplied with warm winter clothing, and they endured without excessive damage the long stays in the dugouts forced upon them by trench warfare. It must be admitted, of course, that the slow progress of Russo-Japanese operations, the long pauses between battles, and the relatively limited area covered by the active operations facilitated clothing supply.

A Nation's Entire Population Must Be Ready to Accept War's Hardships

If war in addition to battlefield and hospital losses necessitates extreme and prolonged exertions and hardships, we should take warning, prepare our minds for the fact, and shape the peace training of our troops accordingly. Universal service fulfills its highest ethical purpose only if all our people understand the inevitable hardships of war and are fully prepared to meet them steadfastly. At the same time the people should be advised that these temporary hardships of war are really of minor consequence compared with the steady wear and tear of the destructive forces in our complicated modern life—forces which continually exact sacrifices in industry and commerce, and which set tasks for whole classes of the people no less difficult than those of war. Every year many explorers and bold sportsmen meet an end which we deplore, but which they willingly risk for adventure and the satisfaction found in any great endeavor.

An age which shows a love of danger and enthusiasm for physical exertion is certainly not an era for the development of pacifism. Among German people, at least, there exists capabilities for the most strenuous warlike endeavors, which will flower at any call to arms. Once in arms, Germans will appreciate the application of these words of Clausewitz: "An army which is strengthened by the habit of temperance and physical exertion as are the muscles of an athlete; an army which regards hardships as a means to victory, not as a curse resting upon its colors; and an army in which all virtues and duties are incarnated in a single goal, the honor of its arms; that is the army that really possesses a true military spirit." [23]

[23] *On War*, bk. III, ch. 5.

CHAPTER 3

War is the Domain of Friction

> ". . . In war, everything is slowed by the influence of innumerable insignificant circumstances which cannot be evaluated on paper, and which lead one to fall far short of his aim."
>
> —Clausewitz, *On War*, book I, chapter 7

ONE WHO HAS HAD no personal experience in war cannot understand the difficulties emphasized about war, and just why the commander needs the genius and the extraordinary intellectual powers he is said to require. To the uninitiated, everything military seems so simple, the required knowledge so slight, all combinations so insignificant that the simplest problem in higher mathematics by comparison seems highly scientific. But when one has seen war, this need for genius and great intellectual power is readily understood. Yet it still remains hard to put into words what it is about war that causes us to accept its need for genius or to identify the separate factors that promote this requirement.

> "In war, while everything is simple, even the simplest thing is difficult. Difficulties accumulate and produce frictions [1] which no one can comprehend who has not seen war. . . . Friction, moreover, is the only term which fully expresses the difference between actual war and a war game [CPX]. The military machine, the army and all that belongs to it, is really very simple, and hence seems easy to handle. But it must be remembered that no part of it is a single piece, each element is made up of individuals, each of whom is subject to friction on all sides. . . . This destructive friction, which cannot, as in mechanics, be assumed to be concentrated at a point, is always distributed by chance, and brings results which cannot

[1] Defined in the U. S. Army as confusion or "snafu."

be predicted because they are in large part produced by chance." [2]

Appreciation of Inevitabilities of Friction a Part of War Experience

In these words Clausewitz explains the reason why our profession is so little understood by those outside it. In time we learn that war training requirements just cannot be comprehended by those outside the military, or even by those who have only casual contact with it. For this reason, works on military history, written by civilians, may be misleading and dangerous unless written with exceptional care and judgment. Here we must of course admit that, although as Clausewitz says, "an appreciation of friction's inevitability and everpresence is one of the principal parts of that experience in war considered indispensable for a good general," very few of us today actually possess it. We have, of course, learned "to plan our peacetime exercises in such a manner that a part of the friction of war is involved in them." That individual commanders are compelled to exercise judgment, prudence, and decision is of much greater importance than can be appreciated by those who have not learned about war's friction by experience; and in our larger troop maneuvers, elements of friction are deliberately introduced insofar as this is possible in peace.

Tactical exercises and war games are all essential aids in training for higher command, and they offer much to officers who are already well-grounded in war's basic fundamentals. But in these games troops are imaginary, and the friction their actual movement would cause can only be imagined. Limiting ourselves to troopless exercises (CPX's) during long periods of peace will lead us to commit one of two errors. Either we will forget these frictions, or we will overestimate their effect. And, as Clausewitz says, "He is not the best general who estimates the effect of war's frictions too highly and upon whom they make too great

[2] *On War*, bk. I, ch. 7.

an impression. This gives us timid generals, and there are too many of these even among trained officers. A general, on the other hand, must at least be aware of these frictions in order to overcome them." A commander learns about them only through the actual handling of the masses of men and transport which make up real troops.

Handling of Large Troop Units Necessary for Effective War Training

There can be no doubt that combined arms maneuvers in different types of terrain, which was practiced first in Prussia, contributed in no small degree to the success of the Prussian arms in 1866 and of the Prussian-German in 1870. The scope of maneuvers today has been greatly increased to conform to an increase in the size of a possible present-day wartime mobilization; but large as these maneuvers are, they still give only a vague idea of what wartime mobilization will be like.

The value of maneuvers appears very clearly from the admissions of British generals, among them Lord Kitchener, who said the British tactical errors in South Africa [3] stemmed largely from a lack of practice in handling large troop units, and from a failure to anticipate the type and intensity of the frictions that resulted during concentrations and subsequent operations.

These difficulties must have been doubly great in an army like that of Great Britain, which is largely a colonial army, and whose higher headquarters and units had to be improvised during the war. With more experienced troops, these frictions would have been overcome more easily.

In this respect the troops in Napoleon's camps at Boulogne [4] possessed a distinct advantage over those of the powers allied against him. This advantage, and the war experience of the commanders and many of the men, were of greater importance than the exercises in the camps along

[3] Boer War, 1899-1902.
[4] In 1805 Napoleon massed large forces at Boulogne on the Straits of Dover for an invasion of England. The destruction of his fleet at Cape Trafalgar, 27 October 1805, ended this effort.

the Channel, which were more or less carelessly done. Nevertheless, even in the victorious campaigns of 1805-6,[5] Napoleon's army had to contend with its share of friction, and it was only because the fortunes of war consistently favored the French that these frictions did not prejudicially affect the general course of the operations. This situation changed as Napoleon's opponents improved by experience, and as the French armies declined in efficiency through continual losses, and through the necessity for keeping a large part of their best troops in Spain. Fezensac obliquely summed up this gradual falling off in efficiency this way: "This habit of attempting anything, with the weakest of forces, this insistence that nothing was impossible, this unlimited confidence in success, which at first gave us one of our greatest advantages, was fatal to us in the end." [6]

Friction Greatest in Improvised Armies

Friction is always greatest in improvised armies. This is shown clearly in the American Civil War. In July 1861, for example, the Northern General McDowell was unable in the first offensive from Washington into Virginia to make his five divisions work together. The Confederate army, 23,000 men, had its main body at Manassas, with one brigade at Fairfax Court House. McDowell planned to attack this exposed brigade with superior force from all sides, and then, under cover of a feint toward Centreville, cross Bull Run lower down and roll up the Confederate position from the flank. His raw troops, however, were not up to this maneuver. On the very first day's march, the intense heat caused great disorder. The men threw away their packs, including the three days' rations they had been issued, and in the evening the trains had to be brought up from Alexandria to resupply them. It was not until the evening of the 17th that the five divisions reached the region of Fairfax Court House, and by that time the Confederate advanced brigade had retired safely. On 21 July,

[5] Against the Russians and Austrians in 1805, and the Prussians in 1806.
[6] Fezensac, *Souvenirs Militaires*.

the defeat at Bull Run brought this first Northern attempt at an offensive to an end.

The next year an attack was attempted in cooperation with the Navy against the Confederate capital, Richmond, by operations on the peninsula between the York and the James Rivers. When this failed, the Confederate Army of Northern Virginia under Lee took the offensive and threw the Union forces back upon Washington. The Northern generals showed a total lack of ability to estimate the situation and to understand what would be possible under a given situation—the faculty which enables an experienced general to reach a correct decision in the field. Tactical insight, coordination of the dispositions of the higher and lower commanders, prompt transmission of orders, maintenance of communications by troop units among themselves and with headquarters—these were all missing in the Union Army for the whole second year of the war, demonstrating that all these things must be studied and practiced in peacetime if they are to be applied properly in war.

The situation did not begin to improve until 1864, when Grant assumed command in the Virginia theater of operations. Corps and division commanders then began to show themselves equal to the ordinary tasks which would have fallen to them in maneuvers. Nevertheless, the Union general in chief shortly before the close of the war addressed a strong protest to the President as to the inadequacy of the training of his subordinates. Until the end, the Union Army remained unfit to conduct a decisive tactical attack efficiently—just as was the case with Gambetta's army. Even this great organizer of the defense of the French provinces lacked an appreciation of friction in war. From this deficiency stemmed his errors in field operations, which nullified all his efforts in organization.

Uniformity of Tactical Training Minimizes Friction

Unquestionably our modern [1911] skeleton armies will experience considerable friction at the outset of war before the troop units have found themselves. This will occur chiefly among reserve units, and may make new leadership measures necessary. However, it is encouraging to note that in our peacetime maneuvers, where we use mixed units assembled for only a few days, we find frictional difficulties of minor importance. Uniformity in the tactical training of our officers and preparation for general staff duty tend to minimize the opportunities for friction insofar as that is possible. It should be remembered, also, that a skeleton army is very far from being an improvised army. It has a good nucleus which gives it strength.

By means of the nucleus saved from the Russian campaign and detachments from the Army of Spain, Napoleon was able, in 1813, to form a new army,[7] which, while not up to the old standard, was nevertheless able, under the leadership of himself and his trusted generals, to win the victories of Lutzen, Bautzen, and Dresden.[8] This nucleus enabled him again, at the end of the armistice in August, to cross the Elbe with over 400,000 men.

A Leader's Strong Will Overcomes Friction

Napoleon's whole military career aptly illustrates Clausewitz's words: "A strong will overcomes friction; it breaks down the obstacles, but sometimes it breaks down the machine also. A strong will and a powerful mind together stand fast, as a landmark for the course of war—or a monument upon which all the streets of a city are oriented." [9]

Toward the end of 1806, Napoleon found himself compelled to place his weakened army, which he had led through an uninterrupted series of victories from the Saale to and across the Elbe, the Oder, and the Vistula, in winter quarters in Poland and West Prussia. Its quality deteriorated further in this inhospitable country. Late in January, when Bennigsen's offensive from East Prussia alarmed the French

---

[7] Following the destruction of the Grande Armee in Russia in 1812, Napoleon was forced to raise new armies to defend himself against practically all the great powers of Europe who were then allied against him.

[8] Cities in eastern Germany.

[9] *On War*, bk. I, ch. 7.

left flank, Napoleon opened his winter campaign of Eylau. Out of the 80,000 men in his troop units at the start, only 60,000 were able to take part in the battle. The loss of 25 percent was due almost entirely to the winter weather. Bennigsen's night retreat left Napoleon the apparent victor at Eylau, but it was a Pyrrhic victory, purchased at the cost of enormous losses. At its end, he could only take his army back into winter quarters. The army, itself, was on the verge of starvation and its horses were unable to travel. Since Napoleon subsequently had to retire, the Battle of Eylau, which cost nearly 30,000 men, must have seemed to everyone a useless waste of lives. It's no wonder the troops fell back behind the Passarge River greatly depressed, and that it required three months' rest to restore their effectiveness. The "powerful, iron will" had worn out the machine in overcoming the friction.

The tragedy of Eylau was small compared with the collapse of the Grande Armee in 1812. Over 600,000 men, including the replacements following in the second line, crossed the Russian border; only about 60,000 returned. This wastage did not begin with the winter retreat. Successive stages in the advance upon Moscow, without any extraordinary battle losses, show enormous reductions in strength. Of the 300,000 men who marched under the immediate command of the Emperor, only 180,000 reached Smolensk. Napoleon fought at Borodino with only 124,000, and reached Moscow with no more than 100,000. In this loss of 200,000 men, battle losses at Smolensk and Borodino account for only 40,000. The losses in minor engagements were slight. All the rest must be accounted for by the general friction of war in an enormous and inhospitable country. The wearing out of the machine is demonstrated by these figures. At the same time, we see in Napoleon, pushing forward to the enemy's capital in spite of all difficulties, the "irresistible will of a powerful mind."

This same irresistible will led him to decline the Austrian intervention for peace in 1813. This action is commonly looked upon as sheer folly; but this view fails to consider that a military ruler like Napoleon could not act otherwise. For him to yield would be to admit defeat. True, his policy was illogical, and his clinging to an imaginary world empire disregarding all historical background and all national sentiment, was a dream. But considering the military situation alone, it is a "hindsight" judgment based upon subsequent events to charge Napoleon with blindness in 1813. So long as the strong will of this powerful mind could bring 400,000 men into the field, against a coalition of varied interests, he had no reason to think he would not succeed. It was this same willpower that enabled him, in 1814, after his defeat at Leipzig, to carry on his supremely powerful offensive-defensive in France with shattered and disorganized troops until he was forced to yield to the overpowering superiority of the allies.

Effects of Human Failures

But the strongest-willed commander, the best organization, and the best discipline cannot always bring about complete unity of thought and action in the multitude of men making up an army. War is "bound by a chain of human infirmity." [10] Oversights, misunderstandings, and misinterpretation of orders, have often had far-reaching effects.

On 16 June 1815, Napoleon discovered during the Battle of Ligny [11] that he was opposed, not by one strong Prussian corps, but by the main body of Blucher's army. He therefore sent orders to Erlon's I Corps, marching upon Quatre Bras, to turn against the Prussian right flank. This corps had been assigned to Marshal Ney, who was then in action at Quatre Bras against a part of Wellington's army. The Corps took the new direction, but Vandamme, who was commanding the left wing at Ligny, took it for hostile troops, and his report led Napoleon to take measures for security which caused some loss of time. Meanwhile Ney, who

[10] *On War*, bk. III, ch. 16.
[11] Napoleon, in June 1815, invaded Belgium in an effort to defeat the Prussian and British armies in detail before they could join. He attacked the Prussians under Blucher at Ligny with his main body, while Ney held the British under Wellington at Quatre Bras.

had no knowledge of Napoleon's new orders for Erlon, ordered the Corps back to Quatre Bras, where it arrived too late to take part in the action. It marched and counter-marched between the two battlefields; and since at Ligny it was mistaken for hostile troops, the Emperor's decisive attack there was delayed a full hour.

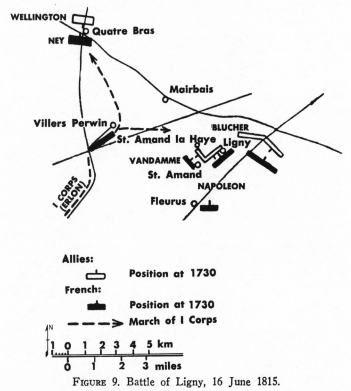

FIGURE 9. Battle of Ligny, 16 June 1815.

In the invasion of Bohemia in 1866,[12] Moltke had planned to effect a junction in the region of Gitschin of the two Prussian armies advancing separately from Lusatia and from Silesia. As these armies moved in compliance with this plan,

[12] Seven Weeks War, 1866.

the Second Army found itself opposed on the upper Elbe by the main forces of the enemy. The advance of the weakly opposed First Army, in the meantime, was progressing much more slowly than planned. Defeat in detail threatened, and it became necessary on 30 June to send renewed telegraphic orders to the First Army to push on without delay in the direction of Koeniggraetz to relieve the pressure upon the Second.

At the beginning of the War of 1870,[13] Moltke's original plan for the deployment of all the German forces on the Saar was not carried out—partly because of the course of events on the front of the Third Army in Alsace, and partly because of the action taken by General von Steinmetz and his subordinate commanders on the German right flank.

On 15 August 1870, it appeared that the French had abandoned the battlefield east of Metz, and under cover of the fortress, had moved off to the west. General Headquarters ordered the Second Army, whose leading corps had already begun to cross the Moselle above Metz, to make a vigorous attack upon the roads leading from Metz to Fresnes and Etain to reap the fruits of the victory of 14 August east of Metz. The army commander was directed to use all available forces as he saw fit. Prince Frederick Charles believed that it was too late to overtake the French main body on the plateau between the Moselle and the Meuse. He therefore directed his main body upon the Meuse above Verdun to cut off the enemy there, and sent only the III and X Corps on 16 August against the roads leading from Metz to Verdun. This right flank of the Second Army thus became engaged in the fierce battle of Thionville, in which it barely succeeded in holding its own against the whole French Army of the Rhine.

Modern means of transport and communication assist the high command today [1911], and it is unlikely a situation will arise again like what occurred in the French army in the Eylau campaign. Here Napoleon was deprived of the

[13] Franco-Prussian War, 1870-71.

use of his left flank corps because an order sent to it on 31 January was captured by Cossacks, and it proved impossible to regain contact with this corps before the Battle of Eylau.

Complete Reliance on Telegraph Undesirable

It is self-evident that control of the allied armies closing in on the main French force in Saxony in the autumn of 1813, would have been infinitely easier with the aid of the telegraph. But it should not be overlooked that in future wars, units must move as rapidly as possible. Hence orders must be transmitted accurately with great speed. Improvements in transmitting methods must also be continuous. Without improvements in this field, it would soon be impossible to handle armies as a unit. In spite of the best work of the telegraph, however, friction will occur, as is shown by the Moltke incidents just described. The individuality of the leaders and differences in their views, which appear conspicuously in war, will always cause friction; and its effect can be overcome in part only by the inculcation of a uniform doctrine for the conduct of war.

Commanders, however, should not permit access to telegraph and telephone to stifle the initiative of subordinates [the radio did not exist in 1911]. These instruments will occasionally fail, as is the case with other modern means of communication, and subordinates will always be called upon to exercise initiative and responsibility. We would be wise, therefore, to recognize this and count upon it, than to depend too much upon technical means of communicating orders.

The Effect of Friction on Tactics

Friction is found not only in the field of strategy but also in tactics. This has always been true, and the condition doubtless will exist to an even greater extent in the future. Modern long-range firearms and smokeless powder make it more difficult to estimate the enemy's situation, and future battles are likely to be fought under very different conditions from those anticipated when orders for them were issued. Troops must learn to adapt themselves to altered situations. The effect of local combat frictions will of course be more localized than in extended campaign operations; but the imminence of danger and the excitement involved make the impressions more acute. Furthermore, combat, once opened, cannot be controlled. It follows its own laws, and for this reason combat frictions can lead to completely unexpected and disastrous results.

How King Frederick's orders for the Battle of Kolin went wrong has been explained previously. At Kunersdorf, unexpected difficulties of the ground interfered with the execution of his plans, while the burning hot weather wore down the strength of the Prussian infantry, already tired from hard marching on insufficient rations.

At Torgau, the attacks of the King and Ziethen on the two fronts of the Austrian position were not properly timed, and the first stages of the battle were a total failure. At Gravelotte and St. Privat, the attacks of the First and Second German Armies could not be coordinated. In the Second Army, there was no unity in the attacks of the Guard in front and the Saxons on the flank. The attack of the Guard Corps was also not properly coordinated in itself. The 4th and the 1st Guard Brigades came into action successively, and each in turn had to meet the full force of the hostile fire.

Size of Fighting Forces Also Increases Friction

The friction of war naturally increases with the size of the fighting forces, and its influence in large units is correspondingly more extensive. It is important, therefore, to emphasize the nature and conditions of mass warfare in the training of the officer corps. Modern warfare on a large scale must not be permitted to surprise us as being something entirely new. The Russian commanders, including the commander in chief, did not fully understand it, and hence were beaten in the Russo-Japanese War. Great armies cannot be assembled in peacetime for training, and the art of leading them must be learned academically. This does not mean from books alone, but also through practical exercises on a large scale without troops.

Supply Difficulties Increase Friction

The best way to overcome friction is to inculcate in every man a grim determination to win at any cost. While this works wonders for the fighting men, behind the lines something more is needed. The will for victory here is powerless. Difficulties of supply are often so great that the war machine simply cannot operate smoothly regardless of personal factors. A theater of war's poverty has often condemned the best plans and the best cooperation to failure.

Supply difficulties may be overcome in part by a commander's forethought. On the other hand, the best human calculations may also fail through sheer accident. Among these accidental conditions, Clausewitz calls especial attention to the weather. Inclement and changeable weather, snow, ice, and fog can upset all calculations. While buildings, vegetation, natural obstacles, and the form of the ground are factors which can be taken into account in a general way, many vital details about them will always be lacking.

The causes of friction are limitless. Theoretically, full allowance can never be made for them. Even if it could, nothing can replace that quality of intuition which is more needed in the presence of a great number of small and varied questions than in great and decisive moments where one may pause to take counsel with himself and with others. Man speaks, acts, and moves largely by an intuition which has become habit. The experienced officer learns to act correctly in emergencies, large and small—one might almost say at war's every heartbeat. Through experience and training, he attains a state where decisions come to him almost automatically; he knows in an instant that one thing will work, another will not.

CHAPTER 4

War is the Domain of Uncertainty

> "War is the domain of uncertainty. Three-fourths of the things upon which action in war is based are more or less hidden in a mist of uncertainty. A keen and penetrating intelligence is necessary to ascertain the truth."
>
> —Clausewitz, *On War*, book I, chapter 3

WE ARE TOLD that Napoleon, when his generals once asked how he always divined the intentions of the enemy so accurately, replied: "I did not know beforehand the mistakes the enemy would make which I took advantage of; I simply studied my map." His successes were not due to the gifts of a magician, but to those of a general who was continuously working out possibilities on a map, and who in this way knew more about the enemy's capabilities and limitations than the enemy did himself.

Napoleon himself, however, systematically tried to lead his contemporaries and posterity to believe that he possessed the gift of prophecy. His secretary Bourrienne writes that the First Consul showed him on the map, in March 1800, the exact point where on 14 June of that year he defeated the Austrians in the Battle of Marengo. Segur tells us that on 15 August 1805, in the camp at Boulogne, Napoleon outlined to his intendant-general Daru the course of the whole approaching campaign against Austria, even to the day of entry into Munich and Vienna. The Emperor himself wrote to Prince Talleyrand on 12 October 1806 of his advance down the Saale River: "The operations here are progressing precisely as I calculated two months before in Paris, march for march, almost incident for incident; I seem to have made no mistakes."

Napoleon Contended With Many Uncertainties

As a matter of fact, Napoleon was surprised by the

Austrians at Marengo. Even the earlier stages of the campaign of 1805, particularly the episode at Ulm,[1] did not conform to his expectation. In 1806[2] he was uncertain as to the movements of the enemy, not only at the time he wrote the above note to Talleyrand, but two days later after the double battle of Jena and Auerstaedt. Napoleon actually achieved his greatest success "in the mist of more or less uncertainty."

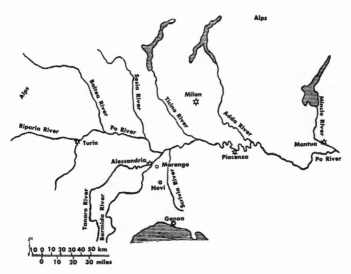

FIGURE 10. Area of Napoleon's Operations in Northern Italy which Led to His Victory at Marengo, 14 June 1800.

In 1800, Napoleon, after crossing the Alps with the Army of the Reserve, turned first toward Milan and cut the main Austrian force at Alessandria off from its communications

[1] Attacking unexpectedly, Napoleon trapped and captured 30,000 Austrians at Ulm in eastern Wuerttemberg (southern Germany). He then moved on to defeat a combined Russian-Austrian force at Austerlitz.

[2] Campaign against Prussia which culminated in Prussia's destruction.

with the Mincio. He calculated that the Austrians would either force their way through, or else pass around the French army by the north, on the left bank of the Po. When he moved from Milan southwestward, and on 12 June failed to find the enemy between the Scrivia, Bormida, and Tanaro, he believed the Austrians were moving upon Genoa [3] by way of Novi, and dispatched 5000 men under Desaix in that direction. He had on hand only 23,000 men, when the Austrians moved out from Alessandria on 14 June with 29,000 men, crossed the Bormida, and would have inflicted a decisive defeat upon him had it not been for the timely arrival of Desaix's division, hastily recalled at the beginning of the action. Desaix's return enabled him to win the victory of Marengo.

In the advance of the French army from the Neckar and the Main toward the Danube, Napoleon knew that the enemy held a position behind the Iller, with his right resting on Ulm. The Emperor expected a counterstroke on the north bank of the Danube for he felt the enemy would not give up his communications without fighting. But the Austrians undertook nothing, and on 7-9 October the French crossed the Danube between Donauwoerth and Ingolstadt without serious difficulty. It then became necessary to deploy the army on the Lech on two fronts, facing the Iller and the Isar, for up to 13 October the Emperor was uncertain as to the position of the Austrian army, as well as that of the allied Russian force which was expected daily from the direction of the Inn. Napoleon looked at first for an attempt by the Austrians to break through at Augsburg or Landsberg. When this did not happen, he thought they might withdraw to Vorarlberg or the Tyrol. When he became confident that the Russians would not soon arrive, he moved his main force against the Austrians, whom he expected to find in position behind the Iller between Memmingen and Ulm, facing east. It was not until 12 October that the actual situation became clear through an engagement on the left bank of the Danube in front of Ulm. This

[3] Where they could be supported by British troops and the British fleet.

action indicated that the Austrian army was probably assembled at Ulm, and all the forces available on the left bank of the Lech were then turned in that direction.

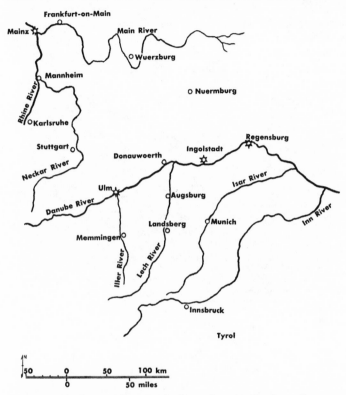

FIGURE 11. Area of Napoleon's Operations in Southern Germany, 7-9 October 1800.

When Napoleon, in 1806, moved his army from the Main, following the general course of the Saale, he knew only that there were strong hostile forces at Naumburg, Erfurt, Weimar, and Gotha, and that there was a detachment of all arms at Hof. At first it seemed probable that the enemy was moving to his left, from the Saale to the

Elster, especially as this would be a natural move for him to make in view of the French threat to his communications. The Emperor therefore decided to concentrate toward Gera. When he received information indicating the enemy's main force was still at Erfurt, Napoleon turned his army on 12 October toward the plateau between the Ilm and the Saale. The unexpected discovery of strong hostile forces at Jena then induced him to send additional troops

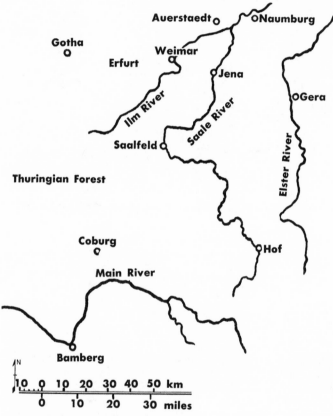

FIGURE 12. Area of Napoleon's Movements in Eastern Germany (Jena campaign), 1806.

to support Lannes in that region, and he became more and more convinced that the combined Prussian and Saxon armies faced him on the heights of the left bank of the Saale, at Jena. On 14 October he believed that he had defeated this whole force. As a matter of fact, however, he had been opposed only by Prince Hohenlohe's 38,000 men and Ruchel's Corps of 15,000. It was not until some time in the morning of the 15th that he learned of the simultaneous victory at Auerstaedt by Davout's left flank III Corps over the main Prussian army of 50,000 men.

Moltke had to cope with similar uncertain situations in

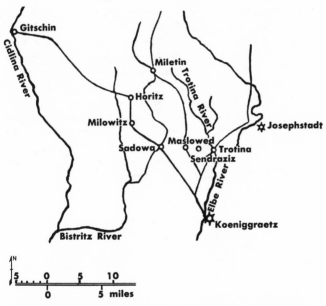

FIGURE 13. Area of the Battle of Koeniggraetz, 2 July 1866.

reaching several of his great decisions. On the day before Koeniggraetz it was believed at G.H.Q. in Gitschin that the Austrians were in position behind the Elbe with their flanks at Josephstadt and Koeniggraetz; when, as a matter of fact, they were in front of the Elbe between Bistritz and Trotina. It was not until 2 July that First Army reports showed clearly that there were strong Austrian forces on the right bank of the Elbe. Even then it was uncertain whether the whole Austrian army was there, or only a part.

The German uncertainty as to the location of the French Army of the Rhine on 15 August 1870, and until the fighting on the 16th disclosed the situation, has already been mentioned. On the 18th, contact with the French was again lost by the German center and left; and on the 18th it was believed in the Second Army that the enemy had already withdrawn to the northwest across the Orne, and that only the rear elements remained on the heights between the Mance and Chatel Valleys. It was only the costly battle in which the IX Corps became engaged, which showed the high command that Bazaine's whole army had taken position on these heights.

In the battle about Liao-Yang, the Japanese attacks of 30-31 August upon the strongly fortified Russian positions south of the Taitzu River had been without success. The situation began to change when General Kuroki, commanding on the right flank of the Japanese First Army, received information which led him to suspect that the Russians were beginning a retreat to Mukden. He therefore pushed a division and a half across to the north bank of the Taitzu. The Russians failed to push the weak Japanese advance guards back across the river, although strong reserves were echeloned back behind the left flank of the bridgehead position. On 1 September, the Japanese succeeded in getting a firm foothold on the north bank. Counterattacks undertaken on the 2d were without cohesion and failed, although the Russians had twice the strength of the Japanese, who by this time did have two and a half divisions on the north bank. Kuropatkin then ordered the retreat to Mukden. The flank attack initiated by the First Army led to decisive results although it was originally based upon faulty information.

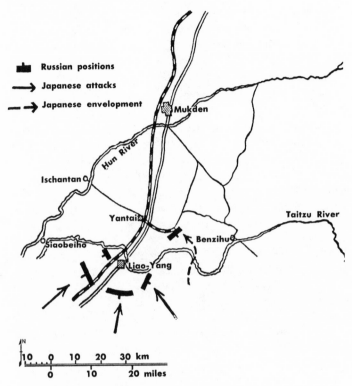

FIGURE 14. Battle of Liao-Yang, 25 August-5 September 1904.

Luck Favors Skillful Commander

Although action in war is always hampered by uncertainty, and some of the weightiest decisions are often made on very uncertain premises, it would be totally false to assume that victory is normally a matter of sheer luck. It is not luck in the ordinary sense that brings victory, but luck in the sense intended by Moltke when he said, "luck, in the long run, favors the skillful commander," In his restrained language and with his usual modesty, the field marshal speaks only of "the skillful commander"; but more than skill in its usual sense is also meant. "A mediocre intelligence may hit upon the truth occasionally, and now and then extraordinary courage may help out dull wits; but in the average case the better intelligence will win." [4] In these words Clausewitz points out that a highly developed mind can plan operations so they will have a greater possibility of success.

At Marengo, even if Napoleon's initial failure had not been transformed into a victory, the Austrians, their communications cut, could not have profited greatly by their victory. Only fragments of their force would have gotten behind the Mincio. Similarly at Ulm, the threat to the hostile communications offset the uncertainty as to his opponent's position which hampered Napoleon for a few days. The success of the double battle of 14 October 1806, fought under such false impression by the French, was possible because the Prussian-Saxon army itself was caught in a most unfavorable strategic situation. Although Koeniggraetz was won through the bold seizure of an unexpected opportunity, the decisiveness of the victory was due to Moltke's basic strategic plans. Premature concentration of the three Prussian armies had been avoided. They all remained mobile and in a position to meet any situation. The few days' uncertainty at Metz had no serious consequences for the Germans, for their tactical actions were based upon a favorable strategic situation. On 16 August the enemy found his communications threatened, and on the 18th he had already lost them.

In all these cases it is true that the high command was aided by the extraordinary performance of the troops. Under Napoleon and under Moltke, "tactics came to the aid of strategy," as Moltke says in the general staff history of the campaign of 1859 in Italy. The arms of the victors were upheld by good fortune, but not by blind luck.

---

[4] *On War,* bk. I, ch. 3.

Weighty Decisions Must Be Made in "Fog of Uncertainty"

No general would go into action carelessly, without adequate preparation or without a general idea of the enemy's position and intentions; but he must bear in mind that it would be an error, because it would be useless, to wait for a situation to clear up entirely. He must remember that the weightiest decisions are generally made in the "fog of uncertainty." If the great generals at Marengo, Ulm, Jena, and Koeniggraetz had waited for the situation to clear up fully, they would have missed the proper moment for action. and military history would be without some of its most brilliant days.

Information in War Often Unreliable

Not only is there often a lack of information, but what information does come in is unreliable. Clausewitz explains the problem this way:

"Our military books tell us that we should act only upon reliable information, and should always be suspicious of reports; but this is ·highly unsatisfactory book doctrine, a maxim behind which the writer of systems and compendiums may take refuge for lack of anything better.

"A large part of the information that a commander gets in war is contradictory; more of it is false; and the largest part is doubtful. All an officer can do is exercise what intuition he has developed through his knowledge of men and affairs and through long training in exercising good judgment. The law of probabilities is his only real guide. Information deficiencies and hazards are present even in the earlier stages of planning, performed at leisure in an office and outside the atmosphere of war; but they become infinitely more difficult to cope with when a stream of messages is being received in the confusion of war . . . Most of this information is false, and faintheartedness augments its falsity. As a rule, everyone is inclined to believe evil rather than good. Everyone is also inclined to exaggerate bad news and false dangers, and, although they disappear like the waves of the sea, they return again like the waves without apparent cause. A leader must therefore stand fast, relying upon his understanding of what is probable and what is not, like the rock upon which the waves break.

"The part is not easy to play. One who is not an optimist by nature, or whose judgment has not been trained by experience in war, must turn resolutely away from the dictates of his timorous instincts and force himself to hope. In this way it is possible to strike a true middle course. . . .

"Ordinary men, who yield to outside persuasion, generally remain continually undecided. They see every situation as different from what they thought it would be. In this frame of mind they yield further to outside persuasion, and become even more uncertain and vacillating. Even a strong, decisive person who has based his decisions on first hand information will often make wrong decisions. But he must not allow these errors to shake his inherent confidence in himself and tempt him to change his well-based decisions to accommodate some fleeting impression."[5]

Initiative of Great Leaders Becomes Uncertainty

Moltke says similarly that from the opening of a campaign everything is uncertain except what the leader himself has of will and energy. An inner understanding, his own intuition, usually provides the only means for penetrating the fog of war and controlling events properly. The instinctive feeling of the proper action to take at the moment has always been present in every great leader. Relying upon this proud prerogative, Frederick drew the sword in 1756 and the next year invaded Bohemia, which was the greatest military operation of his time.

Napoleon's leadership was always marked by his ability

[5] *On War*, bk. I, ch. 6.

to turn the tables on his opponent. This characteristic was especially evident at Ratisbon in 1809 [6] and in the blows which he struck in February 1814 against the Silesian Army. In one case he transformed an unfavorable, in the other an almost desperate situation into its opposite.

Napoleon's Initiative at Ratisbon

When the Emperor on the morning of 17 April 1809 appeared in the theater of operations on the Danube, his understanding of the situation was as follows: 63,000 men of his own army under Marshal Davout were at Ratisbon, and strong Austrian forces were approaching that place from Bohemia; 30,000 Bavarians under Marshal Lefebvre had fallen back from the Isar in the face of a superior enemy to a position behind the Abens; 64,000 men under Marshal Massena were at Augsburg; and 20,000 more were distributed along the Danube between Donauwoerth and Ingolstadt. Napoleon was at first entirely uncertain of the location of the enemy's main forces, but was inclined to believe they were on the north bank of the Danube advancing from Bohemia. In any case it was necessary to concentrate his scattered army, and the Emperor acted at once. He ordered his right, under Massena, to march upon Pfaffenhofen on the Ilm; his left under Davout to fall back on the right bank of the Danube to Neustadt; and the Bavarians together with the available troops between Ingolstadt and Donauwoerth to form a new center behind the lower Abens.

He adhered to these dispositions later in the day even when he learned the main Austrian army, 125,000 men, under the Archduke Charles was approaching from the Inn, south of the Danube, in the direction of Landshut; and that only a small part of the enemy (two army corps, 48,000 men) was approaching from Bohemia. Although the purpose of Napoleon's initial dispositions was to draw his army together defensively, he saw at once when the enemy's

---

[6] Part of the operations against the Austrians in 1809, which ended with the capture of Vienna and Napoleon's great victory at Wagram.

main body appeared south of Ratisbon the possibility of developing the situation for a decisive defeat of the enemy. He directed Marshals Davout and Lefebvre to join, and moved Massena by Pfaffenhofen, Moosburg, and Landshut

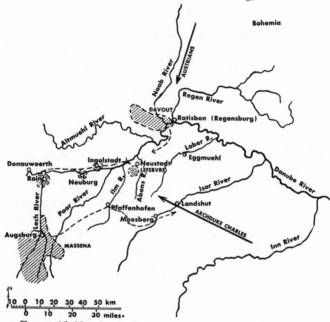

FIGURE 15. Napoleon's Operations at Ratisbon, 17 April 1809.

against the enemy's rear. The Emperor was far from certain of the details of the enemy's position, but he did not hesitate to take the initiative.

He had found the situation badly confused on the morning of the 17th; but by indefatigable study he had reached a definite conclusion by the same evening, when he wrote to the King of Wuerttemberg: "I shall move tomorrow morning and attack the enemy."

Napoleon's Initiative in France, 1814

Napoleon's world power was broken in the Battle of

Leipzig. In France in 1814 he fought only to save his capital and his throne. To accomplish this task he had little more than the strength of a modern army corps against overwhelming superiority. On 1 February, at La Rothiere, he had to give way before the superior enemy, and with 20,000 men fell back to Troyes, where he received 20,000 reinforcements. Marshal Marmont with a few thousand men meanwhile moved down the right bank of the Aube and took position at Arcis to cover the Emperor's left.

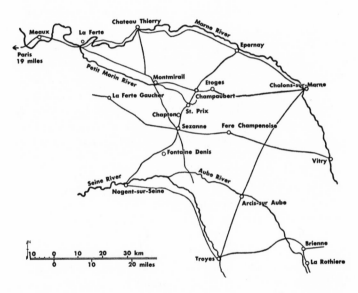

FIGURE 16. Area of Napoleon's Operations in Central France, February 1814.

The allies divided their available force of 150,000 men between the Aube and the Seine. The main army under Schwartzenberg slowly followed the Emperor toward Troyes, while Blucher, with 20,000 Russians of the Silesian Army (the corps of General von Sacken and an infantry division under General Olzuvief), which had fought at La Rothiere, sought to join his remaining corps, those of General von Yorck, von Kleist, and Kapzevich on the Marne. Marshal Macdonald, with 10,000 men, fell back upon Chalons before Yorck's 16,000.

On 4 February Napoleon at Troyes received his first messages from Marmont at Arcis indicating that hostile forces, undoubtedly belonging to the Silesian Army, were moving toward the Marne. Marmont's forces being so small, this move would jeopardize the left flank of the French main army at Troyes and its communications with Paris. The Emperor therefore directed the Marshal to fall back upon Nogent-sur-Seine. On the 6th, Marmont having reached Nogent from Arcis, reported that the Silesian Army, marching on a broad front in several columns, on the line Montmirail—La Ferte Gaucher, was approaching the Marne. The Marshal suggested that there might be an opportunity for a telling blow if the Emperor could at once send 12,000 or 15,000 men by way of Sezanne against the rear of this force, which was moving carelessly and was entirely separated from its main body.

Napoleon acted immediately on Marmont's suggestion. Arriving in Nogent, he directed the Marshal to march with his 6,000 men to Fontaine Denis, and there push forward an advance guard to Sezanne and send cavalry toward Fere Champenoise, Champaubert, and Montmirail. At first, these dispositions were made simply in accordance with Marmont's suggestion; but later, in the course of the 7th, Napoleon developed the idea of broadening the scope of the movement to the north. He wrote to Marmont: "I expect to move tomorrow morning at daybreak with 6,000 cavalry of the Guard and 10,000 men of the Old Guard in accordance with such information as I may receive; but since I do not wish to make any false moves, please send me reliable information from Sezanne."

Napoleon's Intuitive Actions

This note was a hint to Marmont to clear up the situation at once, rather than an indication of any intent on the part of the Emperor to wait until it was accomplished. If the Emperor had waited until he was certain, he would have lost the most favorable moment for action. During the night of the 7-8th, before any further information could come in from Marmont, he decided to act decisively against the Silesian Army with 30,000 men in all, leaving 40,000 on the Seine to cover Paris against the allied main army. On the evening of the 7th Napoleon wrote, "I have had no further reports from the Duke of Ragusa (Marmont), but I am going to attack the enemy decisively and act against his communications."

Note that this decision was made upon fairly sketchy information. The Emperor knew that Macdonald had fallen back down the Marne before superior forces. Parts of the Silesian Army were reported advancing upon Paris between the Marne and the Aube. But further than this everything was uncertain. Moreover, in Napoleon's desperate situation any false step could have destroyed him, and within the next few days the pressure of the hostile main army would undoubtedly have been felt from the direction of Troyes. In spite of all this, he decided upon an advance through Sezanne, even at the risk of striking a blow in the air. He felt instinctively he would succeed if he captured and maintained the initiative. To appreciate completely the full boldness of his decision, one must consider the darkness in which the Emperor was moving. The messages received from Marmont during the night of 7-8 February spoke of the terrible condition of the roads, and of hostile cavalry seen in the region of Sezanne; but they did not clear up the situation. As is always the case with a bold leader, however, he had his reward for not waiting until the fog was completely dissipated.

On the 8th, Marmont was north of Sezanne, and a detachment of Cossacks was driven away by his cavalry. The

Marshal gained the impression that the Silesian Army was moving down the Marne through Epernay, and that an advance by him through Champaubert might do the enemy great damage. On the evening of the 8th, he reported from Chapton, that on the 7th, Russian cavalry had been at Montmirail and infantry at Champaubert. It thus appeared that Sacken's Corps was following the so-called "little Paris Road," south of the Marne. The crossing of the Petit Morin at St. Prix was already in Marmont's hands; and he repeated his suggestion for an attack in that direction.

On 9 February, Napoleon's reinforcing troops, closing up behind Marmont, began to pass Sezanne. Napoleon himself moved to that place in the afternoon. Before he left Nogent he wrote to Paris that he was throwing himself with 30,000 men upon the rear of the Silesian Army, which was then estimated at 45,000 men, but which was actually about 10,000 stronger; and that he expected to gain a decisive victory within a few days.

He thus broadened Marmont's original idea, which was simply to "inflict damage upon the enemy," and planned a decisive blow. He did not as yet know where the individual corps of the Silesian Army were, nor did he know whether he must strike his blow at Champaubert or at Montmirail; but he held firmly to his general purpose, confident that all the details of execution would take care of themselves, and relying upon the strength that follows a definite decision.

This confidence did not desert the Emperor when upon reaching Sezanne on the evening of 9 February he found that Marmont, originally enthusiastic over the idea of an attack upon the Silesian Army, now considered it hopeless. The Marshal was convinced that the hostile column marching by Champaubert and Montmirail had gotten so far to the west that an attack at either place would no longer find the column isolated. It was to be expected that the enemy had concentrated upon news of the appearance of French troops on the flank. Actually, the advance toward Sezanne, however, had only slowed the enemy's movements. According to Marmont's information, Russian infantry under General Olzuvief was following Sacken's Corps by way of Champaubert and should have reached there on the 8th. Marmont for this reason felt that the attack to the northward would come 24 hours too late.

Convinced of the accuracy of his estimate, the Marshal had already, of his own motion, ordered the withdrawal of his troops from the Petit Morin to Sezanne. He believed that the only course for the Emperor was to move west from Sezanne by way of La Ferte Gaucher, effect a junction with Macdonald on the Marne, and place himself at Meaux across the Silesian Army's line of march upon Paris.

The Emperor did not share the Marshal's misgivings, and ordered him to return during the night of the 9-10th to his former positions on the Petit Morin, especially the stream crossing at St. Prix, and to attack the Russians at Champaubert on the 10th without fail.

Here we see the difference between the calculating prudence of a skillful leader—which Marmont unquestionably was— and the intuition and initiative of a great captain. Napoleon did not seek to determine in detail what the enemy would do, how far westward he might have progressed, and whether he was concentrated or not. He struck straight for Champaubert, knowing that he would thus turn the tables on the enemy. He knew that even if the hostile column had already passed Montmirail it would be no blow in the air. The enemy would have to turn back to keep his communications open.

In this case, holding to his own previous decision instead of listening to Marmont brought the Emperor a rich reward. The enemy was not concentrated, as Marmont thought, but was in a most unfavorable situation. The effort of Blucher to pen Macdonald in between Yorck's and Sacken's Corps, to cut him off from the main French army and from Paris, had led Blucher to push these two corps forward too rapidly, without waiting for the arrival of Kleist's and Kapzevich's Corps, which were coming up from the

Rhine. On 9 February, when Napoleon ordered the movement from Sezanne upon Champaubert, the Silesian Army's 55,000 men were scattered for 60 kilometers. Attacked by an enemy such as Napoleon and in such a situation, the result was inevitable. On the 10th, Olzuvief's 4,000 men were badly cut up; on the 11th, Sacken, poorly supported by Yorck from Chateau Thierry, was beaten at Montmirail; on the 12th, both generals were driven across the Marne with heavy loss; on the 14th, Blucher, with Kleist's and Kapzevich's Corps, was defeated at Etoges and compelled to fall back upon Chalons.

Napoleon's action during these February days was a clear illustration of Moltke's words: "Successive acts of war are not premeditated acts; they are spontaneous, dictated by military intuition. In every individual case, the problem is to discover the situation in spite of the fog of uncertainty; to evaluate correctly what is known and to estimate what is unknown; to reach a decision quickly, and then carry it out powerfully and unhesitatingly."[7]

This straightforward carrying out of a decision has nothing in common with false obstinacy, which is an adherence to preconceived ideas with a refusal to take into account the independent will of the enemy. Although a general must always have clearly in mind his ultimate objectives, which he must adhere to regardless of changes in the situation, he must also realize that the roads that must be travelled to achieve them can never be determined precisely beforehand.

Harmful Effect of Preconceived Ideas

Where preconceived ideas control a commander, the army always suffers. Such was the case with the Austrians in April 1757.[8] Its commander shut his eyes to steadily increasing indications of a Prussian invasion, because he was convinced King Frederick, surrounded by enemies, could do nothing but remain on the defensive. In 1805, Mack clung

[7] Von Moltke, *Essay on Strategy.*
[8] Beginning of the Bohemian campaign of the Seven Years War.

to the position which he had taken behind the Iller, and insisted that Napoleon would be obliged to attack him frontally from the west. He completely overlooked the possibility that his right flank might be turned until it was too late to prevent it. In 1813, after Austria had joined the allies, it was generally assumed that because Bohemia flanked Napoleon's concentration on the right bank of the middle Elbe, he would have to evacuate that bank at once. In spite of several defeats, however, he held on there until the beginning of October. In 1866, the main Italian army pushed rashly into the Quadrilateral [9] to take a position in observation in the hill country south of Lake Garda. The Italians thought the Austrian army of the Archduke Albert, which had already penetrated into the same hill country, partly on the flank of the Italian advance, would have to fall back behind the Adise to avoid envelopment by the Italian army of General Cialdini from the lower Po. In July 1877, the Russian command to its sorrow refused to heed the danger Osman Pasha presented in the west. In spite of warnings, his strength was consistently underestimated. The erroneous estimate of the enemy formed by the German Second Army, 15-18 August 1870, has already been mentioned.

One Cannot Fight Successfully By the Book

If persistence in a preconceived idea leads to self-deception and a disregard of the unforeseen, its tragedy is compounded if one tries to fight by theoretical considerations and predetermined forms. He who would be successful in war, must obtain from books only a trained mind. If he brings ready-made plans which have not been shaped by actual conditions, or which he has not produced himself, the current of events will destroy his operation before it is finished. He can never make others understand plans that are not his own, and the better his associates are, the quicker they will recognize his incompetency, and the less they will trust him. "Rigid adherence to dogmas and for-

[9] Area in northern Italy, scene of the Battle of Custozza, 1866.

mulas is the antithesis of proper war planning, which deals
largely with possibilities, probabilities, good and bad fortune. Of all human activities, war most resembles a game
of cards—no human activity is so continually and generally
influenced by chance."[10]

The Russian commander [11] entered the Manchurian theater of operations with preconceived ideas, which prevented
him from utilizing good opportunities. As minister of war
he had previously made an inspection trip through the
Far East, and had returned much encouraged as to the
situation there. Yet he still held to the idea of an unquali-
fied defensive. In his view Port Arthur must be left to its
own resources; South Manchuria was not to be held; the
army must retire to Harbin until it became so strong that
it could pass to the offensive with overwhelming force.
According to mobilization plans, however, this condition
would not be reached until the second half of the year.
As commander in chief, the general could not free himself
from the estimate of the situation which he had made as
minister of war. In his memorandum for the Czar 15 January 1904, he mentions taking the offensive, expelling the
Japanese from the continent, and landing in Japan; yet he
still held to the idea of initial retirement. He still advocated
the construction of strong fortifications at Te Lin, north of
Mukden, and elsewhere and insisted, above all, that care
should be taken not to expose the advanced elements of
the army to decisive defeats, that operations should be
restricted to minor defensive actions to wear down the
enemy. The Russian General Staff official history characterizes this memorandum as a "broad and clear statement,"
although it overlooked entirely the "mixture of possibilities,
probabilities, good and bad fortune" characteristic of war.

The Russians showed this same obstinacy in 1877.[12] After
crossing the Danube in July, they pushed a strong advance
guard across the Balkans under General Gurko. This force

---

[10] *On War*, bk. I, ch. 1.
[11] General Kuropatkin
[12] Russo-Turkish War, 1877-78.

was compelled to fall back before the superior forces of Suleiman Pasha, and found great difficulty in holding Shipka Pass. At the same time, north of the Balkans, Mehemet Ali's main Turkish army held strong forces on the Santra in the east, while in the west Osman Pasha had repulsed the Russian IX Corps with heavy loss at Plevna. The Russians were thus held on all three fronts. This situation was the result of the Russian high command's wish to imitate the bold campaign of Marshal Diebitsch across the Balkans in 1829.[13] Obsessed with this idea, they refused to recognize the danger threatening them from the west. During August, the equilibrium was restored by the alliance with Rumania and the arrival of five more Russian divisions in the theater of operations. The dangerous crisis then passed. Even then, however, the Russian command for some time could not decide to turn its whole force against one of the three separated Turkish army groups, but remained facing three ways on a 200 kilometer front from the Balkans to the Danube.

Rigid Adherence to Original Plans Inadvisable

A mind that adheres rigidly and unalterably to original plans will never succeed in war, for success goes only to the flexible mind which can conform at the proper moment to a changing situation. This is what Napoleon meant when he said he had never had a plan of operations. It also explains Moltke's words, "No plan of operations can extend with certainty beyond the first contact with the main body of the enemy."[14] Man can never fully control chance; he can only succeed in minimizing its effects by making dispositions to meet the various possibilities, and, where he has the strength, by assuming an active not a passive attitude. Moltke restated his idea when he said that we may restrict the independent will of the enemy if we seize the initiative promptly and with determination. Napoleon embodied it also in his letter to Bernadotte 27 September 1805, when

[13] Russian attack against Turkey to aid the Greeks and secure their independence.
[14] Von Moltke, *Tactical and Strategic Essays.*

he said: "When you receive this letter, my army will be on the Neckar, strong, numerous, and ready to face anything." He expressed it again in the letter he wrote to Marshal Soult 5, October 1807: "With our immense superiority of closely concentrated forces you will appreciate that I wish to take no chances, but want to attack the enemy with twice his force wherever he may attempt to hold."

Estimates of Enemy Situation Often Faulty

Not only in the field of strategy, but in that of tactics, we must expect that our estimates of the enemy will often be faulty. If a leader with the experience of Napoleon, concerned only with the limited battlefields of his time, could estimate the Russian army at Friedland at 80,000, when it was in fact only 40,000 or 50,000, it should be evident that in modern times, with the increased range of weapons and size of the battlefields, it has become vastly more difficult to estimate the enemy's situation. This is true not only during the opening stages of battle, but also of later situations, even those which should be perfectly clear to us through extensive combat information. The decisive intervention of the Prussian Second Army in the Battle of Koeniggraetz is a case in point. The Crown Prince's leading divisions (1st Guard, 11th, and 12th) reached the line Maslowed—Sendraziz—Trotina at about 1400. Their flanking pressure compelled the Austrian right flank to give ground. But at headquarters of the Second Army it was not realized that day that their leading elements would still have serious resistance to meet, for there was no way of knowing that the Austrian II and IV Corps on their right flank were changing front to the right and rear to meet the newly arriving Second Army.

General von Verdy writes:

> "As our leading infantry units (1st Guard Division) slowly climbed the heights of Horenowes and established themselves there, almost all of us at headquarters thought the main work of

the day was done and that the decision had already been reached. We attributed the weakness of the resistance which we had encountered thus far to the direction of our march, and to our superior artillery fire, which we thought had compelled the enemy to break off his action with the First Army and to fall back to avoid being cut off. But we were badly mistaken; the hardest fighting and the heaviest losses were still to come. I have often recalled these estimates with interest, because they show how readily an army commander can be led to form erroneous impressions with no one at fault. In formulating his decisions in war, a commander must take into account other elements than appearances, reports, and logical analyses of the situation. Events may appear in a form which he is perfectly justified in considering correct, but which nevertheless gives him a misleading picture."[15]

Difficulties Involved in Forming Correct Estimates of Enemy Situation

St. Privat and Plevna are classic examples of the difficulties an attacker faces in estimating the enemy situation correctly. It should be remembered that in both of these battles lack of familiarity with the effect of the enemy's weapons was a contributing factor. There was also a faulty cavalry reconnaissance, and a lack of the kind of infantry and artillery reconnaissance normal today [1911]. By careful, close reconnaissance with good field glasses and by employing properly our improved means of communication, especially the field telephone, we can today make reasonably accurate estimates of the enemy's position, and to transmit these estimates to those who must use them. It must not be forgotten, however, that modern weapons will greatly impede an approach to the enemy, and offset these modern advantages to some extent.

The advent of smokeless powder has now placed another obstacle in the way of accurate field reconnaissance. The

[15] Von Verdy, *Second Army Headquarters, 1866.*

British in the South African War [16] learned this to their sorrow. On the other hand, we may assume that the airship and the airplane will some day greatly improve the accuracy of reconnaissance.

Warfare of the Future Not Likely to Involve Insuperable Difficulties

In exercising sound military judgment one must continually resist suggestions calling for exaggerated caution, especially advice which paints warfare of the future as full of insuperable difficulties. The capabilities of men rather than weapons will in the future, as in the past, control. The bitter experiences of the British in South Africa resulted primarily from their faulty tactics. In the future, as in the past, war will be conducted man against man; the form will change, the essence will not. General von Kleist's advice still holds, although written in the days when the first suggestions of smokeless powder were giving rise to the most sterile misgivings: "Very well, then, let us pass without hesitation into the age of smokeless powder. The world still belongs to the bold." Today, as always, the way to overcome all our difficulties in war, large or small, is to be found in the proper development of the military personalities of officers and men.

Tactics Must Conform to Armament

Without a doubt our tactics must change with battlefield innovations. Napoleon said, "tactics should change every ten years to maintain even a semblance of superiority."[17] But however tactics change, they will not reduce the need for skilled generals who can act boldly on sketchy information. We shall, for example, always need men like Constantine von Alvensleben; for what would have happened at Thionville, if General von Alvensleben had waited until he was absolutely sure of the situation and had, so to speak, counted his enemy man by man? Problems in

[16] Boer War.
[17] Napoleon, *Maxims of War.*

war can never be solved like those in arithmetic, and we must be ready at all times to act properly despite uncertainties. We must not try either to reduce tactics to mere mathematical and technical formulas. This they can never become; and because they cannot is precisely why our profession is so fascinating. War always has and always will require the best thinking and the most consummate personality development a person is capable of. This is, of course, directly contrary to the negative, leveling, partisan spirit which today poisons our modern life, and which hates, above all things, an independent, strong, soldierly spirit.

Mastery of the Unforeseen Calls for an Artist

The unforeseen, which we constantly encounter in war, calls for the free creative work of the artist. The standardized product of the artisan is doomed to failure. Clausewitz comments on this point as follows:

"If we are to achieve success in this constant strife with the unforeseen, two qualities are indispensable to us; first understanding, which even in the densest darkness never leaves us without some gleam of intuitive guidance to lead us to the truth; and secondly, courage to follow this light, however faint it may be. The first quality is expressed best by the French phrase *coup d'oeil,* literally blow of the eye, or glance. The second is determination, a special quality of the intellect which uses the fear of vacillation and hesitation to overcome all other fears in the human mind, and produces decision in strong minds.

"A man with little understanding, for this very reason, cannot be a determined leader. He may act without hesitation in difficult conditions, but he does it without consideration. Doubts simply do not occur to him. Any man's actions may at times prove correct, but continued success is necessary to prove genius. If one questions this view in light of the number of determined hussar officers he knows who are not thinkers, remember that we are talking about a special bent of mind, not profound intellect. There are men who show an amazing amount of perspicacity, and who do not lack courage to assume responsibility, but who nevertheless cannot make a decision in complicated affairs. Their courage and their insight operate separately, and cannot be brought to work together and between them produce decision as a third factor.

"Determination is an act of courage in a specific case and becomes a trait of character only as it becomes a mental habit. Mere intellect is not courage, for we often see the most brilliant of men without decision. The mind must first arouse the feeling of courage, and must then be inspired or motivated by it; for in critical moments feeling controls men rather than reason.

"Along with *coup d' oeil* and determination, we should also mention *presence of mind,* which helps offset and overcome war's unforeseen difficulties. It is not so much the physical eye we speak of when we use the term *coup d'oeil,* as the inner eye or intuition. As an expression it belongs as a rule in the field of tactics, where the practiced leader can literally sweep the battlefield with a glance."[18]

We find in military history many remarkable examples of determination. Suvorov's march through Switzerland has already been mentioned. Marshal Ney's conduct at Krasny in the retreat of 1812 [19] was just as brilliant. Ney commanded the rear guard of the French army which consisted of 8,000 infantry in three small divisions, 300 cavalry, and 12 guns. He left Smolensk on 17 November by the south bank of the Dneiper, and reached Korytnia on the same day. About 7,000 stragglers, mostly unarmed, joined him

[18] *On War,* bk. I, ch. 3.
[19] Retreat of Napoleon's Grande Armee from Russia during the winter of 1812.

enroute. Detachments of the Hetman Platov's Cossacks followed the little French corps, while the strong advance guard of the Russian army under Miloradovich, which had marched parallel to Ney from Jelnia, took up positions on the Losmina River across his line of retreat.

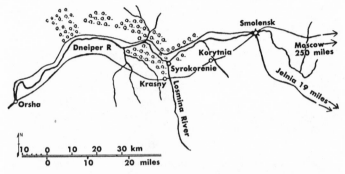

FIGURE 17. Area of Marshal Ney's Operations around Krasny, November 1812.

When Ney on the 18th encountered Miloradovich, he decided to force his way through to the main body of the French army, which he supposed to be still at Krasny. Napoleon, however, thought his rear guard was lost and had continued his retreat to Orsha. Unsupported by Napoleon, Ney's attempt to break through at Krasny after some initial success failed, and a disordered mass, only 3,000 of whom were armed, turned back toward Smolensk. When an officer of his staff asked what he would do next, Ney replied without hesitation, "We shall cross to the north bank of the Dneiper." When it was suggested that the ice was not thick enough to bear their weight, he replied confidently, "it will carry us." And Ney was right. Leaving the main road, he turned northward and reached the Dneiper at Syrokorenie. The ice was so thin that he had to abandon his horses, guns, and wagons; but his men got across, and took up the march for Orsha along the north bank of the river.

Across the river, however, his little band met a new peril. The main body of Platov's Cossacks, with artillery, had come down the right bank of the Dneiper from Smolensk, and several times he had to force his way through them with the bayonet. His force marched without a halt for two nights and a day, 80 kilometers in all, and eventually reached the main body at Orsha. He had only 900 men left; but the "Bravest of the Brave" had not laid down his arms to the Russians, and his rear guard had shown itself truly worthy of the name of the "Grande Armee."

Equally brilliant was the action of Napoleon at the Beresina River. Here his escape from imminent danger was due largely to the magic of his dreaded name.

Clausewitz says of this episode:

> "There was never a better opportunity to force the surrender of an army in the open field. Napoleon had to rely for the most part upon the reputation of his arms; and he made use here of an asset he had been accumulating for a long time. . . . Because the enemy was afraid of him and his Guard, no one dared face him. Napoleon capitalized on this psychological effect and with its assistance worked his way out of one of the worst situations in which a general was ever caught. Of course this psychological force was not all he had. He was still supported by his own brilliant strength of character and the peerless military virtues of his army, not yet destroyed by the greatest of trials. Once out of the trap, Napoleon said to his staff: 'You see how one can slip away under the very nose of the enemy.' Napoleon in this action not only preserved his military honor; he actually enhanced it."[20]

Napoleon succeeded in crossing the Beresina River with 30,000 men, an even larger number of fugitives, and 250 guns despite the fact that its far bank was defended by

[20] Clausewitz, *Campaign of 1812.*

Chicagov with 31,000 men, and he was closely pursued by Wittgenstein with another 30,000 men. This feat was possible only because the Russian commanders were afraid to engage strongly, and held most of their troops out of

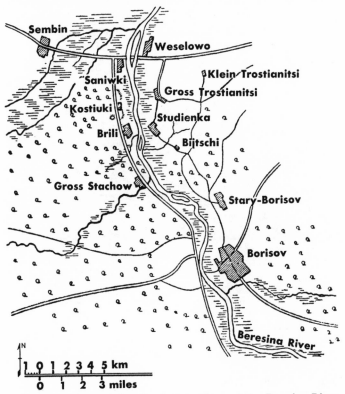

FIGURE 18. Area of Napoleon's Operations at the Beresina River, November 1812.

action. The French rear guard under Marshal Victor, with 6,000 men, had to stand off only 14,000 of Wittgenstein's men on the left bank of the Beresina between Studienka and Trostianitsi, while on the right bank, Marshals Ney and Oudinot with 10,000 men south of Brili had to repulse only 15,000 of Chicagov's men to keep open a route by the Sembin road. Over this route the Emperor withdrew with 40,000 men and 200 guns, although at that time only 14,000 of his men were fit for action.

The Russian attack, it is true, was hindered by the swamps and marshy woods along the Beresina, which hampered the deployment of artillery, but then most armies in difficulties have had some minor terrain advantages to assist them.

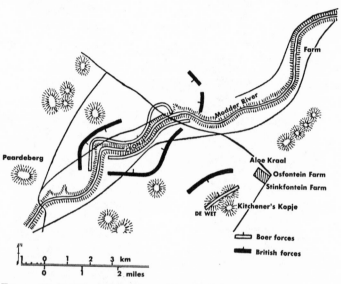

FIGURE 19. Battle of Paardeberg (South Africa), 18 February 1900.

Escape Always Possible

Despite modern firearms, one need not despair of escaping from a perilous situation. This was strikingly illustrated in the British attack on the Boers under Cronje at Paardeberg in the South African War. On 18 February about 17,000 British with 48 guns surrounded 5,000 Boers with 6 guns. The Boers occupied positions in the valley of the Modder River on both sides of the stream. All attempts to capture the Boers had failed, and help was approaching them from the outside. A detachment of Boers, 500 men with 2 guns, under De Wet, seized Kitchener's Kopje, a hill in rear of the British firing line. Within a few days, De Wet's force was increased to 2,000 men, and the British on this part of the field were faced with a crisis. On 21 February they found it necessary to drive De Wet out in order to make their investment of Cronje's force complete. At any time during these three days Cronje undoubtedly would have been able to escape with his mounted men by leaving his women and children behind.

If any body of troops in the peacetime maneuvers had gotten themselves into a situation in open country similar to Cronje's, the umpires, considering fire effectiveness only as it appears on the target range, would certainly have concluded escape was impossible. Outside help such as De Wet brought would have carried little weight either. Yet Cronje could have escaped, and was only kept from doing so by his unjustified fear for the safety of his women and children, and by special conditions existing in the Boer army. Today the word "impossible" is just as inapplicable as ever, although some methods of achieving difficult feats have changed.

Frederick's Coup d'Oeil at Sohr and Rossbach

Frederick's military genius was always evident, but what attracts our admiration most is his *coup d'oeil* in battlefield emergencies, notably at Sohr and Rossbach.

On the morning of 30 September 1745, the main body of the Prussian Army under command of the King—31 battalions, 51 squadrons, 22,000 men—was in camp at Staudenz facing Burkersdorf, where it had been since the 19th. The main Austrian army, 39,000 men, including 12,700 cavalry, was at Koeniginhof, across the Elbe. Its commander, Prince Charles of Lorraine, marching under cover of the great Koenigreich Forest, succeeded in gaining the King's right flank, and by placing a strong artillery force on the Graner Koppe, the hill commanding the Prussian camp, rendered

a Prussian retreat along the Trautenau road impossible.
Since the wooded heights to the King's rear were then
crossed only by the trails to Alt-Rognitz and Rudersdorf, the
fate of the Prussians seemed sealed.

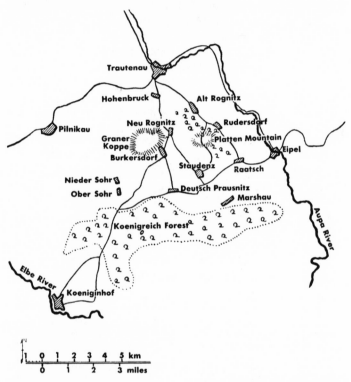

FIGURE 20. Area of Frederick the Great's Operations at Sohr,
30 September 1745.

The King was completely surprised by the report which
reached him at 0530 that the enemy was on his right flank
on the hills beyond Burkersdorf. At his tent door he gave
the necessary orders; and his resolution, together with the
courage of his troops in a few hours changed an apparently
hopeless situation into a brilliant victory over a force double

his own. Marching to his own right flank, he succeeded in turning the enemy's flank and driving the Austrians from the field despite the artillery fire from the Graner Koppe.

On 5 November 1757, the King was north of Rossbach with 22,000 men; the French and Austrians with 41,000 were south of Muecheln. The enemy moved to his right upon Reichardtswerben by way of Pettstaedt in three columns. Meanwhile the King marched in two columns to his own left rear, gained the Janus Hill, then turned east, brought his right flank to Lunstaedt, extended his left toward Reichardtswerben, caught the heads of the allied columns and defeated them decisively before they could deploy.

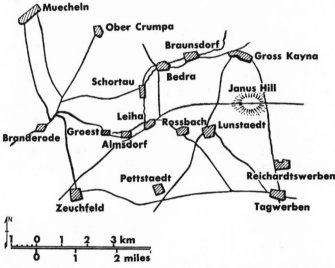

FIGURE 21. Area of Frederick the Great's Operations at Rossbach, 5 November 1757.

Early Leaders Could Observe Entire Battlefield

In the 18th century, the *coup d'oeil* of the leader had its place on the tactical battlefield even in the physical sense. The small armies and the accepted methods of fighting enabled him, as a rule, to watch not only his own troops but also the enemy's, which would be out of the question today for the commander of an army corps, and hardly possible for that of a division. While conducting a battle was easier for Frederick and even for Napoleon than it is today, it should not be forgotten that the annihilating battles fought by these great generals were possible only because they possessed in high degree not only the outer but the inner *coup d'oeil*—because they possessed that power of determination which is always an inseparable part of battle intuition and which guided them not only during, but after the battle as well.

Excellent Tactical Commanders Often Fail in Larger Commands

Great military spirits show the same decision in conducting large operations as small, but as Clausewitz says, "there are innumerable examples of men who have shown great determination in small operations, but lost it in larger affairs."[21] Ney, Steinmetz, and others are examples of this. So is Canrobert, otherwise a distinguished character, both as a man and as a soldier. Canrobert demonstrated he was a good leader on 18 August 1870 in command of the French VI Corps at St. Privat; but earlier in the Crimea, where he took over the French army after the death of Marshal St. Arnaud, his resolution always failed him the moment he put his plans into operation. He realized this himself, and asked to be relieved from command.

Benedek, the unfortunate commander of the Austrian Army of the North in 1866, is another example. Moltke, in the Prussian General Staff history of the campaign of 1859, pays him high tribute saying his "outstanding personality" at the time fully compensated for the disadvantage of having an army corps that was newly formed for the campaign. Since Solferino,[22] where his corps fought victoriously on the right flank, Benedek was regarded as the best gen-

[21] *On War*, bk. I, ch. 3.
[22] A decisive battle in the Italian struggle for independence, fought 1859 between the French and Italians on one side and the Austrians on the other. Won by the Italians and French (largely by the French).

eral in Austria. But he himself did not feel competent to handle an army of 200,000 men, and urgently begged the Emperor to assign someone else to command of the Army of the North. Only after he was told that acceptance of the command was a sacrifice he must make for the Hapsburg dynasty did he accept this command upon which he entered with little hope of success.

Determination Necessary in Strategy as Well as Tactics

Determination is just as necessary in the field of strategy as in tactics, for quick strategical decisions must often be made also. It has been said of one of the army commanders of the French First Republic (Moreau) that "his great fault was indecision. He became excited whenever there was a decision to be made; and as soon as he made one he regretted it, saw only its weak points, imagined it worse than it was, and so missed the right moment for action."[23] Moreau is aptly characterized by Clausewitz's words: "While such men realize they must make up their minds, they are at the same time extremely sensitive to the dangers of an erroneous decision. They are not sure of what is before them; and the more they have been in the habit of acting energetically, and the more they appreciate the dangers of indecision, the more undecided they become."[24]

Napoleon always prepared for adversity, but in quite a different sense. He wrote: "I habitually think of what I must do, three or four months ahead, and I always look for the worst." Thinking things through beforehand is the best possible protection against premature dispositions. Weighing all possibilities also makes it easier to determine the best action at any given moment. Although Napoleon's actions were planned long in advance, they could also be successfully adapted to the exigencies of the moment. He always appreciated the uncertainties of war; but he overcame the difficulties arising from them by remaining complete master of his own decisions.

[23] Count Segur, cited from Pierron.
[24] *On War,* bk. I, ch. 3.

Napoleon's Determined Actions at Ratisbon

The Ratisbon (Regensburg) operation of 1809 is rightly regarded as one of his masterpieces; but throughout this operation he knew little more of the situation of the enemy than he did when he arrived at Donauwoerth. Davout, on 19 April, had joined the Bavarians on the lower Abens after minor engagements with the Austrian main body. On the 20th, the Emperor pushed forward his center, threw back the Austrian left consisting of two corps under Marshal Hiller, and on the 21st drove him across the Isar at Land-shut in front of Marshal Massena, who was advancing from Moosburg. Davout remained facing the hostile forces south of Ratisbon.

Until early in the morning of 22 April, Napoleon believed that the enemy in Davout's front was also falling back across the Isar, and that there was nothing more to do than take up a general pursuit. That morning, however, the Emperor at Landshut learned that Davout was faced by the Austrian main army under the Archduke Charles; and that a corps moving up from Bohemia might reach Ratisbon at any time and be thrown against Davout with overwhelming force. Napoleon left only a detachment to hold the Austrian left, defeated at Landshut, and moved everything else upon Ratisbon. He reached Eggmuehl just in time to check an over-powering attack upon Davout, between the Danube and the Laber, and to defeat the Austrian main army. On the 23d, he compelled the Archduke to cross to the north bank of the Danube at Ratisbon.

While the Austrian commander hesitated and delayed, Napoleon acted swiftly and boldly. By doing this he won all along the line, although the information upon which he acted was vague and erroneous.

When Moltke on the evening of 2 July 1866 discovered unexpectedly strong Austrian forces on the right bank of the Elbe, he acted in much the same manner as Napoleon the evening before Eggmuehl and achieved success also. A commander therefore is often required to change his plans during a battle, just as he is often required to do so before hand. The results of any engagement can never be foreseen with certainty and new dispositions may be necessary at any time.

Every battlefield, moreover, is actually the starting point for a new operation. On the evening of the Battle of Eggmuehl, for example, Napoleon actually took up the advance upon Vienna leaving only two army corps and three cavalry divisions to follow the Austrians through Ratisbon. During the morning of 19 August 1870, reports indicated that the French army had fallen back to the protection of the fortifications of Metz. By 1100, G.H.Q. at Rezonville issued orders which formed three corps and two cavalry divisions of the Second Army into the Army of the Meuse under the Crown Prince of Saxony, and started these troops on a westward advance upon Paris in cooperation with the Third Army.

No victory is complete without a pursuit; but generally this will not be made if the commander has not thought beyond the battlefield itself. Defeats call for even greater powers of decision. The problem in retreat is to give timely effective withdrawal orders which will at the same time aid the general strategic situation and to lay a foundation for a successful continuation of operations.

Fight For Decision War's Greatest Task

Decisions creating these orders, however, must be made in the midst of death and destruction, and under the burden of a defeat which sacrifice and bloodshed has been unable to prevent. To make these decisions when they must be made takes the sternest kind of self-discipline.

Wherever we may serve in the varied situations of war, we will always find the struggle to make a decision the most difficult part of command. A decision demands from any soldier a concentration of all the strength of his mind and spirit. Not everyone has by nature the same power of decision, but by strenuous self-discipline and practice anyone may increase what he has. Thus we may "overcome all other fears, through fear of vacillation, or the fear of fear itself."

CHAPTER 5

The Commander Must Have Imagination

> "The commander in war must work in a medium which his eyes cannot see; which his best deductive powers cannot always fathom; and with which because of constant changes he can rarely become completely familiar."
> —Clausewitz, *On War,* book I, chapter 3

CLAUSEWITZ suggests that the relationship of war to geography and terrain may be regarded, if not as the most *important,* at least as the most *noticeable peculiarity* of military activity.

> "This relationship is permanent. Acts of war take place in specific places. This makes terrain of the utmost importance since it conditions all other factors, and sometimes completely changes them. We are compelled to take into account the smallest features of the ground as well as the salient features of large geographical areas. While both sides must in general contend with the same terrain difficulties, the side with superior skill and talent can transform these difficulties into an advantage for itself. Equality of difficulty, moreover, exists only in theory, for as a rule one of the opponents, generally the side on the defensive, is more familiar with the ground than the other."

The influence of terrain "which conditions all other factors and sometimes completely changes them" has been significant throughout military history. The methods which brought Napoleon his great success in central Europe failed him altogether in Russia in 1812. Not until the Boer War was actually in progress did Britain realize all the difficulties of the South African theater of war.

While the minor features of the ground have always been of the utmost importance in the tactical field, it is hard for us in these days, with our good maps, to realize the unpleasant surprises which commanders often had to meet in earlier times. Personal reconnaissance by the general and his aides had to serve as the foundation for any decision; for only occasionally was some slight hasty sketch of a part of the ground available. At Leuthen,[1] the Prussian dispositions were helped greatly by an intimate knowledge of the ground at this place which Frederick and some of his subordinate commanders had gained in peacetime maneuvers. At Prague,[1] on the other hand, the difficulties of the marshy ground over which the Prussian left wing had to pass in its approach and deployment were much greater than they had appeared from a hasty reconnaissance made by Schwerin and Winterfeldt. The first attack of the infantry on the left wing failed largely because of this unforeseen handicap.

The King criticized himself after the Battle of Kolin for failing to personally reconnoiter the ground to the right front and flank of the Austrians, where the main attack was to be made. In his defense it might be said that such action would have attracted the attention of the Austrians to that region prematurely, especially since it would have been necessary first to drive away the Austrian light cavalry posted there. Actually the King had formed a false impression of that bit of ground and did not realize that the Austrians could extend their right as far as they actually did. By sheer ill luck, also, a sketch of the ground, previously made by an engineer officer, which might have given the desired information, could not be found when a decision had to be made. Although the Battle of Kunersdorf was fought in his own country, a part of the misfortune that befell the King was due to inadequate terrain information.

The fact that the Battle of Bautzen[2] did not end in complete annihilation of the allied armies is often attributed to the slow movement of Marshal Ney, who was charged with the envelopment of their right. Ney, however, had to bring

---

[1] Battles in the Bohemian campaign, Seven Years War, 1757.
[2] Napoleon in this battle, 20-21 May 1813, defeated a combined Russian-Prussian force. Bautzen is a town on the Spree River in eastern Germany, 40 miles east of Dresden.

his untrained troops across the marshy Spree Valley, pass through defiles between large ponds, and deploy on the farther side. The nature of the ground which he had to cross aided the allies, since they had first rate troops and Napoleon did not, even though he was superior in numbers.

Such conditions in earlier battles could never be avoided because of the type of maps then available. Even as late as 1866, the Sweipwald, which was so important in the Battle of Koeniggraetz, did not appear on the Prussian maps. This omission made the handling of the First Army in that battle extremely difficult.

Personal Reconnaissance Still Important Even With Modern Maps

We would seriously overestimate the value of our excellent modern maps, however, to imagine that we can now dispense with personal reconnaissance. No matter how skillfully one may read today's maps of former battlefields, one cannot fully understand, without an examination of the ground, the reasons for events as they actually occurred. At Kolin, for example, the full difficulty of the attack could be appreciated only from the Austrian defensive position.

Actually unpleasant surprises for the attacker are more likely than ever on today's modern extended battlefields, where the attacker, capable only of long distance reconnaissances, gets only general impressions of the enemy's position. On 18 August 1870,[3] the advantage afforded the French by the long ridge between the Mance and the Chatel Valleys could not be appreciated from Verneville and Habonville, especially as to cover. Some of the false steps the Germans took that day may be attributed to this condition.

As the range of modern weapons increases, the scope and frequency of terrain surprises will increase correspondingly. The South African War gives us only a very imperfect idea of what these surprises will be, for there was no great mass of artillery used. This much can be said, however, the defender is definitely gaining an advantage over the attacker

[3] Battle of Gravelotte-St. Privat, Franco-Prussian War, 1870-71.

because of the latter's increasing unfamiliarity with the ground in front of the defender.

Modern Weapons Make Full Use of Ground Necessary

The effect of modern weapons forces the attacker to make full use of the ground's conformation. The slightest bit of cover is valuable. Even our most accurate special maps, however, do not give us the detailed information about the ground we need. In fact, they sometimes lead us to expect more from them than they can give. Detailed map studies can easily divert us from close examination of the ground.

Taine calls our attention to the clarity of Napoleon's insight—a faculty we seem to have been losing for the past three hundred years by reason of our indoor education and studies in the fields of science. He says, "Instead of things themselves we study the conventional signs for them; instead of the ground we study the map."[4]

Acquiring a "Sense of Locality"

On the other hand, although "the relationship of war to geography and terrain covers the widest of fields," its difficulties are much easier to overcome today because we disseminate information more widely and have many more maps.

In many non-European theaters of war, however, conditions may not be as favorable as they are today in Europe. In the American Civil War, for example, the Union armies in Virginia experienced great difficulties working with poor maps or having none at all. The situation was the same for the British in the South African War. In Virginia great wooded areas, and in South Africa the monotonous character of the evenly rolling barren "veldt" made losing one's way easy. In both cases, the defenders' better knowledge of the country gave them tremendous advantages. In Manchuria, both parties were handicapped equally. The Manchurian operations, however, were so slow that the lack of reliable terrain information was less keenly felt.

On this point Clausewitz writes:

[4] Taine, *Origines de la France Contemporaire.*

"Terrain difficulties can be overcome only by a special faculty we sometimes call 'a sense of locality.' It is an ability to form an accurate mental picture of the country, and readily orient one's self with it. This sense of locality is largely imagination, coming in part from actual visual impressions, and part from a mental process which uses knowledge gained from study and experience to fill in missing points and make a complete whole of the fragments determined by physical sight. The power of imagination then brings this whole picture before the mind's eye, makes it into a picture, or a mental map, and maintains it permanently present and unbroken.

". . . Practice and mental application have much to do with the process. Applications of this talent also broaden as rank increases. To find his way readily, the hussar or the chasseur, leading a patrol through all its windings, need only a few landmarks and a small amount of imagination. The general, on the other hand, must project his sense of locality to a point where it encompasses the general geographical features of a whole province or of a whole country. He must be able to picture to himself the general course of the roads, streams, and mountains. At the same time he must be able to envision details of specific localities. While he has a host of reports, maps, books, and memoranda to help him picture extended geographic features, and staff officers to obtain and supply him with details of specific areas, he will find that a personal talent for picturing geographic and terrain situations clearly and rapidly will enable him to act more quickly and confidently, will protect him against a feeling of helplessness, and make him less dependent on others."[5]

Effect of Good Maps on Modern Combat

The idea of "mental maps" was mentioned long ago by Berenhorst, who said an officer's head should be full of

[5] *On War,* bk. I, ch. 3.

maps. Today an accurate sense of locality is just as important as ever despite our improved maps. Maps merely give us more accurate information to fill in gaps in our visual picture, and lead us to better end-results. Like all other technical improvements, they have not made the conduct of war easier; they only enable us to hit harder and move more rapidly. An area covered by a good map, for example, can be reconnoitered much more accurately. At the same time, a general can gain a much clearer picture of the theater of operations, see farther ahead than formerly, and regulate the movement of his armies more effectively—all of which are indispensable necessities, considering the size of present-day forces. All the higher commanders are now in a position to form long-range estimates of the difficulties they will encounter, and can act with greater assurance.

Even With Best of Maps, Effective Imagination Still Necessary

Imagination, however, is still necessary to make full use of our maps. For example, we need to picture troops on maps, if we are to make good use of them. The ability to do this is partly a natural gift, for not everyone can picture troops, invisible to his physical eye, on the ground or on the map. But even though this ability is a gift, as with other things, practice helps us improve it.

Clausewitz says: "The power of quick and clear understanding of the ground must be considered an act of the imagination; but this is almost the only service that we can hope for from this unruly goddess, who generally does more harm than good."[6]

While a leader must be able to bring before his eyes a clear picture of the ground on which he is to fight, he must also at all times be able to picture the positions and movements of his own troops, and those of the enemy to the extent of his information about the enemy. Imagination, Clausewitz's "unruly goddess," helps us to make clear interpretations and accurate assessments. It enables the leader

[6] *On War*, bk. I, ch. 3.

whenever he makes a decision to appreciate the effect of the decision upon all elements of the troops entrusted to him, to see its influence on the last wagon in his train. Such a clear imagination is extremely valuable to all commanders.

Berenhorst gives the following advice for developing imagination as an aid to leadership: "When you have maneuvers on a large scale, when your columns wind over hills and through valleys, then position at least half your officers so they can observe these columns, and form an idea of what various units of an army look like at various distances." One of the important training features of our great autumn maneuvers is the picture they give us of the size and appearance of various types of troop units.

Development of Imagination Essential Part of Staff Training

The development of the power of imagination and its various ramifications is an essential part of general staff training, and an indispensable requisite for leaders of large forces distributed over a considerable area. The ability to form accurate mental pictures of a situation quickly is especially important today when the higher commander cannot hope to see his troops with his physical eyes. Wellington showed a lack of it at Ligny on 16 June 1815, when he assured Blucher of help, when as a matter of fact the armies were in such a position that help from him was impossible.

Uncontrolled Imagination Can Be Disastrous

What Clausewitz had in mind when he spoke of the "unruly goddess" is that form of imagination which fails to see things in their true light, and hence misleads. This mis- or unguided imagination has often led to disaster in war. Mack's preconceived ideas, which led him into disaster at Ulm in 1805, for example, were made more hazardous by his imagination, which was building upon a false foundation.

When the situation began to clear up on 5 August, and he could no longer doubt that Napoleon was moving down the Danube from Donauwoerth to Ingolstadt with the intention of turning the Iller position, he still felt no anxiety. He was convinced that the enemy would be hemmed in between his army at Ulm and the Russians. On the 6th he wrote to Emperor Francis: "More than ever, I hope now for a favorable result." On the 7th he described the desperate position of the enemy between the two hostile armies, overlooking entirely the fact that his army at Ulm, to which Napoleon was immediately opposed, had only half of Napoleon's strength, and the Russians were far away. The mere presence of the two hostile armies on Napoleon's flanks was not dangerous to the French leader, unless these two armies could act simultaneously and in concert. Any threat was further reduced by the Austrian army's intention, as Mack wrote, to hold fast with determination at Ulm until their Russian allies could arrive. On 13 October when the French army was actually closing in on him from the Lech, he believed that the French main body had turned toward the Inn to face the Russians. On the 14th, when he learned of the march of the French upon the Iller, he imagined that Napoleon was giving up his plans and was in full retreat on a broad front, from south of Ulm to the upper Rhine. Mack's plan of holding Ulm seemed to him at that moment brilliantly justified. He was still deep in study of these extraordinary movements of the enemy, when rumors reached him of a landing of the British at Boulogne and of a revolution in France. This news, together with his own personal conjectures of intervention by Prussia, strengthened his belief in an enemy retreat. He admitted later that his conception of the situation might have been a dream; but, he added, "Who can name a commanding general or chief of staff who has never dreamed such dreams?"

The visionary unmilitary imagination of this man brought disaster to the Austrians, and for the same reason a part of the responsibility for the Prussian reverse in 1806 must fall upon Colonel von Massenbach, chief of staff to Prince Hohenlohe, whose character resembled Mack's in many respects. His influence upon the Prince throughout the campaign was most unfortunate. At Prenzlau his excited fancy caused him to see ghosts. Through the false impressions of the enemy which he formed, he became convinced that it was impossible to go farther, and that it was necessary to surrender the Prussian Corps. As a matter of fact, with a little more determination, it was far from impossible to get through to Stettin.[7] Clausewitz says of Massenbach: "It was evident, at first sight, that he was an enthusiast, entirely controlled by his imagination. Such men are never lacking in intelligence, nor in ability to estimate a situation; but they lack tact, judgment, and sound ideas."[8] These "sound ideas," which are evolved from an enlightened imagination, in turn control the imagination and form the best protection against that unwholesome fancy which gains control of readily excitable minds under the pressure of exterior influences and unforeseen circumstances.

With the help of a sound military imagination, an officer can always have a definite picture of the military situation before his eyes, and can therefore make a sound decision. Of course, everything being uncertain in war, the picture may not be entirely correct, and the decisions and dispositions based upon it may not be the best possible; but they will seldom fail completely if carried through with determination, for they have basically a sound foundation.

[7] By reaching Stettin where he could be supplied by sea, Prince Hohenlohe, then in command of what remained of the Prussian main army, hoped to hold out long enough to secure Russian assistance against Napoleon.

[8] Clausewitz, *General Staff, Military History Monographs.*

CHAPTER 6

Ambition is One of the Essential Qualities of a Leader

> "No other feeling, however more common it may be or however more highly it may be generally regarded— patriotism, devotion to an ideal, revenge, enthusiasm of any kind—none of these can make ambition and thirst for glory unimportant. There never was a great leader without ambition, nor is it possible to conceive of such a thing."
>
> —Clausewitz, *On War,* book I, chapter 3

NAPOLEON is reported to have said of himself that he was not ambitious. But he qualified this at once by saying, "or, if I am, it is in the sense that ambition has so penetrated my whole being that it is a necessary element of my life, like the blood in my veins or the air that I breathe."[1] This self-analysis strongly emphasizes the role of ambition as the mainspring of all his actions. Without this spring, history would not contain Napoleon's brilliant chain of victories which still astonish us; the study of which is an inexhaustible source of instruction. On the other hand, there would have been no Leipzig or Waterloo and sudden fall of the Emperor. Ambition of the kind that fired Napoleon can overthrow a world, can bring it under control for a time, but cannot create anything permanent. Defeat and ignominy will always be the end-result of a purely self-seeking military ambition. As soldiers, we cannot afford to look upon such a phenomenon of world history as Napoleon's career "in that moralizing spirit, which sees human greatness only as the opposite of criminality, forgetting the profound truth that every great man is richly gifted for evil as well as for good."[2] Napoleon's extreme egoism, while necessary to set his feet on the road to supreme power, was also one of the principal reasons he lost that power.

[1] Conversation with Roederer, reported in Taine, *Origines de la France Contemporaire.*

[2] Treitschke, *Historical and Political Essays.*

King Frederick was also filled with ambition; but it was a limited and wisely directed ambition which helped him to accomplish things of permanent value. When he seized Silesia in 1740, he spoke to the officers of the Berlin regiments before they moved out of the rendezvous with glory which he had prepared for them, and admitted that thirst for glory and the desire to make his name live had been among the reasons which led him to occupy Silesia. Late in December 1740 he also wrote that he would gladly turn over his duties in the field to someone else, except that the phantom called glory appeared to him too often. "Madness perhaps, but a madness which is beyond remedy when it once has seized upon one." Koser, however, explains this phantom which the young king saw so often, by saying: "It was an ambition justified by a dedication of strength and ennobled by the sacred flame of patriotism. For in Frederick's breast personal ambition was inseparable from the noble desire to make a place for his people in the face of Europe, to wipe out the unfavorable impressions of the past, to determine once and for all the nature of the dubious status between Electorate and the Kingdom, and to place his Prussia among the great powers."[3]

Moral Basis of Frederick's Ambition

It was the ambition for power, characterized by Ranke [an eminent German historian] as one of the chief causes for disturbance in the world, which controlled the King. But neither to this nor to any other question of political power can the yardstick of ordinary civil morality be applied. Only pacifists, who fail to appreciate the real governing principles of the life of nations, attempt to do so. Frederick's attitude toward the state explains the moral basis of his ambition. In Napoleon's case, France was merely a

[3] Koser, *Frederick the Great*. The largest part of Prussia at this time consisted of the Electorate of Brandenburg, a part of the Holy Roman Empire. Its ruling family, the Hohenzollerns, however, had previously acquired control of the small duchy of Prussia, and after a long struggle, been granted the title of "King *in* Prussia," since this part of their domain was outside the Empire. The Hohenzollerns gradually corrupted this title to "King *of* Prussia," although legally they were still only "electors" of the Empire in all areas of Prussia inside the Empire.

tool for the accomplishment of his plans for personal aggrandizement, which were without limit. With Frederick, however, as early as the Second Silesian War he thought only of holding what he had gained; and in the Seven Years War he drew the sword unwillingly, and only to forestall an attack by the enemy. His commendable ambition, in which the state always came first, was the basis of that incomparable boldness of action which we have already noted. His own words, "to live, to think, and to die as a king," furnish the clue to his whole life; and it was only this determination which made it possible for him to make headway against all Europe, with the full determination not to survive a disaster. In this respect he contrasts sharply with Napoleon, who not only survived the collapse of his power, but who, after looking death in the face in so many battles, showed himself a mere adventurer by unworthily seeking to save his own life after his first fall.

Ambition Should Be For Success of Cause and Country

By comparison with Napoleon, King Frederick shows us the more worthy side of military virtue, especially how devotion to a great cause can keep ambition more or less impersonal.

This same impersonal ambition was also found in men like Blucher, Scharnhorst, and Gneisenau, who even in the worst of times remained true to their country. The same spirit strengthened Lee, who, although in his heart he disapproved the secession of the Southern States, nevertheless did wonders in command of their troops. It enabled Moltke to do his duty with great distinction when called to service at an advanced age. The secret of the success of such men is that they were not only great soldiers, but also, in the fullest sense of the word, great citizens. Such men were not uncommon in old France; Marshal Turenne was unquestionably one of the greatest of them. Ranke says of him that no one in the time of Louis XIV did more for the greatness of the French monarchy than he. "No one dreamed less than he of private gain. He never talked about himself. No more frank and modest memoirs exist than those which he wrote on a few of his campaigns. He was one of the few men who, engrossed in great world affairs, entirely forgot himself."[4]

Common Ambition Makes Coalitions a Success

Men of exceptional character sharing a great purpose in common have sometimes brought to coalition warfare that unity of action which it generally lacks. The staggering blows of the War of the Spanish Succession against Louis XIV were possible only because Marlborough and Prince Eugene of Savoy acted so completely in concert. Their relations were based upon the highest and most chivalrous mutual esteem. Prince Eugene's great modesty, and his full and frank recognition of the services of his colleague, made it possible to overcome the difficulties of a situation where neither was under the orders of the other, but everything depended upon voluntary cooperation. The statesmanlike views of these two generals enabled them to disregard all nonessentials and to look only to the great purpose. Our admiration for them grows all the more when we consider the dissensions of the generals of the powers allied against Frederick the Great throughout the Seven Years War, or the obstacles that were placed in the way of unity of action in the armies allied against Napoleon in 1813 and 1814.

Harmful Ambition of Generals Checked by King

It is only human nature for the great powers placed in the hands of a superior commander to lead his ambition into undesirable channels. High place brings a justified self-esteem, which makes it difficult for a successful general to continue to subordinate himself to the general interest. While this subordination can be secured easily when the monarch himself holds the reins of war, rivalry among subordinate generals will always crop out where there is no firm leadership from the throne. The contentions among the generals of the army of the Prince of Prussia after the Battle of Kolin in 1757 was the principal reason for the disaster that befell that army on its retreat from eastern Bohemia

[4] Ranke, *History of France.*

to Lusatia. Many times during the Seven Years War the same troops who had accomplished wonders under the personal command of the King suffered, when he was absent, from the rivalries of his generals.

In Napoleon's armies these personal rivalries stood out even more clearly. There was no feeling of allegiance to a hereditary monarch to make subordination to his authority seem a matter of course. His authority could be maintained only by his personality, which was felt by all. Where he was not personally present, his subordinates regarded themselves as coordinate generals, as they had been under the Republic. Marshal Marmont says in his memoirs that no one but the Emperor had the personal prestige to command several army corps, each of which was commanded by a marshal. Napoleon realized this most painfully in 1813, when he said in conversation with the British commissioner Sir Neil Campbell, "My presence was indispensable at any point where I required a decisive victory. This was the weak point in my armor. Not one of my generals was competent to exercise a large independent command."

This appeared most glaringly in 1811, on the retreat from Portugal to Spain, when Marshal Ney refused to obey the orders of Marshal Massena, who commanded the whole force. Ney went so far as to forbid his division commanders to obey orders from Massena's headquarters. When Massena sent an order relieving him from command of his corps, Ney replied that his command had been conferred upon him by the Emperor, and no other authority was competent to relieve him. Massena finally had to give him explicit orders to return to the rear areas until a reply could be received to the report of the affair which Massena made to the Emperor.

Ney's conduct was not a manifestation of legimate ambition, but of small jealousy. The direct opposite appears in the conduct of General Canrobert in the Crimean War. He voluntarily relinquished command of the French army in favor of a junior, General Pelissier, who had been commanding an army corps under him, and took command, not of a

corps, but of his own old division. While this self-abnega-
tion was due to a fear of responsibility to which the general
did not feel equal, it nevertheless speaks volumes for the
character of Canrobert. It took a genuine, selfless concern
for a cause to freely admit the superior energy of Pelissier
and to silence his own ambition.

A similar situation arose among the Russian superior commanders at Sebastopol. The governor of the fortress, Lieutenant General Moller, and the senior naval officer present, Admiral Nachimov, recognized the superior ability and energy
of the junior admiral, Kornilov. Moller appointed him chief
of staff of the fortress, and both seniors, by common consent, left the conduct of the defense to him. Kornilov then
appointed Lieutenant Colonel Totleben as chief engineer of
the defense, and placed him in charge of all engineering
operations.[5] By this expedient, the right man, the man who
was really the soul of the defense, was brought into the
place he should have occupied without doing violence to the
forms of the military hierarchy. By this voluntary arrangement the same results were accomplished as are secured in
the British Army by the use of "local rank." Russia owes
much to these unselfish men.

Unselfish Action on the Spot No Substitute for Unity Of Command

Command uncertainties, however, cannot always be cleared
up by unselfish action on the spot. In war, everything is
personal, even in this respect. The manner in which the
supreme command in Manchuria was handled warns us never
to let personal considerations control. The Viceroy of the
Far East, Admiral Alexieff, held supreme command of the
army and navy in that region. With and under him General
Kuropatkin held the powers of an army commander over the
troops assembling in southern Manchuria, called the Army
of Manchuria. General Linievich, commander of the troops
of the Amur Military District, and Admiral Makaroff, commanding the fleet, were also under the orders of the Viceroy.

[5] Von Schilder, *Life of Totleben.*

But the commander of the Army of Manchuria had been Minister of War, and moreover was senior to Alexieff, which caused a certain embarassment in their relations. These facts, however, did not justify the final sentence of the Czar's telegram informing Alexieff of the appointments of Kuropatkin and Makaroff: "I am convinced that the appointment of these independent and responsible commanders will facilitate for you, as my Viceroy, the accomplishment of the heavy historic task which falls to you." The Imperial order assigning Kuropatkin to this duty was likewise obscure, for it contains the following sentence: "In the conduct of military operations you are to act according to your own judgment, conforming always to the general plans of the Viceroy." Thus unity of command was lost, as has so often happened before, although theoretically it is universally recognized as being absolutely necessary.

Repression of Personal Ambition Difficult, But Necessary

The common good often requires repression of personal ambition. This is hard to do, for as Clausewitz says:

> "Of all the great feelings that fill the human breast in the midst of hot combat, there is none so powerful and so permanent as the thirst of the soul for glory and honor. This sentiment is unjustly treated in ordinary German speech, which terms it 'ambition' or 'desire for glory,' in a depreciative sense. The misuse of this worthy aspiration in war, without doubt, has caused some of the most shocking of crimes against the human race, but in its essence this feeling is one of the noblest in human nature, and in war it is the breath of life to the most sluggish body."[6]

Although the depreciative connotation of the words to which Clausewitz refers belong to the past—to the adventurer and the mercenary army—these words still retain a certain amount of their former opprobrium. Using "desire

---

[6] *On War*, bk. I, ch. 3.

for glory" and "ambition" in this discredited sense, Taine compares Napoleon with the Italian condottieri[7] of the 15th century, except that his action was on a so much larger scale. In an army organized on the principle of universal military service, and employed only for national purposes, the thirst for glory and honor contains no desire for personal aggrandizement. The ambitions of its members are completely different from those of mercenary soldiery. This is overlooked by those who regard Napoleon as the incomparable model of a great leader. He is the creator of modern warfare, and as such we may admire his military gifts to the full. We may even allow ourselves to be carried away by our admiration for the talents of this great conqueror, and forget all the ills he brought upon Germany. But we must not forget that in him "the misuse of this worthy aspiration has caused some of the most shocking crimes against the human race." As members of a universal military service army, we cannot be motivated by the forces which inspired him, and we would be wise to guard against undue adulation of this superman. It would be best to close our ears to those who, in giving him a place higher than all our own national heroes, are in fact merely seeking for themselves a little of his super-humanity.

Desire for Glory a French Characteristic

Desire for glory of one kind or another has always been conspicuous in the French people. In 1749, the Marshal de Belle-Isle wrote to his son, the Comte de Gisors: "Love glory and always have an ardent desire for it. This passion for glory has sustained me throughout my difficult career." These words are found in a memorandum which the Marshal drew up for his son, who, at the age of 17, was about to assume command of the Royal Champagne Regiment. Rousset rightly says of this memorandum that any soldier who appreciates the high moral significance of his profession will read it with pleasure. It does not touch upon an adventurer's

[7] Bands of 15th century mercenary soldiers whose leaders were called "condottieri," (captain). These leaders sold the services of their bands to anyone who would pay their price.

search for renown, but shows in every line a deep patriotic spirit, as is so commonly found in the old French aristocracy during the decline of the kingdom under Louis XV. By means of it the Marshal shows us that in old France the idea of *"gloire"* was not at all the same as under the First Republic and under Napoleon.

Constructive Ambition Is a Desire to Excel In a Great Enterprise

Real ambition, in its best sense, stems from a desire to take part in a great enterprise, and to excel in it. Without the most exemplary character, ambition in its best sense cannot exist.

> "Patriotism, fanaticism, revenge, enthusiasm of any kind . . . may stir the masses and raise their morale, but these incentives cannot stimulate the leader to do more than any of his following, which, of course, he must do if he is to accomplish anything exceptional. These motivations cannot, like ambition, make a leader seek and exploit every opportunity in war to its fullest extent, as he would his own private property, putting labor and care into his plowing and sowing, in order to reap a rich harvest. This intensity of endeavor is required of all leaders from the highest to the lowest to raise the efficiency of the army and make it successful."[8]

The desire "to outdo others" is characteristic of anyone who seeks to raise himself above the mass. But only the desire to do something really extraordinary indicates leadership, and inspires a feeling of proprietary right in every act of war. Development of this feeling is largely an intellectual achievement. In the higher grades of modern warfare, where the leader cannot so easily see his troops with the physical eye, generation of a personal desire for the success of the cause must be more than ever intellectual.

Every act in war calls for careful study and an estimate of the situation, and the ability to translate thought promptly into action. In the words of Marshal Soult, "What we call

[8] *On War*, bk. I, ch. 3.

an inspiration is nothing more than a rapid calculation."
Such thinking is sharply distinguished from abstract and
philosophical thinking. Learned and philosophical minds are
seldom of use in war. This special war mentality, if any
aptitude for war exists, can be developed by constant practice, as we try to do in tactical problems and war games.
But in these days [1911] of armed peace and railways, military problems come before us with so little warning that
the "property" which is suddenly acquired can be used to
good advantage only if one prepares himself in time of peace,
"putting labor and care into his plowing and sowing."

Ambition of Leaders Raises Efficiency of Army

Great leaders have always endeavored to stimulate the
ambition of their subordinate commanders. Frederick the
Great prided himself upon having restored the morale of
the army by the spring of 1745, after the unsuccessful
Bohemian campaign of the preceding year. After the Battle
of Hohen Friedberg he wrote that the "army had surpassed
itself"; and after Sohr he insisted that there was no difficulty which his troops could not overcome. His officers strove
to outdo each other in seeking distinction. With justified
pride in the accomplishments of his army, he wrote, after
the Second Silesian War: "A general who would be looked
upon as rash in any other country is taken as a matter of
course with us; he may undertake anything that is humanly
possible." The generals he entrusted large independent commands to in the Seven Years War did not always succeed
in satisfying him, but they always attempted "anything that
was humanly possible."

Napoleon's Genius Developed by Ambition of Revolutionary Armies

Napoleon's genius was aided by the military ambition
which inspired the armies of the Revolution. Domestic unrest
had brought many valuable elements into the army, and as
a rule their ambition took a truly chivalrous form. Avarice
was not the mainspring of the action of the French leaders
of that period, although it played its part with many of them.

Twenty years of war also tended to produce harsh characters. This ambition, allowed full scope under direction, was the driving force which passed from the Emperor to the subordinate commanders and from them to the troops. This force was evident even among the German contingents from the Confederation of the Rhine, which were grateful to the Emperor for bringing them out of their position as insignificant states, and giving them their opportunity for glory in the great war. The magic of victory always rouses an ambition which gives a great momentum to military operations We saw the same thing in our [German] armies of 1870.[9] They entered that war knowing their task was a difficult one, but with a complete confidence in themselves derived from the battlefields of 1866.[10] The commendable desire of our generals to close with the enemy and to give each other support had a salutary effect and readily cleared up temporary misunderstandings. It was not by sheer luck that General von Alvensleben and his III Corps gained glory at Thionville. It has been said with considerable truth that: "Whatever one seeks with all his strength, that he shall have; for the desire for it is an expression of one's very nature."[11] At Thionville the right kind of military ambition proved its value in the face of the enemy.

Creation of Right Type of Ambition Duty of Leaders in Peace

To create this constructive type of ambition in time of peace and guard it against harmful influences, is the duty of all leaders. Here we must distinguish between a mere satisfaction of vanity, and rewards justly due for honest efforts.

Without a doubt, virtue is its own best reward, and ambition is in itself a satisfaction, for it springs from the need which everyone feels to know his own nature. But for continued effort in time of peace, none of us can dispense with the approbation of superiors. It is the nature of any strong personality to seek to show its strength. Peacetime service,

[9] Franco-Prussian War.
[10] Seven Weeks War.
[11] Feuchtersleben, *The Nature of the Soul.*

however, offers only limited objectives for ambition, and as the prospect of distinction in war seems to recede further and further, one comes to feel that his opportunity will never arise. Those who are best fitted by nature for war feel most keenly at times that their service in peacetime is utterly unreal, and only a consciousness of duty well performed can overcome this feeling. For weaker characters, the temptation is strong to be content with the little ostensible triumphs of peace.

It is the duty of superiors to prevent this feeling and to keep the eyes of all subordinates fixed upon the requirements of war. Only in this way can they act in the spirit of Frederick the Great, who wrote these words for his successor's eye: "Honor, love of glory, and the good of the Fatherland must inspire all those who devote themselves to the profession of arms, and ignoble passions must not be allowed to take hold. Such qualities render soldiers worthy of respect, and make them supports of the Kingdom and bulwarks of the State."[12]

[12] Frederick the Great, *Military Testament*.

CHAPTER 7

Only a Strong Mind Can Resist the Impressions of War

> "A strong mind is not one which is simply capable of strong exertion. It is one which, in the midst of the strongest exertions, can maintain its equilibrium, so that in spite of internal tumult, power of decision and insight remain as steadfast as the needle of the compass, which, regardless of the tossing of the ship, retains its accuracy."
>
> —Clausewitz, *On War*, book I, chapter 3

WAR as the domain of danger, physical exertion, and uncertainty, taxes the determination of the leader to the utmost, especially in actual combat. In pointing this out Clausewitz said:

> "As long as troops fight enthusiastically, no great display of willpower is necessary. But when the going begins to get difficult, where exceptional results have to be accomplished, the fighting force loses the characteristics of a well-oiled machine. Friction begins to appear, and great determination on the part of the leader is required to overcome it. This friction is not characterized by actual disobedience and resistance, although these may appear in a few individuals. Rather it is the collective effect of flagging physical and moral strength, the heart-breaking sight of the sacrifice of life, which the leader has to fight in himself, and then in all others who immediately or mediately pass on all their feelings, cares, and exertions to him. When the strength of individuals begins to flag, and can no longer be stimulated by their own will, the resulting mass inertia falls more and more heavily upon the shoulders of the leader. By the fire in his own heart, by the strength of his own determination he must rekindle enthusiasm and reinstill hope in all the others. To the extent he can do this, he main-

tains his ascendancy over the masses and remains their master. But when his own courage is no longer strong enough to stiffen the courage of others, then the weight of the mass drags him down to its own level, to the depths of mere animal nature, which flinches from danger and knows no shame. These are the burdens the courage and willpower of the leader must bear in action if he is to accomplish anything worthwhile. Since these burdens increase with the size of one's command, a corresponding increase in strength must accompany every increase in a leader's rank."[1]

The burdens described by Clausewitz weighed upon the German leaders on 16 and 18 August 1870[2] with a force unknown in the days of less destructive armament.

General von Alvensleben at Thionville

When General von Alvensleben in the course of the initial skirmishes on 16 August realized he was opposed by greatly superior forces, if not by the whole French Army of the Rhine, he did not hesitate to go into battle with a reversed front, although at the outset he could count only upon his own III Corps. His one idea was to overcome his lack of physical strength by the moral power of the offensive. By 1230 he had pushed back the French II Corps; but this was supported by a division of the Imperial Guard and the VI Corps, and the pressure of the approaching French III Corps was beginning to be felt seriously by the German left wing in the Tronville copses. This required him to commit his last remaining infantry reserves. General von Alvensleben writes of the situation at 1400:

"The ascendancy which the III Corps had thus far maintained over the enemy appeared to be threatened by the offensive preparations of the enemy in the front of the 6th Division . . . Since it seemed to make little difference where the enemy's westward movement was

[1] *On War*, bk. I, ch. 3.
[2] Battles of Gravelotte-St. Privat, Franco-Prussian War.

stopped, provided it was stopped, a retirement was proposed and considered. But the idea of leaving the battlefield with our wounded in the hands of the enemy was intolerable . . . To give up the initiative would also have risked the outcome of the whole day's battle, a peril in comparison with which minor risks became insignificant. I decided, therefore, to attack again before the enemy could do so; this time with cavalry, for the 6th Division was so weakened and exhausted that nothing more could be expected of it."

This decision occasioned the famous charge of Bredow's cavalry brigade, which gained a little relief for the hard-

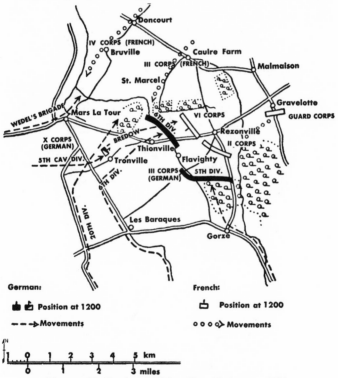

FIGURE 22. Battle of Thionville, 16 August 1870.

pressed left wing of the infantry north of Thionville, and checked the advance of the French. The arrival of the German X Corps on the left of the III gave further relief, and in spite of a few counterattacks both corps succeeded in holding their ground.

The superior range of the Chassepot rifle[3] had been reported to the Germans before the war; but only on the battlefield itself was it possible to really understand the destructive effect of this weapon, particularly the hail of lead it made possible, which was almost as heavy as in our own times [1911]. This Chassepot fire beat upon our III Corps furiously, but fortunately the infantry that day was excellently supported by skilfully handled artillery. Since the situation called for holding a greatly superior enemy our commanders had no choice but to bring the attack up to the effective range of our needle gun [600-700 yards].

General von Pape at St. Privat

At St. Privat on 18 August the 1st Guard Division was not so fortunate as the III Corps. Difficulties of various kinds in this battle prevented proper coordination between the infantry and artillery.

When General von Pape whose 1st Guard Division was assembled at St. Marie was ordered by the commander of the Guard Corps to attack St. Privat on and north of the highway he pointed out the difficulty of such an attack. First the attack had to be made up a perfectly open glacis. Second the strongly built village of St. Privat had not yet been taken under artillery fire and the enemy there were entirely unshaken. Third the Saxons who were to envelop the enemy's right were still far behind. The 4th Guard Infantry Brigade, however, was already advancing south of the highway and the order stood. Under a withering fire from front and flank, the 1st Guard Brigade crossed the highway and deployed north of it facing St. Privat. After heavy losses, the two regiments succeeded in advancing to within 500 or 600

[3] Effective up to 1,300 yards. This rifle was greatly superior to the German needle gun in rapidity of fire, flatness of trajectory, and penetration.

meters of the village, where they formed a single skirmish line with their right flank about 600 meters north of the highway. The division commander then sent the 2d Guard Regiment into the gap between the 4th and the 1st Guard Brigades; and this regiment also worked forward toward the enemy. The 4th Guard Regiment then came into line on

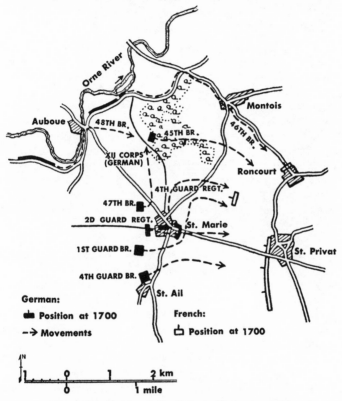

FIGURE 23. Battle of St. Privat, 18 August 1870.

the left of the 1st Guard Brigade, which was bent back toward Roncourt. This regiment was able to make its initial deployment under cover, in a ravine running from St. Marie to the Orne, and thus reached the firing line with much smaller losses than the other regiments of the division suffered.

Most of the losses occurred during the advance to the fire position just indicated, up the St. Privat glacis. They were, for 18 August—

> 1st Guard Regiment, 36 officers, 1056 men.
> 2d Guard Regiment, 36 officers, 1060 men.
> 3d Guard Regiment, 39 officers, 1076 men.
> 4th Guard Regiment, 29 officers, 524 men.

The gallant Guard battalions succeeded in establishing themselves on the St. Privat glacis at needle-gun range, and partly enveloping the village, but their offensive power was practically exhausted. The enemy, however, was also badly shaken, and when envelopment by the Saxons finally became imminent, and the artillery had an opportunity to fire briefly on St. Privat, the strong point of the enemy's right, the remnants of the Guard skirmish lines were able to make a decisive attack upon the village. The effect of the uninterrupted hostile fire during the advance of these battalions is graphically described in volume V, *Studies on Military History and Tactics,* from the recollections of General von Kessel, commanding the 1st Guard Brigade, and other eye-witnesses: "Both skirmishers and formed bodies often had to halt and lie down to get their breath, but they always sprang up again at the word of command. Each man marched stooping over, with his face turned to one side, as if to protect himself against a hailstorm; the expression of their faces was almost unrecognizable. All trumpets sounded and drums beat. General von Kessel continually shouted forward." This quotation shows how severely the nerve of a leader is tested in a modern battle which lasts for hours. Both at Thionville and St. Privat "the men's energy began to fail," and the inertia of the whole mass bore down more and more heavily on the shoulders of the commanders.

Defeat and Length of Modern Battle Impose Added Strains

A burden far heavier than that of the fiercest offensive

battle, however, has to be borne by the leader when the battle takes an unfavorable turn. Sheer tragedy is his lot when he can no longer rekindle enthusiasm and reinstill hope in all others by the fire in his own heart, by the strength of his own determination; when he can no longer maintain his ascendancy over the masses and remain their master.

The first attack of the Prussians against the right of the French army at Waterloo, was temporarily checked at 1900, and Napoleon sent in his last reserve, ten battalions of the Guard, for a decisive attack upon Wellington's left. When this last effort to turn the fortunes of the day had failed, when these picked troops whose eagles bore the tradition of invincibility had fallen back, the Emperor cried at last, "C'est fini." This expression showed that the moment had come "when the weight of the mass had dragged him down to its own level, to the depths of mere animal nature, which flinches from danger and knows no shame."

When, at Koeniggraetz, the Austrian Army of the North broke under the pressure of the Prussian double envelopment, Benedek left the battlefield with the last organized infantry brigade, which had been designated as support for the cavalry divisions left to cover the retreat. In passing, he rode through the long lines of artillery, posed to check the Prussian pursuit; and, with what little was left of his staff, exposed himself coolly to danger. "Never in all his campaigns had he looked more boldly into the face of death. When he was asked later if he purposely exposed himself to fire, he denied it, saying, 'I never thought of myself at all, only of my men.' "[4]

Effect of Decisive Battles on Men and Leaders

The following words of Clausewitz apply to all great decisive battles:

> ". . . The morale of the defeated party always falls below its original level farther than the morale of the victor rises above it. Hence, when we speak of the moral effect of victory, we generally have

[4] Friedjung, *The Struggle for the Hegemony of Germany.*

in mind the morale of the defeated force. This effect is more pronounced in a large engagement than in a smaller one, and overwhelming in a great decisive battle. The decisive battle is fought for a specific purpose— to obtain victory at that spot, a victory that must be won there at all costs. All prior sacrifices and hardships are endured for its sake. It is a winner-take-all effort, and the hopes of the present and future hinge on its outcome. With stakes so momentous, it is no wonder the decisive battle is a time of extreme tension not only for the commander, but for the last driver in the train.

"Decisive battles actually are never unprepared and unforeseen. They may be forced suddenly, and at a place not exactly of either side's choosing, but as soon as the stakes are apparent, both sides commit everything they have to win, and the fight quickly passes beyond the commonplace and increases the tension of everyone."[5]

Higher Commanders Must Not Lose Sight of Battle as a Whole

Defeat in a decisive battle weighs most heavily upon the commanding general himself. The load which his courage and determination must carry increases with the masses involved. His strength must be equal to the burden of his high office. This was not the case with the unfortunate commander of the Austrian Army of the North, as was shown at Koeniggraetz. Instead of continuing to the last to bear the burden of his position, he threw himself into the fight and left his corps commanders without orders for the retreat. Blucher too was wrong when as commander in chief at Ligny he allowed his hot temper to control, and joined in the cavalry charge in the evening. Higher commanders, especially commanders in chief, must restrain themselves if they are to retain their broad concept of the whole situation. A commander who goes personally into the frontlines is likely to be overimpressed by the requirements of one area and lose sight of the needs of the battle as a whole. Napoleon

[5] *On War*, bk. IV, ch. 10.

understood the importance of this detached attitude perfectly. At Bautzen he sat quietly on a camp chair and remained deaf to all calls for help from his hard-pressed right; for he intended to strike the principal blow by an enveloping movement by Marshal Ney.

It is easy to understand how men like Blucher and Benedek would seek to relieve their feelings by personal participation in the action. General Kuropatkin, too, often exposed himself to imminent danger in critical situations, as at Mukden. Even his severest critics have never found any fault with his personal conduct under fire. We honor the instinctive soldierly feeling of these men, which brought them under hostile fire at such moments. To expect the commander to remain cool and reserved in such a situation is asking for a superhuman effort; for as Clausewitz says,

> "The feeling of defeat is not a figment of the imagination which one may control. It is a clear realization of the fact that the enemy is superior for reasons which were previously unforeseen, but which now have become clearly evident in the results of the action. The enemy's superiority might have been recognized as possible beforehand. Yet in the absence of proof there was every reason to believe this was not so, that good fortune, foresight, and unhesitating boldness would enable us to prevail. Now truth stares us in the face. Our great faith stands betrayed, our supreme, heroic sacrifices are revealed as fruitless. Now no one cares much what happens outside the army, to the people and the government. There is a sudden collapse of all hopes, a breaking down of all self-confidence. Instead of working energetically together to stem the tide, each man fears that his efforts will be useless, hesitates where he should hasten, or lowers his arms in despair and leaves everything to fate."[6]

We make no mistake in assuming that Clausewitz had

[6] *On War*, bk. IV, ch. 10.

the collapse of Prussia in 1806[7] in mind when he wrote the above words. Where a whole governmental system collapses at once, as was the case with old Prussia, the effect of great defeats will always be the same. France in 1870[8] illustrated this point again.

In these days of universal military service [1911], where everyone has a direct tie with the battle, the results of a decisive defeat may be the same without a complete collapse of the governmental system. The first blow could decide the ultimate result, and all subsequent sacrifices, such as those made by France in the second period of the war of 1870-71, may well be in vain.

Wars of Complete Annihilation Not Possible

The sacrifice of human life is much less likely to prevent a long war, than the economic difficulties a civilized country experiences in such a war. The expression "war of annihilation" can be used only in a relative sense. Clausewitz calls our attention to this fact when he says: "Savage as may be the nature of war, it lies within the sphere of human weakness";[9] and "War assumes human weakness, and is directed against it."[10]

Resistance to the last, by any state, is almost unknown to modern history [1911]. The American Civil War is the only exception. In the end, the Confederacy fought a war of desperation. Army and people were lumped together, and all were looked upon by the Union as rebels. There was no possibility of negotiation or of compromise, as there always is in a war between two separate nations. Victory or destruction were the only alternatives and this dilemma was clearly understood by all Southerners.

If a modern civilized state cannot resist to the last, the results of the first great battle assume tremendous importance.

---

[7] Following the defeat of Prussia in the Battle of Jena, Napoleon imposed so many restrictions on this country that its government virtually ceased to govern.
[8] After the defeat of the French armies in 1870, Emperor Napoleon III, a nephew of the great military leader, was overthrown and France again became a republic (Third Republic).
[9] *On War*, bk. III, ch. 16.
[10] *On War*, bk. IV, ch. 10.

As a consequence, both sides will endeavor to be as strong as possible at the outset. Developing into a "nation in arms" is the only means by which a resolute and honorable people can provide for further resistance and influence the fortunes of war. Droysen [German historian] discerningly remarks that while the fortunes of war are not the only controlling element in the fate of nations, defeat in a war for existence shows flaws or weaknesses which history cannot pardon. But where there is a sound foundation, where the motives for action are just, a temporary misfortune in the life of a nation may be corrected, as in the life of an individual. Droysen goes on to say:

> "Riches, material possessions, numbers are not the only things that count; there are other non-physical elements which may bring victory—the education of the people; order and subordination, which give form to the mass; discipline, which renders the mass utilizable and which, even in misfortune, enables it to have confidence in itself; emulation of noble lives, which strengthens the spirit; determination, which controls all; and intellectual power, which directs toward the desired goal."[11]

This is as true in our days [1911] as in those of Hohen Friedberg, for which the words were written; for the power of personality, rooted in strength of character, is as effective now as in Frederick's day. This is our reason to model ourselves after Frederick, of whom it has been so aptly said:

> "When Gneisenau studied men to see if their spirit was capable of 'elevation,' it seemed that Frederick's spirit had attained the zenith of its influence. Frederick possessed and worked with an inexhaustible determination; and as Fichte said, it is this and not strength in arms that wins victories. It was this strength of mind that supported Frederick in his deepest misfortunes, caused him to rise higher than ever under

[11] Droysen, *Frederick the Great*.

adversity, and gave him his claim to the title 'The Great.' The story of Frederick's misfortunes illustrates a poet's description of destiny, as that which exalts a man although it crushes him."[12]

Clausewitz's Four Classes of Men

According to Clausewitz, "Differences in mental abilities are closely related to the relative physical strengths of human organisms; these differences are exposed by the nervous system, which connects the physical and mental elements of man."[13] From this point of view he goes on to set up four classes of men.

"First is the phlegmatic and indolent. Their equilibrium is not easly disturbed; but one can hardly call this 'determination' since there is no opportunity for any external manifestation of power. Such men, however, from their very stolidity, have a certain one-sided value in war. They often lack energy and activity, but they are very seldom total failures.

"The second class are either excitable men whose feelings never reach a great intensity, or calm, sensitive men. Both are readily moved to action by small circumstances, but they cannot control great affairs. Although in war they lack neither activity nor solidity, they can accomplish nothing really great.

"In the third category are highly excitable men, whose feelings flare up quickly, like powder, but do not continue. Such a temperament is in itself ill adapted to practical life in peace or war. Its impulses are strong but transient. But if in such men their excitability is combined with courage and ambition, they may accomplish valuable results in the lower grades, since the specific actions called for in the lower grades are naturally of short duration. At this level, a single bold decision or a psychological gesture is often sufficient to change the outcome of a battlefield action.

---

[12] Koser, *Frederick the Great.*
[13] *On War*, bk. I, ch. 3.

"Men with such swiftly changing feelings, however, find it difficult to keep their equilibrium, and are inclined to lose their heads, which is one of their worst failings in war. But it would be contrary to all experience to say that such excitable temperaments are never strong—that is, that they never retain their equilibrium in spite of excitement. While men of this type generally lack confidence in themselves initially, they can through study, training, and experience acquire a form of self-confidence, which they can call to their aid in crucial moments."

A sharp distinction between classes of men, as indicated by Clausewitz, is of course out of the question, since it may often be doubtful in which class a particular man belongs. Clausewitz himself says that it is contrary to all experience to say that excitable natures may not even in their excitement maintain their equilibrium. If the proper counterpoise can be found through training, self-study, and experience, men of this class are hardly distinguishable from those of the fourth class; that is, those who "are not readily moved by small matters, and who are not to be set in motion suddenly, but only gradually, whose emotions are powerful and lasting. Their feelings are strong, but lie deeply concealed. Such men are to the other classes as a glow is to a flame; they have the power of Titans to move massive weights, which may be likened to military difficulties."

Excitable Natures Valuable in Secondary Positions in War

The element of genius which overcomes military difficulties is clearness of thought, which highly excitable natures seldom possess. Such men, however, often accomplish great things in war, especially in a secondary position. Clausewitz describes General Yorck, the famous commander of the Prussian I Corps in the Wars of Liberation, this way:

"A strong, passionate will, which he concealed under an appearance of coldness; great ambition, which he concealed under an apparent reserve; and a strong, bold character. General Yorck was an upright, honorable man, but he was surly and obstinate, and so made a poor subordinate. . . . He was unquestionably one of the most distinguished men of our [Prussian] army. Scharnhorst, who appreciated his capabilities at a time when so few showed themselves capable and appreciated him all the more because he hated the French, always tried to keep on friendly terms with him, although Yorck always had a thinly concealed dislike for Scharnhorst. From time to time, this dislike almost showed itself actively; but Scharnhorst always acted as if he did not notice it, and used Yorck wherever a man of his type could be useful."[14]

Yorck showed himself a particularly poor subordinate in the campaigns of 1813 and 1814. Sometimes he carried his opposition to the command of the Army of Silesia to the point of open disobedience, but Blucher and Gneisenau overlooked it for the good of the country. They knew that from a patriotic point of view they could count upon "the old grumbler," the hero of Wartenburg.

Buelow, the commander of the Prussian III Corps, also had a fiery temper, and was often at odds with his superiors. At times his anger against them was so violent he would tear the buttons from his uniform while pacing up and down in his room. But he was still living verification of Clausewitz's belief that such men as a rule are to be classed among the nobler natures; for harsh as he was, he was frank and generous in the highest degree. It was fortunate for the allies that he held command of the III Corps, for otherwise, considering Bernadotte's conduct of operations, the Corps would not have won the victories of Gross Beeren and Deenewitz.[15]

Excitable Natures Difficult to Deal with in Peace

In time of peace such excitable natures are hard to deal with, either as superiors or subordinates; but if they really

[14] Clausewitz, *Russian Campaign of 1812.*
[15] German cities near Berlin. Marshal Ney was defeated at Deenewitz and French Marshal Oudinot at Gross Beeren, both in the summer of 1813.

possess skill and desirable qualities of character it is best to ignore their peculiarities so long as no actual damage is being done, and to take Scharnhorst's attitude toward Yorck as our model. Moreover, since the levelling tendencies of peace do not favor the development of strong personalities, it is best not to discourage such development when it appears, but direct it instead into proper channels.

The tensions of our times also should lead us to study ourselves carefully as the most effective means of strengthening our minds and making ourselves like those "whose feelings are strong, but deeply concealed." Evenness of temper, natural or acquired, is of the greatest importance in war, and may often make up for the absence of other qualities. Clausewitz tells how the Russian commander in chief at Valoutina-Gora,[16] in 1812, displayed in this battle "his best quality, a quality which alone would have justified his appointment to a high command—that is, great calmness, firmness, and bravery."[17]

Summarizing the ideal leader, Clausewitz says: "When we must in war entrust the safety of our brothers and children and the honor and safety of our country to some leader, we prefer to find the critical rather than the creative intellect, the broad rather than the narrow mind, the cool rather than the hot head."[18]

[16] General Barclay de Tolley.
[17] *Russian Campaign of 1812.*
[18] *On War,* bk. I, ch. 3.

CHAPTER 8

No One Can Be a Leader in War Without Strength of Character

> "One must believe strongly in the value of well-tested principles, and remember that momentary impressions, however strong, are unreliable. Then when we are tempted to doubt the correctness of our decisions, our faith in these principles and our engrained distrust of transitory sensations will help us hold fast to basically sound decisions, and our actions will thereby gain that steadfastness and consistency we call 'character'."
>
> —Clausewitz, *On War,* book I, chapter 3

"B Y THE EXPRESSION 'strength of character,' or simply 'character,' we mean a firm adherence to one's convictions, whether those convictions are the result of one's own reasoning or another's, and whether they are classed as principles, opinions, or aspirations of the moment. The expression can be applied only to those who stand by their convictions. A man who continually changes his mind does not have character."[1]

"He who understands the nature of a decision in practical affairs, especially in war where it must be made under the pressure of great responsibility and in the midst of a thousand uncertainties and contradictions, will appreciate that decisions cannot be made without many doubts; and what may seem a very simple problem often cannot be decided without the exercise of great determination. Conceiving plans for military operations is therefore the easiest part of a planning task, although to succeed the plan must of course be sound."[2]

Strength of Will Especially Important in Utilizing Staff Advice

The preponderance which Clausewitz gives to the de-

[1] *On War,* bk. I, ch. 3.
[2] Clausewitz, *Campaign of 1799 in Italy and Switzerland.*

termination to go ahead with a plan, as compared with the plan's conception, explains why he defines determination or strength of character as holding fast to a conviction, even though the subject of the conviction may have been suggested by another. Theodore von Bernhardi expresses much the same idea in speaking of Prince Schwartzenberg, commander in chief of the allies in the campaigns of 1813 and 1814.

> "He was not a general in the true sense of the word, for he required guidance. But we must repeat that it is far more important than is commonly supposed for a man to be capable of being guided consistently in a given direction. This takes a firmness and certainty on the part of the one guided, which only a few men possess. If a general who is already in doubt listens to too many counsels, he is likely to become even more uncertain and end up in a position where he can form no coherent judgment, no conviction, and therefore no decision."[3]

Moltke's famous comment on the organization of headquarters is in the same vein:

> "There are generals who need no advice; who judge and decide for themselves, and their staffs merely execute orders. Such generals are stars of the first magnitude, appearing only once in a century. In most cases, commanders of armies feel the need of advice. This can be given in conferences attended by large or small groups of men whose training and experience qualifies them to give expert judgment. But at the conclusion of such a conference, a single opinion should prevail to facilitate the infinitely more difficult task of deciding to execute the proposed plan. This responsibility rests solely upon the commander."[4]

[3] Memoirs of General Count von Toll.
[9] Von Moltke, *Italian Campaign of 1859*, ed. 1904.

Commander's Deficiencies Cannot be Corrected by Chief of Staff

Archduke Albert of Austria, the victor of Custozza, made a similar comment upon the personal responsibility of the commander. He said:

"It has sometimes been thought that the defects of an army commander, such as inexperience, inadequate training, weakness of character, may be made good by assigning an exceptionally qualified man as chief of staff. Experience, however, has shown that these attempts invariably fail. Why the experiment has been tried so often through history calls for study.

"All men have some weak points and the more vigorous and brilliant a person may be, the more strongly these weak points stand out. It is highly desirable, even essential, therefore, for the more influential members of a general's staff not to be too much like the general, or the shadows will be even more distinct. Ideally, the general and his principal assistants should in a sense supplement one another. Such a mutually supplementary relationship, however, produces desirable results only when the general himself is fully qualified for his office in all professional respects. Mutual supplementation is often misinterpreted, however, to mean that a lack of some indispensable quality in the general may be compensated for by some special talents in the chief of staff. This is a dangerous error.

"As illustrations of complementary personalities, we usually think of Radetzky and Hess, Blucher and Gneisenau. But it should not be forgotten that Radetzky, a general in the fullest sense of the word, was over eighty years old at the time of the campaigns of 1848-49, and hence required some support, both physical and mental. For this there could be none equal to his old confidant Hess—a noble, self-sacrificing, devoted, and modest character, thoroughly competent for this work.

"Blucher, although he was much younger and more

vigorous at the time of the Wars of Liberation than Radetzky was in 1848, was of limited education; but he had great experience in war, clear insight, sound knowledge of men, great perseverance, and an iron will that could not be shaken by any difficulties. He was no mere thrusting trooper; and his deficiencies could be fully compensated for by the highly qualified and modest Gneisenau. There can be no doubt that these famous chiefs of staff could not have made full use of their brilliant qualities had they served with officers without moral authority, accessible to irresponsible and incompetent influences, instead of with highly talented generals.

"There are things that no one can give to the general, if he does not possess them himself. If he does not have the independence of mind to select the most appropriate course from among the many that are possible, if he lacks the firmness to carry out his decision, and under all conditions to maintain obedience and discipline in his army; then no one can help him."

In Frederick the Great's time, there was no position equivalent to our [German Army] chief of staff. But the King expressed the same idea as Clausewitz and Moltke when he said:

"I believe that a general who receives good advice from a subordinate officer should profit by it. Any patriotic servant of the state should forget himself when in that service, and look only to the interests of the state. In particular, he must not let the source of an idea influence him. Ideas of others can be as valuable as his own and should be judged only by the results they are likely to produce."[5]

Great Leaders Have No Fear of Responsibility

Even the best chief of staff cannot bear the responsibilities of the general. Where the general is also the monarch, he is responsible only to his own conscience; but in every other

[5] Frederick the Great, *General Principles of War.*

case he is a subordinate responsible to a human superior.
If he is to perform successfully in action he must have no
fear of this responsibility. This is a quality possessed only
by strong characters who have no fear of men. In this respect, Blucher is the incomparable model. His unreserved
acceptance of responsibility is his most commendable quality,
which makes him great despite the fact that the operational
ideas for the Army of Silesia originated with Gneisenau.
Blucher had not the slightest fear of Napoleon, whose approach terrified other allied generals; and in his dealings
with his own king, his allies, and the commander in chief,
Prince Schwartzenberg, he never hesitated to be frank.

Blucher opposed the idea of taking the bulk of the Army
of Silesia into Bohemia to reinforce the allied main army
after its unsuccessful thrust toward Dresden.[6] The independence which he thus maintained he used later, marching
his army on his own initiative from Upper Lusatia to the
Elbe. Here he forced the crossing of the river at Wartenburg and enabled the allied Army of the North to cross at
Roslau and Aken. Blucher's independent action furnished
the impetus for the final decisive advance of the allies which
in turn led to the defeat of Napoleon at Leipzig.

The allied main army took up its advance across the Erz
Mountains in the general direction of Leipzig. Napoleon left
a detachment to observe it, and early in October moved his
main body down the Mulde against the Army of Silesia and
the Army of the North. In conjunction with the commander
of the Army of the North, the Crown Prince of Sweden,
Blucher retired behind the Saale, and prevented a retreat
of the Crown Prince to the Elbe. For the second time in the
autumn campaign of 1813, Blucher cut loose entirely from
his communications. Although he commanded the weakest
of the three allied armies, he took it upon himself, by independent action, to determine the course of the campaign for
the others. In the same way in the 1814 campaign in France,
the Army of Silesia was the driving force in the conduct of
the war by the allies.

[6] Campaign of the Allies against Napoleon in 1813.

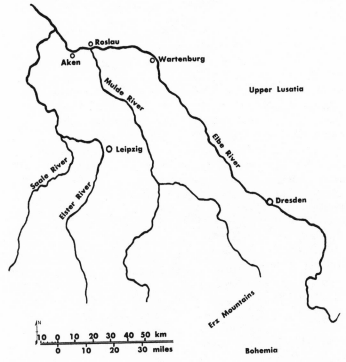

FIGURE 24. Area of Napoleon's Operations around Leipzig, October 1813.

Spirit of Initiative Must Not Be Lost in Times of Peace

The results obtained by Blucher's ready acceptance of responsibility, and his absolute frankness should spur efforts to develop and maintain initiative in our [German Army] officers during periods of peace. Initiative has always been one of our most distinguishing characteristics. To quote Frederick on this subject: "A general to whom the sovereign has entrusted his troops should act on his own initiative. The confidence which the sovereign reposes in the general's ability is authorization enough to conduct affairs in his own way."[7] The King continually demanded that his officers do things "on their own." We also owe most of our successes in 1870[8] to the ability of [German Army] commanders of all grades to act independently.

The [German Army] Field Service Regulations [of 1911], in keeping with this tradition, require "every officer, under all conditions, to exercise initiative to the maximum extent, without fear of the consequences. Commanding officers must encourage and require this." This requirement is especially important during long periods of peace, when the necessity for maintaining discipline has a tendency to discourage independent action. All commanding officers, especially the higher ones, must, as their duty, make every effort to develop initiative in their subordinates, and oppose indifference and routine service. They must also restrain their supervisory activities and avoid too frequent visits to troop instruction, which sometimes causes embarrassment.

The ill effects of a fear of responsibility were glaringly apparent in the action of the Russian commanders in the Manchurian war. Accustomed to working under orders which laid down what was to be done in minutest detail, they carried out their orders literally, exercised no initiative, and lost favorable opportunities for action. And in this war such opportunities occurred often in spite of the bravery of the Japanese.

Staff Must Be Given Opportunity to Exercise Initiative

Blucher required the assistance of Gneisenau; but, on the other hand, it was only because Blucher accepted responsibility fully and freely that his chief of staff could make full use of his own great talents. Gneisenau needed this freedom, for he was an exceptionally able organizer and inspiring individual himself.

Blucher not only granted freedom of action to his chief of staff, but to his other officers as well. Droysen shows us how sharply conditions at Blucher's headquarters contrasted with those at Yorck's.

[7] *General Principles of War.*
[8] Franco-Prussian War.

> "Blucher, entirely without jealousy, gave full freedom of action not only to Gneisenau but also to Muffling and even his junior officers, who vied with each other in independent action. Yorck, on the other hand, insisted upon rigid discipline and order. Each man was required to attend strictly to his own duties. One of his aides wrote that Yorck gave all the orders himself, and wanted nothing from his staff except reports and obedience. No one, from the highest to the lowest, had any influence upon him."

By granting this freedom of action, Blucher secured the highest quality of service from his staff. While he depended greatly upon his staff, nevertheless his deeds were his own and bear the unmistakable stamp of his will. Blucher, more than any other general, shows us that the distinguishing feature of a great soldier is a bold and ardent heart rather than a superior brand of cold, intellectual effort.

Suvorov possessed a unique personality. Clausewitz describes him this way:

> "If we overlook his affected eccentricities, he may be compared very closely with Blucher. In both men the subjective side of generalship was highly developed; but both lacked a clear insight into the objective world, and hence both needed advice and guidance . . . Suvorov was a man of fiery will, with great strength of character and excellent natural intelligence. He had passed through a hard school in the wars with the Turks. This training, however, did not fit him for conducting war against French armies, and his rough eccentricities often placed difficulties in the way of simple and logical solutions to problems which arise in wars between civilized peoples. Undoubtedly these eccentricities were intentionally assumed. His keen intelligence allowed them scope only on the surface and never permitted them to affect his serious decisions. We may assume that the Austrian general staff, whose chief was the distinguished General Chasteler, was of great assistance in handling the problems arising out of these

complexities of civilized warfare; but this does not detract in any way from Suvorov's brilliance.

"The most highly trained general staff, with the best of ideas and principles cannot guarantee good leadership in an army by itself. It must be backed by a great general who serves both as its leader and counterbalance, who from time to time prevents the staff from entangling itself in its own red tape. A good staff on the other hand is an indispensable aid for a general."[9]

Modern War Makes Trained Staff More Important Than Ever

A trained general staff is even more necessary to a commander today than when Clausewitz wrote, because of the greater masses of men involved in operations today. There is little danger that such a staff will, as with the opponents of Napoleon, "entangle itself in its own red tape"; but there is another danger which has resulted from the highly technical character of general staff training. This is the tendency to overemphasize detail. We must take care that the mass of minutiae required in modern-day planning does not overshadow the spirit of the operation itself, and cause us to judge the operation by the excellence or insufficiency of its staff work, rather than by its scope and daring, as we should. To use Boyen's words, we must see that "industry without talent is not unduly rewarded." There is no better way to prevent this than to study the leadership of great generals of the past and endeavor to follow the workings of their minds. Only in this way can we gain for ourselves some part of the insight and determination they possessed.

To Hold to Consistent Course of Action Difficult in War

To hold consistently to a plan once adopted is especially difficult in war. The great number of strong impressions that are made upon the mind, the uncertainty of all information and all conclusions, creates more of danger that a man may allow himself to be turned from his course and go astray than in any other human occupation.

[9] *Campaign of 1799.*

Clausewitz says:

"In the presence of danger and suffering, one's feelings can readily overcome one's intellectual convictions; and in the dim light by which everything is seen, clear insight becomes so difficult to maintain that vacillation appears natural and excusable. There is always a seeking and groping for the truth, upon which to base action, and for this reason, differences of opinion are never so great as in war. The stream of impressions eating at one's convictions never ceases. Even the greatest stability and determination cannot protect one completely, for these negative impressions are strong and vivid, and affect the mind almost unconsciously."[10]

Leaders With Strong Feelings Must Have Great Strength of Character

All this might lead us to believe that men of deep feeling are not fitted for serious military operations; and yet history shows us the contrary. In Frederick the Great we find "sentimentality, even to tears and a reveling in grief."[11] Like the King, Moltke and Lee were extremely kindhearted men in private life. But, like him also, they were able to master their feelings; and where the military purpose required it they could show that ruthlessness which is so essential in a real warrior. Deep as their feelings were, their minds kept their poise. "The great strength of character required to accomplish this is evident. Men of strong feeling, therefore, must also have great strength of character."[12]

Highly intellectual men, on the other hand, usually have little strength of character, and, generally, the greater the intellect the less the strength of character. The intellectual mind carefully arrays all the weaknesses of any situation side by side with all the strong points and leaves one irresolute.

Genius is, of course, an exception to all rules and is in a

[10] *On War*, bk. I, ch. 3.
[11] **Koser**, *Frederick the Great*.
[12] *On War*, bk. I, ch. 3.

category by itself, as we see from the personality of Frederick, whose versatility is unequalled among military men. The Comte de Segur, as quoted by Pierron, says very pertinently: "Tremendous intellect, plus a vast amount of good sense, coupled with great strength of character add up to genius. The first two of these characteristics make it possible to see the critical point in any affair; the third enables one to employ all his force to reach it."

Hold First Decision Until Positive Conviction Forces Change

Clear insight is not enough to prevent irresolution. Clear insight can help us chart an excellent course of action, but adhering to this course is another matter. As soon as a decision is made, and throughout the life of any plan based on that decision, a steady stream of ideas and events tending to refute the basis of the decision impinges on the leader's consciousness and weakens his determination. Often, too, a decision is made which cannot be justified by any accepted principle, and the urge to modify such a decision, no matter how well-thought-out it may have been, becomes particularly hard to resist. Remaining steadfast here calls for a vast amount of confidence in oneself, as well as a certain degree of skepticism. One's main help, as we have indicated previously, is faith in the time-tested principles used to frame the original decision, backed up by this maxim: In case of doubt, hold to your first decision, and make no change until positive conviction forces it.

Knowing When to Change Plans Also Important

By and large, adherence to one's first carefully calculated opinion is a proper and desirable action, but at times it may be carried too far. When Napoleon struck the advanced troops of the Army of Silesia in February 1814, who were then advancing in separated columns, the prudent course would have been to withdraw the separated corps across the Marne. In this way no definite objective would have been offered to Napoleon, and the junction of the separated corps could have been effected behind the Marne. During the previous autumn, the Army of Silesia had always been able to avoid serious danger by well-timed withdrawals; but here a different course was taken. Yorck and Sacken had orders to make their way to Vertus by the southern Paris road. When Olzuvieff was beaten at Champaubert, and nothing was heard from Sacken and Yorck, the corps of Kleist and Kapzevich were held at Vertus until the situation could be cleared up. Napoleon, when he turned from Champaubert toward Mont-mirail, had left Marmont with 5,000 men at Etoges to watch Blucher; but no attack was made upon Marmont, and the two rear corps were not brought back behind the Marne.

Clearly the original plan was adhered to too long; although Blucher and Gneisenau were probably justified after a long series of victories in taking more chances than at the beginning of the campaign. They were understandably reluctant to retire voluntarily behind the Marne and give up their march upon Paris. They had just beaten the enemy at La Rothiere, and too great caution would mean surrendering the fruits of that victory. This undoubtedly led them to feel they were justified in continuing the original plan, but at a little slower pace.

The opportunity for making the concentration behind the Marne that the situation actually required was lost. But again we must remember that the situation for a commander in the field is never as clear as it is to us after the event when we know the exact situation on both sides. This delay on the 11th and 12th was an error on Marshal Blucher's part; but in the uncertain situation that faced him, most generals would have done the same thing.

Clinging Too Closely to Original Decision Lesser of Two Evils

While one will not always be justified in clinging too closely to one's original decision, the errors involved in such action are usually small compared with the benefits that generally result from it. An illustration in point is the attitude of Blucher and his advisers, Gneisenau and Grolman, after the Battle of Ligny.

The first three corps of the Prussian army were beaten there on 15 June 1815 by Napoleon's main army. The fourth corps, under Buelow, was still on the march up from Liege. On this same day, Ney, with the separated left wing of the French forces, had fought a drawn battle at Quatre Bras with the leading elements of Wellington's army. Napoleon assumed that the Prussians, although during the battle they naturally fell back in the direction of the attack upon them; that is, northward, would immediately attempt to regain their natural line of communications which led down the Meuse to the lower Rhine. This would have given him complete

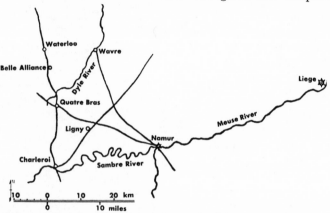

FIGURE 25. Area of Marshal Blucher's Operations in Belgium, 15-18 June 1815.

freedom to turn his main forces against Wellington. His whole plan of campaign depended upon separating the allies, and it seemed after the Prussians at Ligny had been compelled to abandon the field that he would succeed. During the 17th, however, the Prussian army concentrated at Wavre, and it was not until the 18th that a pursuing French column under Marshal Grouchy regained contact with it there.

> "Blucher had given up his natural line of retreat in order to keep in touch with the Duke of Wellington. Although the first battle had been more or less a failure, he was determined to attempt another, and informed

the Duke of Wellington that he was coming to his assistance with his whole army. This decision of Blucher's deserves the highest praise. Contrary to all expectations, and all established rules and techniques, but following his own sound common sense, he decided to join Wellington on the 18th and if necessary to go outside his own boundaries rather than do things half way."[13]

This adherence to the controlling idea of the campaign, which was a joint operation with Wellington's army, was crowned with the complete success at Waterloo.

Stubbornness a Perversion of Strength of Character

Stubbornness is classed by Clausewitz as a perversion of determination: "It is often difficult to tell, in a concrete case, where one leaves off and the other begins; but it is not difficult to explain the difference in theory. Stubbornness is a defect of temperament. It is an inflexibility of will, a resistance to outside influence fathered by a special type of egotism which delights in exhibiting intellectual superiority.

"Stubbornness actually might be called a form of vanity, although it is something more than that. Vanity, for example, is content with appearance, stubbornness goes deeper. Stubbornness also is not a mere excess of determination, for there are stubborn men who, for lack of intelligence, have little genuine determination."[14]

Stubbornness often results from a certain narrowness of mind, which views the relinquishment of any of its own ideas as a weakness. It is sometimes found in men of the highest attainments. Its presence at this level, however, is due largely to their ingrained habit of assuming the superiority of their views.

Suvorov, along with the most ruthless military determination, showed a great sensitiveness and a great stubbornness. His pleasure in his victories in Italy, gained with the assistance of Austrian troops, was marred by the general feeling that his conduct of affairs was influenced by the court of Vienna, in which political views he did not concur. The

[13] Clausewitz, *Campaign of 1815.*
[14] *On War*, bk. I, ch. 3.

nature of his reports on this situation to Czar Paul tended to weaken the coalition.

Suvorov's stubbornness manifested itself not only in the strategic handling of the army, but in its tactical operations on the battlefield as well. The Battle of Novi[15] opened under conditions which he had not foreseen. Kray's Austrian Corps became heavily engaged and was hard-pressed for several hours. Its commander sent one officer after another to ask the Russians' assistance, but without success. Their generals dared not move without orders from the Marshal; but he had shut himself up in his quarters and had given orders that he was not to be disturbed on any account. It took a long time to secure Russian help.

Stubbornness Leads to Lost Opportunities

Stubbornness, too, may sometimes cause a general to miss golden opportunities.

In February 1814, Yorck's Corps was marching in second line, echeloned to the right and rear of Sacken's. It had reached Chateau Thierry when Napoleon's attack from Sezanne was made. Yorck estimated the danger more correctly than the army commander, who was farther to the rear, and proposed a junction with Sacken behind the Marne. At army headquarters, it was correctly estimated that Yorck and Sacken together outnumbered Napoleon, 30,000 to 20,000; and for this reason the two corps were ordered to join on the left bank of the Marne at Montmirail, and then to break through to Etoges. Yorck adhered obstinately to his own view, and took only half measures to carry out these orders. Knowing that Sacken was turning back toward Montmirail, he did not support him with all his force, but merely made dispositions to receive the Russian corps after its defeat, and enable it to cross the river at Chateau Thierry. This enabled Napoleon to defeat the two corps separately, and throw them back across the Marne with heavy loss. Von Bernhardi was right when he said:

[15] City in northern Italy, site of an early Napoleonic battle between the Austrians (assisted by the Russians) and the French.

"Among the many effici-
ent commanders in the Prussian Army at that time,
Yorck was one of the best—perhaps the very best in
handling troops on the battlefield; but he was discon-
tented, and believed himself entitled to a higher position. Here at the Marne a rare opportunity was offered
him to place himself in the very first rank of army commanders, and by independent action to strike Napoleon
a crushing blow—but he did not see the crown of glory
prepared for him."

CHAPTER 9

The Essence of Military Personality

> "The military virtues are for all individuals what the genius of the general is for the whole army."
> —Clausewitz, *On War,* book III, chapter 5
> "Military genius is a harmonious blending of forces."
> —Clausewitz, *On War,* book I, chapter 3

CLAUSEWITZ here uses the term "military virtues" to classify habits and traits of character that make soldiers successful. He says:

> "War is a separate activity, distinctly different from other human activities. To be thoroughly imbued with the requirements of this activity; to implant and develop within oneself the abilities that are demanded by it; to acquire an intellectual appreciation of it; to gain ease and certainty in it by practice; and to completely reconcile oneself to the duties involved in it— these are the military virtues of the individual.

> "Widely as national wars may differ from the campaigns of the old condottieri, nevertheless those who follow the trade of war come to look upon themselves as a sort of guild in whose ordinances, laws, and customs the military spirit is incarnated. One who is seeking a profound understanding of the fundamentals of war, therefore, must understand *esprit de corps*. This spirit is the cement which binds together all qualities which taken together give an army military value. In the presence of this spirit, the military qualities also unite more freely. What has been accomplished in the past by this combination of qualities which gives solidity to the army, which refines crude ore into brilliant metal, is illustrated by the Macedonians under Alexander, the Roman legions under Caesar, the Spanish infantry under Alexander Farnese (Duke of Parma), the Swedes under Gustavus Adolphus and Charles XII, the Prussians under Frederick the Great, and the French under

Napoleon. We would be ignoring history if we failed
to see that the successes of these leaders and their greatness in overcoming difficult situations would have been
impossible with anything but an army of this stamp."[1]

These words of Clausewitz present the value of military
esprit de corps in a very clear light. To ignore or underrate
its importance is to disregard the teachings of history. De-
preciation of the so-called "military caste spirit" is largely
the work of those who wish to destroy the *esprit de corps*
of the army because it is the strongest possible protection
against their designs.

Volunteer and Mercenary Armies Lack Esprit de Corps of Nation in Arms

Perversions of this spirit inconsistent with the nature of
universal service should of course be eliminated, for the egotism and vanity of mercenary armies is not comparable to
the broadened ennobled spirit of the "nation in arms." The
French Imperial Army of 1870, with its system of substitu-
tions and its great number of men who had grown old in the
ranks, was an example of misdirected *esprit de corps*. It
fought with brilliant gallantry in the August battles, but its
egotism and vanity were all out of proportion to its real
value. Its corps of officers, too, especially in the higher
grades, was not up to requirements.

The British volunteer army failed at the outset of the
South African War when opposed by a civilized and equally
well-armed enemy. Although the difficulties encountered in
that theater of operations must not be overlooked, it is still
accurate to say that an army raised through universal service
would have done better against the Boers. A volunteer army
also must always be comparatively weak in numbers.

In dealing with civilized enemies, the defects of the volunteer army have always been conspicuous. They appeared
in the British army in the Crimea, as well as in South
Africa. A volunteer army cannot possess the spirit of a
"nation in arms" fighting for its existence. In a small, per-

[1] *On War*, bk. III, ch. 5.

manent army, which is not required to train large numbers
of universal service soldiers, the concept of war on a large
scale is soon lost, as was the case with the French Army in
1870. Sound military ideas also take root more readily in an
officers' corps which knows that the whole mass of the people
is behind it, and which is accustomed to work with the people
and to count upon them. It is only in a dynamic type of
service, where an officer can feel he is training his nation for
its defense, that he can develop that idealism he must have
if his service is not to grow monotonous during long periods
of peace, and if he is not to fall into dead routine which
Lloyd calls the worst of tyrants.

A trained "nation in arms" is the correct middle ground
between the professional army and the undisciplined mass
typified by the Boer forces. To such forces these words of
Clausewitz apply: "Men may fight gallantly like the Ven-
deans, and accomplish wonders like the Americans and the
Spanish, but still achieve nothing of military value, for it
takes accomplishments of value to give an army real
morale."[2] Morale did develop in the course of the war among
those Boer commandos which kept the field after the break-
up of the main armies and carried on guerrilla warfare under
bold leaders; but it was not present in the mass of the armies.

Spirit of an Army Different From Morale

Universal military service developed in Prussia from
necessity. With its help, the state atoned in 1813 for the
errors of 1806 and before. The qualities of military value
which existed in Frederick's army disappeared after his
death and only by making everyone a part of the defense
of the state could these qualities be re-instilled. While
strenuous discipline and training may help to maintain these
military virtues, they cannot create them.

> "These virtues come
> only through the development of a burning desire to
> see one's army and nation strong and respected. Order,
> skill, a certain pride, and high morale are highly prized

[2] *Ibid.*

peacetime qualities, but they provide no spur to excellence and sacrifice. Each of the former qualities depends upon the other; and, as with poorly tempered glass, the smallest crack may extend itself at once through the whole mass. The best morale in the world may, at the first reverse, readily turn into cowardice, and to an exaggeration of fear—the French 'suave qui peut.' Such an army may accomplish something through the character of its general, but nothing of itself. It must be led with the utmost of care, until, gradually, victory and exertion give it real strength, real fighting spirit. This spirit should not be confused with morale."[3]

Object of Training Should Be Early Victory in War

The first part of this quotation is an apt characterization of the Prussian army which was defeated at Jena; the latter part is borne out by the events on the French side in 1870. The armies that were beaten at Jena and at Sedan both fought gallantly; their misfortunes were due to faulty leadership and training. This should warn us to exert every effort to maintain a true military spirit in peacetime. Under present conditions [1911] we cannot be content with an army that "must be led with the greatest of care," and whose morale is easily broken. We cannot wait until "gradually, victory and exertion have given it real strength." The first shot must find us strong enough to meet any emergency. We must have victory at once; hence we must prepare for it continually in time of peace and keep it firmly before us as the sole object of our training. Convinced of this necessity for immediate and complete victory, we will in any great national war have that vital inspiration "which enables us to do more than our military honor requires, and which makes us attempt the impossible if it will aid our cause."[4]

This inspiration is both the goal and justification for the profession of arms, which in our times should not be satisfied with outward personal military honors, but pride itself

---

[3] *Ibid.*
[4] Von Moltke, *The Italian Campaign of 1859*, ed. 1904.

instead on the extent it is able to instill the highest military virtues in its members and in the people as a whole.

Meaning of Honor to a Soldier

The moral significance of war is manifest in everything that appears in connection with it [not in it]. Wherever in human life a conflict arises, dealing with anything better than blind avarice or ferocity on both sides, wherever there is even the feeblest spark of what men call duty, there is always found that mysterious and exalted feeling called honor, with whose bitter sweetness nothing else that is human is comparable, since by comparison with it life itself has but a feather's weight of value. The sentiment of personal honor, of self-respect, which raises man above the conditions of ordinary life, is nothing else than a concentration of nobility in the individual. To the soldier, it appears as a sacred trust and a special prerogative. The soldier watches jealously over his honor, for he feels that it is the only thing that sets him above his caricature, the gladiator.

Pacifists seek to lower the soldier to this caricature, for they have no conception of true manhood. They have no understanding of the greatness of the sacrifice and suffering which war demands. Nor can they understand that there are men who can look upon a glorious death as the great achievement of their lives.

Moral Significance of War

Consciously or unconsciously, such a misunderstanding of the moral significance of war shows a failure to comprehend human character; it comes from a purely materialistic philosophy of life. The real foundation of the doctrine of eternal peace is nothing more than selfishness and love of comfort, hidden under a vague idealism. This tendency ignores entirely the fact that a much more wholesome idealism is to be found in accepting life as it is.

History teaches that nations which are not ready to defend their honor with arms invariably decline. It is fortunate, then, that whenever society turns to careless luxury, restrained by no moral considerations, there appears on the horizon that specter of political anxiety, that restorer of civic duty—war. Eternal peace would be an evil fate, for it could be purchased only at the price of man's noblest qualities and highest destinies.

Necessity for Developing and Maintaining Warlike Spirit

We should, then, be mindful of our duty to rouse and develop these noble qualities, and to guard against unwholesome sentimentality. "If bloody war is a horrible spectacle, it should admonish us to raise war to a higher plane, but not to blunt our own swords through false sentimentality; for there may come an enemy whose sword is still sharp."[5] World conditions are certainly not such today [1911] as to encourage us to think that armed conflicts between nations are a thing of the past. We have already seen in our own country [Germany], the effects of the deceitful doctrines of pacifism, now so widely disseminated, and we have been cruelly punished for it. The weak philanthropic theories which controlled the upper classes of our people in 1806 were largely responsible for the disasters of that year. Many of that generation had entirely lost their comprehension of real war, and of the real military character; but they remembered it again in the years of foreign domination.

Henrich von Treitschke strikingly characterizes the disaster of 1806, when he says we feel it even today in the midst of our glorious military history [1911] "like personal suffering." From this we should take warning to guard against those tendencies which lead away from the true objectives of our profession. Such tendencies manifest themselves in many ways. Sometimes they are hidden in clouds of pseudo-philosophy, where they weaken our sense of military duty, destroy our pleasure in our work, and even suggest to us that what we are working for is already obsolete.

[5] *On War,* bk. IV, ch. 11.

To guard against these influences there is no better protection than Clausewitz's vigorous ethics. His work is founded upon the experience of an age which saw the sudden fall and the immediate and astounding rise of our country. In 1813, Clausewitz saw universal service develop from the necessities of war. Our duty today is to maintain the valuable military qualities which grew up in our national army at that time, and which, three generations later, inspired us in three victorious wars. It is our duty to train this "nation in arms" for modern war. Hence we must strive to develop a singleness of purpose in this respect in spite of the disruptive tendencies of the times. Establishment of a national belief in the paramount necessity for victory in war should be our real purpose in life; for this conviction is the essence of a military character.

The methods we use to accomplish our great goal will be as different as the methods by which this conviction is established in different persons. Men like Scharnhorst, Gneisenau, Lee, Moltke, acquired the ability to inspire great effort and self-sacrifice in others by strict self-discipline and strong religious faith. The purity of their characters was so evident that they seemed to be the incarnation of the ideal leader formulated by Clausewitz. The religion of these men was the truest Christianity; and from this they drew that humility which made them strong against all difficulties.

Military Leaders Must Be Judged Largely by Results

Familiarity with combat often engenders a certain fatalism, which for many great soldiers becomes a substitute for religion. Life in war tends to harden men, and even in peace the environment in which a soldier spends his earlier years determines much of his character. Therefore greater allowances should be made for this than is sometimes done in judging military men. To judge Blucher, in whom the whole military spirit of our people was once incorporated, solely from a Philistine and moralist point of view would be a gross error. The rude life of the camp, in which Blucher delighted, was repugnant to his chief of staff,

Gneisenau. But he understood his chief, overlooked his minor weaknesses, and regarded only his great and heroic qualities. Like Gneisenau, we should render honor to great military virtues, even if within the man greatness is not fully attained in every respect.

The essential point is, and always must be, that a man shall give himself up wholly to a great cause; that he shall not seek to satisfy his vanity and achieve personal advantage. Regarded in this light, the effort to express one's own personality is not an object in itself; it is merely a means to prepare us for the one thing that measures the value of a man in war—that is, what he does in action.

SURPRISE

General Waldemar Erfurth

First Translation, 1943,
by
Dr. Stefan T. Possony
and
Daniel Vilfroy

CONTENTS

Translator's Comment

GENERAL Erfurth's book on "Surprise in War" is the first treatise on the importance of surprise in modern military literature. Surprise was considered as an essential element of victory by almost all ancient military writers. Frontinus and Polyaenus, for instance, had written a whole collection of ways and means of surprise—almost text books for victory. These books, especially Frontinus', were known to every military commander in the later period of antiquity and throughout the Middle Ages. Machiavelli, the founder of modern military science, heavily drew on Frontinus. During the eighteenth century, the problem of surprise again attracted the attention of military writers. The Chevalier de Cessac wrote an entire book on surprise. Frederick the Great never tired in advising his generals on the importance of surprise and declared that in war one should alternately don the skin of the lion and of the fox.

Yet the military school which began with Guibert and ended with the generals of World War I did not fully understand the role which surprise may play in war. For them, as Napoleon pointed out in a famous dictum, only one thing counted: mass. To be sure, almost every one of these military writers did mention surprise. Clausewitz himself, as can be seen from the quotations which General Erfurth faithfully collected, insisted on the importance of surprise. Occasionally surprise methods were applied on the battlefield.

Yet surprise was not considered as the basis of military planning nor as the *conditio sine qua non* of victory. Rather, it was considered as a welcome by-product which sometimes completed and facilitated victory. Surprise was luck, but not the result of strategy. The generals of the nineteenth and early twentieth century were more concerned with the problem of the inner and outer lines, with the principle of concentration which had been first formulated by Carnot, at a time when the role of surprise was almost completely forgotten. Later on, the attention· of military thinkers centered on the importance of the flank.

To assess the real value of General Erfurth's book, one must realize not only that it was written before the outbreak of World War II, but also that it amounts to a more or less complete break with traditional military thinking. To be sure, General Erfurth tries hard to prove that his ideas completely tally with the doctrines of Clausewitz, Moltke and Schlieffen. Yet, whatever his quotations may say, it is easy to realize that the doctrine of surprise and the doctrine of the flank attack, as propounded by Schlieffen, do not go together. Either surprise is "the key to victory" or the attack against the enemy's flank is. This does not mean that surprise and flank attacks cannot sometimes be combined. Yet it is obvious that surprise cannot, on principle, always and exclusively be achieved on the enemy's flank. If it is known *a priori* that whatever else one does, one attempts to launch a flank attack, obviously surprise can never be accomplished. After all, the enemy knows where his flanks are.

Where To Attack the Enemy

If we assume that the enemy can only be defeated by surprise operations, it is clear that he should not know where these operations are going to take place. A strategy which is based upon the principle of surprise can therefore not be bound by Schlieffen's doctrine. Instead, the general who relies on surprise must have a completely open mind as to whether he should attack on the flank or at the center or somewhere else. The strategy of surprise replaces the traditional principle: "Attack on the flank" by the broader and more general principle: "Attack wherever the enemy is off guard."

Besides, General Erfurth makes a rather loose use of the term "flank." The flank of a Roman legion or of Napoleon's army can hardly be compared to the flank of a modern army which usually rests upon the frontier of a neutral country or upon impenetrable terrain. It is hardly an exaggeration to say that, under modern condition of continental warfare, flanks in the traditional sense do not exist or do not offer any prospect for envelopment maneuvers. In modern war flanks are available only at bulges and wedges, but the sides of a wedge are not necessarily more vulnerable than its peak or other sectors of the front.

As a matter of fact, modern strategy, including German strategy, has liberated itself from the dogma of the flank.

General Wetzell, Ludendorff's Chief-of-operations, writes: "The enemy is not necessarily weakest on his flanks, nor will he make most of his mistakes on the wings. His weakness and his errors may occur at other places. The main condition of success is to discover weaknesses and errors wherever they are" and to attack the enemy wherever he is weak and whenever he has committed an error.

"It is remarkable," Wetzell continues, "that Field Marshal Count von Schlieffen in his war games of 1904 and 1905 soon discontinued his flanking attack through Belgium in order to exploit mistakes which had been committed by the enemy. After discovering the enemy's mistakes, he immediately regrouped his entire forces and tried to decide the war by partial victories west and east of the Moselle, and renounced seeking the decision in Belgium and northern France. There is a tendency to overrate the importance of envelopment and flanking attacks. Instead, one should do what Schlieffen himself did: exploit the mistakes of the enemy."

In other words, there is a difference between Schlieffen the theoretician and Schlieffen the soldier. The soldier Schlieffen was a pupil of Moltke and the Germans, on the whole, are going back to Moltke's concept: "Strategy is a system of expedients and makeshifts." Rommel, says Fuller, "has never worked on what may be called a fixed plan." We are thus coming back to Napoleon's: *"On s'engage et puis on voit."* Wetzell summarizes this new, or old, strategical thought as follows: "The greatest surprise for the enemy is a lost battle, wherever this battle takes place. Victory can be achieved by many different methods and sometimes by mere luck. But the surest way to win is to exploit the enemy's weaknesses and errors by the immediate forming of a center of gravity at the enemy's vulnerable points."

Even a casual glance at the history of the two World Wars

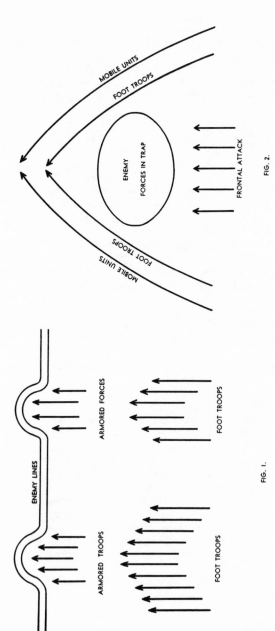

FIG. 2.

FIG. 1.

WEDGE AND TRAP

The *keil und kessel* (wedge and trap) tactics used by the Germans in Russia stem directly from the classical German strategy of destroying the enemy by encirclement resulting from outflanking action. *Keil und kessel* is the process of taking huge bites out of the hostile position, destroying the enemy forces in a given sector, and then repeating the process in another sector. The *keil* or wedge, Figure 1, is driven by strong armored forces, supported by motorized and foot troops, which push deep into the enemy rear. Usually two such wedges are driven, at a considerable distance from each other. The operation then develops into a double pincers movement. The mobile forces spearheading the original wedges turn to meet at some point deep in the hostile rear. Figure 2: The slower foot troops turn inside the mobile forces, forming an inner set of pincers. This encirclement forms the *kessel* or trap.

shows that many offensives had been directed against joints, hinges or pivotal points. The big German offensive of March, 1918, was launched against the joint of the British and French armies. The German attack against the Allies in May, 1940, was directed against Sedan, that is to say, against the point around which the offensive wing of the Allies turned and which separated the defensive army group and the Maginot Line from the offensive left wing. Other attacks were directed against points upon which the entire front of the defender depended and whose fall necessitated a general retreat. Other operations again were break-throughs. If in modern war the flank had maintained its traditional vulnerability, break-through operations were hardly possible, let alone the formation of "kessels."

General Erfurth's reliance upon the flank should therefore not be taken as a reflection of modern German strategy. Instead, wherever he says "flank," one should read "vulnerable point." The character of the vulnerable point may change. Sometimes it may be a long fortification line, or only a strong point like Eben Emael. Sometimes it may be an important railway junction or a bridge like the Moersdijck bridge in Holland. At another time, it may be a front where the enemy does not expect an attack, as at the Chemin des Dames in May, 1918. Enlarging our views as to the necessities of "combined operations," one may also say that the vulnerable point may be on the sea or in the air, in the ports or in the factories.

Economy When Striking

At bottom, the strategy of surprise is nothing but an application of the principle of the economy of force. Obviously, it is more economical to strike at vulnerable points than at points which are not vulnerable, as it is more economical to strike when the enemy is not prepared for the blow than when he has taken all precautions to parry the expected stroke.

It may be useful to supplement General Erfurth's discussion by several arguments which have been set forth by the Austrian, General Alfred Krauss. Krauss, who repeatedly is quoted by General Erfurth, played a major role in the famous battle of Caporetto: he is also known as one of the most important modern military writers in the German language. His points are as follows: Surprise does not depend upon lack of care or complete ignorance on the part of the enemy. To achieve surprise, it is by no means necessary that the enemy dreams or sleeps, but that one undertakes an operation which he does not expect. According to Krauss, the enemy may well know many important details about the attack in preparation and still be surprised by its location and timing.

With respect to the two major elements of surprise, secrecy and speed, General Krauss points out that secrecy cannot be maintained by hiding one's intention from subordinates. One should not believe that secrecy can be maintained if only a handful of superior officers know of the battle plan. (This is a point which has also been strongly emphasized by Lord Fisher). Such secrecy is not desirable, because any operation must be thoroughly trained and rehearsed if it is to be successful. Besides, many people must be in on the secret, anyway, and to a watchful enemy the secret is usually given away by numerous preparatory measures. Secrecy sought by not informing subordinates does not prevent the enemy from knowing what is afoot, but it does prevent subordinates from doing a good job. By this method the enemy usually learns more of our intentions than our own army. "Real secrecy," says Krauss, "can only be achieved if, in addition to the correct information which the enemy receives, he is also provided with incorrect information. Confusion is the only effective method of maintaining secrecy."

Meaning of Speed

Speed, on the other hand, is not necessarily identical with quick marching and exhausting troops. Speed is merely being "quicker than the enemy." Forced marches may be an important component of speed. Yet the essential point is to have everything ready before the operation begins and to carry it out without interruption and delay. To attack with tired and hungry troops who do not have enough ammunition and lack the support of heavy arms is not a correct application of the principle of speed. Seldom can such an attack be successful.

The idea that something "cannot be done" is one of the main aids to successful surprise. It frequently happens that military experts consider particular operations as not feasible. Logistical difficulties, roughness of terrain, military traditions— all these elements are often over-emphasized. Experts tend to forget that most military problems are soluble provided one is willing to pay the price. Many problems are soluble by new methods. If one has a list of the enemy's prejudices and knows what he considers as being "out of question" or as "impossible," and has in addition some new ideas, one is almost sure to catch the opponent by surprise. This is the essence of General Krauss' opinions.

Throughout the whole book, General Erfurth, makes the *a priori* assumption that every battle should be waged with a view to the enemy's destruction. It does not require many words to demonstrate that annihilation under any circumstances, cannot be the only objective. Regardless of whether war should ultimately lead to the destruction of the enemy, it is quite clear that in some periods of the war, annihilation cannot be attempted because the available forces, even in their best possible disposition, would not be sufficient for so ambitious a goal.

This does not mean that surprise should not be attempted by an inferior army. Quite to the contrary, surprise will be one of the important means by which the weaker army may compensate for his weakness, at least partly. Yet it does mean that concentration of "everything one has" should not be applied on all occasions, lest a stronger enemy may annihilate one's own concentration at a stroke. There are cases in which concentration may actually be extremely dangerous and wherein an army can be saved only by dispersal. Hannibal, for instance, would have desired nothing better than the concentration of Fabius Cunctator's army, as Napoleon prayed for the concentration of the Russian forces under Kutusov. Guerilla tactics have often been successfully used and have come as a surprise to a superior opponent. But the essence of guerilla warfare is dispersion and not concentration.

Length of Modern Wars

General Erfurth very often conveys the idea that the enemy's destruction should be attempted by one single blow. He apparently considers "victory through a single battle" as the ideal form of war. As a matter of fact the *Vernichtungsschlacht* [annihilation by *one* battle] was for a long time considered as the main element of war. Schlieffen advised to aim at one single *Vernichtungsschlacht* because, in his opinion, a modern war should, or could, not last for a long period of time. This

idea has been abandoned by many modern military writers in
Germany who substituted the *Vernichtungsfeldzug* [annihilation
by a *series* of battles] for the battle of annihilation. Wetzell
is of the opinion that the doctrine of the single *Vernichtungsschlacht* is an exaggeration of the Cannae concept. "The destruction of a modern mass army cannot be accomplished by
a single victory, however overwhelming. The final decision
is dependent on numerous partial victories. This is the essence
of Moltke's teachings and of the experience of World War I.
The partial battles and partial victories must be integrated into
one big operation. In this case they will be of decisive importance." As a matter of fact, General Erfurth himself, in a
later publication, admits that under present conditions the
Cannae concept has more tactical than strategical significance.
This, of course, amounts to a definite farewell to Schlieffen's
idea.

General Erfurth refers to deceptive methods which were
employed by the Germans during the last war. By mounting
several secondary or sham operations, the enemy is deceived
as to the time and location of an impending offensive. It is
indeed true that the enemy can often be deceived only if he does
not know which one of several offensives will turn out to be
decisive. Here activity behind the lines and sham attacks will
hardly neutralize the enemy's reserves which, as Erfurth rightly
points out, is one of the main conditions of a successful offensive. Hence the main offensive should be supported by secondary offensives of inferior, although considerable, strength.
This does not mean, of course, that one should not use maximum force for the main drive. Nevertheless, this constitutes an
important qualification of the principle of concentration.

Use of Strategic Reserves

A problem which General Erfurth fails to discuss is the
question of whether strategic reserves should, or should not,
be thrown into the surprise operation, so as to provide for the
greatest possible strength. It is clear again, that there are cases
in which reserves must be spared. The mobility of modern
armies makes it possible to achieve surprises merely by with-
holding strong strategical reserves which are used only after
the enemy has revealed his counter-moves. In other cases, it
may be impossible to know beforehand where the weak points

of the enemy's lines are. These points can sometimes be determined only by attacks along the entire front. The reserves should be used where the enemy shows least resistance.

General Erfurth is not very communicative concerning the methods by which surprise can be achieved in case the enemy commander has no preconceived ideas and is not willing "to contribute his own share" to one's victory. He makes casual reference to radio-listening and ruses of war, in addition to the aforementioned sham operations. It must be pointed out that ruses of war have a much greater importance than his remarks convey. On principle, it can be said that surprises are only accomplished if and when by some kind of a ruse the enemy has been deceived, or confused, as General Krauss emphasized.

In his discussion of the German operations in Belgium during August, 1914, Erfurth repeatedly alludes to the apprehensions of the German army commanders as to the location of the British Expeditionary Force. He forgets, however, to tell that these apprehensions were not as unfounded as his recital would suggest. As a matter of fact, the British had sent a small force to Ostend whence it had to advance on bicycles to give the Germans the impression that the British would attack from that region. In addition, stories were circulated about the arrival of strong Russian forces on the Belgium front and the British censorship had taken care that these rumors were through "reliable sources" quickly transmitted to the Germans. The British marines who performed this operation wore uniforms resembling the Russian attire. They themselves spread the rumors that they were the Russian advance guard.

Ruse at Gaza

To quote another example, the famous Battle of Gaza by which General Allenby hastened the end of World War I. If Allenby had attacked on the left flank of his front, in the region of Gaza, he would have encountered strong Turkish resistance. The Turks assumed that on account of the water supply this was the only sector where the British could attack. Allenby therefore decided to attack on his right wing in spite of the scarcity of water in the desert. Still, it was necessary to get quickly to Beersheba, the only oasis in that region, if he was to advance further with sufficient forces against the strongpoints of the Turkish lines. Since Beersheba was a junction of good roads, secrecy was indispensable if a *coup de main* on that oasis was to be successful. This secrecy, of course could not be guarded merely by silence. The enemy had to be led to believe that the main blow would fall near Gaza.

A whole month was spent in sending "misleading messages by wireless telegraphy in a code which the Turks, by various ruses, had been taught how to solve, without realizing the situation." In addition, a British staff officer on patrol ride let himself be surprised by a Turkish guard. He feigned to be wounded and ostensibly lost his haversack with an especially prepared note-book, including money, love-letters and several purported orders and military documents. The haversack was picked up by the Turks. The next morning, a notice appeared in the paper that was issued to the Desert Mounted Corps, stating that a notebook had been lost by a staff officer on patrol and that the finder should return it at once to Allenby's headquarters. "A small party was sent out to search the country for the pocketbook. . . . An officer was stupid enough to wrap his luncheon in a copy of these orders, and to drop it near the enemy."

These ruses were successful. The Turks prepared themselves for an attack on Gaza and to make the deception complete the British actually began to attack Gaza. After Turkish reserves were rushed to the ostensibly menaced front, the real British attack started on the other end of the Palestinian front. Almost without effort, the British took Beersheba.

Frequent use has also been made by dummies, such as dummy camps, dummy tanks and dummy artillery. In 1914, after the German cruisers "Goeben" and "Breslau" had fled to Turkey, the British watched the exit of the Dardanelles with a considerable naval force. The approach of Admiral Count von Spee's squadron to the South Atlantic made it necessary to bring all available British naval forces into the Atlantic. The British war-ships before the Dardanelles were secretly replaced by ships with exactly the same appearance. The British victory of the Falklands was due to this ingenious use of dummies. Incidentally, the German squadron had been mislead by their deciphering of falsified messages from the British Admirality. Otherwise, it would hardly have obligingly waited for superior British forces to surprise it as it lay immobilized, at anchor.

Surprise requires extensive and efficient espionage and other form of intelligence work. For, if one wishes to surprise the enemy, one must know what he intends to do and how he is likely to act.

New Technique and Weapons

General Erfurth, comparatively speaking, gives little attention to surprise which may result from new weapons and new fighting techniques. He somewhat discounts this kind of surprise by saying that within a short time the enemy will also adopt the new weapons and tactics. This argument is scarcely valid, for it is enough if a surprise play works once. After all, neither can strategic surprise be repeated, no more probably than surprise which results from new techniques and weapons.

In reality, the constant change of tactics offers especially good opportunities for surprise. The Battle of Caporetto, for instance, was won by a new technique of combat. In this battle, it was considered as an axiom of mountain warfare that the heights dominate the valleys and that, therefore, the heights should be attacked. General Krauss, however, pointed out that although the fire from the heights may control the valleys, it is also true that the party which is in control of the valleys controls the supply and conmmunications of the heights. If the fire from the heights cannot eject the enemy from the valleys, the troops on the heights must capitulate. Krauss concluded from this that one should attack only in the valleys and not bother about the mountains, an idea which led to the complete surprise of the Italians and almost annihilated their army.

The change from mass-attack to infiltration tactics was the major reason of the German successes in March, 1918.

General Erfurth entirely fails to realize that the difficulties of modern armament production have introduced new problems into the art of war and opened up wide possibilities for technical surprises. It is well-known that mass-production "freezes" the armament, at least to a large degree. For this reason, technical surprise may have much more lasting effects than General Erfurth suggests. Unless the enemy knows of the new weapons beforehand (in which case the surpriser may be surprised, as happened apparently with the magnetic mines) new technical surprises can be applied repeatedly.

If today an army uses a superior weapon on the battlefield, it may take the opponent months, if not years, to produce a similar weapon or an effective counter-weapon. During this time of adaptation, the happy owner of the new weapon has all the advantages and may win one battle after the other. This is not only true for quality, but also for quantity, for it is next to impossible quickly to step up armament production and to overtake a substantial lead of the enemy. It is not different with new fighting techniques, though the time-lag may be shorter in this case. Experience shows that it often takes rather a long period of time to re-educate troops for new tactics. And it is sometimes also difficult for general staffs to adapt themselves to new and unforseen situations.

The reader will see from General Erfurth's description of how Moltke deduced the French war plan from a cheap French railroad map. While technical progress has made production more rigid, it rendered transportation much more flexible. It would be impossible for a present-day Moltke to deduce a war plan from a railway and road map, for the simple reason that there are too many railways and too many roads. With the existing transport facilities, almost any point can be chosen as basis for an offensive; retreat can be effected in almost any direction. Besides, so-called natural obstacles now do not constitute such problems as they formerly did, disregarding the sea and the desert, but even these have lost much of their obstacle-value.

Time and Space In Surprise

In other words, the possibilities of surprise *in space* have improved. That motorization and the conquest of the air also improved the chances of surprise *in time* goes almost without saying. Future perfection in handling and training air-borne troops will improve both kinds of surprise. And it has already been mentioned that technical surprise has also been perfected and, on account of industrial rigidity, has become more durable. Only surprises by new ideas and ruses seem to have become more difficult, although radio offers large and new opportunities for ruses of war, at least technically. But there is little doubt that on the whole General Erfurth underestimated rather than overestimated the possibilities of surprise in modern war.

One important, although obvious, point still must be made:

It is not sufficient to attempt only one kind of surprise for one operation. On principle, every detail and every part of any operation should spring surprises upon the enemy. The attack should come from an unexpected quarter at an unexpected time, with unexpected violence; new tactics, new techniques and new weapons should be employed. The important point is to overthrow all plans and preparations of the enemy. For the outwitted enemy will lose confidence, hence the surpriser will establish moral ascendancy, which is the main condition of victory.

Key to Victory

The first few years of the Second World War thoroughly justified General Erfurth's statement: "Surprise is the key to victory." Surprise could even be achieved in operations the feasibility of which Erfurth tended to discount, as for instance, naval surprises. Pearl Harbor is ample evidence of the possibility, not only of naval surprises, but even of repetition-surprises. We are lucky that the Japanese shared Erfurth's skepticism and therefore probably did not expect their surprise-attack to yield such unprecedented results. Pearl Harbor was thus a double surprise: for us and for them. The Japanese success was as unexpected as the Japanese failure to exploit it. Pearl Harbor may well serve as an example for General Erfurth's pet theory that an attempt undertaken to annihilate the enemy should be made with "everything one has." What was the use of knocking out the Pacific Fleet and the most important mid-Pacific base, and not having ready a superior force to conquer control over the entire Pacific area?

Turning to the European battlefields, we observe that the war was conducted chiefly as a war of surprise, at least from the German side. First of all, the Germans persistently planned their wars as *Ueberfallskrieg.* They attacked without warning and without delivering any declaration of war *before* the actual attack. They timed the beginning of their operations in such a way that the fighting started before the opponent had completed his armaments and his mobilization. It must be added that the Germans hereby used a rather novel form of surprise, which could be called the "open surprise." By applying political pressure and by maneuvering they prevented, for instance, the Poles, Dutch and Belgians from taking defensive measures and fully mobilizing their armies. The result was that these countries fought only with a fraction of their actual strength, and whatever force they brought to battle was used up in a planless way, or, at any rate, not according to a plan concerted with their Allies.

Coups de main were frequent and successful during this war, particularly during the early phases of new campaigns. It may be enough to recall the Norwegian campaign which was nothing but a sum of many different smaller *coups de main.* In the west, the Germans applied particular care to the seizure of important bridges before the enemy was able to destroy them. These operations, particularly those against the Meuse-bridges, were conceived as *coup de main* tactics. It is, however, also true that some *coup de main* operations were unsuccessful as, for instance, the attempted capture of Queen Wilhelmina and from the British side, of Marshal Rommel.

Surprise During Approach to the Battlefield

On the whole, there was no real "approach" on land during this war, for the simple reason that most battles began at the frontier. Nevertheless, the Battle of Holland was preceded by a kind of approach, as was the Battle of Norway, insofar as both battles began at unexpected places and as the attacking troops were transported to the main battlefield in an unexpected way. In Norway they arrived in freighters, disguised as sailors, and in planes; they attacked at places (Narvik) which were believed to be safe from any attack. In Holland, parachutists and "tourists" carried out attacks against focal points which were considered as safe. On the other hand the Allies' approach to the Flanders battlefield did not contain a single element of surprise, but was effected in exactly the way the Germans expected. Hence the Allies' crushing defeat.

The Allied landing in North Africa may, on the contrary, be considered in almost every respect as a surprise approach.

The itinerary, the points of attack, its time, the strength of the attacking force and, to a certain degree, the method of transportation (air-transports), all these remained hidden from the Germans. The secret had been kept by use of many effective deceptions and ruses. In particular, the enemy was induced to believe that the Allied convoys would go either to Dakar or to the eastern Mediterranean.

Surprise of Concentration

In the Polish war, the defender's plan of concentration was so obsolete that it gave surprise every chance to display its effectiveness. The Polish General Staff had placed the small Polish army in a linear formation along an extremely lengthy border, one of the longest in Europe. There was no concentration of force on the Polish side. The deployment of the Polish army was a classical example of dispersion as it should never be attempted. For political reasons, the Poles tried to defend everything.

The Germans, however, had concentrated their forces into four different groups, two of which attacked from unexpected directions. For the first time in the history of war, the Germans applied the principle of concentration in armored warfare by organizing armored divisions which they sent out in well-chosen strategical directions. Due to the thinness of the Polish lines, the German panzer formations accomplished easy break-throughs, carved out large masses of Polish troops, isolated them and progressively reduced all the Polish forces. The delaying tactics which the Poles in their headless bravery tried to apply until the last did not serve any reasonable military purpose.

The hitherto most successful strategic concentration was, beyond any doubt, the German maneuver of Sedan, in May, 1940.

One may consider this operation as among the leading successful surprise blows of all history. This operation affirmed one of General Erfurth's basic theories, namely that surprise requires the opponent's "collaboration."

Former Slow Mobilization

Germany in 1914 had taken advantage of the element of surprise by launching her troops through Belgium. The opposing armies met when they had fully developed and taken up battle position. They came into close contact as late as August 26; the first battle took place near the Franco-Belgian border. Such was the slowness of mobilization in 1914, that the Germans needed three weeks to concentrate, to move less than 100 kilometers and to begin combat. When battle was joined, to the surprise of the French, it appeared that the Germans enjoyed an enormous superiority in heavy artillery and that cohesion and coordination in the German army were better than in the French. Despite these weaknesses the Allies were able to avert defeat. Why? Because both armies were more or less identical in nature, having the same mobility and maneuverability and because the power of machine gun defense made the rupture of any front impossible. Consequently, no large elements of any army could be encircled, immobilized and trapped in one region, and then annihilated.

The lessons of the German failure in 1914 had not been lost. In 1940 the *"idée de manoeuvre"* was to break into the French disposition at its very center, while preventing any coordination by swift infiltration. By the same token, the northern group of the Allied armies sent into Belgium would be cut off from the eastern and southern Allied forces by a resolute and concentrated attack towards the west. The plan of 1940 was altogether different from the plan of 1914 when the Germans had even thought of leaving Alsace-Lorraine to advancing French formations (with the idea of immobilizing the French by permitting offensive action in a direction with no strategic importance). The Germans in 1940 met the French on the second day and as close to the French bases as possible, thus paralyzing the French transportation system and impeding the movements of the French army. In 1940, the French army failed to win a new Battle of the Marne because, unlike 26 years before, it had been immobilized and because from the beginning the German army possessed superior mobility.

Ardennes No Obstacle

On the tactical field, the main surprise was the German attack through the Ardennes, a deeply cut and wooded plateau which is a considerable obstacle to movements with strong mechanized elements. The French believed the Ardennes mountains were not suitable for large-scale operations. This firm conviction that no strong enemy attack could ever come from across the Ardennes is expressed by almost all decisions which the French took during the critical phase of the operation. The French Intelligence Service on May 12, advised the Bureau of Operations of the French General Staff that the main German attack would be delivered against the hinge of the Allied fanwise movement at Sedan. This information did not find credence, and no step was taken to thwart the German maneuver.

The French not only expressed their opinion of the obstacle-value of the Ardennes quite openly, so that the Germans knew about it, but they also failed to take precautions in case the Germans might not also believe in the French doctrine. The French assumed, or were led to assume by various German ruses that the Germans would, on the whole, repeat the Schlieffen plan. That is, concentrate their main forces on their right wing. In this case, the main battle was to be expected between the Belgian fortifications and the river Dyle. The Germans, when drawing up their war plan were sure that the French would neither attack through the Ardennes, nor have forces enough ready for a strong defense of that region. The Germans, while also considering the Ardennes as difficult country, believed that by good planning and after thorough preparation, a strong attack could be delivered in that sector. The Germans knew quite well that they took a considerable risk by sending strong mechanized formations through a region full of fosses, woods, deep valleys and steep escarpments. But they decided on it because they were sure the French air force was not able to interfere with their movements. They selected the Ardennes as the point of the essential attack, because it was there that surprise was most likely to be effective. It was an attack directed at the joint between the offensive and defensive wings of the Allied army. All other attacks were made in part to protect the flanks of the main German offensive group, in part to draw the Allied forces on to a battlefield where no decision was sought. The Allies were induced to advance as far as possible into Belgium; the main blow was delivered only four days after the offensive had begun.

The "collaboration" of the French went as far as it could. The French High Command, it seems, refused to believe reports of the presence of strong German units in the Ardennes. The French forces assigned to defend the Meuse, weak as they were, did not arrive in time. French reserves were not available for the defense of the decisive point. On account of their disposition, the re-grouping of the Allied armies was no longer possible once the break-through had occurred.

Belgium a German Trap

The Germans effected a noteworthy surprise by luring the Franco-British army into Belgium. They were careful not to impede the seemingly offensive move of the Allies and refrained from bombing the advancing Allied left wing. The farther the Allies moved into Belgium, the easier it would be for the Germans to crush them. By their inconsiderate advance, which was facilitated for them to the utmost, the Allies immobilized themselves. This shows that surprise can also be achieved in other forms than by concentration and attack.

The disposition of the Anglo-French armies was indeed singular. If the Allied generals had the intention of helping their enemy, they could not have acted differently. The battle was to be fought defensively. The advantage of defense, as Erfurth reminds us, is that the attacker must reveal his plan first. Yet this advantage exists only if the defender can profit from this revelation. And he can profit from it only:

(a) if he concentrates his main forces behind;

(b) if he forces the enemy to deploy his forces at an early moment;

(c) if he has strong reserves which can quickly be thrown at menaced points.

The French followed none of these rules; they neither held substantial forces in reserve, nor did they put their reserves in the right place. There were three groups of reserve forces in the rear. One was centered around St. Quentin and Laon; the second east of Compiègne and the third around Chalons-sur-Marne. All of them faced northward and were earmarked to follow the movements of the French First Army in Belgium. No mobile reserve was held behind the Ninth and Second Armies, or in the region of Montmédy-Caregnan. Two armored divisions attacking from that sector could have seriously compromised the German advance. If the left flank of the German troops advancing through the Ardennes had been attacked, General Gamelin could have practically profited by the military advantages which theoretically were gained by the advance into Belgium.

It is still more astonishing that on their left wing, which was supposed to fight the decisive battle, the Allies concentrated approximately only one-third of their army. The remaining two-thirds were in and behind the Maginot line. Besides, this weak offensive wing was not used, as it could and should have been, because one entire army, the Seventh Army under General Giraud, was given the insoluble task of fighting in southern Holland, with the result that this army practically did not intervene in the decisive fighting. According to their own assumptions, the French should have had concentrated two-thirds of their armies, or even more, behind the Belgian frontier and before moving them ahead they should have waited until the Germans had revealed their plan.

But whatever the French disposition, it is hard to explain why in the most critical sector, at the hinge of Sedan, there were only reserve divisions and some motorized divisions but no strong mobile force which could have effectively counterattacked. The basic idea of French strategy was to abandon the artificial and weak positions at the Franco-Belgian frontier and to fight instead on the stronger as well as shorter line of resistance which is marked by the river Meuse, by the fortress of Namur and the river Dyle. Unfortunately, this plan left the center door of the French house wide ajar.

Erroneous Assumptions

Part of these strategical errors may, however, be traced back to erroneous tactical and technical assumptions, or in other words, to surprises of a tactical and technical nature. Among these assumptions were the belief that:

(a) the Belgian fortifications would hold out at least five days, giving the Allies enough time to advance into Belgium and occupy the Dyle line;

(b) the speed of the German army would not exceed the speed of the Allied army;

(c) the Allied·tank defenses, in spite of their short-comings, would considerably reduce the striking-power of the German army.

The disregard of the principle of concentration is even more pronounced if we consider what use the Allies made of their tanks and planes. Briefly, they never concentrated their tanks, although, in fact, they had considerable numbers of excellent tanks (most of which have later been used by the Germans). The tanks were dispersed in many units, and even the available armored and mechanized divisions were used in driblets. Besides, many of them were wasted in defensive operations instead of being held for concentrated counter-attacks. The air force, small as it was, was squandered in operations which could have no immediate effect on the battle that was proceeding, as in bombing of the Ruhr; or in useless work, like bombing bridges which were either not used by the Germans or which, in case they were hit, were repaired within a few hours. Every available Allied aircraft should have been used instead against the German air force itself.

The essential causes of the French defeat are extremely few. The Germans attacked at an unexpected place; the French fought on the passive and static defensive by sitting tight behind the natural obstacle of the Meuse; the French forces were excessively dispersed; there were no reserves. For these reasons, the German surprise attack was successful beyond expectation. At the first blow, the French were completely immobilized, the German exploitation was immediate and irremediable. After the breakthrough at Sedan, the French army no longer existed. There were only numerous separate and independent French units which bravely fought according to circumstances and possibilities.

There is hardly a more successful case of surprise in any war.

Russians and French

The beginning of the war in Russia is quite different from the initial phases of the French campaign of 1940. Terrain conditions are not the same. The Russian army is both stronger and more modern than was the French; the possibilities of retreat are much greater. An invader cannot reach the heart of Russia in one good stroke as can be done against France. In France, the German victory was consummated on May 13, 1940, at 4 o'clock in the afternoon, less than three days after the start of active hostilities. Against the Russians, such speed could not be dreamed of. On May 10, 1940, the Allies had massed 101 divisions along the Franco-Belgian frontier. (91 French, 10 British). They had practically no reserves. They had approximately 3000 tanks and less than 2000 first-line planes. On June 22, 1941, Russia had 215 divisions immediately available, more than 200 other divisions available within a few weeks, plus a considerable quantity of non-divisional troops. The Soviets had probably 14,000 planes both in line and in reserve and more than 15,000 tanks. With these quantities, they had a considerable numerical, though not qualitative, superiority over the Germans both in personnel and in materiel.

From the start, the Germans proposed to deal a blow to the Russians from which they could not recover. The Germans also planned to attack in such way that the Russian disposition would be disrupted and at the same time large and efficient Russian formations annihilated. The German plan was a combination of many different surprise attacks. Tactically, they had perfected the team-work between plane-tank-gun. They had also perfected the method of launching attacks against the enemy's rear. And in addition, they did make effective use of the Pripet marshes which cut the battlefield in two. Tannenberg was repeated on an immense scale.

The Germans almost succeeded. Their tactics and strategy were well worthy to match the blows they had dealt to France. Russia was saved by the valor of its men; but the bravery and tenacity of the Russian soldier would have been of no avail if behind the positions overrun by the Germans other positions could not have been found on which the Russian army could consolidate. Russia was saved primarily by her spaces, the area for maneuver at her disposal.

The Russian General Staff committed similar mistakes as the French. The Russian generals were confident that the advance of the armored columns which the Germans launched forward as in Poland and France, could be checked by allowing them to venture into the Russian rear. With depots and commando posts protected against sudden attacks, the defending troops would close behind the armored invaders, cut them off from their bases and infantry support and destroy them. This concept of defense in mechanized warfare had already conspicuously failed in the Polish war. The Russians also sent their troops too close to the German main concentration, not realizing that the mobility of the German army was much greater than theirs, so that the enemy's armored columns were able quickly to eleminate all forces imprudently sent ahead of strong defensive zones.

Defense Helped Attack

The defenders played into the hands of the attacker by concentrating too near the Pripet marshes. These rendered any lateral shifting of forces impossible. Thus the Germans were able to attack large Russian units separately with superior strength and to apply Napoleon's strategy to tackle the different enemy armies at different times, and each of them with overwhelming force. The initial German strategy in the Russian campaign was a classical application of the principle of concentration.

On the contrary, if the advanced flat regions were strongly held by the Russians, the Stalin line was undermanned. The largest reserve forces were concentrated west of Moscow. The attacker could penetrate quickly into the Russian defense system, annihilate strong forces and considerable equipment and gain contact with the main line of resistance without loss of time. This line was almost as easily reduced as was the futile line of the Allies in 1940, the K. W. line between Antwerp and Sedan. At the beginning of the war, the Russians showed themselves unable to concentrate sufficient forces at the right time and at the right place. During the Battle of Moscow they accomplished their first strategically correct concentration, obviously because they knew the main objective of the German offensive. But at that time the Germans had already conquered the Ukraine.

German Indecision Fatal

The Germans, although convinced partisans of the principle of concentration, frequently failed to apply it. In particular, they were unable to make up their mind as to where the decision of their struggle for world hegemony was to be sought. The attack on Britain was not undertaken with a real concentration of force, because the air-force alone was thrown into the fight. Regardless of whether the German army was ready to attack Britain or whether after the naval defeats during the Norwegian campaign, enough naval forces were available for amphibious attack, the offensive should never have been undertaken unless the whole strength of Germany could be used against the then main and strongest enemy.

After the failure of the Battle of Britain, the main German strength should have been used for the conquest of the Near East. The Balkan campaign was useless, the Libyan position was not properly employed, and the operations in Syria and Iraq were stopped before they really began. The offensive against Russia was launched before the Germans had secured their rear. This sin against the principle of concentration was only surpassed by their folly in declaring war on the United States before Germany's European enemies were liquidated. Since Germany had no chance whatsoever to strike at the United States, her declaration of war also was a radical abandonment of the principle of surprise.

On the other hand, dogmatism is never effective in military matters. Deviations from the principle of concentration may sometimes be justified. The dispatch of the British Eighth Army to Egypt during the worst military crisis of British history was beyond doubt not compatible with the principle of concentration. This decision required high courage and it may be presumed that the Axis powers based their plans on the assumption that Britain would keep all her soldiers at home. They were much surprised when they discovered their error. And this British heterodoxy led to remarkable success. Indeed, it saved the Near East and Africa and thereby—who knows?—prevented the Allies from losing the war.

Incidentally, the principle of concentration must also be applied to production. One must produce most of that weapon, or those weapons, which one considers as decisive. The Germans first considered the plane as their basic weapon. Later on, it seems, they gave preference to the tank, and finally halved their main effort between land weapons and submarines. The Allies were likewise frequently shifting their main effort from one weapon to the other. The fact, however, that they were able to maintain their shipping production must certainly have surprised the Germans and upset parts of their strategic calculations.

Evacuation At Dunkirk

No data are available as yet relating to the development of the battles which took place during World War II. Yet the main facts concerning surprises in retreat operations are known, and we may briefly mention them.

There were no surprising features in the retreats of the Polish, Dutch and Belgian armies, none of which chose the right moment and the right direction of retreat. Dunkirk, however, is a different story and certainly a remarkable example of effective surprise.

First, it may be presumed that the Germans counted upon either the annihilation or the destruction of the trapped Allied forces and did not expect them even to attempt to get away.

Secondly, the technical feasibility of embarking more than 300,000 men was certainly questionable, in particular, because the Germans could hardly expect the British to risk substantial naval forces within the reach of the victorious German Luftwaffe. That the performance of the Parisian taxicabs of 1914 [in quickly transporting troops to the battle front and stopping the German rush] could be repeated with British yachts and motor launches was indeed an unexpected occurrence.

Thirdly, the British surprisingly used their Spitfire fighter plane which up to Dunkirk was held in reserve. The mastery of the air over the Dunkirk region was wrested from the Germans and a heavy defeat was inflicted on the Luftwaffe which may be considered as the main reason for this successful retreat. It may be added that the Allies were also luckily favored by weather: calm sea and poor visibility.

The other phases of the Allied retreat in France are, however, characterized by all the mistakes which General Erfurth rightly castigates. The Allies merely fell back from one line to the other, without ever attempting to maneuver. Besides, they committed other serious blunders which by no means can be justified or explained away by their lack of armament and their general inferiority.

For resistance, the French High Command did not select defense lines with strong natural obstacles, but those which actually had little tactical value. The Somme, for instance, is no real obstacle. The Seine and Paris, however, offer strong defenses. Yet the French chose to fight the last decisive battle on the Somme, and not on the Seine behind which they should have withdrawn after performing widespread demolitions in the fore-field. A second mistake was not to shorten the lines and to evacuate the Maginot Line when it was still possible, so that the eastern army group could still be used in the decisive battle.

It has also been argued that the line of retreat was badly selected and that instead of retreating to Bordeaux, the French army should have gone to Britanny where it could have found strong positions and good communications with Great Britain. There is little doubt that the Bordeaux maneuver would have made sense only if the French had reasonable hope of accomplishing a sort of military come-back. But if this was impossible, as it indeed was, the only reasonable strategy was to maintain a French bridgehead. This could only have been done in Brittany. It is true, however, that retreats require careful planning and advance thought. The French had made no preparations for retreat in any direction. Hence they would have hardly been able to disengage their troops from the enemy and to ship large parts of them to Africa.

Defensive-Offensive Doctrine

The first Battle of El Alamein is almost a perfect illustration of the doctrine of the defensive-offensive. Here the offensive party, although victorious, grew disorganized and tired during the pursuit and offered thereby a chance to the defender, provided he disengaged himself in time and made a deep withdrawal. Against an exhausted pursuer a successful stand is possible even with small forces especially if the defense rests upon strong natural positions which cannot be turned. However, one should not forget the role airpower played in this battle. If the British had also lost their air supremacy, they would have hardly been able to recuperate.

The battles in Papua (New Guinea), the ill-fated Japanese thrust at Port Moresby and the subsequent annihilation of the entire Japanese detachment at Buna were certainly other master-pieces of defensive-offensive strategy. The surprise for the Japanese apparently lay in the fact that the Australian-American troops could stand the strain of jungle fighting and that, in addition, they were able to improvise an air transport system far superior to anything the Japanese could muster.

The crown for retreat-strategy goes, however, to the Russians, and particularly in connection with the Battle of Stalingrad. The surprise for the Germans was that Stalingrad, unlike Verdun and Sebastopol, did not offer special limited targets, such as forts. The major military targets in Stalingrad were dispersed and not discernable and could, therefore, not be destroyed by German heavy artillery. In addition, the battle was fought out over an immensely wide area. Even day-long mass attacks of the German air force sometimes 1000 or more in a day, could not destroy the invisible Russian defense system.

On the contrary, the wholesale destruction of houses proved to be a most efficient antitank protection. Another important point was that the Germans were unable to cut the Russian supply line across the Volga. When it became clear that Stalingrad would not fall, an immediate German retreat was indicated. This was not done, with the result that the German Sixth Army was annihilated. One is reminded of General Erfurth's description of Falkenhayn's strategy in 1914, when he refused to give up

conquered soil and to retreat voluntarily in order better to prepare
for a new offensive.

Voluntary retreats to prevent enemy offensives, in the style
of the German retreat in April, 1917, also apparently occurred
in this war. Some of the German maneuvers in Russian in
the winters of 1941-42 and 1942-43 fall into this category. On
the contrary, Wavell's offensive in the winter of 1940 against
Libya caught the Italians before they were ready and during
their own offensive preparations. This operation may be characterized as a "preventive offensive."

Surprise Tactics and New Techniques

We shall conclude this cursory glance at the history of World
War II by mentioning briefly the different surprises which have
been effected during this war outside the realm of strategy. On
the whole, it can be said that none of the weapons of this war
is entirely new.

Only the efficiency which modern armament acquired since
its birth in World War I is new. The tank, for instance, is an
old acquaintance, yet the armored division, the mechanized
and motorized divisions are new comers which behaved in a
quite unexpected, though highly successful, manner. The same
is true of the dive-bomber which dates back to 1919, and to
air-power with all its implements and potentialities, including
paratroops. The Germans succeeded in the first surprises with
these weapons and the new techniques. The second round in
aircraft competition was won by the British during the Battle
of Britain, characterized by superior British fighter planes, by
effective and constantly improving night defenses (night-fighters,
radio location) which made possible superior air tactics and
strategy.

The Germans soon had used up their major surprises, with
the exception of the wolf-pack submarine tactics which were
perfected only later on. The only important surprise in land
warfare which they developed after the Battle of France was
in connection with the Battle of Crete, although, of course, at
that time, paratroops were no longer a surprise. Nevertheless,
this operation showed that maneuvers on the strategical scale may
be undertaken with air-borne troops and that the plane may
serve as a useful means of transport in the case of amphibious
operations. Crete, on the whole, was nothing more than an

experiment. It can be presumed that the results of this experiment were more profitable to the Allies than to the German, which again proves General Erfurth's opinion that one should apply surprises with new weapons only for decisive operations and always be careful not to give away technical secrets.

In the case of amphibious warfare, most surprises were ,developed by the Allies, from the creation of the "Commandos," to the tactics which the American Marines used at Guadalcanal and the landing operations in north Africa.

German Errors In Russia

The longest list of successfully accomplished surprises, however, can be presented by the Russians. Generally speaking, their very resistance is altogether the biggest surprise of World War II. Surely, the Germans did not expect to crush the Russians within three weeks or three months. But would they have attacked had they not been fairly certain that the Red Army would be crippled or annihilated within a reasonable period? Is it not probable that Hitler hoped to be in Moscow at the same time the Japanese attacked in the Pacific? Disregarding all Nazi doctrines bearing upon the inefficiency of the Russian political system, the probability of major political changes in the Russian government, once war had broken, one may list the German military expectations and the surprises that came to them as follows:

1. The Germans depended upon annihilating the strong power of the Red army near the frontier. They hoped to be able to repeat the strategy so successfully employed by them against Poland. In the heyday of their advance in Russia they considered that the Battle of Kiev would prove to be as successfully decisive as was the Battle of Kutno; that after that anticipated defeat the Red Army would be virtually destroyed and unable to throw large reserves into battle.

2. Though the Germans expected a "defense in depth," they never expected that the Russians would organize a defense in *extreme* depth, in such a way that the Germans would practically never be able to operate with their tanks through open and obstructed country. They were merely prepared for a more difficult blitz than previous ones; and they were being surprised by the Russian method of "blitz-grinding."

3. The Germans believed that their *"kessel"* tactics would

have the same efficiency in Russia as in western Europe. This was, however, an error. The encircled Russian units almost never capitulated, but fought to the last cartridge, thus substantially reducing the speed and power of the German offensive on which everything else depended. This Russian "stubbornness," as the Germans called it, compelled them to disperse their forces, and prevented strong German concentrations. On the other hand, the Russians showed themselves able to withdraw in time, sacrificing territory for time and man-power.

4. The Russian partisans revealed themselves as a very efficient weapon. Their activities also resulted in German dispersal and—this is of equal importance—made the Germans fear that their communications were insecure.

5. The Russians showed that big cities are considerable military obstacles, the reduction of which is extremely costly and laborious.

6. The Germans did not believe in the value of Russian strategy and considered the leadership of the Red army as clumsy and incapable of maneuver.

7. The Russians were better equipped for winter warfare than the Germans.

8. The Russian artillery was much more efficient than expected. This was one of the main reasons why the German tactics did not work against the Red army.

9. Russian matérial was greater and of better quality than the Germans thought.

10. The Germans did not expect that after and despite their conquest of the most important industrial regions of Russia, the Red army could be constantly equipped with new weapons. They were surprised that Russian industry continued to operate. In all likelihood, they never reckoned with the possibility that the Russians would receive considerable equipment from Britain and the United States.

11. In particular, the Germans assumed that the Russian transport system would break down, or work ineffectively. It was not forseen that, despite indubitable weaknesses, the Russian transport system would continue to operate and that whenever necessary the Russians would transform themselves into sorts of Chinese coolies and on their own backs carry the materiél to the battlefields.

12. Finally, the Germans underestimated the endurance and the courage of the individual Russian soldier.

Conclusion

If the history of World War II ever becomes known in its exact details, the importance of many more military surprises will be revealed. At present we must content ourselves with recognizing that a. surprises occurred more often in this war than in World War I; b. the results of the surprises were usually far-reaching.

Consequently, we are justified in saying that surprise has indeed become one of the essential factors of victory. Whether or not it is the "key to victory," there is little doubt that it is one of its main conditions. Wherever possible, surprise should be made the basis of military planning. Successful surprise will not spare fighting. But, most certainly, it will spare blood.

DR. STEFAN T. POSSONY.

The Institute For Advanced Study,
Princeton, New Jersey,
May, 1943.

Author's Introduction

THE principle of annihilation is the fundamental law of war. It is intimately connected with the principle of surprise.

Surprise is a particularly efficient means of defeating the enemy and as old a method as war itself. The history of war shows that through the centuries, almost all decisive victories have been preceded by successful surprises, despite tactical and strategical changes.

The great importance of surprise in war was strongly emphasized by Clausewitz: "Surprise is more or less at the bottom of all military enterprises." However, Clausewitz asserted that surprise can be better applied in tactics than in strategy. According to him, it is rare that surprises are achieved in the field of grand strategy and military politics.

It is obvious that military surprises can be easily accomplished only if small forces and limited spaces are involved and there are merely minor obstacles to be overcome. That is why tactical surprises occur more often than strategical surprises. In every engagement one should try to surprise the enemy by the deployment of one's own forces and by the unexpected use of one's weapons. This rule is generally accepted and it is hardly necessary to illustrate it by examples taken from recent wars.

Surprise is necessarily less frequent in strategic operations, nor can one take advantage of surprise in the general conduct of war. The history of modern wars shows that the chances of strategic surprise are small indeed. The question might therefore be asked whether in a war which is fought by many millions of soldiers strategic surprises are still possible at all.

This is one of the fundamental questions of modern strategy. For annihilation—which is the chief objective of war—cannot be achieved unless the enemy has previously been surprised. German military regulations consider surprise as "a decisive means" for obtaining great successes. If the possibility of surprise is questionable, the possibility of decisive victory must equally be doubtful. Consequently, the question arises whether with modern mass-armies decisive victories in the style of Cannae can still be won.

Count von Schlieffen[1] who taught the German Army the art of waging war with mass-armies believed in the possibility of strategic surprise under modern conditions. The strategy he had in mind did not aim at the destruction of smaller enemy units, but at the annihilation of the total enemy force. War should be decided in one gigantic battle. Schlieffen tried to understand the fundamentals of a battle of annihilation, not in order to enrich his historical knowledge, but in order to outline the character of future battles. "The basic laws of battle," as Schlieffen summarized the results of his historical research, "remained unchanged since Hannibal's victory over the Consul Terentius Varro at Cannae. A battle of annihilation can still be fought according to the same plan which Hannibal devised many centuries ago. The enemy front should not be the objective of the main attack. Neither the main concentration of force nor the reserves should be used against the enemy front. Only the smashing of the enemy's flanks is essential. Annihilation is complete if the enemy is also attacked from the rear." Schlieffen did not particularly stress the importance of surprise. In his numerous historical examples he mentioned surprise only casually, although he sometimes emphasized the importance of taking the enemy by surprise.

Battle's Decisive Factor

Schlieffen was chiefly concerned with the general aspects of the battle of annihilation. He did not discuss problems of a more specific character, because he feared that details would obscure the clarity of his vision. He sought to answer only one question: What is the general form of a battle of annihilation? How must an army be deployed and what form must the attack take, if the enemy is to be annihilated? But Schlieffen by no means disregarded the preponderant role of surprise.

Hannibal won the battle of Cannae because the Roman commander had been surprised by the deployment of the Carthagian army. Numerical superiority was always "the most decisive factor in battle." (Clausewitz). The Roman leader counted on the vast superiority of his forces. In a speech he delivered before the battle, the Roman expressed full confidence in his coming victory. He expected to defeat the numerically weaker Carthagian army in the Roman tradition, by a heavy frontal attack.

Terentius Varro was surprised when Hannibal weakened his center and dared to encircle his much stronger opponent in spite of the numerical inferiority of his own forces. The previous battles of the Ticinus and the Trebia had been won as the result of victories of the Carthagian cavalry over the Roman cavalry. In these battles Hannibal also used encirclement tactics. Then he detached for the attack against the enemy's flanks only cavalry and light troops which made it possible for the Romans to break through his pincers and to salvage a large portion of their army.

At Cannae[2], a Carthaginian victory was already assured when Hannibal's cavalry attacked the Roman rear. Yet the new and therefore surprising feature of this battle was the fact that Hannibal deployed his best troops, not at his center, but on both of his flanks, where during the first phases of the battle he hid them behind his mounted troops. At a favorable moment, these troops attacked the flanks of the Roman legions. It was only this attack against both flanks of the Roman army that made possible the total annihilation of the enemy. Hannibal lacked absolute numerical superiority, but by his unorthodox arrangement he established relative superiority at the decisive point. When the surprised Roman commander finally realized what the intentions of his opponents were, it was already too late to avoid disaster.

The battle of Cannae clearly shows that decisive victory is not the result of a brilliant strategic idea, nor of its effective and skillful execution alone. Victory is also dependent upon the attitude of the enemy commander, who must be caught unawares and ignorant of the true intentions of his opponent until it is no longer possible for him to act on his own initiative. The blow must fall swiftly and unexpectedly; strength must be met by weakness if a battle of annihilation shall materialize. "To obtain a perfect Cannae it is necessary to have a Hannibal on one side, a Terentius Varro on the other. Both of them, each in his own way, contribute together to the great achievement." (Schlieffen). One belligerent must surprise, the other must be surprised. Only and when the two commanders play these respective roles will a battle lead to the annihilation of one army.

Fencers' Surprise Tactics

In the introduction to "On War," Clausewitz compares war to a gigantic duel. In a duel for life and death, the normal rules of fencing are not observed. Rather, the fencers try to deceive and fatigue each other by feints and to hit suddenly and surprisingly at a vital spot. It is not different in war. Great commanders always distinguish themselves in the art of surprising their enemy. They hide their intentions and measures until the hour of decision comes. Only those commanders act openly who are absolutely certain of victory.

In Clausewitz' opinion, surprise is possible only under favorable conditions. In addition to a good strategic idea and its energetic execution, many conditions are necessary which cannot be influenced or changed by the commander. Luck and merit on one side, mistakes, negligence and ill luck on the other, are the conditions in which surprise may be successful. The effects of surprise are multiplied by the mistakes of the opponent. This is the reason why Schlieffen taught that to achieve victory, it is merely necessary to exploit the enemy's errors. The enemy must be attacked if he has exposed himself by his own mistakes. The attack on unexpectedly exposed weaknesses is a particular form of surprise operation which, however, requires quick action. Otherwise the opportunity may be lost.

The tactical and strategical problems which Schlieffen discussed with his pupils have often been criticized on the ground that he assumed situations which resulted from mistakes committed by both parties. Schlieffen justified himself by pointing out that military history is nothing more than a chain of mistakes and, consequently, every military situation is the product of previous errors. Above all, the soldier must learn to recognize the mistakes of the enemy and to exploit them, though this may sometimes require departure from accepted military rules. The military leader must indeed be able to rid himself from traditional precepts, yet in doing so, he should never forget that heterodoxy has its limits beyond which it is no longer effective, but becomes dangerous.

"Consul Terentius Varro had many pupils at all times," while examples of Hannibal are much less frequent in the history of war. Can the great Carthaginian leader still serve as a model for modern strategists? Can a decisive victory still be won with the means which have so effectively been applied by his military genius? Are the principles which Count Schlieffen developed in his study on the battle of Cannae still valid under present day circumstances? Is successful surprise still the necessary condition of annihilation? Is annihilation the essential objective in the wars of mass armies? Is superior generalship today characterized by executing maneuvers which the enemy does not expect? And is even the most brilliant strategic idea futile if the enemy prematurely learns of it? These questions shall be answered in this book.

NOTES, INTRODUCTION

1. Schlieffen: Count von Schlieffen (1833-1913) is the master and to a certain extent, the creator of the German army. Many of the present generals still received part of their military education from him, or were, at least, educated in his spirit. Schlieffen tried to imbue the German Staff with one doctrine and one spirit, so that leadership would never break down even if the communications between the different leaders were severed.

The reactions of all German leaders were to become identical. In order to achieve this goal, Schlieffen frequently played war-games with his officers and undertook trips to prospective battle-fronts where practical field studies were made. Schlieffen is also the father of the German war plan of 1914, although his plan was applied in a modified form. He had forseen a war on two fronts against France and Russia and advised the use of three-quarters to four-fifths of the German army against France.

Since the German-French frontier was heavily fortified, thus making quick victory improbable, he planned to use the main strength of the German army for an attack through Belgium by which the French were to be enveloped and possibly encircled. Later on he even thought of marching through Holland so that his offensive wing could still further be strengthened. After his retirement new army corps were raised in Germany and at the beginning of World War I used on the left flank of the German army, which thereby acquired enough defensive power to beat back a strong French offensive. It has been argued that these forces should have been employed on the German right wing, for the attack through Belgium and the decisive battles north of Paris. However, it has been shown that the available transport facilities were already overtaxed and would not have permitted a further strengthening of the German right wing. Ludendorff was the author of the modified Schlieffen plan.

Despite all shortcomings, Schlieffen's doctrine must still be considered as one of the best military doctrines which exist, if not the best. It can be summed up as follows: Form a center of gravity; concentrate there the greatest superiority you can; attack in the direction of the enemy's flanks and rear and try to envelop and encircle the enemy army; above all, maneuver incessantly.

Negatively put: Do not disperse and do not attack frontally; be not afraid of weakening parts of your front if you need strong forces for concentration; do not wait passively, but take and keep the initiative.

2. Cannae: The battle of Cannae (216 B.C.) in which Hannibal inflicted a major defeat upon the Romans has been discovered as a model of battle strategy by the German historian, Hans Delbrueck. Field Marshal Count von Schlieffen the German chief of staff, 1891-1906, framed the German war doctrine according to this model and tried in his war plan against France to imitate Hannibal's example. The most important characteristic of the battle of Cannae, according to the German doctrine, is the attack against both flanks and the rear of the Romans.

It must, however, be pointed out that the Germans over-simplified the story of Cannae and that the usual description of this battle is partly not correct and partly unproved by the sources. In particular, it is doubtful whether the Romans actually had substantial numerical superiority.

The orthodox figures are: 80,000 Roman infantry plus 6000 Roman cavalry against 40,000 Carthaginians and 10,000 cavalry. These figures have been computed by assuming the size of a Roman legion as ten thousand men. However, more recent studies refute this assumption. The most probable figures are: 40,000 to 50,000 Romans against 35,000 to 40,000 Carthaginians, plus the cavalry as indicated above. This makes the Roman superiority much less impressive, and particularly so because Hannibal was superior in cavalry, the decisive weapon.

To the Roman defeat many more factors contributed than the attack on the flanks. First of all, the two Roman commanders were on bad terms, each of them pursuing his own strategy. Terentius Varro was a political general who had been appointed through public pressure and who was being forced to accept battle on account of the home situation.

Hannibal's battle plan on the other hand, was successful because the disposition of his troops was skillfully concealed from the enemy. However, had the Roman infantry which broke the Carthaginian center not been seized by panic, Hannibal would hardly have won his battle. Panic, therefore, is certainly as important a factor as the attack on the flanks. So far as the attack on the Roman rear is concerned, it must be emphasized that according to some sources Hannibal actually used a ruse for getting behind the Roman lines. Just before the battle began, parts of his cavalry pretended to desert to the Romans who had no time in which to investigate thoroughly. They placed the "deserters" behind the battlefield. When the battle was approaching its climax, the "deserters" drew short swords which they had hidden and charged the Romans from the rear.

At any rate, there is little doubt that the victory of Cannae was due to rather exceptional circumstances. The Germans themselves acknowledge that in the time between 216 B.C. and 1914 A.D. only the battle of Sedan in 1870 can be compared to it. Consequently, many victories were won according to quite different patterns. And it must be added that Cannae did not decide the war, though this battle figures in history as a "decisive" victory.

Hannibal could not beat the Romans. Fourteen years later he was himself beaten by Scipio. This is to show that foreign readers of German military literature should not accept the German tradition of Cannae without qualification. Cannae may well be the pattern of an ideal battle; it is certainly not the pattern of battle as such, nor is it the only way to victory.

I

Surprise as Means for Victory in Recent Wars

SURPRISE, in Clausewitz' opinion, is a product of secrecy and speed. Is is of extreme importance to hide one's own plans from the enemy until he is unable to take effective counter-measures. This can be done either by concealment and camouflage or by deception. The enemy is easily deceived if he does not expect a particular decision. Yet if the existence of a decision is in the air, if everybody talks and knows about it, the enemy is seldom deluded. If a military decision is executed with the utmost speed, the chances are that the enemy will be surprised. Secrecy and speed are mutually dependent upon each other. If secrecy cannot be maintained, speed must be increased; if speed is not practical, the enemy must be kept wholly ignorant of the impending operations. Otherwise surprise can never be achieved.

In modern times, secrecy can be maintained only with great difficulties. Too many persons know of the decisions which have been made, even the most secret, inasmuch as the High Command is organized according to the principle of division of labour.[1] As a remedy, every military plan should be executed with extreme speed. Unfortunately at present ideas can not be followed by action as quickly as in earlier wars. The movements of mass armies and the re-grouping of large forces require much time. A great time-lag between the conception of a plan and its execution is inavoidable. This time-lag evidently must affect secrecy. For it will often provide an opportunity for the enemy to discover and frustrate our plans.

Strategic surprise, therefore, in the 20th century became the most difficult military undertaking. The often-discussed mediocrity of generalship in modern wars is to a large degree due to this time-lag between decision and execution which makes strategic surprise next to impossible. In the wars of the 19th century and, of course, in previous wars, strategic surprises were rather frequently accomplished, because wars were then fought in small spaces and during short periods of time. Surprise is obviously much easier under such conditions. But when military preparations must be undertaken in vast areas and over many months, if not years, the maintenance of a military secret must be regarded as an extraordinary achievement.

Time-lag Grows Greater

The time-lag seems to have much increased during and after World War I. In the last decade, it became more and more difficult to hit the opponent mortally by surprise. Very few brilliant strategic ideas could effectively be put into operation. The danger arose that mass and matériel dominated the ideas of the general, the military machine became too cumbersome for swift adaptations and flexible plans. In one word, the tools became dominant. In Clausewitz' terms, one could say that ideas were being frustrated by frictions of the machine.

What are the result of surprise? Clausewitz asserts that surprise may create the effect of numerical superiority. Without successful surprise no superiority at the decisive point can be achieved. Superiority of numbers is the most general requisite for victory. Absolute superiority *everywhere* is unattainable; hence it must frequently be replaced by relative superiority *somewhere*. To achieve relative superiority somewhere is the main objective of almost all military movements and the essential purpose of generalship. Since relative superiority will hardly be accomplished if the enemy knows the plan of concentration before the hour of attack, the principle of surprise is of importance equal to that of the principle of concentration. To defeat the enemy, he must be attacked with superior numbers at the decisive point; but to possess superior forces at the point of attack, the enemy must be surprised. Annihilation is not possible without previous surprise.

Surprise, however, is not a means for the offensive only. An army on the defensive fights for victory as well as its opponent and must therefore also try to surprise the enemy. Surprise deployments are a particularly effective method at the disposal of defensive armies.

Surprise is thus an element of equal importance to offensive and defensive warfare. All kinds of surprise can be applied in both forms of war, except the surprise of a sudden and unexpected onslaught at the beginning of war, *Ueberfall* which is an important element of offensive warfare exclusively.

The intellectual consequences of surprise are sometimes as important as the surprise concentration, or application, of force itself. "When surprise is highly successful," says Clausewitz, "it leads to confusion and breaks the enemy's courage." Usually the intellectual and material results of surprise supplement each other. Together, they are capable of completely reversing a given military situation.

Conflicting Orders

Frequently, surprise reduces the unity of the enemy forces and induces the commanders of the enemy army to issue conflicting orders. Under modern conditions, this danger is particularly great because the direct influence of the High Command on the battlefield is comparatively weak, modern dispersion-tactics giving subordinate leaders a rather large measure of independence. The general can, but seldom is, personally able to, restore the morale of his troops if their will to fight is paralyzed. Modern wars offer many examples of panic which led to the frantic flight of whole armies. One is reminded of Schiller's Talbot, the commander of the English forces, who exclaimed at the sight of his routed and fleeing army:

> "They will not hear me—not a man will stand;
> Clean-loosed are all the bands of discipline.
> As if Hell's self had vomited around
> Its legions of the damned, delirium wild
> Blends in a desperate and senseless rout
> The coward and the brave alike. In vain
> I strive to muster e'en a tiny band
> To rally round me and confront the flood
> Of foes who waxing surge into the camp."
>
> *(Maid of Orleans, Act II, scene 5.)*

General Archduke Joseph Ferdinand might have spoken similar words when large parts of his panic-stricken 4th Army were thrown back behind the river Styr by the Russians under Brussilov. The Italian General Capello had a like experience in the autumn of 1917 when at the Isonzo his army was seized by panic and could not be halted in its retreat[2].

Clausewitz was quite right when he asserted that a commander who possesses moral superiority over his opponent is particularly apt to discourage and outwit the enemy and often even wins when, according to the rules of military art, he should lose. ' Military disasters are usually preceded by moral collapse on the part of the leaders.

To quote one of Clausewitz' *dicta* which is characteristic of his military ideas: "Only he can surprise who imposes his law on the enemy." "To impose one's own law on the enemy" for Clausewitz is not identical with having the "initiative" in military operations. The offensive party usually possesses the initiative, but offensive operations are not necessarily advantageous. In Clausewitz' opinion, they are only profitable if there is some chance that the enemy might be surprised by the offensive moves. If this is not possible, it is preferable to make decisions later than the enemy and to take the enemy's previous decisions into proper account.

The general who can execute his decisions imposes the law on the enemy. If the enemy is able to carry out his own decisions, the opposing army loses its freedom of action. But which side can execute its plans? That side which makes the least mistakes. A military decision which is poorly performed will miscarry. Faulty dispositions will enable the enemy to take effective counter-measures and may thus lead to reverses. If both sides try to surprise each other, the army that commits the fewest errors will be successful.

NOTES, CHAPTER I

1. A strategic decision can be taken by a few individuals. Yet many more persons are necessary to draw up detailed battle orders, and numerous are those who are in charge of preparations and who therefore must gain knowledge of the plan, whether directly or indirectly, by deduction. It has been asserted that approximately 2000 persons knew in advance of the Anglo-American operation against North Africa. This, obviously, is the number of persons who had been officially informed of the enterprise. The number of those who deduced the Allied intentions from many not uncertain indications was probably higher. Thus secrecy can not be obtained by merely "saying nothing". Secrecy requires the systematic confusion and deception of the enemy.

Secrecy is one of the main conditions of success in war. Yet it is also true that nothing is more abused than the principle of secrecy which frequently serves as a shelter for incompetence. Very often, secretiveness is fantastically exaggerated and without deceiving the enemy, serves only to impair the efficiency of one's army. Sometimes, information about the enemy is withheld from their own officers. Many persons think that a secret or confidential document is for their own use only. "Secrecy" is also an effective instrument for interdepartmental competition. It is therefore in order to quote Lord Fisher's remarks on "secrecy and secretiveness":

"There are three types of secrecy: I, The Ostrich; II, The Red Box; III, The Real Thing.

"I. The ostrich buries his head in the sand of the desert when pursued by his enemy, and because he can't see the enemy concludes the enemy can't see him! Such is the secrecy of the secretive and detestable habit which hides from our own officers what is known to the world in other navies.

"II. The secrecy of the Red Box is that of a distinguished Admiral who, with great pomp, used to have his red despatch box carried before him (like the umbrella of an African King), as containing the most secret plans; but one day, the box being unfortunately capsized and burst open, the only contents that fell out were copies of "La Vie Parisienne! Such, it is feared, was the secrecy of those wonderful detailed plans for war we hear of in the past as having been secreted in secret drawers, to be brought out when the time comes, and when no one has any time to study them, supposing, that is, they ever existed; and, remember, it is detailed attention to minutiae and the consideration of trifles which spells success.

"III. There is the legitimate secrecy and secretiveness of hiding from your dearest friend the moment and the nature of your rush at the enemy, and which of all the variety of operations you have previously practised with the fleet you will bring into play! But all your captains will instantly know your mind and intentions, for you will hoist the signal or spark the wireless message, Plan A, or Plan B, or Plan Z!"

2. The "intellectual consequences of surprise" which General von Erfurth mentions may more accurately be described as "panic". Panics occur very frequently in war and play an important role in almost any battle in which a numerically not inferior army is decisively beaten. In spite of the frequency and importance of panics, few military writers and even fewer official military publications mention or discuss panics which apparently are considered as something shameful and unmilitary. Panics happen with unseasoned and under-armed soldiers and in case troops have not been prepared for the fighting methods of the enemy. They also happen with experienced armies, particularly when the troops

are tired and hungry. Generally speaking, panics are the result of bad leadership and of lack of confidence on the part of the troops. Good leaders may be transformed into bad leaders, if a successful surprise has overthrown their calculations and sapped their self-confidence.

II

Strategic Surprises, Early Phases of War

AT THE beginning of a war the enemy can be surprised either with respect to time or to space. The enemy should be ignorant of the date of the zero hour as well as of when hostilities will start or what the deployment of the attacking forces will be. Surprise can also be accomplished by new implements of war and by new fighting-methods. Any one of these surprises may if successful, put the enemy in a difficult position.

Almost all great commanders attempted to surprise their enemies by and at the very outbreak of war. Frederick the Great began every one of the Silesian wars with a surprise attack. Napoleon always tried to take the lead over his enemies by sudden onslaughts. Moltke won his decisive victories in the early phases of his wars—a fact which is the basis of the erroneous belief on the part of many pre-World War I writers that quick decisions can still be won as in the period of mass-armies.

After the naval surprise with which Japan in 1904 began the war against Russia, the question whether war should be begun with or without a formal declaration of war was being widely discussed. The Japanese attack without the formality of first declaring war was, however, not a historic novelty. In former times, diplomatic niceties in this connection were rarely observed, and even in the so-called "progressive" centuries many governments failed to deliver a solemn declaration of war. When in 1801 England intended to break the alliance with the Scandinavian countries, the British navy first took up battle positions, and only then, in order to save appearances, was an ultimatum delivered to the Danish government. This ultimatum contained terms which the Danes could not be expected to accept. After, as foreseen, the Danes rejected the

British ultimatum, Nelson began immediately to attack the Danish fleet and bombed the fortifications of Copenhagen. (April 2, 1801). This action is a good example of a naval surprise-offensive in peacetime.

War In Peace-Time

Some years later, Denmark was again the object of precipitate military violence in time of peace. In order to increase the effectiveness of the *guerre de course* against Napoleon I, the British government on July 19, 1807, decided to ask the surrender of the Danish fleet. The ships were to remain in British custody for the duration of the war against Napoleon. After this decision was taken, the royal navy anchored in the harbour of Helsingor. Transports carrying 20,000 soldiers followed the navy. The British envoy presented terms to the Danish government and warned that, should the ultimatum be rejected, violence would again be used. The Danish government again refused to submit. Thereupon the British expeditionary forces were landed. On August 24, 1807, Copenhagen was encircled. In the evening of September 2, (that is, technically speaking, still in time of peace) bombardment of the city began. Immense fires were started and many persons were killed. Finally on September 7, an agreement was drawn up according to which the Danish warships and all naval matériel and installations in Danish possession were surrendered to the British. Danish sea power was annihilated for the time being and was never fully restored. Daird Clowes, the greatest British authority on naval history at the beginning of the 20th century, considers the legality of the British attack on Copenhagen as open to discussion, but thinks that this attack was a wise and indeed necessary measure.

The sea battle of Navarino which preceded the Russian-Turkish War of 1828-29 was also a battle in peacetime. This battle was the outcome of political tension which resembled somewhat the political situation at the time of the Spanish Civil War, 1936-39. Great Britain, France and Russia had signed a pact to protect Greece from Turkish oppression. Thereupon the Turkish-Egyptian navy, accompanied by an Egyptian landing force under command of Ibrahim Pasha, entered the port of Navarino at the western coast of Morea. Admiral Codrington, commander of the British naval forces in the Mediterranean, informed the Turkish Pasha that the Allies would not permit the Turkish-Egyptian navy to support Turkish land operations against the Greeks. During several weeks the British and French squadrons stood guard over Ibrahim Pasha's navy. On October 14, 1827, a Russian squadron joined the Allies and the Bay of Navarino was effectively blockaded. However, the prospect of maintaining a winter blockade did not particularly please the Allied admirals. They decided to force Ibrahim Pasha to give in. On October 17, 1827, they sent him an ultimatum of sorts. Unfortunately, their communication did not reach the Pasha who was ashore and thus unable to reply promptly. Disregarding this particular circumstance, the Allied warships sailed into the bay. The Turks notified the Allies that the entry of the whole Allied fleet into the bay would not be permitted, although some of the Allied ships might enter if they liked. The British admiral curtly replied that he came to give, not receive, orders. Should a single shot be fired against Allied warships, he added, the Turkish fleet would be destroyed. The Allied ships continued to move in closer to the Turkish navy. Codrington's flagship "Asia" set anchor alongside the Turkish flagship. Again, the vice commander of the Turkish navy officially demanded what were the intentions of the Allies. Suddenly shots were fired and a general engagement began. The Turks fought as well as they could. Finally they succumbed to the superiority of the Allies.

The net result of this surprise attack was the destruction of the Turkish fleet which, without previous declaration of war, was sent to the bottom. The British admiral who was responsible for this deed was decorated by the Allied governments. Yet he was severely reprimanded by British public opinion and eventually he was recalled. After all, the destruction of the Turkish fleet served better the interests of Russia than of England. The liberty of movement which the Russians enjoyed in the Black Sea during the Russian-Turkish War was granted to them by the British admiral.

Official War Declarations

After the battle of Navarino none of the Allied Powers delivered an official declaration of war; nor did Turkey. It was only half a year later, on April 26, 1828, that Russia formally declared war on Turkey.

The Japanese attack on the Russian navy at Port Arthur, of all the powers, particularly offended Great Britain. Article 1 of the Third Agreement of the Second Hague Convention, signed on October 18, 1907, was largely due to British influence. It provided that "the contracting Powers recognize that hostilities between them must not commence without previous and explicit warning, in the form either of a reasoned declaration of war or of an ultimatum with conditional declaration of war."

This agreement is probably the reason why, at the outbreak of World War I, declarations of war were delivered in volume for which there is hardly a historical precedent. Any delivery of a declaration of war obviously has definite disadvantages. The power which delivers the first declaration of war is often held responsible for the war itself, although it hardly needs elaboration to show that war guilt not necessarily must have relationship to the first declaration of war. Outsiders and the general public prefer to overlook the true causes of war, particularly in a period of political tension. The factors which really are at the bottom of war are revealed only when secret archives have been opened to historical research. Wise and far seeing governments will therefore avoid taking upon themselves the blame of delivering the first declaration of war. Public indignation can be so easily aroused that it is not advisable to take such a risk.

Pre-War Diplomacy

The prudence with which, for instance, Bismarck always dealt with this difficult problem is instructive. In 1870, by artful maneuvers he forced the French government to declare war on Prussia, though he himself considered this war as unavoidable. In 1866, he was particularly careful to prevent Prussia from being considered the aggressor, thus taking into account the political situation in Europe and Germany as well as the wish of his king who desired that "the honor of firing the first cannon shot should be left to the Viennese court." Bismarck treated each of his prospective opponents with special and appropriate methods and succeeded in outwitting every one of them.

Even though by May, 1866, the armies of Austria and her Allies feverishly were preparing for war against Prussia, Bismarck did not yet resort to military counter-measures. He preferred to continue diplomatic conversations, which he could exploit for putting the responsibility for the war on the shoulders of his opponents. Despite the fact that Austria's military preparations were far in advance, Prussia mobilized her forces only step by step, always taking a new provocation on the part of Austria as a welcome pretence for proceeding further.

From a military point of view, the Prussian army's position became more and more difficult. The Austrian army was at last entirely ready for attack, together with the armies of other German states which had had enough time for completely mobilizing their forces and which could, in Moltke words, "measure up to realities." Prussia was thus menaced by war on many fronts, an unpleasant situation which, from the narrow point of view of the army, would have required immediate action. Bismarck did not accede to the desires of the soldiers. Here Prussia purposely renounced the advantages that may result from a surprise attack. Her soldiers were not permitted to begin active operations before Bismarck was convinced that he had exhausted all diplomatic possibilities and that the war guilt was definitely put on Austria. The Austrian government, in order to counteract Prussian pressure on smaller German states, saw itself obliged formally to declare that Austria would give assistance to all countries at war with Prussia. This statement was interpreted by Bismarck as an Austrian act of aggression. According to him, Austria had proved her "hatefulness by aggression."

In Bismarck's interpretation, the Austrian statement was almost a formal declaration of war. At any rate, it was depicted as a notification that a state of war *did* exist between Prussia and Austria. Hence there was no reason why Prussia should furthermore retard her military operations. Bismarck informed the commanders of the three Prussian armies earmarked for operations against Austria that a state of war had come into existence between the two countries and directed them to act accordingly. He also directed the military authorities to deliver to the Austrian advanced guards a letter for the Austrian commander-in-chief. This letter in which the Austrian statement was quoted closed with the following words: "This declaration [of the Austrian government] officially announces the existence of a state of war between our two countries. The

signer of this letter [that is, a Prussian officer] has the honor
to notify Your Excellency that the Royal Prussian Army has
received orders to act accordingly." This method of beginning
war by delivering a *lettre d'adieu* to the enemy commander, his-
torically speaking, was extraordinary and unique. Usually events
move much too quickly to permit so slow a procedure.

Serbia's Hard Problem

During World War I the advantages of strategic surprise-
attacks were considered on several occasions. To the beginning
of September, 1915, the Serbian army concentrated its main
forces against Austria-Hungary. Bulgaria entered the war on
the side of the Central Powers. The Serbian High Command
planned to attack Bulgaria before the mobilization of the Bulgarian army could possibly be completed. The Serbs occupied
strong defensive positions covered by the three rivers, Drina,
Save and Danube. The strength of the Serbian positions would
have made possible the concentration of large forces against
the Bulgarians without exposing the Serbian army to an Austrian
attack. Such a maneuver was the best possible way to forestall
a concentric attack from several directions by superior forces.
Serbia's allies, however, Russia in particular, objected, in the
vain hope that the Bulgarian government might at the last
minute change its mind. In view of the future policy of
Greece, it was deemed advisable to let Bulgaria, and not Serbia,
play the role of aggressor.

Only the Russian High Command whole-heartedly supported
the Serbian plan and denounced these delaying tactics. Not to
undertake a promising preventive offensive, and to leave Bulgaria complete freedom of action, appeared to be a serious military blunder. The Russian Foreign Minister, Sasonoff, did not
share this opinion and even declared that he would consider a
preventive attack on Bulgaria a "crime". The Serbian High
Command was thus obliged to defend a line of more than 650
miles by means of passive defensive only. Hence the Serbian
army was confronted by an insurmountable task. By a purely
passive attitude, the approaching concentric attack of the Central Powers against Serbia could not be thwarted, nor could an
effective surprise be staged. Schlieffen warned against static defense when he said: "If the enemy is to be surprised, one must
not stay in fixed positions, but unceasingly move and maneuver."

After World War I the question whether war should be begun by surprise attacks was widely discussed in military literature. Time and again, French military experts discussed this problem and developed the new theory that future wars should and probably would begin by sudden and unexpected attacks *("attaque brusqué")*.

An Italian, Ulisse Guadagnini, has given a particularly radical form to the concept of the surprise war. He developed the interesting idea that war should be planned like an ambush. On principle, the first attack of the war should only be launched when and if the opponent does not expect it, thinking that peace is not menaced by any military design on the part of the neighbor. War should erupt suddenly, as a thunderstorm develops in the mountains or as an earthquake occurs, not preceded by warning signals. The army, the navy, the whole people even, must be able to transform themselves with the shortest delay from potential into actual energy—like an explosive charge.

Moral considerations have validity only in civilian life and should not interfere with preparations for war. There are no international laws to prevent a stronger and more powerful people or a better-equipped army from attacking and defeating an inferior opponent. He who would win should not suffer from moral inhibitions. A sudden and unexpected attack is a decisive factor of victory and it will necessarily apply in any future war.

"Without giving the opponent the slightest cause for apprehension beforehand, the aggressor must strike with all his forces and with extreme violence at a previously determined day and at a pre-arranged hour." The mortal blow must be struck before the enemy even knows that war is on. The enemy's military power must be so severely hit that he will be unable to retaliate. Guadagnini emphasized the necessity of striking by surprise with both land and naval forces. He was more skeptical with respect to the chances of surprise by aviation.

In sharp contrast to Guadagnini, another Italian, Giulio Douhet, firmly believed in the decisive role of air-power. According to him, air battle must precede battles on land and sea. After the airpower of one belligerent has been destroyed, his land and sea forces are at the mercy of the master of the air[1].

Exploiting Surprise

Once the decision has been taken to wage war, all air forces must immediately attack the enemy nation and, without bothering about declaring war, exploit the possibilities of surprise to the utmost.

The theory of victory through an unexpected offensive in time of peace has, however, obvious weaknesses.

Under modern conditions, thorough large-scale military preparations can hardly be undertaken without knowledge of the enemy. It will be extremely difficult to accumulate a large amount of "potential energy," as Guadagnini wishes, and keep this accumulation secret. At present, and probably also in the future, distrust is a very powerful factor in international relations. The neighbor is often suspected of having evil intentions which actually he does not have. Large-scale preparations for big offensives are likely to be discovered almost immediately, and one may be sure that such a discovery will lead to counter-measures[2].

On the other hand, moral considerations retain a greater importance than many modern writers are inclined to admit. After all, one can never be sure of victory. Even a statesman who is firmly convinced that his country is going to win will hesitate to disregard entirely moral traditions. A country which launches a surprise attack will internationally be denounced as the aggressor and, in case of defeat, may be held fully responsible and to account for its actions. If the surprise attack is not wholly successful, severe reprisals will be taken against the country guilty of the breach of peace. The theory that might is identical with right and that the stronger can do with the weaker whatever he likes, has not been universally accepted in the history of mankind. For all these reasons, it is easier to advise that moral standards be disregarded than to accept such counsel. Few statesmen will be willing to embark upon a surprise-attack in the midst of peace.

The doctrine of the ambush-war has assumed many different forms. Some of its partisans concede that a single surprise-blow, however strong, is unlikely fully to defeat a strong enemy. Yet a surprise offensive may make possible the seizure of important regions near the frontier and of objectives of high military value to the opponent. The Austrian, General Alfred Krauss, was of the opinion that in 1914 Austria should have begun the war by the immediate occupation of Belgrade. According to him, the capture of this city would have been the best start for the Austrian army. "Serbia's capital, with the headquarters of all Serbian authorities and with its important archives was separated from Hungary only by the river Save, that is to say, by approximately 600 yards. The seizure of the Serbian archives would have been of inestimable political value, while the early crossing of the Save and the establishment of a bridgehead in Belgrade would have been of equally inestimable military value.

Another Austrian, General Conrad von Hoetzendorf, on August 10, 1916, proposed to the German Chief of Staff to march into Rumania immediately after the conclusion of an alliance between Rumania and the Entente should officially be confirmed by the Rumanian radio. His plan was to attack with the German forces under Mackensen from northern Bulgaria across the Danube and to advance toward Bucharest. At the same time, Austrian and Hungarian units, reinforced by German detachments, would attack eastward from Transylvania, moving equally to Bucharest. The Austrian was convinced that this operation would catch Rumania napping and lead to important quick successes. The German High Command, at first, did not expect Rumania to enter the war. On August 18, they sent a belated and dilatory reply and practically declined Hoetzendorf's idea. His plan was critized by the official Austrian publication on the history of the World War, on the ground that it would have required the presence of ready and powerful forces in Transylvania and northern Bulgaria which were not available at that time. Still, it is conceded that an attack of that kind could have been very successful[3].

Mission of Frontier Troops

Swift action at the outbreak of war is generally considered as an indispensible feature of effective defense. Very early it became customary to station troops near the frontier. In case of enemy attack, these covering units were assigned to the task of disrupting the enemy's mobilization schedule and, if possible, pushing his forces back. The experience in 1870 that France had with such an arrangement was far from satisfactory. The hasty advance of French units not yet fully mobilized caused general confusion. The mobilization centers and railway stations were crowded with reservists unable to join their units, because they did not know where they could find them. The army corps and divisions lacked the most essential transport services, their field hospitals and administrative personnel. No provisions were made for the feeding of the troops. Maps were not available.

After some days, the Ministry of War in Paris did not know what to do; they left all decisions to the troops and the field-officers themselves, hoping that they would be able to muddle through. However, the confidence in the *"on se débrouiller"* was disappointing. The chaos was not disentangled. At last, the French High Command realized that, instead of taking the war quickly across the Rhine into Germany, the French army had to defend French soil in France. The strategic surprise-attack which the French had planned in 1870 thus was frustrated by the frictions of their own military machine.

The German *coup de main* against Liège in 1914 is an example of a successful surprise operation at the beginning of war. The troops selected for this enterprise were assembled during the third day after the proclamation of general mobilization (August 4), while still in their peace-time formation. In the night of August 5-6, they were ordered to surprise and break through the outworks of the fortress and to seize the town and its transport-facilities. This bold and reckless operation was accomplished despite almost insurmountable difficulties and local setbacks. It could easily have failed. Its success was chiefly due to the energy of one man, Ludendorff, who had conceived the whole plan himself. Besides, it was executed by first-class units and, in some respects, favored by luck. The *coup de main* against Liège is one of the very few successful examples of its kind. Consequently, it must be considered as an exception, not as a generally applicable precept[4].

For sometime prior to World War I, the concentration of Russian cavalry divisions near the German eastern frontier often gave cause to apprehensions on the part of the German government. In his time, Bismarck, as Chancellor, felt himself responsible for the military preparedness of the Reich and repeatedly drew the attention of the German War Minister to the possibility that East Prussia might be invaded by Russian cavalry. He prevailed upon the Minister to take necessary precautions against that danger. The German General Staff was, of course, constantly concerned with the same problem. In 1894, Count Schlieffen travelled with the General Staff in eastern Germany in order to study the problems which would arise for Germany's defense in case Russian cavalry had invaded Prussia and accomplished the partial destruction of the railroad system before the German army was mobilized. Schlieffen did not consider a Russian cavalry offensive as likely, or dangerous. The events of August, 1914, showed - how right he was in this assumption. To be sure, Russian cavalry tried to cross the boundary and, by destroying railroad facilities, to disrupt mobilization and deployment of the German army. But the German frontier-guards were prepared, and the Russian cavalry achieved but poor results. One Russian cavalry division was beaten on August 5, near Soldau, another on August 9, near Bialla.

Defense Becomes Stronger

In modern military literature surprise raids across the frontier during the first days of war are frequently discussed and sometimes recommended, because, under modern conditions, they can be carried out by mechanized and motorized units. Speed and the fire-power of modern mechanized equipment are, of course, incomparably stronger than those of the old-time cavalry. The power of mechanized weapons is sometimes considered as a promise that surprise raids, which formerly were seldom effective, can now be successfully performed. One should, however, not forget that the defense against modern offensive weapons also has become much stronger than it was in 1914 and that no country will neglect the protection of its frontiers. Provided both sides are equally cautious and either side is unable to begin its mobilization substantially in advance, modern mechanized units are not likely to be more successful than the Russian cavalry in 1914.

The early beginning of the Russian offensive in August, 1914, was largely due to French pressure. The French needed a strong diversion on the eastern front in order to resist the German attack in the west. The director of the Russian Bureau of Military Operations, General Dobrorolski, reported that the Russian army was not prepared to take the field before August 28. The French, however, insisted on accelerating the Russian operations. General Shilinsky, a former chief of the Russian

General Staff, who had negotiated the military alliance with France and who in August, 1914, was the commander of the Russian armies operating against East Prussia advanced the date of his offensive to August 17.

The Russian First Army began to move; the Second Army crossed the frontier on August 18 and 19. The results of this precipitated action were far from satisfactory. As a consequence of their forced marches, the Russian troops, in particular those of the Second Army, were tired and insufficiently supplied. Nevertheless, the Second Army continued its marches across the difficult and almost roadless regions near the German frontier. The Russian troops suffered from the immense heat of August. On August 24, the Chief of Staff of the Second Army, General Posdovsky, was forced to declare that, due to the exhaustion of the troops, the continuation of the advance would be "an adventure". General Samsonoff, commander of the Second Army, shared this opinion and asked the High Command for one day's rest. This request was rejected. Consequently, the Russian Second Army entered the battle of Tannenberg in a state of exhaustion and with insufficient supplies. Under the circumstances, catastrophe was hardly avoidable.

A postponement of the Russian offensive by four days would not have been a disadvantage for the Russians. Our present knowledge about the battle of Tannenberg certainly justifies this conclusion.

The history of modern war offers not a single example of a successfully precipitated offensive undertaken with units either not yet fully mobilized or mobilized more quickly than the rest of the army. There are many examples to the contrary. In the most favorable cases, precipitated offensive action led to momentary and local advantages, but only at the cost of disturbing one's own mobilization and deployment.

Precipitation will hardly yield better results in future wars. Success in war usually goes to the side which uses its power in a premeditated and coordinated way.

Surprises By Sea

The obstacles which prevent quick and early land operations are insignificant in comparison with the obstacles to surprise-attacks over sea. In an illuminating article, entitled "Naval Surprise Attacks at the Beginning of War," General von

Janson discussed Japan's naval surprise attack against Russia in 1904. The success of this operation, which actually started the war, was due to exceptional conditions. It is unlikely that similar conditions will ever exist again before a war between the great western powers. Besides, the distant coastal areas of Asiatic Russia are hard to defend from European Russia where the sources of Russia's military power are situated. The geographical conditions of the Russian empire permitted the Japanese to dispense with a general mobilization of all their forces. Instead, they mobilized their divisions successively and even dispatched them successively to the front. To be sure, their landing forces in neutral Korea on the Asiatic mainland did not have to fight, but only to secure bases for later operations. A landing on the shores of a western country would immediately be followed by a difficult battle with a strong military force. The Russians were unable quickly to counter-attack the Japanese in Korea, but under normal conditions, the defender will not be slow in concentrating a strong force against the invader.

The mobilization of large landing forces can remain as little a secret as the assembly of a big convoy of transport ships. Only a direct attack against the enemy navy itself can be carried out with surprise. Before extensive landing operations can be undertaken the enemy fleet must be paralyzed if not annihilated.

But such an ambitious goal cannot be reached unless the attacker is assisted by criminal negligence on the part of the defender. And yet, notwithstanding the extraordinary negligence of the Russians, the Japanese did not succeed in completely crippling the Russian navy in Port Arthur. General von Janson proved the hopelessness of a naval surprise-attack under normal western conditions by the indecisiveness of Japan's surprise in 1904. The events of World War I did not refute General Janson's thesis of the impracticability of naval surprise attacks. In the meantime, the appearance of military aviation which enables an effective control of all main sea-approaches has facilitated the defense of coastal lines. Naval and air-attacks, even if launched only to gain temporary mastery of the sea and air require extensive preparations. Too, these preparations take such time that their premature discovery can hardly be avoided. Large scale surprise-landings must practically be considered as an impossibility. They are not an appropriate method to win a war during and by its very start[5].

Aviation offers, however, a better chance for surprise than land and naval weapons. Douhet, the advocate of a surprise offensive with large fleets of aircraft, has still many partisans. Indeed, an air-force is able swiftly to attack unsuspecting opponents, although during a political crisis no country will neglect to perfect extensive air-raid precautions.

Many plausible objections have been raised against an air strategy in Douhet's style. The danger of reprisals, for instance, should not be overlooked. On the whole, it is not altogether probable that future wars will be started in accordance with Douhet's recommendations.

Abyssinia, Italy and England

The question must also be asked whether future wars, like World War I, will be preceded by the usual diplomatic formalities, from the recall of Ambassadors to the official declaration of war. Every government will leave it to its opponents formally to declare war while the latter will, of course, try not to fall into the trap. The relations between Great Britain and Italy during the Abyssinian War showed that one may even resort to open economic warfare without either side recognizing the existence of a state of war. The history of Far Eastern wars also indicates that a state of war may actually exist, screened as frontier incidents, although no state of war is recognized by the belligerents or the neutrals.

These examples seem to demonstrate that initial surprise attacks are of questionable military value and can be successful only under rare and exceptional circumstances.

The question then arises whether the enemy can be surprised by a particular and unexpected disposition of the military forces. Schlieffen remarked that the disposition of an army is largely dependent upon the peace-time location of troops, the railroad system and the shape of the frontiers of the attacked country. "If these three factors are known, the offensive deployment of any army can be calculated in its general outlines."

Field Marshal Count von Moltke in 1870 indicated the exact disposition and concentration of the French army. "In order to learn the French war plan," commented Schlieffen, "Moltke paid neither many spies nor did he bribe high officials. To get knowledge of the most important French state secret, he limited his expenses to the price of a cheap railway-map. In the area of railroads the deployment of every army is conditioned by, and dependent upon, the existing railroads[6]."

Before the First World War, the German General Staff deduced the deployment of the French and Russian armies in the same way and later events proved their deductions to have been largely correct. Similar deductions are obviously more difficult with respect to a country fighting on several separate fronts because, comparatively speaking, it is free to decide by its own will against which opponent it shall first concentrate the bulk of its forces. Consequently, Germany's enemies in 1914 were at a loss correctly to foresee the German war plan. The Russians assumed that the main German forces would be tied up in the west. The Russian General Staff therefore intended to throw its main forces against Austria-Hungary while Germany was to be attacked only by limited forces. Yet the Russians were not sure of their own deductions and prepared a second substitute war plan in case the Germans should carry their main effort to the east. Then the mass of the Russian army would take the offensive against eastern Prussia.

Effective Secret Service

In order to gain the necessary information in time, the Russians had placed secret agents in all German cities with big garrisons, particularly in Stettin, Posen, Breslau. The agents had to ascertain in what directions the German corps were moved. On August 6, that is to say just four days after general mobilization had been proclaimed, the Russians already knew that Germany would leave only small forces in the East. The original Russian war plan could therefore be put into operation.

Nor did the French General Staff dare rely on its own guess. To be sure, most French officers were convinced of a German attack through Belgium. However, opinions were divided with respect to the numbers which Germany could spare for the Belgian operation, to the direction of their advance (in particular whether they would operate only on the eastern or on both banks of the Meuse) and to the German attitude in Lorraine. The French therefore devised a plan with two variations. The second variation was to be applied in case of a German attack through Belgium. In addition, they put a whole army in second line for use where needed. The second variation of the French plan was set in motion by August 2, when the Germans asked the Belgian government for free passage through Belgium. Though the uncertainty of the French General Staff was thus dispelled, they continued to ignore the true German intentions. The French persisted in their belief that large German forces would be concentrated in Lorraine and that the German right flank would not extend beyond the Meuse. "The advance of our strong right flank on the left bank of the Meuse," writes General von Kuhl, "completely surprised the enemy and disrupted his plan of operations."

Surprise through unexpected disposition and concentration of forces is certainly a difficult undertaking, yet it is possible and can be very effective. An army battling on several fronts has the advantages of the inner lines and can, within limits, freely choose the direction of its main effort. The disposition and concentration of armies fighting on the outer lines can, however, be deduced with some probability although, of course, such deductions may be wrong. It follows that surprises can also be performed by an army operating on the outer lines.

The tendency to begin war with surprise attacks was a standard feature of many former wars and still exists in the present period, even though initial surprise-attacks become more difficult. An unorthodox and unexpected disposition of the army puts a means of surprise at the disposal of the commander. On principle, the army should be deployed with a view to surprising the enemy, even if the chances are small that the attempted surprise will succeed.

NOTES, CHAPTER II

1. Douhet: The Italian, General Giulio Douhet, (1869-1930), is usually considered as the prophet of air power. He indeed was one of the first professional soldiers who recognized the vast military potentialities of aviation. However, his contributions to the emergence of air power were not considerable, except in the field of propaganda. His forecast of future wars and future types of military aircraft were not borne out by facts. He was an enthusiast of his weapon, who had lost almost all sense of proportion, asserting, for instance, that land offensives could be no longer decisive. Yet he was indubitably also a man of vision.

2. Guadagnini: It is obvious that the chances of such a war are much better than General Erfurth assumed. It may be true that preparations for attack are detected before the attack is launched. Yet the defender may not be able to catch up with the advance of the attacker. A mobilization with a lead of only a few days may be of inestimable value, at any rate in a war against a country without space. On the other hand, one has seen that for political reasons the defender sometimes does not dare to take counter-measurers and actually may fail to mobilize fully his forces. This happened with Poland. Germany could not be angered with "provocation."

3. Ambush War: Despite General Erfurth's arguments, in the present war Germany as well as her co-belligerents began all their campaigns with a surprise attack, and delivered their official declaration of war only after the operations had already started. And there is no doubt, either, that most of the attacks occurred when they were not yet expected. There is, of course, never a complete surprise. But an advance of a few hours may decisively influence the first battles and enable the attacker to seize immediately important territory.

4. Liege: It is quite true that the *coup de main* on Liège was a hazardous undertaking, for the simple reason that it had not been thoroughly rehearsed and that the troops did not know their tasks. Liege was almost a failure, because the principle of secrecy had been exaggerated. Many of the officers did not know what they were supposed to do and had only insufficient knowledge of the situation. The much more difficult *coup de main* on Eben Emael which the Germans performed in 1940, after thorough rehearsing, shows that similar operations are not chiefly dependent upon luck, but can be successfully accomplished, provided they are carefully planned and studied.

5. Naval Surprises: It is hardly necessary to show that actually the chances for naval surprises are much better. Norway, Pearl Harbour, North Africa would not have been possible, if Erfurth's pessimism were justified.

6. Moltke: Today, Moltke would be hardly as successful with a cheap railway map. There are too many railways and too many highways and military concentrations can be accomplished wherever one likes. Under modern conditions, motorized and mechanized units can partly liberate themselves from railroads and highways. Hence, war plans may now be kept secret easier than they were in Moltke's time.

III

Surprise, War of Movement

INFORMATION gathered in peace-time about enemy country is not only incomplete but loses its value after the enemy army has been deployed and begins to move. With the beginning of hostilities, however, information of the enemy army and country becomes constantly available.

Yet little military information, whether secret or not, can ever be accepted as definite and reliable. For war takes place in the realm of uncertainty, hence of surprise. "A good deal of the information gathered during war is contradictory; a still greater part of it is erroneous and the bulk of military information is of dubious reliability. Plans which are built upon such ground may fail."

Services of intelligence, whatever their reliability may be, are indispensable in time of war. The more that is known about an opponent, the better are the chances that strategic intentions against him will be effectively carried out and that the enemy will be surprised. Consequently, intelligence and information services should be as effective and efficient as possible. Yet it is one thing to collect abundant detailed information and another to synthesize it into a general picture correctly reflecting the general conditions on the enemy side. The commander-in-chief has the ungrateful task of distinguishing between correct information, willful lies, exaggerations and errors. From among the numerous and contradictory pieces of information he receives, he is supposed to make a correct selection[1].

The talent to see things rightly is very rare. Napoleon exclaimed: *"Mais c'est la realité des choses qui commande,"* thus criticizing commanders who base their decisions not upon facts, but upon their own wishful thinking. Most people are more impressed by dramatic events than by sober calculations and cold reasoning. In serious situations they tend to see things as worse than they actually are, while they like to exaggerate their own successes if the developments are more favorable. They lack the quality which Marshal Pilsudsky characterized as a good *"tête froide d'un chef."* This quality is inborn, but can also be acquired by a long experience in war.

Military situations change rapidly. Very often a commander has taken a decision in view of a given situation. But when he begins to execute his plan, the situation has developed further and he is already confronted by a totally different set of circumstances. Unless he has self-confidence and liberates himself from the impressions of momentary conditions, he will become undecided and hesitate. Clausewitz therefore asked that a true military leader must have confidence in his superior knowledge and be "like a rock that shatters the waves."

Objective Self-Confidence

Obviously, self-confidence goes hand in hand with the faculty of objectively and soberly appreciating a given situation.

The commander should be able correctly to appraise new information which may modify or change the situation and he must examine it without prejudice to decide whether his original decision is still applicable. It is as wrong to adhere too long to a previously made decision as to relinquish it too early. The history of war shows that self-deception on the part of the High Command is a very definite danger, especially for strong personalities.

Count Schlieffen ironically described the type of military leader who puts trust only in his own intuition and dismisses any information which does not tally with his dreams. "It is wrong to assume," he writes, "that information gained by the cavalry does invariably influence military decisions or is even acceptable. Military leaders often like to depict the situation in a way compatible with their own wishes. If the information they receive strengthens their belief it is joyfully accepted. But if it contradicts their assumptions, it is rejected as entirely wrong and used to prove that the cavalry has again failed in its duties."

Count von Schlieffen wrote these words at a time when cavalry still was the main instrument for reconnaissance. At present, reconnaissance is carried out by other branches of the army.

But the experience of former wars which Schlieffen thus described is still valid. The World War I offers many examples of how superior commanders rejected information from their subordinates with the remark that it be only the product of "imagination and pessimism." Warnings were often credited only when it was too late. Commanders suffer frequently from the tendency to be over-optimistic. The consequence usually is that the enemy is able to achieve a surprise, if not against the troops themselves, then against the commanders. A commander who fails to accept warnings, facilitates the winning of a great victory—for the enemy. An erroneous appreciation of the situation is an essential factor of defeat. In recent wars, many successful surprises were made possible by the incredulity of commanding officers.

The difficulty of correctly appraising a military situation is still one of the main bottlenecks in war. It will continue to remain an essential bottleneck in all future wars.

Note, Chapter III

1. Intelligence Service: One of the reasons why high commanders are likely not to accept incoming information must be attributed to the fact that the chief of the intelligence department seldom has equal rank with the commanding officer. In some armies, he is not even a general officer. It also happens that he is sometimes insufficiently informed of the intentions of the operation department. Care should be taken that close collaboration and incessant consultation between the department of military operation and the intelligence department are assured, and that not as in the French army during World War I, when the Operation Bureau on principle distrusted any information it received from the Intelligence Service. (cf. Pierrefeu).

IV

Deployment for Battle

UP TO the time of Moltke, an army usually marched a considerable distance before it reached the battlefield. Since 1914, the open space which formerly separated two fighting armies before they joined in battle has been narrowed down. Railroads have been developed to make possible the deployment of the armed forces in the immediate vicinity of the frontier. The increasing size of armies has made the former assembly in different groups impractical. Continuous fronts are now being established on the very first day of hostilities.

At the beginning of World War I the German and French armies deploying at the Franco-German frontier were separated from each other by a small distance. Therefore deployment in depth was not possible in this area. Further to the north, however, the two armies were separated by the whole width of Belgium.

The right wing of the German army was consequently compelled to march a considerable distance until it could reach the battlefields of the Sambre and Meuse. The corps at the extremity of the German flank between August 12 and August 22 marched approximately one hundred and forty-five miles.

When hostilities began, both sides ignored the condition of the enemy army. Hence both sides, at least in theory, had a good chance of surprising the opponent. Yet none of these many chances was exploited by either side, as we shall see presently.

The German High Command on August 20, learned some important details of the French plan of concentration. A strong French army was being assembled between Charleroi and Dinant in the triangle between the Sambre and the Meuse. The Belgian army had retired into the fortress of Antwerp. The location of the British Expeditionary Force was not known to the German High Command. A Belgian newspaper on August 19, had published an official London dispatch on the landing of the British army in France. But the German High Command still ignored the reference to the port of disembarkation as well as the whereabouts of the British units.

The concentration of strong Allied forces at the Franco-Belgian frontier confronted the German right wing with the prospect of a big battle. The German High Command took measures to ensure a well-concerted attack of the three armies forming the right German flank against the enemy forces west of Namur. The difficulties of this task are not always fully appreciated today because we are influenced by our historical knowledge about the events. In actual battle the situation can never be appraised so easily as is possible later by study of historical books. The exact strength of the opponent, the direction of his movements and his intentions are apt to be unknown during actual operations. Movements in war strongly resemble a passage through wild, primeval country.

"War is like sailing across an unexplored sea full of reefs which the captain may well divine, but which he has never seen and amongst which he now must navigate in a dark night." (Clausewitz). German leadership had to coordinate the advance of the three armies so that they could effectively be concentrated on the battlefield itself. Field Marshal Count von Moltke considered such a coordinating task as the most difficult undertaking of strategic leadership. Indeed, history shows that a similar task has only seldom been successfully performed.

Shortening Time-Lag

The difficulty lies in the inevitable time-lag between the arrival of one formation at the front and of other formations at the enemy's flank or rear. Count von Schlieffen taught that this time-lag should be shortened by appropriate arrangements on the part of the different army leaders. If the armies approach the battlefield and battle becomes imminent, energetic leadership is necessary to maintain cohesion between the different units. In such a situation the movements of the advancing armies must be coordinated by a strong central command, even if at the cost of interfering with the independence of the army commanders. At least, this was the opinion of Field Marshal Count von Moltke. His own nephew, General von Moltke, however, did not conform to his uncle's precept and assigned the central command of the movements of the German right wing to the senior among the three army commanders, General von Bulow. Since the three German army commanders had different strategic intentions, this solution increased friction on the German side.

Buelow, the commander of the Second Army, did not believe in an early intervention by the British Expeditionary Force. He ordered on August 20, the First and Second Army to move on to the south and then to wait until the Third Army which was still operating in the area of Namur and Givet, could catch up with them. He planned for a later concentric attack against the enemy forces assembled between the Sambre and the Meuse. The First and Second Armies were to attack in a north-southern and the Third Army in an east-western direction. By the evening of August 21, the Second Army had turned around and was facing south. Its advanced guards had crossed the Canal du Centre and the Sambre, where as a consequence of the rashness of subordinate leaders, some fighting had taken place. Bulow on August 22, ordered the First and Second Armies to stop the southward advance and instead to close the gap between the two armies.

All three armies on August 23 were to effect a simultaneous attack on the French south of the Sambre and west of the Meuse. But during the morning of August 22, General von Bulow changed his mind. He had gained the impression that only weak French forces stood south of the Sambre. He could thus hope to win an important success by launching an immediate attack. Without hesitation, he ordered the resumption of the advance and the capture of the difficult terrain south of the Sambre. The Third Army was directed to attack quickly in the direction of the Meuse. Bulow ignored the fact, however, that the commander of the Third Army could be informed about his new plan only around 12 noon, of August 22. Bulow also counted upon the full cooperation of the First Army.

In the course of August 22 the true disposition of the French Fifth Army became increasingly clear. The Second Army did not meet weak French advanced guards south of the Sambre, but with the mass of the French Fifth Army occupying positions, "worthy of a Terentius Varro." The French positions invited encirclement. The German armies were thus certainly well placed to inflict a crushing defeat on the French Fifth Army. The eastern flank of the French could have been attacked by the Third Army. Had the German First Army advanced quickly, where necessary by forced marches, it could have attacked the western flank of the French positions. Too, had strong available cavalry units been concentrated on the German right flank in order to attack the enemy's rear, all essential conditions for the annihilation of the French Fifth Army would have been created.

Difficulties of Envelopment

In order to achieve a complete Cannae against the French Fifth Army, a frontal attack of the German Second Army, tieing up the main French forces, was indispensable. The frontal attack was the very condition of successful attacks against the French flanks. But the German assaults on the flanks and the rear of the French Fifth Army failed to develop satisfactorily and were too weak to achieve an annihilating victory.

Schlieffen pointed out that to begin envelopment at the right moment and to direct attacking forces in the right direction is the most difficult part in any battle of annihilation. The battle of Mons and Namur proves the accuracy of this view.

Germany lacked a Hannibal who would have been able to coordinate the operations of the three armies. It was wrong to deliver the main attack at the Sambre near Namur and Maubeuge. The main attacks should have been directed against the French flanks. If, to their surprise, the French and British should have been outflanked, a definite success was assured. Yet it was essential that the German flanking marches were carried out during the night of August 22-23. The attack had to be launched on August 23. Had it been retarded longer, the enemy would have avoided the trap. The time-lag between the beginning of the frontal attack and the first attacks on the flanks could under no circumstances be extended beyond that date.

At the end of his study on the Battle of Cannae, Count von Schlieffen summarized the conditions of a successful battle of annihilation. He emphasized that the commander must be assisted by sub-leaders with a strong sense of discipline and a good understanding of his intentions. Only if the situation of the enemy is interpreted similarly by all commanders and if the sub-leaders agree with the commander-in-chief on the plan of operations, is the battle likely to end successfully. Such an agreement was entirely lacking among the German commanders in the battle of Mons and Namur.

General von Kluck held opinions about the enemy situation that differed from those of von Buelow. Von Kluck was convinced that the British Expeditionary Force would soon attack north of Lille. In the hope of avoiding a British attack against his right flank, he stopped his advance on August 21 and left his right wing as a protective force behind his main forces, although, according to Bulow's directions, this wing was to proceed hurriedly to the south. Indeed, a surprise attack against the Allied left flank could not be accomplished by keeping these forces back.

The opinions of the two commanders were not harmonized during the next days. A staff officer from the High Command tried to adjust the existing differences, but failed to coordinate the strategic ideas of the two generals A coordination would have been possible only by a clear and incontestable order which Bulow, for lack of authority, could not issue. Bulow was merely a *primus inter pares* and could not prevent General von Kluck from making faulty dispositions.

Thus, Kluck maintained his arrangements, although in the meantime it had been ascertained that the British had taken up positions on the western flank of the French Army and could therefore not attack the right wing of Kluck's forces. Still, Kluck was not yet convinced and held that the positions of the British left wing were not yet sufficiently known. Consequently, he continued to protect his right flank with considerable forces which he left far behind his front, instead of dispatching them as quickly as possible to the battlefield. This arrangement was maintained on August 23[1].

Napoleon Demanded Speed

In a similar situation Napoleon had found impressive words to assure absolute obedience to his orders and to make his marshals act with indicated speed. Before the battle of Ligny, Marshal Soult, upon Napoleon's command, sent an urgent appeal to Marshal Ney to direct his immediate advance on to the battlefield: "You must immediately maneuver to envelop the flank of the enemy . . . . If you act vigorously, his army is lost. The fate of France is in your hands." On the eve of the battle of Mons a similar order should have been sent to Kluck.

A commander with the necessary *coup d'oeil* was also lacking on the left flank of the German forces. It is a frequent occurrence in the history of war that reality and its recognition through the commander are two entirely different things. The commander of the Third Army did not realize the tremendous possibilities which offered themselves during the battle of Namur. His attention was fully absorbed by the difficulties of his imminent attack across the Meuse near Dinant. To be sure, the Meuse in this region is a very considerable obstacle. The attack had therefore to be methodically prepared. Haste would have been dangerous. Or so it seemed.

August 22 was spent in preparing for the crossing of the Meuse. The attack against the hills dominating the regions west of Dinant was ordered for August 23. Yet, on August 18, it had already been ascertained beyond doubt that the regions south and southeast of Givet were not occupied by the enemy. According to information obtained on August 22, mutually corroborated by cavalry and air reconnaissance, it was confirmed that both banks of the Meuse between Givet and Charleville were free from the enemy[2].

This valuable information failed to cause the commander of the Third Army to change his plan. However, it should have convinced him that it would be more effective to launch a surprise attack in direction of the gap south of Givet, instead of concentrating the main effort against the strongest part of the enemy front near Dinant. An attack against the open flank of the enemy could have smashed the entire Allied defense position on the Meuse.

Germans Missed Chances

The dense forests southeast of Givet would have made possible a secret southward advance of strong German formations. Enough time was available to prepare a surprise crossing of the Meuse near Fumay during the night of August 22. This attack would have aimed at the rear of the Fifth French Army. It would have been the most important contribution to a battle of annihilation, in the style of Cannae. The historical evidence conclusively shows that the French would have been totally surprised by a German attack south of Fumay. And they would have been hit at the most decisive point.

German leadership during August 23 lost the last opportunity to impose its law on the French army.

The previous night the commander of the First Army received a very important message. He was notified that British troops had occupied positions on the Canal du Centre, that is to say, north and northeast of Mons. Early in the morning a cavalry division reported by radio that the British were in Maubeuge and that the whole territory up to the Scheldt was free from enemy forces.

But even now no decision was taken to accelerate the advance. The commander of the First Army did not think to proceed *"sur-le-champ"* on to the battlefield and without further delay attack the enemy's flank. Instead, he still persisted in waiting for more complete information. In particular about the left wing of the British Army. Complete and detailed information about the enemy is, however, never available in war, unless the enemy himself takes the trouble to furnish it, as the Russians did during the battle of Tannenberg and during the campaign of Lodz by broadcasting it by radio. Normally, "imagination and combination have an important role to play" (Schlieffen).

Before noon on August 23, the commander of the First Army received a report that since August 22, strong enemy forces were being detrained near Tournay. It was not said whether these troops were British or French. This news caused further confusion and hesitation; the advance of the First Army was again stopped. It is opportune here to recall Schlieffen's dictum that "nothing is more dangerous in war than reliable information." For "reliable" information very often turns out to be either wrong or out of date.[3] In point of fact, information did come in which dispelled definitely all doubts about the location of the British forces. After 12 noon the commander of the First Army conclusively knew that the British stood near Mons. He learned in the afternoon that information of the arrival of troops near Tournay had been erroneous. Cavalry reported that no enemy forces were present in the area of Thielt-Kortryk-Tournay. French troops were in the vicinity of Lille.

At last all concern about the security of the First Army was removed. The advance was resumed. Yet the corps in the second line of the First Army were not ordered to push quickly forward, despite the fact that they still lagged far behind. The advance of the right wing of the First Army was also retarded by different counter-orders. Nevertheless, on August 23, the British front near Mons was strongly attacked by the left wing and center of the German First Army. Yet a decisive victory was impossible without a simultaneous attack by the right wing of the First Army against the enemy flank. This attack could not be launched in time because on the evening of August 23 this wing was still at a distance of twenty to thirty miles from the front.

The German High Command on August 23 twice notified the Third Army of a big gap in the enemy front south of Givet. The High Command advised the Third Army to cross the Meuse south of Givet "in order to cut the retreat of the enemy forces."

On the other hand, the commander of the Second Army pressed General von Hausen, the commander of the Third Army, to advance rapidly in a westerly direction. Obviously, these two requests were somewhat contradictory.

Hausen was thus faced with the alternative of continuing his frontal attacks near Dinant towards the west or of following the advice of the High Command, cross the Meuse south of Givet and then attack to the northwest. Hausen first decided to accede to the request of the Second Army and to continue his frontal attack near Dinant. After a second message from the High Command he modified his decision and ordered those parts of his forces which were not tied up at Dinant to proceed to Fumay. Since the mass of his army was pinned down in the north, not much could be done in the south. Moreover, the columns which advanced to Fumay during the day could not get far beyond the Meuse. The only result of all this was the establishment of a German bridgehead on the western bank of the Meuse. The French apparently were retreating from the Meuse, though their rear guards still put up a stiff resistance. An important success seemed to be in the offing for the following day. In order to harrass the French by a quick pursuit, the commander of the Third Army on August 24 ordered a continuance of the advance in a general southwestern direction.

This decision was altered on the morning of August 24. The commander of the Second Army dispatched a staff officer to General von Hausen. This officer requested the Third Army to move westward in order to assist the Second Army which was somewhat exhausted by the heavy fighting of August 23. Hausen felt that he was obliged to give Buelow, whom he believed to be hard pressed, all the assistance for which he had asked. He changed his dispositions and thus abandoned the last chance of strategic pursuit. After several hours, German aircraft reported that the enemy forces in front of the Second and Third Army were in full retreat. Consequently, Hausen reverted to his original plan and ordered a new change in the direction of the advance. This general confusion caused much friction and a considerable loss of time. The Third Army on August 24 did not succeed in forcing the retreating enemy to accept battle.

Poor Results Obtained

The battle of Namur and Mons yielded only mediocre results for the German army, though the relation of force was not unfavorable for the Germans. The respective dispositions taken on the eve of the battle would have made possible a repetition of the methods applied in the battle of Cannae. On the central front 137 German battalions with 820 cannon fought against 188 French battalions with 748 cannon. Yet on the Meuse, 101 German battalions confronted only 17 French battalions while on the western battlefield, the First Army, in theory at least, could have thrown 120 German battalions with 748 cannon against 52 British battalions with 336 cannon. The Germans had undoubtedly enough strength for smashing both Allied flanks. It was only necessary to use the German forces at the right moment and in the right direction.

The Allies had done nothing to prevent the Germans from winning a Cannae. Like Terentius Varro, they were ready "to contribute their share to the great objective."

The French Fifth Army under General Lanrezac which proceeded northward along the Sambre, west of Namur, on August 21 was informed by the French High Command that the Germans advanced with strong forces on both banks of the Meuse. The Fifth Army was directed to attack the northermost German units by wheeling around Namur. To the British, who had finished their concentration on August 20, the French High

Command suggested that they follow the movements of the Fifth Army by forming, so to speak, the left wing of that French unit.

When on August 21 the Second Army began its attack across the Sambre and when the French cavalry corps under General Sordet was pushed back from the Canal du Centre, General Lanrezac stopped his advance beyond the Sambre. It seemed preferable to him to let the enemy attack across the river and then to strike a strong counter-blow. He considered his positions south of the river as sufficiently strong for such strategy, and failed to recognize that the movements of the German Third Army threatened his right flank. He even reduced the strength of this flank at the Meuse in order to strengthen his positions south of the Sambre. By replacing a whole corps through a reserve division, he virtually opened the door of the Meuse front to the German Third Army. After the evening of August 22 the flank and the rear of the French Fifth Army lay open to German attack.

Two French corps on August 22 had suffered considerable losses in the valley of the Sambre. For the next day, Lanrezac intended with his main forces to remain on the defensive and to undertake only a local offensive with one army corps against the east flank of the German Second Army. Yet when the German crossing of the Meuse south of Dinant was reported, this attack stopped after it had scarcely begun. In other words, Lanrezac ordered the same corps which originally were to fight offensively to protect his flank and rear.

During the evening, General Lanrezac also learned that the French Fourth Army had been forced to retreat toward Mézières. Besides, Namur had fallen to the Germans. The British had been attacked by heavy odds near Mons.

Directions from the French High Command were lacking. Consequently, the commander of the French Fifth Army decided, on his own responsibility, to retreat to the line Givet-Maubeuge.

The cooperation between the French Fifth Army and the British Expeditionary Force was still less effective than the cooperation between the different German armies. The British Field Marshal, Sir John French, was an entirely independent commander. The French High Command and the Commander of the French Fifth Army could transmit only suggestions, not orders to the British leader, which he was free to accept or to reject.

After the completion of the British concentration on the evening of August 20, the British commander intended to advance in the direction of Mons. He received on August 21 excellent reports which gave him a correct picture of the situation of the German First and Second Army. Marshal French had also ample information of the German strength and knew that his opponents had six corps in the first and five other corps in the second line. Nevertheless, the British Field Marshal, evidently encouraged by French suggestions, persisted in continuing with his offensive operations. The British Army late on August 22 had reached the Canal du Centre between Nimy (north of Mons) and Thulin; the British right flank was still somewhat lagging behind. Incoming information made it clear that the British were going to be attacked by the Germans and that their left flank was particularly menaced.

British and French Retreat

Marshal French therefore ordered the advance stopped and the present positions held, thus giving the German First Army a good opportunity to outflank the British army during August 23, provided, of course, the Germans had quickly taken the necessary dispositions for such manoeuver.

The British front on August 23 was strongly attacked. The Germans entered Mons and put the British forces east of that town in a difficult position. The British also lost Jemappes and St. Ghislain.

Despite these reverses, French on August 24 still intended to hold on to his positions. As a consequence, the Germans had a second opportunity to envelop the British army. When on the following night French was informed that Lanrezac had begun to retreat, he at last also decided to do the same. The British retreat was ordered at the very last minute and some British units had already difficulties in disengaging themselves from the enemy.

We have seen that the German army had a good chance to score a decisive victory at the expense of the British and French on August 23. The Allies, like Terentius Varro, had strengthened their front and weakened their wings. Besides, they had chosen to attack the strongest points of the German positions, thus again imitating the tactics of Terentius Varro. The Allies did not use the British Expeditionary Force as a mobile wing operating independently from the French Fifth Army against the axis of the German advance. To be sure, the British may not have been able to execute such complicated strategy. The mere lengthening of the French front by simply adding the British to the French line facilitated the outflanking of the Allied armies by the Germans.

On the other hand, the presence of strong British forces near Mons surprised the First German Army. Yet the British were not able to exploit this successful surprise because their positions offered no opportunity for effective maneuvers against the German flanks. Throughout the whole battle, the German Army was able to impose its law on the enemy. It would have been possible to apply Count von Schlieffen's doctrine and to attack the enemy's flanks with the main German forces, provided the necessary orders had been issued in time and energetically carried out. The two British corps were held up by the frontal attack of two German corps. Thus, three German corps and three cavalry divisions were available for an attack on the British flanks. The British could have opposed only one infantry brigade against these strong German forces. This brigade, just arrived from England, began to move forward on August 23. The Germans were thus undoubtedly in a position to win a quick and important victory. It is even probable that they would have cut off the British retreat.

Timorous Generalship

In World War I, envelopment was usually avoided by immediate retreat. Most generals became apprehensive of the security of their flanks and withdrew their forces when a threat against the flanks materialized. During the initial operations in this war, British generalship was still rather clumsy. It is questionable whether the British forces would have escaped from a German pincer-attack. Besides, Marshal French was quite willing to let himself be surprised. He worried so little about the situation on his left flank that as late as the evening of August 23 he intended to remain in his positions, assuming, however, that the French would also continue to hold to theirs.

On the Meuse, German leadership could have taken advantage of equally good opportunities. The German attack south of Dinant took the French completely by surprise. As we know, Clausewitz taught that surprise is the chief means of achieving numerical superiority at the decisive point. By their successful surprise, the Germans had indeed concentrated vastly superior numbers at the Meuse, which was the decisive point of the whole battlefield, though here again their superiority existed only in theory. Had the Germans attacked in greater strength—which was possible—and had they extended their offensive further to the south, the French could not have warded off the threat against their flank and rear. Nor could they have retreated to the south and southwest. The French would have been obliged to accept battle on a reversed front. Large forces would have undoubtedly been encircled by the Germans. The hesitations and the confusion on the part of the German commander prevented the harvesting of the fruits of successful surprise.

It appears that the British and French formations were menaced by an attack on their both flanks. If the Germans had been able to complete their deployment, the Allied forces in northern France would have been eliminated. As it was, the German army made, so to speak, only a feint along the lines of the battle of Cannae. But this feint induced the Allies to retreat.

The following day, the French High Command again did its best to help the Germans win the decisive victory which had escaped them on August 23. The French High Command was not in agreement with General Lanrezac's decision to break battle and to retreat. In their opinion, an attack of the French Fifth Army could have been successful on August 24. There is little doubt that a French offensive move would have persuaded the British Field Marshal to stay in his positions at Mons and thus to offer his flank to a German blow. Nor can there be any doubt that the strategy devised by the French High Command would have led the French Fifth Army and the British Expeditionary Force to disaster.

German Movements Ignored

The history of the German advance through Belgium shows that the Germans had good opportunities to deceive their opponents and to surprise them by the disposition and the concentration of their forces, despite that the Allies fought in a country almost entirely inimical to the Germans. An army fighting on its own, or in a friendly country is always better supplied with information. Still, the French and British ignored the German movements for a considerable period of time.

Up to August 18 the French High Command was not yet sure whether the Germans would operate with strong forces on both sides of the Meuse or concentrate only small forces on the left bank of that river and deliver their main attack against the French Fourth Army. It was not until August 21 that the French Fifth Army received word from the French High Command that the Germans could be expected to launch their main attack in the region between Brussels and Givet.

By that time General Lanrezac already knew that the same German army which had taken Liège had occupied Brussels and that another German army was about to cross the Meuse near Namur. He rightly deduced from these facts that the Germans would soon appear on the Sambre. However, General Lanrezac ignored the situation on the Meuse front south of Namur. He did not know that the Third German Army approached the Meuse on both sides of Dinant. Instead, he assumed that only one or two German corps operated in that sector. Besides, he underestimated the total strength of the three German armies which he thought to be composed of nine or ten corps. In reality, the Germans had twelve corps available for their operation on the Sambre and Meuse front while Lanrezac could muster only seven corps, including the British.

The British, up to August 20, remained totally ignorant of the location of their enemy. Until the evening of that day, British cavalry had met with no Germans. On the same day, air reconnaissance observed a German column marching westward through Louvain. The British on August 22 had full information of the German movements.

On the German side the lack of information was even worse. They knew by August 20 that a strong French army was being assembled in the Sambre-Meuse triangle between Charleroi and Dinant. However, many important points remained obscure. On the morning of August 22 the commander of the German Second Army still believed that only weak French forces, chiefly cavalry, stood south of the Sambre. General von Hausen ap-

pears to have been ignorant that the French positions opposite
the Third German Army on the Meuse were undermanned.
His information service failed to inform him of the highly
important replacement of a whole French corps by a reserve
division, although this movement was carried out in broad
daylight. General von Kluck was taken by surprise when British troops appeared before his front. And it took him quite
a few hours definitely to convince him that he was opposed
by the bulk of the British Expeditionary Force. All in all,
none of the commanders of the three German armies got a
clear picture of the situation. Every one of them was highly
surprised when, on the morning of August 24, the Allied retreat was revealed.

Each General His Own Judge

The lack of sufficient information of the German commanders was largely responsible for the disappointing outcome of
the battle. Each German commander interpreted the general
situation according to the particular situation at his own front.
The commander of the Third Army was overimpressed by
the natural strength of the French Meuse positions near Dinant
as well as by the repeated requests of the Second Army to
lend assistance for the attack in the Sambre sector. The commander of the Second Army was strongly affected by the violence of the battle south of the Sambre. The Second Army
had clashed head-on with enemy forces of equal and at some
places even superior strength. Besides, the French positions
were covered by the Sambre; Namur and Maubeuge, two big
fortresses as yet uncaptured, constituted a virtual threat against
the flanks of Bulow's army. It must be admitted that the Second Army was in a difficult position. It is understandable why
Bulow exerted his main efforts to secure first of all tactical
safety for himself. Overestimating the strength and power of
his opponent, he wanted to concentrate all available German
units for achieving a tactical victory in his sector. He demanded that the First and Third Army close in with his forces
as much as possible, without considering that by doing so he
narrowed the German offensive front and hence reduced the
possibility of maneuver against the enemy flanks. Bulow paid
more attention to the tactical situation of his own army than
to the strategic opportunities of the whole German force.

The commander of the First Army, on the contrary, thought more in strategic than in tactical terms. However, General von Kluck was guided less by the desire to attack the open flank of the enemy than by anxiety to dispel his uncertainty concerning the location of the British Expeditionary Force. He thus tried to solve two different and more or less incompatible problems.

To command an open and moving flank of the strength of a whole army is a very heavy responsibility. The right combination of boldness and prudence cannot be determined by intellectual reasoning alone. Divination and intuition are likewise necessary. In difficult situations, the intellect of a military leader is less important than his character. Yet he will listen chiefly to reasoned arguments. Flanking and encircling attacks involve heavy risks; a skillful and daring opponent may be able to launch a counterflanking attack against the flanking force.

Prudent leadership is in fundamental contradiction with the idea of annihilation. A prudent general will never be able to surprise his opponent. This is why Count von Schlieffen time and again emphasized audacity and preferred bold solutions for his tactical and strategical exercises. He emphatically warned of prudent solutions which would never lead to a decisive victory. "A military decision must be determined by the burning desire to beat the enemy and not by the wish to avoid defeat."

An Important Principle

In his last discussion of military problems, he once more drew the attention of his student-officers to the importance of his principle: "It seems that the idea of the battle of annihilation which permeated the strategy of Frederick the Great and Napoleon and which is at the bottom of Moltke's incomparable successes, begins to fall into oblivion and disregard. In the numerous compositions which you handed to me I found mention only twice of the intention to annihilate the enemy. On the contrary, most of your studies are concerned with precautionary measures and do envisage only a slightly energetic blow."

It must be recognized, however, that the German commanders during the battle of Mons could only guess of their opportunities. In war, complete and reliable information about the enemy is always lacking. Clausewitz even went so far as to assert that three quarters of the facts which one should know in order to make the right decision remain shrouded in uncertainty. He who waits too long for better information risks the loss of a good opportunity. Thucydides' famous saying that good opportunities do not wait is still valid in modern war.

One important lesson must be drawn from the battle of Namur and Mons, namely that a modern battle of annihilation should never be commanded by three commanders of equal rank.

In every war, the absence of one single will was a clear disadvantage. A divided High Command rarely led to great success. It is true that Prince Eugène and Marlborough together won the battles of Hoechstaedt and Malplaquet. This was, however, predominantly due to Eugène's adaptability and personal modesty. Personalities like Eugène are extremely rare among great captains. Most soldiers have it in their blood to stress their independence and object to division of command as well as to subordination which is not based upon the ordinary military hierarchy.

A military duumvirate was still possible in the War of the Spanish succession, but is no longer practical at the present time. Two hundred years ago, armies were small when measured by today's standards. Battles were fought on a terrain of the size of a modern drill-ground. The entire battlefield could be overlooked from a small eminence. Battles did not differ radically from drill movements. If two commanders were agreed upon the general plan for the battle, the divisions of command could hardly interfere with the actual fight.

In this period of mass armies, divided leadership is no longer feasible. The three German commanders had to improvise the function of the German High Command which had eliminated itself. They cannot be reproached if they did not perfectly fulfil their unexpected task. Modern battles cannot be fought with a deteriorated High Command.

The commander-in-chief must be the only commander and every operation must be conducted by a single leader with absolute authority. For only a leader with ample authority will be capable of mustering the superhuman strength necessary for commanding a modern battle.

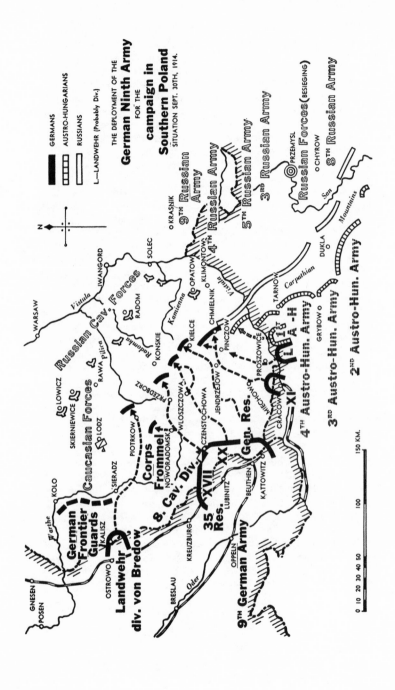

THE DEPLOYMENT OF THE
German Ninth Army
FOR THE
campaign in Southern Poland
SITUATION SEPT. 30TH, 1914.

GERMANS
AUSTRO-HUNGARIANS
RUSSIANS

L-LANDWEHR (Probably Div.)

N

WARSAW
LOWICZ
SKIERNIEWICE
LODZ
RAWA
Pilica
KOLO
SIERADZ
KALISZ
OSTROWO
GNESEN
POSEN
BRESLAU
KREUZBURG
LUBINITZ
BEUTHEN
KATTOWITZ
OPPELN
Oder
Warthe
Vistula
IWANGOROD
SOLEC
RADOM
Radomka
KONSKIE
Kamienna
PIOTRKOW
NOWORADOMSK
PRZEDBORZ
WLOSZCZOWA
CZENSTOCHOWA
JENDRZEJOW
MIECHOW
CRACOW
OPATOW
KLIMONTOW
KIELCE
CHMIELNIK
PINCZOW
PROSZOWICE
Vistula
KRASNIK
TARNOW
GRYBOW
DUKLA
Carpathian
Mountains
San
PRZEMYSL
CHYROW

Russian Cav. Forces
Caucasian Forces
German Frontier Guards
Landwehr div. von Bredow
Corps Frommel
8. Cav. Div.
35 Res.
XVII
XX
Gen. Res.
XI
XII
LA-H

9TH German Army
9TH Russian Army
4TH Russian Army
5TH Russian Army
3RD Russian Army
8TH Russian Army
Russian Forces (BESIEGING)
1ST Austro-Hun. Army
4TH Austro-Hun. Army
3RD Austro-Hun. Army
2ND Austro-Hun. Army

0 10 20 30 40 50   100   150 KM.

It may be questionable whether a future war will again begin with lengthy marches to the actual battlefield, as in August, 1914. Probably, a future war will begin under conditions similar to those which at the opening of World War I prevailed on the German-French frontier. Advances in depth will in future occur only after a gap has been opened in frontier fortifications. Consequently, the advance to the battlefield will be but the second act of a future offensive following a victorious struggle for positions near the frontier.[4]

During World War I, many offensives were carried out on the Eastern front through regions not yet affected by the war, such as the advance of the German Ninth Army to the middle Vistula in October, 1914, and the German advance to Lithuania and Curland in the spring of 1915.

Campaign On the Vistula

The German campaign in the loop of the Vistula in October, 1914, ended undecisively. We propose to examine whether surprise was an important factor in these operations.

General von Conrad on September 1 asked the German High Command to send strong and fresh German forces to the Galician front. He asked for two corps which should move towards Przemysl. The Austrian chief-of-staff expected these German forces to change fundamentally the situation on this front. The German High Command repeatedly discussed the question of German assistance to the Austrian army during the first half of September. It was agreed in principle on September 14 to accede to the Austrian request. At the same time, it was stipulated that no German troops should be taken from the western front.

A new German army, the Ninth, on September 15, was formed for cooperation with the Austrian forces. In an order of the German High Command, dated September 17, the tasks of this new army were formulated as follows: "To operate independently, although in conjunction with the Austrian High Command, against the flanks and rear of the Russian armygroup which is in pursuit of the Austrians."

The transportation of the Ninth Army began on the night of September 16-17 in East Prussia. The mass of the Ninth Army was massed in the region of Gleiwitz-Beuthen-Czenstochowa-Lublinitz. One corps was directed to Cracow, and

other troops into the sector of Kalisz-Ostrovo. The detrainment
began on September 18 and was ended on October 2, when
the ammunition supply had arrived. The assembly of the troops
on September 28 was begun behind the positions from where
their offensive was to be launched.

According to the agreement with General von Conrad, the
mass of the German Ninth Army reached the line Chmielnik-
Kielce on September 30. The left wing of this German army
had already reached the regions west of Konskie, Piotrkow
and Novo Radomsk. The German Ninth Army and the Austrian left wing north of the Vistula began to advance on
October 1. The mass of the Austrian-Hungarian army south of
the Vistula began to move forward on October 4.

The offensive aimed at the two flanks of the Russian forces
which, on the left banks of the San and Vistula, occupied a
line from Przemysl to south of Ivangorod. The German
units had to envelop the Russian northern flank, while the
Austrian Second Army in the sector of Przemysl had to outflank the Russian left wing.

This plan had fair chances of giving good results, provided
secrecy to the last minute could be maintained. Its chances
were dubious in case the deployment of strong German forces
north of the upper Vistula and their advance through Poland
became prematurely known to the Russians. For the Russians
would hardly have permitted the Germans to threaten their
right flank without reacting forcefully and speedily.

Radio Messages Unciphered

In effect, the Russians were quickly informed about the
German troop movements in upper Silesia. And this was only
natural, since the assembly of the German Ninth Army was
not effectively screened by Austrian forces. On the other hand,
the Germans and Austrians were equally well informed of the
Russian moves. In that territory, secret agents played an important role for both parties. Besides, the Russians still stuck
to their habit of not enciphering important radio messages, a
habit which already during the battle of Tannenberg proved to
be very helpful to the Germans.

The commander of the Russian southwestern front received
early intelligence of the appearance of German infantry units
on the river Warthe and of the "daily arrival of thirty-seven

troop trains" in Czenstochova. He took this information as pretext to protest against the weakening of his right flank which was planned by the new commander of the Russian northwestern front, General Russki, who at that time, envisaged his retreat from the line of the Narev.

The first German units, on September 20, arrived in Czenstochova. The first strategic Russian countermove came on September 22 when the Russian High Command intervened in the dispute between the commanders of the northwestern and southwestern fronts.

In view of a probable German offensive in the direction of the bend of the Vistula, the Russian commander-in-chief, Grand Duke Nicolai Nicolaievitch, on September 22 prohibited the retreat of the northwestern front. At the same time, he promised to re-enforce Russki's left wing near Warsaw by two Siberian corps already *en route.* He also directed the commander of the southwestern front to send three army corps and one cavalry division to Ivangorod. Thus, the Grand Duke had already done much to frustrate the German offensive which had not yet begun.

Nevertheless, the Russians did not yet fully realize the meaning of the German maneuver. In particular they failed to understand the unexpected dispatch of German troops to the Austrian front. The Russians had counted on a German offensive from East Prussia in direction of the Narev.

The Russians should not be blamed for their lack of understanding, for the German High Command did not know just what was the sense of a joint German-Austrian operation on the Austrian left flank. The reasons for which General von Conrad had supported his request for German troops no longer existed; the Russian forces formerly in pursuit of the Austrian Army had already been stopped on the line of the river San. There was no longer any danger of an envelopment of the Austrian fronts.

Offense Changed to Defense

At the time of the German deployment, the Russians had five and one-half cavalry divisions on the left bank of the Vistula. Originally, this force had been assigned the mission of outflanking the retreating Austrians. Yet after the appearance of German troops in southern Poland, this offensive mission was changed into a defensive one. Instead of the previously planned crossing of the Vistula, these cavalry divisions were ordered to remain where they were and to protect and screen the Russian positions north of that important waterway.

On the same day, September 22, when the Russians began to organize the defense of the Vistula position, General von Hindenburg energetically requested the Austrian High Command to send strong Austrian forces to the northern bank of this river. This move would be a necessary complement to the movements of the German Ninth Army and would be indispensable to an effective attack against the Russian flank. On the next day the Austrians promised to dispatch considerable forces across the Vistula.

On the evening of September 24, Russian reconnaissance units established the presence of strong German forces along the line Sieradz-Novi-Radomsk-Miechov. A German prisoner informed the Russians moreover of the arrival of a German corps in the sector Beuthen-Tarnowitz. This corps had formerly been stationed in eastern Prussia.

From this available information, General Ivanov, the commander of the Russian southwestern front deduced—one week before the actual beginning of the German offensive—that the imminent German attack would be directed against the great bend of the Vistula. To counter the German move effectively, he proposed to retreat behind the Vistula, San and Tanev rivers. General Ivanov's plan, however, was badly received by the Grand Duke who still on September 25 expected a German offensive from East Prussia to the south. The Russians had received ample information of the railroad traffic behind the German lines. They were convinced that no strong forces had been sent from France to the eastern front.

The Grand Duke on September 26, discussed the situation with General Ivanov. They decided upon an active defense of the Vistula line and reinforced their units on both sides of the river, placing reinforcements chiefly in the northern and western sectors of the front.

At the same time the Germans learned of the regrouping of the Russian forces. In particular, that the Russian Ninth Army with at least three corps would open a new front on the Vistula west of Krasnik, although mainly with a defensive mission, though this army could develop a big offensive.

The commanders of the German and Austrian armies thus had to acknowledge the impracticability of their original plan. The attack intended against the flank of the southwestern Russian army group was made impossible by the strong forces which the Russians had brought up to cover the threatened areas. It remained dubious whether the Russians would accept battle on the left or the right bank of the Vistula.

Russians' Successful Parry

The Russians received final and definite information of the disposition of the German and Austrian forces on September 30, when they discovered in the diary of a slain German officer that of the six German corps which had fought the battle of the Masurian Lakes only two still remained in East Prussia. Thus, the Russian High Command realized that the main German forces were concentrated along the line Lodz-Kielce, while other strong forces were near Cracow and behind the Carpathian mountains. The German concentration between Lodz and Kielce was rightly considered as extremely dangerous. The Russians understood that they had to neutralize this threat by a strong counter-blow and they prepared an attack against the front of the German Ninth Army. They took measures to attack the German left flank by a whole army reinforced by two or three corps. The Russian counter-blow was therefore ready before the German operation had even begun.

When, on October 1, the German Ninth Army began to move forward, a strategic surprise against the Russians in southern Poland was already out of question. The Russians parried effectively every German move and finally imposed their own law on the Germans. At long last, the Germans had no other way out of their difficulties than to retreat into upper Silesia. This unexpected failure of the campaign in southern Poland must be ascribed chiefly to the previous failure to surprise the Russians.

The Germans did not succeed any better with their offensive in Lithuania and Courland in the spring of 1915. The commander of the German eastern front intended by a surprise-offensive to push the Russians back from the Njemen and from Kowno, with the hope that during the operation strong Russian forces could be caught in a trap. Precautions were taken to concentrate the German attacking forces only shortly before the

zero hour. On the evening of April 26, the German units were
ready and on the following night the offensive began. Much
had been expected from it. Yet the offensive did not succeed.

The Russians had received timely warning of the German
preparations. They frustrated the planned destruction of their
troops by methodically retreating before the German advance.
Despite their desire, the vastly superior German forces could
not catch up with the Russians, although the Russian retreat
was by no means quick. Surprise is an essential condition of
victory.

Our examples reveal that during World War I the surprise
of the enemy during the advance to the battlefield was possible
in theory, but could be scarcely achieved in practice. In the
present, the difficulties of surprise have become even greater.
In particular, the means and methods of reconnaissance have
improved. If surprise should be attempted in future, it will be
necessary, on one hand, to keep utmost secrecy by improved
camouflage and by executing movements only during the night.
On the other, the speed of operations must be increased by
the use of motorized units hurled against the flanks and the
rear of the enemy. But it is essential to exploit a successfully
achieved surprise by concentrating strong forces at the point
where the decision shall be won. Modern strategists have
sinned much too often against the principle of concentration,
although this principle has been valid at all times and is now
as valid as ever before[5].

NOTES, CHAPTER IV

1. Kluck's halt: The nervousness of the German commanders was
due to a cause which is rarely mentioned in German publications, but
which was of decisive importance: The size of the German Army and
its speed was inadequate for the successful execution of the German
war plan. Besides, forced marches had over-strained the troops as well
as the staffs. There seems to have been a widespread fear among the
German superior officers that a continued advance would necessarily
weaken the German army and make their lines so thin that they would
not be able to resist a strong counter-attack. Before 1933, the
Militaer-Wochenblatt repeatedly declared that, if the Germans had not
lost the Battle of the Marne, they would have lost the Battle of the
Seine.

The insufficient strength of the German offensive wing was the main
reason why the Germans did not attempt to envelop Paris, but to by-

pass it in the east, a movement which enabled Galliéni to attack the German flank.

Many German writers have criticized the German war plan of 1914 on the ground that the German offensive wing was not made stronger. That, in particular, two army corps which had been created after Schlieffen's retirement should have been used on the German right wing. This theoretical view however, is hardly borne out by the facts. The Germans had actually used all the troops which they could possibly transport through Belgium. There is a limit to any concentration, which limit is usually determined by the existing transport facilities.

2. Crossing of the Meuse: During the Battle of Flanders in World War II German armored units which had reached the Meuse more quickly than expected, renounced organizing a systematic crossing, but improvised a swift crossing in order to keep up with the speed of operation.

3. Reliable Information: The facts related above conclusively show the necessity of systematically deceiving and confusing the enemy. It has been reported that during 1942 the Germans added a section for *Irrefuehrung* (that is, for confusing and misleading the enemy) to their General Staff. There is no reason to assume that the Germans in August, 1914, were confused by mere accident. On the contrary, the British had put an elaborate scheme for misleading their enemy into operation. They were successful because they had discovered the German espionage system in England and used, or rather abused, it without knowledge on the part of the Germans. During the first days of the war they transmitted to Germany the information that the British army would not leave Great Britain. Later, they spread false information of the size of the British Expeditionary Force and the points of disembarkment. During the critical phase of the operations in August, 1914, they made the Germans fear a British attack from Ostende, that is to say, against rear and flank of the German First Army. Moreover, they spread the rumor that strong Russian forces, recently landed in England, would attack the Germans in the same region.

4. Approach to battle: The modern defense organization of extreme depth does prevent big battles at the frontier. In order to forstall surprises, the defender forces the attacker to advance deeply into enemy territory and to reveal the articulation of the offensive army. Consequently, surprises during approach are still possible.

5. Concentration: General Erfurth's examples show that surprise has become more difficult for the attacking, but not necessarily for the defending, army. It is possible to let the offensive army advance and to trap it according to a pre-conceived plan. In August, 1914, the

French intended to let the Germans advance beyond the Sambre and to attack the German units south of that river with superior forces. In October, 1914, the Russians planned to permit a German advance from eastern Prussia to the east and to counter-attack the German rear flank from the direction of Warsaw. However, advancing armies did not lose all possibilities of surprise. If an offensive army will accomplish surprise also during approach, it is only necessary to screen effectively the main concentration of force.

V

Battle

IF SURPRISE is really indispensable to a battle of annihilation, we should *a priori* assume that surprise played an important role in the battle of Tannenberg. For this was a most perfect example of a modern battle of annihilation. The German official history of World War I goes so far as to rank Tannenberg higher than all other battles of envelopment in history and rates it above the classical model of Cannae itself.

The greatness of that German victory is by no means diminished if we acknowledge that faulty Russian leadership considerably facilitated the task of the German command. The outcome of that battle was dependent as well on the mediocrity of Russion generalship as on the high quality of that of the German. The main merit of the German command consisted in having discovered, and exploited, the errors of the opponent, thus multiplying the consequences of the accomplished strategic surprise.

The Germans in August, 1914, were favored by all the advantages of the battlefield in East Prussia, while the disadvantages of terrain operated against the Russians. In addition, the staff of the German Eighth Army read all the important Russian radio-messages and thereby had exact and complete knowledge of the enemy's intentions. There is hardly a historical precedent for this. The commanders of the two Russian armies on August 25 informed each other by radio of the disposition of their forces and the objective of their movements. The Germans intercepted these radiograms and thus were able to base their own decisions upon invaluable complete information. Hence a surprise move could be attempted under excep-

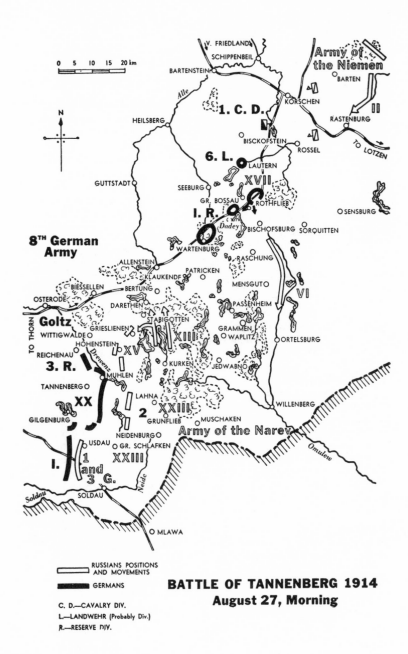

BATTLE OF TANNENBERG 1914
August 27, Morning

RUSSIANS POSITIONS AND MOVEMENTS
GERMANS

C. D.—CAVALRY DIV.
L.—LANDWEHR (Probably Div.)
R.—RESERVE DIV.

tionally favorable conditions. The "Cannae of Eastern Prussia" was the result of a combination of merit, luck and surprise-methods on the one side and of mistakes, omissions and ill luck on the other.

In the preceding battle of Gumbinnen the Russians had suffered severe losses. They therefore did not expect the German retreat which they discovered early in the morning of August 21. They were somewhat suspicious because they did not understand why the Germans retreated for a second time, inasmuch as they had delivered a serious blow to the Russian army. (On August 17, German forces had retreated after a successful engagement near Stallupoenen.) The Russian command expected the Germans to make a new stand on previously fortified positions behind the Angerapp river. During the next day, however, they found that the Germans had evacuated this position.

Thereupon, the commander of the Russian Army of the Niemen assumed that the Germans were retreating behind the Vistula, although he was prepared for strong German rearguard actions and delaying tactics in prepared positions. After two days of rest, the Army of the Niemen began its advance to the west.

Russian Commander's Belief

When General Shilinski, commander of the Russian northwestern front, received information of the evacuation of the Angerapp line, he became convinced that the Germans were retreating behind the Vistula. Since the German civilian population began to flee, he expected the total evacuation of East Prussia, with the exception of the fortress of Koenigsberg which was the apparent objective of strong retreating German forces. In the belief that the Russian Army of the Narev was being opposed by weak German forces, General Shilinski directed this army to cut the retreat of these German units which were being pushed back by the Army of the Niemen. He hoped to annihilate them before they could make their escape across the Vistula.

In the night of August 23-24, after an engagement in the Lahna-Orlau sector, the German XX Corps withdrew its left flank to a position on both sides of a lake near Muehlen. This move led the commander of the Russian Army of the Narev erroneously to believe that the whole XXI Corps had retreated in the direction of Osterode. General Samsonov thereupon decided to concentrate his army further west and to march forward to the Allenstein-Osterode line, instead of continuing his former advance toward Sensburg-Allenstein. To protect his right flank, he left his six corps and one cavalry division near Bischofsburg.

General Samsonov on August 25, saw that his interpretation of the German disposition had been incorrect. He now believed the XIX German Corps to stand near Allenstein or Osterode, the XVII south of Gildenburg, and other German forces farther west of this area. This new error was due to the concentration of German landwehr and reserve formations west of Gildenburg. For the first time Samsonov vaguely suspected that those German units which some days ago had fought near Gumbinnen had been moved by rail to another sector. He remained entirely ignorant of the presence of strong German forces east of Gildenburg, but expected a German advance from the general direction of Thorn on the Vistula, that is to say, far from the southwest of Gildenburg.

The attack of the German Eighth Army on the left flank of the Narev Army did not catch the Russians by surprise. General Samsonoff awaited the German attack with confidence and was convinced that the Russian forces concentrated in the region of Usdau would be strong enough for any emergency. These Russian troops had two days in which to take appropriate defense measures. Yet the Russian leaders still had a wrong picture of the German dispositions in the Muehlen and Hohenstein-Allenstein-Osterode sectors.

German Movements Missed

As a matter of fact, the German attack on the eastern flank of the Narev Army developed a complete surprise to the Russians which they themselves had facilitated. For their reconnaissance units failed to notice most important German movements, in particular the march of the XVII German corps from the north to the sector of Bischofsburg. This march was a rather remarkable military exploit since the German unit marched along the front of the Russian Army of the Niemen, thus offering an open flank to the enemy. It is still more remarkable that the Russians remained ignorant of this movement and completely disregarded any possible danger that might threaten the Narev Army from the north. On the night of

August 25-26, the Russian VI Corps still stood near Bischofsburg, without even taking the precaution to reconnoiter the
areas farther north. The Russians, therefore, learned of the
German advance only on the morning of August 26, when
they were surprised and defeated near Gross-Boessau. This
setback forced the Russians to retire in the direction of Ortels-
burg. This local retreat opened the way for a German attack
against the flank and rear of the Narev Army whose commander
for a long time remained in total ignorance of that important
development. Not in the least did he imagine that the German
units which he supposed to be west of Usdau had actually advanced behind the flank and rear of his army, let alone that
they were about to begin the very attack essential to winning a
battle of annihilation, namely, an attack against his flanks.

General Samsonov learned of the Russian defeat near Gross-
Boessau around noon on August 27. In the evening of the
same day he received the additional bad news that the Russian
1st Corps had been beaten near Usdau and was falling back on
Mlava.

The Russian commander did not immediately realize the
full implications of these defeats on his both flanks. He gave
orders to continue with the attack during the next day. It is
true that on the morning of this day he at last understood how
disastrous his decision had been. In his last report which
he dispatched to his superiors in the morning of August 28,
he characterized the situation of his army as "extremely dangerous." Despite this correct appreciation, the retreat of the
Narev Army was not ordered until the evening of August 28,
much too late to save the mass of the Russian forces.

Mission of the Russians

At the outbreak of the war, the northwestern group of the
Russian army had been charged "to annihilate the German units
in East Prussia" or to cut them off from Koenigsberg and
the Vistula. The Russians therefore had to operate on outer
lines. In our discussion of the battle of Mons and Namur,
we have already pointed out that the coordination of the movements of different and geographically separated units constitutes
the main difficulty of such an operation. The commander of the
Russian northwestern front was not equal to this admittedly
difficult task. The operations were executed in vast spaces

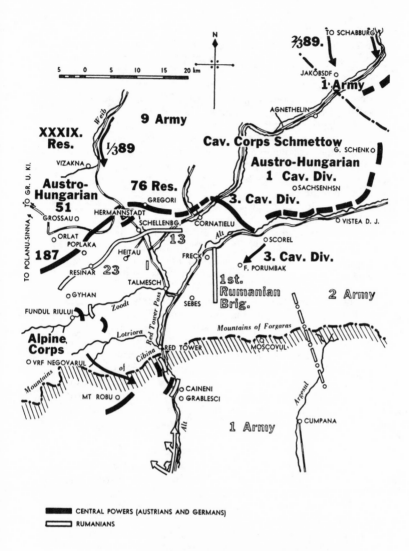

CENTRAL POWERS (AUSTRIANS AND GERMANS)
RUMANIANS

The BATTLE OF HERMANNSTADT
Situation September 26, evening.

and he was unable to get a correct view of them. Besides, he lacked the energy which is so necessary for simultaneously conducting large-scale operations on different fronts.

Nor had the commanders of the two Russian armies the correct appreciation of the situations involved, thus failing at a similar task which, during the same weeks, also proved to be beyond the capacities of the German leaders on the Sambre and Meuse.

If the Russian generals had been in possession of better information, a quick advance on the part of General von Rennenkampf and a cautious defensive on the part of General Samsonov would have avoided the catastrophe of Tannenberg. In this battle the Russians possessed huge numerical superiority. Approximately 485,000 Russians were confronted by only 173,000 Germans of the Eighth Army. However, General Shilinski, as a disciple of Terentius Varro, did not use his superiority to concentrate overwhelming forces at decisive points, for the simple reason that he did not believe that the Germans would accept a big battle east of the Vistula. After the battle of Gumbinnen, General Shilinski considered the German Eighth Army as already beaten and mentally prepared himself for the operations supposedly imminent on the Vistula. Underestimation of the opponent is always highly dangerous. The Germans were lucky to have in General Shilinski an opponent who split his armies and dispersed his forces for secondary operations. That is the main reason why General Samsonoff had to fight the battle of Tannenberg alone. During the decisive operations, 153,000 Germans, 296 machine guns and 728 cannon were opposed by 191,000 Russians, 384 machine guns and 612 cannon, although they could have been opposed by at least twice that number. The Germans possessed one superiority only. Leadership. It enabled them to strike decisively at the vulnerable points of the enemy. Incidentally, Tannenberg is the only battle of World War I in which separate advances of different armies and an attack from two independent fronts led to victory[1].

Originally, the German Eighth Army's mission was only defensive. The Germans had practically no chance to hold the German territory east of the Vistula unless they separated the different Russian armies and defeated them successively. For that purpose the dispositions of the German forces had to remain hidden from the enemy. In point of fact, German leadership was able thoroughly to deceive the Russians on all important German dispositions and movements[2].

Speed in Inner Line Moves

The German Army operated on inner lines. Since the enemy cannot be deceived for long, such operations must be executed with the utmost speed. But once the offensive has begun, the enemy receives the information he needs by the very movements of the attacking troops. Consequently, surprise can only be utilized during the preparatory phases of the attack. "Almost the only advantage of attack," says Clausewitz, "is the possibility of surprise with the first blow." The German forces that won the engagement of Gross-Boessau delivered such a first blow. Their attack came suddenly and was pressed home without giving respite to the enemy. Thus it led not only to the defeat of the Russian VI Corps, but eventually to the annihilation of the entire Russian Army of the Narev.

Several other attempts were made during World War I to defeat a numerically superior enemy by an offensive on inner lines. But a complete victory like that of Tannenberg was not accomplished a second time.

Some similar attempts led to ordinary victories, as at the battle of Hermannstadt. But other attempts repeatedly miscarried, as the Rumanian offensive west of Bucharest in the winter of 1916. In the battle of the Arges, the Rumanian High Command intended to beat the Army of the Danube and to drive it back across the river before the right wing of the German Ninth Army under the command of General Kuehne could intervene. The Rumanian forces formerly entrusted with the mission of defending the Danube and a *masse de manoeuvre* constituted for the same operation together had to take the offensive against the Army of the Danube of the Central Powers. The three divisions of the Rumanian right wing had to operate in the direction of Draganescii, while one division and one infantry-brigade of the Rumanian left wing had to attack in the direction of Giurgiul. The Rumanian First Army had to protect the *masse de manoeuvre* offensive against the German units under General Krafft. Between the left wing of the Army of the Danube and the right wing of General Kuehne's forces was a wide gap, which apparently favored the intentions of the Rumanian commander, General Presan. The Rumanian High Command hoped that on receiving the news of a defeat of the Danube Army, General Kuehne would stop and possibly retreat. They underestimated the danger which menaced the Rumanian forces from Kuehne's group. Consequently, they failed to protect the area between the Rumanian First Army and the Rumanian *masse de manoeuvre* with sufficient forces However, the arrival of several Russian divisions and of one Rumanian division on the battlefield was imminent. In the opinion of General Presan, these reinforcements would give the Rumanians numerical superiority even in case General Kuehne should continue to advance, after a defeat of the Army of the Danube.

Both opponents lacked sufficient information about each other. Foggy weather made air reconnaissance difficult. The advance of Kuehne's forces was effectively screened by the cavalry corps under General Schmettow. On the whole, the German leaders had the trump cards in their hands and were in a more favorable situation for achieving surprise than the Rumanians, although the Rumanians, too, tried to surprise their enemy. In effect, the German commanders ignored the fact that forces of the left flank of the Rumanian *masse de manoeuvre* advanced southward. This southern move, according to Presan's plan, was the most decisive one; it was frustrated, although only in the last hour, when most unexpectedly General Kuehne appeared on the focal sector of the battlefield. Thus, the Rumanian surprisers became the surprised.

Luck an Element

It must be admitted that in this battle the Central Powers were favored by luck. The headquarters of a Rumanian division which fought on the open flank of the *masse de manoeuvre* had on December 1, been effectively bombed by German aircraft. Consequently, the leadership of this key division became wholly insufficient. On the same day, General von Falkenhayn, commander of the German Ninth Army, gained full knowledge of the Rumanian battle-plan by the seizure of a written order carried by two Rumanian staff-officers who were taken prisoner. To this moment, Falkenhayn had been entirely ignorant of the Rumanian intentions, but after a thorough analysis of the captured orders he realized that

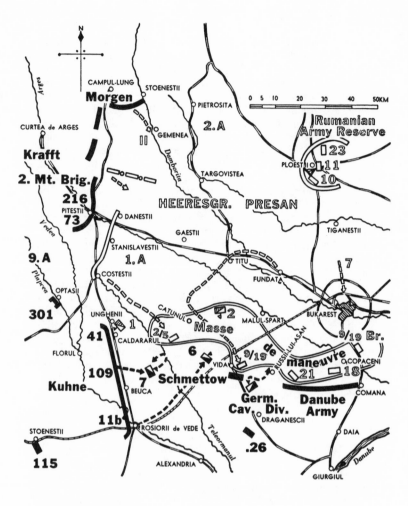

The BATTLE of the ARGES

Situation on November 29, evening.

Legend:

CENTRAL POWERS
(AUSTRIANS AND GERMANS)

RUMANIANS

FORCES UNDER GEN. MORGEN
FORCES UNDER GEN. KRAFFT
FORCES UNDER GEN. SCHMETTOW
FORCES UNDER GEN. KUHNE

General Kuehne's forces were in an exceptionally favorable position not only to parry a dangerous Rumanian blow against the left wing of his Army of the Danube, but also to hit the enemy strongly and offensively at a decisive point. For the Rumanians, while attacking, opened themselves to attack on their flank and rear. Falkenhayn, therefore, ordered General Kuehne to hurry to the battlefield.

Incidentally, before the capture of the two staff-officers, another Rumanian order had fallen into German hands. This was an order from General Presan himself, dated November 29 and addressed to the division on the open flank of the *masse de manoeuvre*. The order contained ample information of the Rumanian plan and in particular of the mission of the *masse de manoeuvre*. Yet, the staff of the cavalry division which came into its possession apparently failed to transmit this valuable document to General von Falkenhayn.

Such incidents are typical and inavoidable in a war with mass-armies. Every student of World War I will know many other examples of the kind. Important orders, even those emanating from the highest military authorities, were captured by the opposing army during practically every big operation. In former times, operational orders were seldom lost to the enemy. This particular danger to secrecy arose under modern conditions, when it became necessary to multiply important orders because numerous persons must know them. There is hardly a way of dispensing with the multiplication of orders, although this will certainly continue to be the source of difficulty.

Care should be taken to inform subordinate commanders only of the most necessary details and to reveal to them only those points which they must know for accomplishing their particular tasks. The enemy should be unable to deduce the whole plan from a single captured order. To give orders in such a way is certainly a laborious process, but the additional troubles which the staff must incur when editing such orders will undoubtedly be worth while. The orders for the Rumanian First Army carried by the two captured staff-officers contained the orders for all divisions of the *masse de manoeuvre*. This, of course, was unnecessary. Since the advance of the open wing of the *masse de manoeuvre* and its reinforcement by a division from the First Army clearly constituted a heavy risk, as do all marches along the front of the opponent, it was of extreme importance to keep these movements as secret as possible. Yet they were mentioned in the captured documents.

Transylvanian Campaign

The campaign of the German Ninth Army in Transylvania began with a surprise. In September, 1916, the Rumanian army stood in a semicircle around the units of the Central Powers in Transylvania, threatening to annihilate them by concentric attack. The situation was similar to that in which the Austrian-Hungarian Army found itself on the Russian southwestern front in the summer of 1914. The Rumanians were numerically much stronger than the forces of the Central Powers. Yet in order to attack they would have been obliged to travel over several mountain-passes and to divide their forces. Thus, the Central Powers could find a chance successively to beat the different parts of the Rumanian army.

To avoid the danger of a Rumanian concentric attack on the German Ninth Army, a German offensive had to be undertaken against the westernmost Rumanian units. General von Falkenhayn decided to strike his first blow against the Rumanian forces near Hermannstadt. He estimated the Rumanians at twice the number of his own force. This, of course, ruled out a frontal attack, for by attacking frontally, General von Falkenhayn would have had no troops left for an operation against the Rumanian flanks and would have run the risk of being attacked himself on his own wings by superior forces.

General von Falkenhayn was informed that, contrary to expectation, the mountains of Cibina could be negotiated by strong detachments, comparatively speaking. If it was possible to advance through these mountains towards the Red Tower Pass, the enemy could be outflanked and his only supply road cut. If this was done, there was a good chance that a frontal attack would also be successful, despite numerical inferiority.

General von Falkenhayn did not plan the battle of Hermannstadt as a battle of single or double encirclement. Instead, he attempted to combine an attack against the enemy's only supply line with a rather reckless frontal attack.

Falkenhayn on September 20 discussed his plan with his commanding generals. General Krafft von Dellmensingen was directed to prepare the attack of Alpine troops through the mountains of Cibina. Two days later the mountain troops began to move while other German forces were being concentrated north of Hermannstadt.

General von Falkenhayn intended to launch his attack on September 26. A whole corps was to move forward on both sides of Hermannstadt in the general direction of the Red Tower Pass. By the same date, it was expected that the Alpine detachments would approach the pass, and also attack. German cavalry units, supported by Austro-Hungarian infantry, were directed to divert from the battlefield the Rumanian Second Army which had taken up positions east of Hermannstadt. For an intervention of the Rumanian Second Army would have endangered the whole position of the German Ninth Army.

Mountain Operations

The crux of Falkenhayn's plan depended upon whether the Alpine detachment would arrive in time in the enemy's rear and would be able effectively to close the Red Tower Pass. True enough, the Rumanians were surprised by the unexpected raid of these troops across mountains over six thousand feet high, using mule-tracks and stony paths as roads. The commander of the Rumanian First Army, General Culcer, had given orders to watch the mountains of Cibina, yet the officer in command of this front, who did not believe in the practicability of an enemy thrust through these inhospitable mountains, had recalled all guards to reinforce his positions near Hermannstadt. The history of war offers many examples of a sector which is reputedly not negotiable being passed by strong forces and thus used for surprising the enemy. Some Rumanian guards were still in the mountains when the first Germans appeared. One Rumanian position fell to the advanced guards of a Bavarian brigade, but its garrison escaped. Rumanian shepherds also informed the Rumanian command of the German advance, but the Rumanian commander whose attention was concentrated on other operations, did not consider these reports as important. Some types of military commanders prefer to believe in their own intuition rather than in reliable intelligence. Only one battalion and some guns were diverted for the protection of the Red Tower Pass; another battalion was dispatched to protect the regions west of the pass. These two battalions were attacked the next day by the German mountain troops.

At long last, the Rumanian commander realized the situation and hurriedly dispatched reinforcements to the pass. On September 27 further Rumanian reinforcements arrived at the southern exit of the pass. They immediately counter-attacked through the pass as well as through the mountains farther west, while additional reinforcements arrived from the north.

The German units were much too weak effectively to close the pass and to defend many miles of the pass road against an enemy, by now numerically superior and trying his utmost to reopen his only supply line. Besides, the supplying of the German detachment through the mountains was extremely difficult. The Germans in the pass were soon in a critical situation. They were unable definitely to disrupt the enemy's communications, although they effectively disordered them. Falkenhayn's plan was not a complete success, but this menace against the rear and the Red Tower Pass communications of the Rumanians considerably helped the Germans in the battle of Hermannstadt.

Falkenhayn was more successful with his plan to keep the Second Rumanian Army far from the battlefield. The Rumanian High Command and the commander of the Rumanian Second Army realized the difficulties of the First Army too late. During the afternoon of September 27 the Second Army was ordered to move to the west and to begin a powerful westward offensive which, at first, made good progress. But on September 29 the right wing of the Rumanian army was stopped and finally beaten back. Other Rumanian forces on both banks of the river Alt could make but little progress against German cavalry and were unable to intervene in the battle of Hermannstadt. On the other hand, the units of the Rumanian First Army which had fought north of the Red Tower Pass were exhausted and had already begun to retreat.

As a result of the incomplete control of this pass by the German mountain troops, the Rumanian retreat succeeded, although the Rumanians lost most of their vehicles. Too, the morale of their troops was seriously impaired by this operation.

Forces Too Weak For Task

Falkenhayn's plan to cut off the Rumanian communications near Hermannstadt and to encircle strong Rumanian forces failed.

True, the Rumanian commanders had been surprised by the un-expected dash of the mountain units through the mountains of Cibina. But the German detachment was too weak for its task. It was not strong enough at the beginning of the operation, let alone after the Rumanians had been reinforced.

We remember that, according to Clausewitz, surprise should be the means to achieve local numerical superiority. An opera-tion which had not been expected by the opponent is only effec-tive if undertaken by really superior forces. The degree of numerical superiority of the forces executing the surprise move must be determined by the opportunity to reinforce speedily, and also by the ability of the opponent to bring up reinforce-ments.

In the battle of Hermannstadt both parties, numerically speak-ing, were more or less equal, although the Central Powers had vast superiority in artillery. It was probably impossible to throw stronger forces against the Red Tower Pass. A decisive victory was therefore beyond Falkenhayn's powers and he was unable to harvest all the profits from his successful surprise. Nevertheless, the daring move through the Cibina mountains facilitated the frontal attack and made the Rumanian retreat very difficult. The Rumanian First Corps was thoroughly beaten in this battle. But the German forces which operated against the enemy's rear were too weak to achieve the annihilation of their opponent.

In his study on the Battle of Cannae, Count von Schlieffen emphasized that a battle of annihilation was rarely won by in-ferior forces. If the enemy's numerical superiority is too great, his front cannot be attacked and no forces can be spared for a flanking operation. In such a case, the only expedient left is *to launch the main attack against the flank,* or, if possible, against the rear and to push the enemy against an unpassable natural obstacle and to outflank him after he has been immo-bilized. In that way Frederick the Great once tried to win a battle of annihilation against an army twice as strong as his. But in his time, the envelopment of the enemy was a difficult undertaking. Unless the turning movement remains a secret to the enemy, its success is doubtful. If the enemy has time to take appropriate counter-measures, the flanking maneuver must fail. And only if secrecy can be combined with speed, is sur-prise possible.

During World War I strategic envelopment was repeatedly

attempted. We will examine some of these attempts in order to determine just what role surprise played in them.

Before and during the battle of the Masurian Lakes both sides had incomplete knowledge of the impending movements of the enemy. The Germans were no longer assisted by Russian radio messages in plain language.

The commander of the German Eighth Army was under the impression that the Russian Army of the Niemen prepared for a long stand northwest of the Masurian Lakes. Yet the possibility of offensive moves on the part of the Russians could not be ruled out. The exact strength of the enemy was unknown. In particular, the Germans disregarded the distribution of the Russian forces east and south of the Masurian Lakes and the question of whether reinforcements were approaching. As it so often happens the Germans overestimated the Russian strength, believing that they were opposed by twenty infantry divisions. In reality, General von Rennenkampf, who in the beginning of September had sixteen and one-half infantry divisions and five and one-half cavalry divisions, began the battle with only fourteen infantry divisions.

Flank and Front Attack

The main Russian forces stood between the Kurische Haff in the north and Lake Mauer in the south. A mere frontal attack against their strong positions did not offer promising prospects. An enveloping movement against the Russian northern flank, which was protected by the Baltic was, for geographical reasons, out of question. The German commander, therefore, decided to combine a frontal attack with an attack against the Russian southern flank. The difficult terrain south of Loetzen, however, made a flanking maneuver extremely complicated. The numerous lakes in this sector necessitated a division of the German attacking forces, so that the Russians could find an opportunity to fall upon the German units piecemeal. Those German troops which had to advance south of the lakes were particularly in danger of being attacked by strong Russian units from the area of Lonsza and Grodno.

During the early phases of the battle, the German command apprehended a Russian counter-attack on the German northern flank, although, with our present knowledge of the situation, this fear is hard to understand. For in this case the Russians would have been obliged to evacuate very strong positions and to attack the German forces supported from the fortress of Koenigsberg. However, the German command was justified in taking precautions. An army concentrating the bulk of its forces against one of the enemy flanks always risks a heavy counter-attack from the enemy's other flank. These apprehensions were strengthened by the report of German flyers, according to which the Russians had concentrated large forces far behind their northern flank. The German leaders, therefore, decided to reinforce their left wing. Yet it proved to be impossible to divert units from the right to the left flank because the right wing had already advanced too far to the east. This impossibility of reinforcing the left wing at the expense of the right flank was very fortunate for the Germans, for they saw themselves compelled to resort to a ruse of war which not only deceived the Russians into taking faulty positions, but also enabled the Germans to achieve a sucessful surprise. It was particularly important to prevent a Russian attack on the German left flank. The German radio on September 7 transmitted a message *en clair* suggesting the arrival of two corps from the western front behind the German left wing.

The exact timing of the German frontal attack with the attack against the Russian flank proved to be a major difficulty. It was hard to tell just how long the crossing of the lake sector would last, since the terrain offered good possibilities for delaying defensive action by even weak forces. In point of fact, the enveloping movement was too slow for a decisive German victory against the Russian Army of the Niemen.

The battle began on September 8 with the capture of the Russian advanced positions. The main frontal attack was to begin on September 9, yet the speed of its execution was to be timed with the operations against the Russian flank. The lake sector was crossed during September 6 and 7; the German troops had been opposed only by weak Russian forces. Serious opposition had been encountered only on the right flank, but had been overcome.

On the evening of September 9, the German right flank had arrived near Lyck and in the zone of Kruglanken-Possessern.

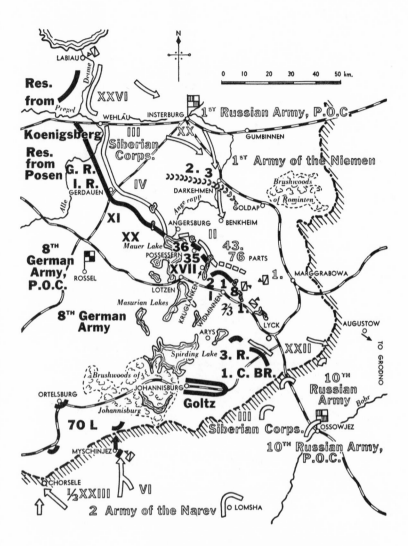

BATTLE OF THE MASURIAN LAKES

Situation, Sept. 9th, 1914, evening

☐ RUSSIAN

■ GERMAN

43. RUSSIAN DIV. AND PARTS OF 76 DIV.
3RD. RESERVE DIV. AND 1ST. CAV. BRIG.

P. O. C.-POST OF COMMAND
FORCES UNDER THE COMMAND
OF GEN. VON DER GOLTZ

The German command had the impression that the flanking operation proceeded according to plan, but thought that the capture of the Russian main positions would require a major effort. It seemed advisable to postpone the main frontal attack until the German flank had advanced still farther.

An Unexpected Evacuation

To the great surprise of the German leaders, the Russians evacuated their main positions on September 10. This complete and unexpected change was not immediately comprehensible. In view of the strength of the Russians the German command did not dare to begin a swift pursuit. Instead, they ordered a limited advance and strongly admonished the troops to be cautious.

Only after Rennenkampf's retreat had clearly been established by air reconnaissance was a quicker pursuit ordered, yet it did not get under way before September 11.

How did the Russian leaders interpret the German strategy before and during this battle? Still influenced by memory of the catastrophe of Tannenberg, the Russians were uncertain whether the Germans would turn against the Army of the Niemen or that of the Narev. They also considered the possibility of a German thrust against Warsaw which, after the arrival of German forces from the western front, was certainly within the realm of possibility. The Russian press by August 30 had already reported this important German troop movement from the western to the eastern front.

Originally, General von Rennenkampf planned to fight defensively and to hold his strong natural positions behind the line of the Deime-Alle-Omet rivers and to cover his left flank by the Masurian lakes. He expected a German attack in the vicinity of Loetzen, but not a flanking movement farther south which turned around the region of the lakes. He concentrated his reserves behind his northern flank, fearing German amphibious operations across the Haff and perhaps by the Baltic. On September 7 to his surprise he learned of the German movement to the east along the southern frontier of East Prussia. Realizing that the Germans were attempting to envelop his weak southern flank, he gave orders to attack strongly on a broad front the open flank of the wheeling Germans.

Rennenkampf's Irresolution

On the same day, however, the Russians received the German radio-message about the alleged arrival of two German corps behind the northern flank. Rennenkampf became irresolute and could not make up his mind whether he should accept battle or withdraw. In the hope that the Germans had made available for their flanking maneuver only weak forces, he finally resolved to make a stand.

The hope of stopping the envelopment attack of the German right wing by a strong attack against its open side soon proved vain. The Germans speedily overcame the Russian resistance, did not bother about the Russian forces in their flank and rear and hurriedly proceeded northward.

This unexpected development obliged General von Rennenkampf to withdraw strong forces from his right flank and to reinforce his threatened left wing. Yet this move came too late to prevent the defeat of a Russian division on September 9 near Possessern. But on the next day the Russian left flank had been reinforced by four infantry and three cavalry divisions. The Germans had not yet launched a really serious attack on any of the Russian positions. The Russian general had therefore no reason prematurely to break battle. Nevertheless, he preferred to extricate his troops from the threatening envelopment. During the afternoon of September 9 he ordered the retreat of all Russian units north of the lakes. This order came as a surprise to the Russian troops in the first lines as well as to the Germans who just prepared their main effort. The Russian retreat began in the night of September 10 and was completed without incident.

The Germans had thus won a victory. They had been victorious in an ordinary battle, but they had not achieved a decisive success. The result did not correspond to the hopes of the German leaders. The Russians could not be compelled to fight the battle out to the bitter end. They maintained an open line of retreat and withdrew undisturbed, according to their own will.

Numerically speaking, the situation was much more favorable for the Germans than at Tannenberg. The Germans had 184 battalions, 99 squadrons and 1074 guns against 228 Russian battalions, 173 squadrons and 924 guns. Nor did the quality of Russian leadership prevent the Germans from winning a more decisive victory. The Russian commander saw dangers which actually did not exist and put his reserves behind his right flank which never was in danger. On the other hand, he failed to protect his left wing and was caught by surprise when the Germans began their envelopment maneuver. Consequently, the responsibility for the unsatisfactory outcome of the battle does lie on the German side.

According to the German plan, two thirds of the German forces had to deliver a frontal attack on the Russian front; the last third was ordered to outflank the Russian position. If General von Rennenkampf had continued to fight until September 10 the German leaders would have discovered that their enveloping flank was to weak to achieve a quick and definite success. By then they would have met strong Russian reinforcements and in all probability would have been stopped.

Reserves Were Lacking

The Germans did not possess enough reserves to maintain the superiority of their flank after the Russians had thrown in their reserves. After all, since numerical superiority was lacking in the battle of the Masurian Lakes, it was indispensable to achieve at least relative superiority at the decisive point. The envelopment operation was conceived as the most important part of the German attack. The decisive point, therefore, was on the German right flank. Consequently, according to theory, the bulk of the German forces had to be used on the right flank.

The commanders of the German Eighth Army disregarded Count von Schlieffen's doctrine in many essential points. Schlieffen considered the flank attack as the essential operation and advised that, in case of insufficient numbers, the necessary numerical superiority must be made available for the flank by delivering the frontal attack with minimum strength. But even with very weak numbers, the forces of the center have to do more than merely immobilize the enemy by long distance artillery fire. "The enemy front," wrote Schlieffen, "must under all conditions be attacked." The postponement of the German frontal attack during the Masurian battle enabled the Russians to move their reserves behind their left flank. One can be sure that General von Rennenkampf would not have dared to risk his reserves had he envisaged a German onslaught against his center. A German attack against the Russian northern flank would have been particularly helpful, since it would have incited the Russians, who were already confused by the German radio message, to keep at least some of their reserves in the north.

When on the night of September 9-10 General von Rennenkampf began to retreat, the German offensive against the Russian front had not begun. The German flanking move had not yet progressed sufficiently to deprive the enemy of his initiative. The Russians were not yet enveloped, the German flank was still far from advancing perpendicularly against the Russian positions. Annihilation can only result from an attack from two or three fronts. In the battle of the Masurian Lakes the envelopment of only one flank was feasible. The Germans should therefore have pushed the Russians back to another line and forced Rennenkampf to retreat in an unfavorable direction, preferably to the north against the Haff and the lower Memel. But this was not possible before the German flank, comprising the majority of the German forces, had wheeled around Lake Mauer and was progressing northward. The German offensive never matured. When on September 9 the Russian retreat started, the German center as well as the German flank still faced due east.

None of the many attempts in World War I to inflict a decisive defeat on the enemy by an attack against one single flank was entirely successful. Most of these attempts led to a greater or smaller victory, but none ended with the annihilation of the enemy. The battles of Leuthen and Zorndorf cannot be easily imitated in modern war. The turning marches which Frederick the Great was still able to perform within a few hours in the immediate vicinity of the battlefield, at present take days, if not weeks; moreover, they spread out over vast expanses of terrain. Surprise can hardly be achieved under these circumstances. The opponent prematurely recognizes our intentions and prepares appropriate counter-moves. The enemy can either evade the flanking attack or withdraw his endangered flank. He may also extend his front and counter-attack with new forces.

Successful Counter-Moves

In recent wars such counter-moves were frequently and successfully executed; for instance, by the Russians near Lodz and Wilna. Even in wars under more primitive conditions, it proved to be difficult to annihilate the enemy by a double flank attack. In the Abyssinian War, particularly in the second battle in Tembien and in the battle of Schiré, Badoglio tried to annihilate his enemy by a pincer-attack. He could not accomplish his purpose since the Abyssinians slipped away before the Italian forces joined. In the Chinese War, the main Japanese army under the leadership of General Terauchi could not destroy the Chinese by a combined flank and frontal attack in the battle of Paoting which took place in September, 1937. The Chinese realized the Japanese's intention and retreated before they were effectively turned. Some weeks later the battle of Jengding took a similar course.

The experience of the Germans in the battles of Mons and the Masurian Lakes caused the command of the German Ninth Army to begin the frontal attack in the battle of Vloclavek one whole day earlier than the flank attack. In addition, they placed chiefly cavalry forces on their enveloping flank. However these forces proved too weak to accomplish their task. The Russian leader had enough time to extend his threatened wing and so to forestall any envelopment. Besides, the supporting strong infantry forces, despite a forced march, did not reach the battlefield in time to defeat the Russian forces which successfully held up the German cavalry. The Russians had enough time to retreat, because the Germans were unable to advance deeply into the enemy's flank. All the battles mentioned above show that an enveloping force can never arrive in time if it is organized in deep echelons. Echelon formations with the main forces in the second line are good only for defense, for it is very difficult to transform them quickly into a formation with the strongest forces in the first line, that is to say, into an offensive echelon. Flanking attacks with defensive echelon formations were rarely successful in recent wars, despite the fact that they sometimes mislead the enemy.

The method of outflanking the enemy with troops taken from the first center lines, which the Germans tried before Vilna, is still more unsatisfactory. On September 8, 1915, on the eve of the battle of Vilna, seven German divisions (four of which had little value) stood against fifteen Russian divisions south of the river Vilia. North of the Vilia eight and one-half Russian divisions were confronted by ten and one-half German infantry and four cavalry divisions.

The German offensive against Vilna was planned as a decisive operation which should lead to the annihilation of the Russian units. Obviously, the relation of force did not favor such an ambitious undertaking. Already on the first day of battle, September 9, the German northern flank was being immobilized by strong Russian resistånce. Only three infantry divisions and one cavalry unit could be made available for the attack on the flank. The German commanders intended to reinforce their attacking flank gradually by units no longer needed on the central front. But superiority on the flank could not be achieved by this method. It is true that the Russians were surprised by the speed of the German wing, but its numerical weakness enabled the Russians to deprive the German flank attack of its strategic potentialities.

Overlapping of Fronts

Instead of letting the encirclement proceed the Russians retreated. At the same time they dispatched strong forces from their central front to the threatened wing. Having all transport facilities of their own country at their disposal, they were quicker than the Germans and, despite almost incredible marching performances of the German troops, extended their line more speedily so that the Russian front soon overlapped the German formations.

Finally, the Russians launched a counter-offensive against the other German flank and on September 26 obliged the German commander, General von Eichhorn, to cease his offensive moves altogether. By this time Eichhorn's forces were confronted by almost double Russian numerical superiority ($18\frac{1}{2}$ German infantry and five cavalry divisions against 34 Russian infantry and six cavalry divisions.) The battle of Vilna had taken a course exactly contrary to that planned by the German command.

This battle suggests the conclusion that any attempt to evolve flanking attacks from the first center lines must prove futile.

An imitation of Frederick's oblique order was never tried

in World War I, though this would have been possible by using an echelon formation with its main forces in the first line for the envelopment attack. If an offensive echelon can operate from an angular position against the enemy center, the chances for decisive victory are much better than if only a defensive echelon is used, as in the battle of Vlocavek. However, such a disposition will not remain secret for long. The enemy will soon find out about the movements of the flank and, since the main forces are in the first line, he will be able to deduce the intended maneuver without difficulty. By using offensive echelons, the attacker plays his trump-card first. This is a definite disadvantage which demonstrates the value of the use of offensive echelons for flanking maneuvers only under exceptional circumstances.

The chances of flank attack would be considerably improved if turning movements could be accomplished more quickly than the advance of the frontally attacking center. The motorization of modern armies which permits the setting up of formations with a speed superior to that of the infantry, opens vast new possibilities. The speed of the new land weapons and of the air force has given back to military leadership the chance of surprising the enemy by speed, so that he may be prevented from organizing an appropriate defense in time. An attack from two or three sides against the wings of the enemy has therefore better chances in a future war than during World War I. However, sufficient offensive striking-power of the flanking units, which must at least be strong enough to smash weak and defensive flanks, is still an essential condition for a battle of annihilation. In addition, leadership has to perform the difficult task of coordinating the movements of several units with different speeds and of timing effectively frontal with flank-attacks.

Concentric Movements

A battle of annihilation can also result from concentric movements of independent armies coming from different directions. This strategy led the Prussian Army "from Belle Alliance via Koeniggratz (Sadowa) to Sedan." Theoretically, today it is still the simplest and most promising way to gain a decisive victory. Yet, a concentric operation of the kind requires secrecy. To maintain the secrecy of approaching armies in the era of air power will be more difficult than ever before. In World War I, this strategy was successfully applied at Tannenberg, while in the campaign against Serbia in the autumn of 1915 and during the offensive of the Central Powers against Bucharest at the end of 1916, effective junctions of the independent armies on the battlefield could not be achieved. The encirclement of the Serbian army failed on account of the difficult terrain and the tenacity and skill of the Serbs in defense and retreat. Besides, one of the Austrian flanking armies possessed only insufficient strength while the Bulgarians advanced much too slowly. Nevertheless, the concentric attack pushed the Serbians back into inhospitable regions and put them practically out of the war. In the campaign against Bucharest the Central Powers were hindered by the terrain, the weather and the opponent himself. In particular, the skill and mobility of the Rumanian High Command frustrated the German plan to maneuver the Rumanian army into a strategic situation where it could be encircled and destroyed. When the intentions of the Central Powers became clear, the Rumanian commander broke battle and saved his army.

In an operation on outer lines, energetic and unified leadership is indispensable. This has already been pointed out. In both campaigns against the Serbs and the Rumanians, leadership on the side of the Central Powers was much less unified than on the side of their opponents who moreover were fighting on the inner lines. The German and Austrian commanders agreed on the unification of their command only after the decisive battle for Valachia had already begun. Modern technical facilities will certainly help to improve the coordinated command of separate units.

It is no longer necessary, as in the nineteenth century, to issue "directives" in order to regulate the movements of separate units for several days[3]. Operations on outer lines are therefore favored by technical progress. On the other hand, the technical power of the defense, which is so characteristic for modern war, facilitates operations on inner lines more than concentric attacks. Operations on outer lines are purely offensive enterprises while operations on inner lines are a combination of offense and defense. Considering all elements, a concentric offensive of several armies was more difficult to execute with the weapons of World War I than in the period between Leipzig and Koeniggratz (1815-1866). Schlieffen had foreseen this development and had trained his students for operations on inner lines. Moltke, however, had won his classical victories by operations on outer lines. Since in all modern armies weapons have been introduced to increase the power of offense, the chances of the outer lines have been improved.

The rarity of concentric attacks in World War I must, at least in part, be explained by the fact that the essential conditions for such operations were usually lacking. Shortly after the beginning of the war, the continuous front led to the re-emergence of linear strategy. Independent armies were not created and gaps were filled before they even occurred.

Separation and Union

Moltke's doctrine that the art of leading big masses consists in having them separated as long as possible and in quickly uniting them on the battlefield soon fell into oblivion. In the autumn of 1914 the art of war fundamentally changed after the battle of the Marne when new methods had to be adopted. The German victories up to this moment were possible because the Germans could impose their law on an enemy entirely taken by surprise. It was clear, however, that the enemy could neither be surprised again on the same front, nor with the same methods. The French had strongly reinforced their left wing and they were careful to prevent new German victories on that flank. Consequently, the Germans could achieve new successes in that sector only if they were able by surprise to concentrate vastly superior masses. Yet the attack by larger forces would have required larger spaces than were at the disposal of the German troops. It would therefore have been necessary to give up a good portion of the conquered territory and to withdraw the whole German army over a considerable distance. Otherwise the necessary space could not be made available. The moral and political consequences of such a bold decision had courageously to be accepted.

It was particularly necessary to prevent the establishment of a continuous front, because flanking attacks are only possible if the front is not continuous. New military units should have been formed and put together in one big shock army. This new army should then have been assembled far behind the

front and of course, should have operated independently from
the already existing and fighting German units. This is self-
evident, according to all military theory. "If one undertakes
large scale strategic operations," said Moltke, "the separation
of the different armies must be maintained."

The strategic decision which General von Falkenhayn made
in the night of September 14-15, 1914, marks a turning point
in the history of strategic thought. At first, remaining within
the framework of military tradition, he envisaged a continuance
of the war of movement and attempts at a new enveloping offensive against the open flank of the Entente. For this, he
wished to take the German Sixth Army out of the front in
Lorraine and to concentrate it in the vicinity of Maubeuge, where,
as a sort of shock army, it was to operate independent of the
rest of the German right wing.

It is doubtful whether this army would have been sufficiently
strong for this task. To fill the time-lag between the moment
when this decision was made and the moment when the Sixth
Army would have been ready to take the field, the right wing
of the German army had to retreat in an excentric direction.
This was an excellent solution and quite in the spirit of German
military tradition. Yet, new strategical ideas determined Falkenhayn's decision. He decided against withdrawing the right
wing of the German army and refused to relinquish conquered territory. He was particularly anxious to avoid gaps between his different units, and after some hesitation, dismissed
the idea of an excentric retreat. Instead he resolved to wage
a new battle on the Noyon-Reims-Verdun line and to keep
the German army as close together as possible.

A Contradictory Task

The Sixth Army was transported to the sector of St.
Quentin, that is to say, much closer to the German right wing
than was originally intended. It was no longer to be used
for the offensive exclusively, but also to protect the right wing
of the German army. The explanation for this somewhat contradictory task lies in the fact that on September 15, General
von Falkenhayn became convinced that Joffre's intentions were
similar to his own. The envelopment of the German flank by
the French and British could only be avoided by reinforcing
the German wing and by extending the front-line.

This was the origin of that singular and fateful operation known to history as the *course à la mer*, the race to the sea. Surprise is, of course, impossible in a race. Both sides know the intentions of the opponent and both sides have the same strategic objective. One is astonished to detect how small a force each of the commanders employed for a battle which both of them considered as decisive and final. Rarely in history were military leaders confronted with a similarly gigantic task and, at the same time, with similarly even chances. But the means both of them employed were insufficient. Joffre and Falkenhayn failed, therefore, by necessity.

The main forces must fight on the front where the decision is sought. If the main attack is to be delivered against the enemy's flank, the main forces must be thrown against it, if possible in a direction perpendicular to that of the central front. There was little chance in September, 1914, to surprise the French by attacks at unexpected times or places. They could only be surprised by superior numbers which should have attacked at a point where a decision was possible. But numerical superiority on the German right flank was impossible without recklessly weakening the center and the southern flank of the German army.

As a matter of fact, this recklessness was the quintessence of Schlieffen's doctrine. But none of the two commanders dared to concentrate sufficient numbers for the decisive operation, thereby risking the weakening of his other fronts. General Joffre did not find any impressive solution for his strategical problems despite the fact that he was in possession of an excellent railroad system which still was unimpaired. Both commanders committed the same errors and thus prevented a decision on either side. The mistakes of one side were neutralized by the mistakes of the other.

Forces Dribbled Away

In the race for the open flank, the method of "too little" prevailed. The forces of both armies were used up in driblets. Despite the bloody sacrifice of the troops, the operation ended in a draw; nowhere a real success was gained. At the end, the original plan to outflank the opponent had evaporated and was replaced by a simple purpose, running faster than the opponent. The race led to the exhaustion of both armies. When it came to a stop, both commanders were confronted with the new and unexpected problem of how to launch frontal infantry attacks against an enemy equipped with modern rifles and machine-guns. An open flank no longer existed.

The *aide de camp* to the German Emperor, General von Plessen, noted on September 28 in his diary: "It is incomprehensible why our right wing cannot defeat the French. Five army corps are unable to inflict a definite defeat on them, though the French do not have numerical superiority." This remark shows that the problem was not properly understood. Von Plessen ignored that, as a result of the efficiency of modern weapons, defense had become, technically speaking, more powerful than the offensive. Moreover, the difficulties of attack had been considerably increased by the unfortunate strategic dispositions of the German High Command and the complete absence of strategic surprise.

If generalship yields disappointing results, it is habitual to appeal to the morale of the troops. In former times, this expedient was sometimes quite successful. In the battles of Leopold of Dessau and Frederick the Great, the Prussian troops, after patriotic appeals, were sometimes capable of taking by a "brutal offensive" even "impregnable positions." In the war of 1870, it was already rather difficult to rely exclusively on heroism and to ignore the deadly effects of modern weapons. Nevertheless, the impressive victory of Gravelotte-St. Privat must largely be ascribed to the valor of the German troops who defeated the enemy despite bad leadership and numerical and technical inferiority. For a long time this "victory put the German army at the top of all European armies" (Count von Schlieffen).

Success at Heavy Cost

One should not forget, however, that Gravelotte-St. Privat was one of the bloodiest battles of the nineteenth century, nor that the German success was extremely costly. In modern times, even the utmost bravery is not an efficient expedient against quick-firing artillery and machine guns in prepared positions. German subordinate commanders in 1914, had considerable difficulty in explaining the new situation to their superiors who could not understand why the advance of the troops was so slow in comparison with the speed shown in former wars. If the German leaders had taken into account the incomparable efficiency of modern material, they probably would have understood that appeals to the morale of the troops are futile and that victory is exclusively dependent upon appropriate strategic dispositions, that is to say, upon surprise and concentration of force. Masterly generalship usually has immediate positive effects on the morale of the troops and is much more capable of increasing their courage than even the most impressive and convincing appeals in the order of the day.

On the other hand, unjustified optimism on the part of the High Command has a very negative influence on morale. The troops quickly lose their confidence if reality substantially differs from the situation as it has been depicted to them by their commanders. Generals who lack the sense for the *realité des choses* tend to wishful thinking, especially in difficult situations.

It must be admitted that during the difficult weeks of 1914, the German High Command and some army commanders indulged in undue optimism. Time and again they were convinced that they had smashed the flank of the enemy and that decisive victory was within their grasp. When a new unit, however small, was thrown into the battle, General von Falkenhayn was confident that it would tip the balance in his favor. He consistently believed that the enemy was exhausted and that his lines were about to crack. Falkenhayn's optimism prevented the German commanders from concentrating a numerically decisive superiority of force on the German right flank.

But the strategy of the French Command in like manner failed. On October 5, 1914, when the battle of Arras had reached its peak, fourteen German divisions fought against fifteen French divisions north of the Somme. That is to say, on the very battlefield where both sides were out to gain a decisive victory, both sides threw approximately only one-sixth of their total strength into this supposedly decisive battle. At that moment, the German Army had a total strength of $83\frac{1}{2}$ divisions; the Franco-British Army was composed of $85\frac{1}{2}$ divisions. Under such circumstances, definite results cannot be achieved by either side. The only result of this battle was a steady expansion of the front line. Never in history had a similar battle been fought. Commanders of the past would have not understood a battle fought against all the rules of art, developing mechanically and automatically without showing the influence of any strategic idea. Both commanders lacked a creative mind which is so necessary for the solving of new military problems.

On account of technical progress, the art of war had not become inapplicable during World War I. The art of war had not been applied. The principles of concentration at the decisive point and surprise as the means of achieving relative numerical superiority were replaced by the undefinable rules of linear strategy. The war of movement had come to an end.

Instead, a disastrous war of position was fought which could never yield any clear decision.

NOTES, CHAPTER V

1. Battle of Tannenberg: The Battle of Tannenberg must indeed be considered as a strategic masterpiece. Had the Russians not decisively lost this important battle, they could have continued their offensive into eastern Germany and should have been able during the first weeks of World War I to advance at least beyond the Vistula. This advance would have fundamentally changed Germany's strategical situation and might have led to an early victory of the Entente.

At the end of August, 1914, the Russian Army of the Narev moved forward to the west. It was first attacked on its left flank, while its center continued to advance successfully. When the German attack did not develop satisfactorily, the center of gravity was shifted against the Russian right wing. Later, the Germans also launched an attack against the rear of the Narev Army. This latter attack was made possible by the previous Russian advance which had driven a wedge into the German lines. The German forces used for the attack on the Russian right wing and rear had been taken out of the front opposite the Russian Army of the Niemen. This army therefore was opposed by practically no German forces.

The Germans would never have taken the risk of leaving the Niemen Army alone if they had not by their radio monitors learned all important details of the Russian disposition and intentions. If the Russians had attacked with the Army of the Niemen, the Battle of Tannenberg would probably have ended with a German defeat. According to some sources, the inactivity of General von Rennenkampf was due to personal enmity against General Samsonoff.

2. German War Plan: While the German war plan of 1914 against the western powers is usually considered as a strategic masterpiece (despite the fact that driving Great Britain into the war definitely resulted in Germany's defeat) the German war plan in the east was wholly insufficient. The Germans were favored by luck. Had Russian

leadership been more capable, the Germans should have lost the Battle of Tannenberg and would have got into a very difficult situation.

The main criticism made by the Germans themselves is that they failed to cooperate closely with the Austrian army and to have one single Austro-German war plan against Russia. Both countries together would have been able to oppose the Russians with adequate forces, particularly so if the Austrians had not undertaken the superfluous campaign against Serbia. As it was, each of the countries operated according to its own plan. The consequence of this faulty strategy was that the Austrian army lost its striking power in an unequal offensive fight against Russia.

It is hardly an exaggeration to say that Austria was destroyed during the fall of 1914. It is known that the breakdown of the Austrian empire precipitated the German collapse. Incidentally, it is characteristic of German strategy in 1914 that the Germans had built numerous and strong fortifications in the west, where they intended to fight offensively, but had almost no fortifications in the East, where they planned to remain on the defensive.

3. Speed of Fighting: General Erfurth does not take into consideration that the speed of fighting has considerably increased, so that even with the most perfect communications it will be difficult to receive detailed orders in time. "For every sixty minutes we had at our disposal in muscle-moved warfare, in machine warfare we have nine when faced by tanks and two when faced by aircraft. The old system of command is therefore manifestly useless; for once things get moving there is no longer sufficient time to make out detailed operation orders and filter them down to the troops, the men of action.

"To do so in a division normally took about eight hours in the last war, and in eight hours a tank may have moved 100 miles or more and an airplane 2,000 . . . In watching and studying (Rommel's) several campaigns it has become clear to me that, so far, he has never worked on what may be called a fixed plan . . . He has relied on rapid decisions, spontaneously made to fit changing events. Instead of working on detailed orders, it would appear that his subordinate commanders have been taught to elaborate their actions from simple ideas and in accordance with a few simple rules . . . It would appear that the secrets of his tactics are to make fuller use of intelligence than of obedience; to impregnate his soldiers with his ideas and then leave it to the men on the spot to elaborate them" (Major General J. F. C. Fuller).

VI

Pursuit, Retreat, Diversion, Counter-Attack

BEFORE the First World War, pursuit was considered one of the essential elements, if not *the* most essential element of war. Clausewitz pointed out that victory without pursuit never yields great results. Schlieffen, too, thought highly of an energetic pursuit which he regarded as the necessary complement of a battle of annihilation. Pursuit must be undertaken, he taught, irrespective of the fatigue of the troops. No attention should be paid to commanding officers who, on account of the exhaustion of their soldiers, would like to discontinue pursuit.

Nevertheless, "a direct pursuit, however energetically it may be carried out, offers little chance of success." The pursuing infantry as a rule is unable to march quicker than the retreating enemy. The opponent cannot be forced to accept battle anew, consequently his annihilation cannot be completed. Any pursuit must stop after a short while. Direct pursuit should only be undertaken by weak forces in an effort to win all successes they can without spending themselves in excessive efforts. But the bulk of the pursuing army must not advance in the same direction as the fleeing enemy; instead there should be attempt to cut the enemy line of retreat. Such a pursuit against the enemy's communication line is indispensable if the battle is to end decisively.

The theories of pursuit which date from the time before World War I can be supported by many examples from Napoleon's campaigns, but by not a single example from the wars in the second half of the nineteenth Century. No pursuit occurred in the war of 1866, disregarding one insignificant exception. In the war of 1870-1871, the Prussian army was equally unable to pursue the fleeing enemy, at least not in a manner that would have corresponded to theoretical exigencies. Moltke explained this by his subordinate commanders' lack of understanding of the importance of pursuit.

But other reasons may have been more effective. The most efficient form of pursuit is a march almost parallel to the enemy's line of retreat, aiming at an important objective in the rear of the retreating army. But such a march is possible only under exceptional conditions. On the whole, it is only possible if a strong and early attack has been launched against the enemy's flank and rear. Where the battle consists of frontal operations only, a pursuit to overtake the enemy should not be undertaken.

After a frontal battle, pursuit consists of nothing more than a mere following of the beaten enemy by the victor; both victor and vanquished have to take the same road. This kind of pursuit occurred frequently during the fifty years previous to World War I. In the period of linear strategy, the "frontal pursuit" became the rule. Recent wars re-emphasized the old experience that in a pursuit in which the enemy is merely followed, instead of being cut off from his line of retreat, the vanquished army is soon able to outrun its pursuer, to complete its retreat undisturbed and even to resume battle whenever it choses and its commanders think it is in a position to do so. In the years following the 1914-18 war, however, several classical pursuits were accomplished in minor wars. In August, 1922, the Turks were able to annihilate the Greak army by an effective pursuit which cut the Greek line of retreat. Similarly, the Abyssinians were annihilated while retreating after the battle of Lake Ashangi.

Pursuit Difficulties Increased

The strong defensive power of modern armament is a new element which further increases the difficulties of pursuit. Generally speaking, most pursuits stop after dusk, or are halted at the next more or less strong natural position defended by a few rearguards. If a pursuit is interrupted once, it is extremely difficult to resume it. Modern technique has not only weakened the attack, but also paralyzed pursuit while it favors the possibility of retreat. It may be said that by the development of modern matériel, the whole strategy of retreat has been fundamentally changed. This statement, however, loses its value if the pursuer possesses mastery of the air and large superiority in mechanized and motorized equipment as well. The pursuit operations in the Abyssinian War were exceptionally effective because the Italians could attack the helpless Abyssinians from the air. After the battle in Schiré, the flight of the Abyssinians before the Italian planes assumed "a tragic character." The Abyssinian retreat after the battle of Lake Aschangi became disorderly, not only on account of a successful Italian flanking maneuver, but chiefly because of the incessant air attacks[1].

Before World War I military theory strongly opposed any form of retreat, without even distinguishing between voluntary retreat and a retreat due to, or forced by, enemy superiority. Even the breaking off of minor engagements was considered a risk. According to the official German doctrine, a unit which with its major forces had been involved in a fight could only under rare circumstances dare a discontinuance of the struggle. Unless the disengaging maneuver was protected by terrain or by strong cavalry, it was said to involve great dangers. Movements to the rear were supposed to be morally disintegrating even if ordered without previous enemy pressure. It was held that voluntary retreat would be equal to an avowal of defeat. Prewar manuals therefore advised that any fight should be continued up to its final decision and, if necessary, by throwing all available reserves into the struggle. Moltke formulated this doctrine in a rather dogmatic way: "He who waits until the opponent has closed, must fight it out." This opinion was perhaps still justified in Moltke's time; yet the disintegrating effects of retreat were certainly overestimated before World War I.

At any rate, Moltke's doctrine lost validity after the machine-gun was introduced into modern warfare. For this weapon enables the retreating army to stop the pursuer with only weak rear guards while getting away with its main forces. An orderly and well conducted retreat must be no means lead to a moral crisis. This has repeatedly been proved during World War I. Nevertheless, the official German doctrine stuck to Moltke's formula and even Schlieffen still considered it as valid. He usually refused to accept from his students any solution of military problems in which voluntary retreats were envisaged, regardless of whether the situation would be improved by the proposed retreat. For Schlieffen any retreat was a defeat.

Offensive Retreat Principle

This attitude on the part of the German authorities was the main reason why the strategic potentialities of voluntary retreats were not understood. In France, the principle of the *retour offensif* was generally accepted, while German writers emphasized only in rare instances that a combination of retreat with counter-attack could be highly effective. In contrast to German conceptions, French strategy and tactics tended to confuse and deceive the opponent. According to the French, the *retour offensif* is one of the most effective means of deception; an especially appropriate method for achieving surprise. Consequently, the army has to be trained not only for attack, but also for retreat and in particular for the difficult switch from retreat to counter-attack.

The French doctrine of strategic retreat was one of the main reasons why, after the loss of the battle of the frontiers, the French High Command quickly determined "to give up terrain in order to organize a counter-attack farther inland," as General Joffre telegraphed to the French Minister of War. The Germans were entirely mistaken about the character and the purpose of the French retreat. They overestimated the significance of their own successes and thought that they had already imposed their law on the enemy. The official German attitude with respect to retreats also influenced General von Falkenhayn when, in September, 1914, he rejected the idea of withdrawing the German right flank in order to gain increased strength for a renewed attack and, instead of such mobile strategy resolved to fight on in the positions he occupied at the time.

As long as World War I still remained a war of movement, voluntary retreat and pursuit, diversion and counter-attack played an important role on all theatres of war. Modern weapons seemingly eliminate the war of movement in favor of a war of position. But in reality the war of movement was preserved, at least to a certain extent, in operations of elusion and in retreat-counter-attack combinations which, in some instances, must be considered as a particularly energetic form of the war of movement. This is not an entirely new phenomenon; former wars offer many examples for successful counter-attacks after retreat. Clausewitz compared the retreat of a great leader commanding an experienced army to the exit of a wounded lion.

Modern warfare offers good opportunities for retreat-counter-attack combinations.

In point of fact, most of the really great battles of our time have actually been waged as a counter-attack after a retreat (for instance, the Battle of the Marne, the campaign of Lodz, the Serbian counter-offensive late in 1914, the Battle of Warsaw in August 1920). In all these battles, the factor of surprise assumed an important role. Each of these battles began with the unexpected decision to disentangle an army from a difficult position by voluntary retreat. These retreats, if begun in time and commanded skilfully, usually succeeded—contrary to the expectations of pre-World War I military theory. Even if the enemy had envisaged the possibility of retreat, he was usually surprised when the retreat actually started. And from the very beginning of retreat the retreating party usually improved its situation.

Retreat Confused Russians

During the night of August 20-21, 1914, the German Eighth Army retreated from the battlefield of Gumbinnen. The Russians were highly surprised next morning, when they discovered this sudden change. However, the Russian command became confused by that unexpected development and ordered that the offensive should not be resumed before the Russian units had rested, reorganized and received reinforcements.

The German leaders on September 10, 1914, were surprised by the unexpected retreat of the Russian Army of the Niemen. Since they did not grasp the intentions of the Russians, they kept their troops back and waited for a further clarification of the Russian tactics.

The Germans had been surprised by the Anglo-French retreat from the Sambre on the night of August 23-24, 1914. The retreat of the Central Powers from Poland in October, 1914, came as an equal surprise to the Russians. General von Mackensen, on October 17, while still attacking Warsaw, confidentially informed his subordinate commanders that a retreat was imminent. After the thorough destruction of railway, telegraph and telephone facilities, the blowing up of bridges and the evacuation of all other military equipment the retreat commenced on the night of October 20. General von Mackensen vanished like a ghost and left nothing behind. Only a few stragglers remained.

The retreat of the Austrian First Army of October 26 on the next day was discovered by the Russians. It was similar to the retreat of the German Eighth Army from the Lötzen-Angerapp position, after the Germans had delivered a successful blow near Stallupoenen on November 7 and 8, 1914. Similarly, the Germans learned about the Russian retreat from Lodz, which began in the evening of December 5, 1914, during the following morning.

The German retreat from the Marne on September 9, 1914, was a complete surprise for the French High Command. General Joffre did not understand the new situation until a whole day had elapsed. On the evening of September 10 he issued a general instruction in which, for the first time, he informed the French Army of the German retreat and directed an energetic pursuit from the French center and left flank.

Voluntary elusion and evasion from the enemy is, however, merely the first step towards a greater success. Disengaging from the enemy may bring about a certain easing of a difficult situation. Yet the gain of time which results from voluntary retreats may be partly cancelled by loss of terrain and thereby of space which is necessary for maneuver. Retreat can alter a military situation only if it is used for re-grouping one's forces and for launching a new attack in the right direction. The counter-attack should provide a second opportunity to surprise the enemy (the first surprise having been the timely disentangling from the enemy). This surprise should be accomplished with due regard to time and terrain as well as to the numbers which are required for making the counter-blow sufficiently powerful.

Military writers of pre-World War I times usually recommended retreat in an excentric direction. An excentric retreat was supposed to screen one's own intentions better than a simple retreat along the axis of the previous advance. Moreover, the excentric retreat was believed to render pursuit more difficult. Yet, during World War I, the simple retreat expedient everywhere enjoyed marked preference. One usually withdrew on a broad front, without the idea of launching a new offensive from a rear-position. The intention was merely to continue with a passive defense farther back. The essential factors of strategy—maneuver and movement—were discounted by the tactical conceptions of trench-warfare.

Retreats in Depth

The deep retreats of the Russian Army in 1915 were simple backward movements to new positions. Danilov, the Russian general, rightly considered the absence of maneuvering as the chief reason why the Russian retreats were so exceptionally deep. Linear strategy, however, reached its peak in the Russian-Polish War of 1920. After the Russian offensive in July north of the Pribjat, the Polish army without offering resistance fell back first on the old German positions from the World War, then with increasing speed to the line Szczara-Niemen, later to the line Bug-Narev and finally almost to the Vistula. This enormous retreat of nearly four hundred miles brought the Polish capital and the battlefield closely together. Marshal Pilsudski blamed the far-reaching results of the Russian victory on the Auta to the trench warfare tactics dear to the heart of the commander of the Polish northern front. Indeed, this officer did not act in accordance with Schlieffen's precept that in order to surprise the enemy one should never take up fixed positions, but must keep moving. He was satisfied with falling back from one fortified line to the other, instead of trying to stop the Russian offensive (as Pilsudski had recommended) by maneuver and counter-attack.

Tuchatchevski, the Russian commander-in-chief admitted that after the Russian victory of July 4, 1920, he had no clear ideas about the intentions of the Poles. It was therefore difficult for him to take appropriate measures. After any success, he wrote some years later, the commander of the victorious army is confronted by a difficult choice. Shall he continue his offensive in the former general direction and maintain the existing disposition of his forces, or shall he re-group and select another direction? Shall he leave all his forces in the front-line or shall he form a reserve force? Shall he, therefore, pursue with weak forces and have strong reserves ready in case the reinforced enemy strikes back or shall he recklessly advance? Tuchatchevski rightly emphasized that an army can hardly be re-grouped during a speedy offensive, particularly if the destruction of railway facilities makes the shifting of large units almost impossible.

These were the same difficulties which in August, 1914, confronted the German chief-of-staff after the Franco-British army had begun to fall back on the Marne. Actually, the Russians did

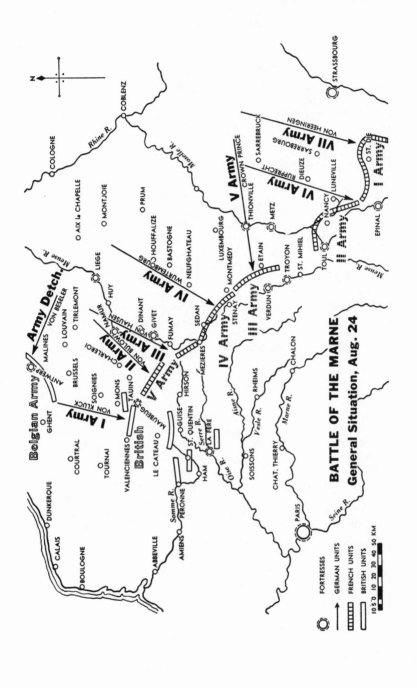

BATTLE OF THE MARNE
General Situation, Aug. 24

FORTRESSES

GERMAN UNITS

FRENCH UNITS

BRITISH UNITS

10 5 0 10 20 30 40 50 KM

not expect that the Poles would still be able to execute strategic maneuver. They counted upon a simple retreat on a broad front which, at the beginning, the Poles carried out. The Russians hoped to disintegrate the Polish army by merely pursuing them. Neither side ever thought of surprise operations, though the possibilities for very effective surprises were certainly not lacking for either army. In particular, the Poles would have been able to lay a trap for the Russians. The retreating army is usually better informed about the opponent and what he is doing than the pursuer, especially in the former's own country. During the advance to the Marne, the German Army could learn many details about the advantages of fighting in their own country.

Doubts and Possibilities

Military writers sometimes tend to doubt the possibility of strategic surprise. They allege that surprise can never be achieved, unless the opponent has previously been forced to occupy those very positions which the surprising party wants him to occupy. Otherwise the opponent could never be out-maneuvered and surprise accomplished. The opponent must either be immobilized or else completely unable to move and to maneuver. It is asserted that unless he passively permits himself to be enveloped, surprise is out of the question.

These doubts seem to be partly justified, yet history shows that not only surprises have effectively been staged, but that also the attacked army usually contributed its own share to the success of the attacker. Nevertheless, the switch from retreat to attack is an extremely complicated maneuver and is dependent upon some kind of aid from the pursuer. According to Schlieffen, the main difficulty is to deprive the enemy of his initiative and to regain the initiative for oneself after it had been lost in previous phases of the battle. To remain on the defensive and to continue with a retreat until the favorable moment arrives, requires strong nerves and Napoleon's *coup d'oeil* for strategic possibilities. The decision must be made at a moment when possibilities can only be dimly discerned.

The difficulties which oppose the strategy of counter-offensive revealed themselves clearly during the operations of August, 1914, in Alsace-Lorraine. During these operations, the opinions, orders and counter-orders of the highest German military

authorities did not cease wavering[2]. Count von Schlieffen was
certainly justified in saying that lack of harmony between the
intentions of the commander-in-chief and the independence and
initiative of subordinate commanders constitutes the main trouble
of big armies. Harmony may only be achieved, says Schlieffen,
if the commanders of the different army groups adapt themselves to the ideas of the commander-in-chief, so that only one
single thought directs the entire army.

In Alsace-Lorraine, the divergence of views had to be eliminated by a clear order from the High Command. But on both
German flanks, the necessary energy of command was lacking.
Instead of issuing clear and binding orders, the High Command
contented itself with "wishes" and "proposals" and timidly gave
in when the subordinate did not deign to accommodate himself
to the desires of the chief.

Traps and Their Chances

Military theorists are fond of asserting that successful surprises are more or less improbable because the enemy rarely
runs into a trap which has been set for him. This prejudice
was the main reason why at the outbreak of World War I in
1914, the commander of the German Sixth Army gave up the
promising plan of falling back behind the river Saar and withdrawing on the Lorraine front in order to lure the French
into Germany and to attack them at both flanks after they had
driven a sufficiently deep wedge into the German lines. True,
Marshal Joffre after the war affirmed that he would not have
marched into a sack which the Germans had obligingly opened
for him. This statement, however, does not prove that he
would not actually have helped the Germans by walking into
the trap. At any rate, he had given orders to the French First
and Second Army to attack in direction of Saarburg. These
orders permit us to question whether his post-war assertion has
any real historical value.

To choose the right moment for the start of an undertaking
of any kind is very difficult. But in strategy the choice of the
right moment is particularly hard and, moreover, is of crucial
importance. Striking too soon means spoiling even a perfect
chance. The commander must not permit himself to be taken
in by the enthusiasm of the troops. He should not follow their
natural impulse to advance but, if need be, should be able to

check his troops and curb forward movements, however promising they may look to victorious soldiers.

The German Army began the Battle of Lorraine too soon, hence it could win only an "ordinary victory." The French did not expect a German counter-attack on August 20, and were effectively caught by surprise. But the German counter-attacking forces were too weak and the direction of the German move did not correspond to the strategic plan. It proved to be impossible to force the enemy into a different position. The French were attacked only frontally. Therefore, they were able to disengage and to withdraw to their original positions. The German attempt at least to cut the retreat of some French units was unsuccessful, in spite of the fact that the German units were ordered to pursue relentlessly in the direction of the Meurthe.

A counter-attack by an army retreating on a broad front is not easy. It is particularly difficult to choose a direction that may yield strategic results. Frequently, the counter-attacking units will crash head-on into a strong enemy line. It is also possible that two attacks clash and that no result will be achieved despite a bloody and exhausting fight.

Results at St. Quentin

This, for instance, was the fate of the counter-attack of the French Fifth Army near St. Quentin on August 29-30, 1914, the failure of which was easily predictable. It may be presumed that General Joffre intended at first merely a diversion-attack to relieve the hard-pressed British army. However, General Lanrezac objected to this project with apparently rather good reason and the French generalissimo had to use strong language to make himself obeyed. He declared that the fate of the whole campaign depended upon Lanrezac's attack on St. Quentin and that, by means of surprise, this move could give "decisive results." He asked General Lanrezac to execute his orders *"sans discuter."*

Lanrezac was not convinced, but began the attack in the morning of August 29. The course of events proved him to be right and disproved General Joffre. It is true that the French counter-attack was a complete surprise for the German command and for most of the German divisions. On the western bank of the Oise, a serious crisis occurred in the

The Battles on November 7th and 8th,
1914
in EASTERN PRUSSIA

German ranks. However, the situation was soon well in hand again and the French did not succeed in forcing the Germans on the defensive. On the second day, the attack of the French Army petered out and the Germans launched an attack of their own from the southern bank of the Oise near Guise.

Some hours later, the French Fifth Army was already in difficulties; General Lanrezac reported to the commander-in-chief that his army might be cut off, if it remained much longer in the present position. Since he was under formal and strict orders to attack he would continue to do so, but not on his own responsibility. Instead, the French High Command itself had to assume the responsibility for this operation. General Joffre was not prepared to accept such a heavy risk. During the night of August 29-30, he ordered the French Fifth Army to resume its retreat. General Lanrezac received this order late in the morning of August 30, and was obliged to break off battle in plain daylight. During the disengagement, the French suffered heavy losses and could retreat but slowly.

As a consequence of this two-day-battle and the subsequent retreat, the French Fifth Army had lost much of its striking power. Yet the Germans let the French go and most of the German soldiers were permitted to rest. The German commanders were content with pursuing the French with artillery and smaller infantry detachments in light marching order. Such a pursuit, of course, could not lead to any real success. One may be sure that under similar circumstances Count von Schlieffen would have driven ahead and paid not the least attention to the fatigue of the troops and the apprenhensions of the commanding generals.

Incidentally, the conduct of the Battle of St. Quentin was greatly facilitated for the Germans by the seizure of important documents. On the evening of August 29 they captured the chief-of-staff of one of the French corps who carried the complete French order of attack in his pocket. This order revealed every detail of the French plan and informed the Germans of the numerical strength of the French. The information proved to be very helpful on the second day of the battle.

Results in East Prussia

In East Prussia the Germans were more successful with a combined retreat-counter-attack than the French near St. Quentin. On November 6, 1914, they stopped their retreat beyond the Prussian eastern frontier. On November 7, 1914, they launched a counter-attack against the Russian forces in the vicinity of Stallupoenen. Because the region of Lake Wysztyt and the brushwoods of Rominten can hardly be negotiated by strong formations, the commander of the German Eighth Army had correctly foreseen that the Russians would divide their forces into two parts. This was a good opportunity to attack the Russian units which passed north of this impenetrable sector, namely the Russian Third Corps. This corps could be attacked from the region of Stallupoenen on both flanks by a corps under General von Bulow and in addition by the German First Corps which proceeded by forced marches into the vicinity of Tollmingkehmen. On November 7, the Germans attacked the advancing Russian Third Corps (which had just been reinforced) on both sides of the Wirballen-Stallupoenen railroad and also the Russian Cavalry Corps near Mehlkehmen under General Gurko which protected the Russian left flank. The Russians were hard hit by this surprise attack and after having suffered heavy losses retreated beyond the German frontier. The engagement of Stallupoenen may serve as an example for a well planned and executed diversion attack. Despite numerical inferiority, the Germans were able to concentrate superior numbers in the region where they intended to strike. Their surprise attack was therefore successful.

The Austrian offensive in December, 1914, which was aimed at the southern wing of the Russian army under the command of General Dimitriev and which led to the battle of Limanova-Lapanov shows strategical similarities. It also ended with a marked success. According to the testimony of General Russki, who at that time commanded the Russian northwestern front "this dashing operation completely surprised the Russians and hit them at the most vulnerable spot of their entire front." General Russki rightly called the battle of Limanowa "a strategical masterpiece."

Reasons for Results

On the whole, a strategic counter-attack after a preceding retreat is a more ambitious, and hence more difficult, enterprise than a diversion-attack with limited objectives. In recent wars, a *retour offensif* has been sometimes attempted in order to alter the strategic situation as a whole. We shall now discuss some of these attempts and see why they have or have not been successful. In particular, we shall try to determine what role the factor of surprise played during these operations.

The analysis of the Battle of the Marne in September, 1914, yields interesting results. First, it shows that the French made their counter-attack with astonishingly weak forces which were certainly not in proportion to their task; and, secondly, that the Germans really had been surprised by the French maneuver.

The French generalissimo was not alone responsible for the assembly of a new army in the region of Paris. This measure must in part be attributed to the French Minister of War, Messimy, who claims to have been solely responsible for it. However this may be, Messimy asked on August 25 that three French corps should be earmarked for the defense of Paris. The next day, the Governor of Paris, General Galliéni, who worried about the security of the French capital, insisted on the urgent dispatch of additional troops to Paris. Had these troops not been formed into the Army of Paris, the French attack on the right German wing would have been still weaker than it actually was. As it was, the old principle that one must be strongest at the decisive point was by no means adhered to.

At the end of the five-day battle on the Ourcq, the German First Army comprised 128 battalions. These German battalions were attacked by 127 French battalions, and at the beginning of the battle even by a lesser number. It is true that the French fought in conjunction with 64 British battalions, yet at the most decisive point of this battle, at the extreme left wing of the French army, the Germans possessed almost threefold superiority.

The German command had thus accepted the risk of being numerically weaker on most parts of the front in order to concentrate a real striking power at the focal point. If the French desired to win a final victory on the Marne, they should have attacked with overwhelming odds. In discussing a similar strategic situation, Schlieffen once remarked that a flanking attack against the enemy's line of retreat should never be launched "with four corps, but with everything one has[3]." With a superiority of a few divisions the French could not expect to disrupt the German front, let alone overthrow the German army. It is true that the French commander did not have so ambitious a plan. He did not wage a decisive battle north of Paris; he merely attempted a limited counter-attack against the two German flanks on the Meuse and near Paris respectively, without forming a center of gravity on either spot.

Galliéni vs. Joffre

General Galliéni had a much clearer view of the German situation, but Joffre was not at all pleased with the former's proposal to attack strongly the flank of the German First Army. At first, Joffre even refused to be dragged into a "premature offensive." Galliéni, however, accepted no refusal and insisted that the circumstances were favorable for a counter-attack, since the flank of the German Army was protected by only one single corps. Joffre finally realized the opportunity himself and on September 4 accepted the plan of his subordinate.

The Germans made many contributions of their own to the success of the French counter-attack. After the battle of the frontiers, the German High Command believed the French to be in full retreat towards Paris. They expected the French to make several stands, first behind the Aisne and then behind the Marne. They also considered possible a French concentration on the lower Seine and believed in a French diversion-offensive in Lorraine. The German Army was therefore ordered to pursue the French to Paris. The German High Command evidently exaggerated the importance of the victories which had already been won. The French were supposed to be exhausted and a *retour offensif* was considered out of question.

According to the German High Command, relentless pursuit would definitely break down French resistance. Consequently, no re-grouping of the German forces nor a concentration of strong forces at one point was deemed to be necessary. On the evening of August 30 the German High Command changed the direction of the advance and turned the wing of the German army from southwest to south. On September 2 the German High Command announced its intention to push the French back to the southeast, instead of forcing them into Paris. The German First Army was ordered to advance more slowly than the Second Army whose flanks it had to cover.

At that moment, however, the German chief-of-staff received advance warning of impending misfortune. Air reconnaissance disclosed that the French had begun to move large bodies of troops to the southwest. In spite of the hot German pursuit, the French, with the help of their railways, were apparently still capable of re-grouping. On the next day, these reports were confirmed and the Germans suspected that the French withdrew troops from Lorraine, a conjecture which was confirmed on the afternoon of September 4. The German commander could no longer doubt that the French were preparing a large scale counter-blow.

On the same day serious trouble arose for the German chief-of-staff. He suddenly received unexpected information that the German First Army, instead of following the German Second Army farther behind, had crossed the Marne west of Chateau-Thierry. In the evening of September 4 he had a radio message from the First Army informing him that this army had continued its advance during the whole day. The First Army tried to envelop the French Army in a southeastern direction, while the protection of its flanks had been entrusted to small forces.

Attack From Paris Feared

What would happen if the French launched a strong attack from Paris? Was there still a chance to forestall the danger which menaced the German right flank? The moment had come to reconsider whether the operations just in execution were to be continued, or if the maintenance of the original plan would not lead into serious trouble. Had the German operation still a good chance to warrant the acceptance of heavy risks? The German chief-of-staff was confronted by the alternative of either stopping the pursuit of the French army and re-grouping his forces for a new operation, or of leaving everything as it was and continuing the advance. He adopted the latter solution and thus contributed to the success of the French counter-attack.

The French enterprise was also being favored by unexpected luck and favorable circumstances. Still, as late as the evening of September 4 it was possible to protect effectively the German right wing against a French blow from Paris. It was merely necessary to re-group the German First Army. The German commander-in-chief issued an order to that purpose, but unfortunately worded it in so complicated a way that it was not understood by his subordinates. The order ran as follows: "First and Second Army remain in front east of Paris, the First Army between Oise and Marne, the Second between Marne and Seine."

When Moltke wrote this order he already knew that a great part of the First Army stood south of the Marne and had advanced far away from the Oise. Instead of ordering the First Army to remain east of Paris, he should have ordered the retreat to the positions between Oise and Marne. This retreat was unavoidable, if the German flank was to be protected at all. Besides, the commander of the First Army should have been informed about the re-grouping of the French army, but for some reason or other he never received this vital information.

Air Survey Incomplete

To make things even worse, the First Army completely failed to reconnoiter in direction of Paris. The available aircraft was used only for reconnaissance to the south. The Second Army reconnoitered in the same direction; the extreme German flank had no aircraft at all. Only one corps reconnoitered to the west and indeed did not fail to report the concentration of strong French forces northeast of Paris. This report, however, was not transmitted to the commander of the First Army. The lack of information was therefore exclusively due to the faulty use of air reconnaissance.

Yet the commander of the First Army interpreted it as proof that the German flank was safe. Consequently, General von Kluck on September 5 continued his advance to the south, thus getting further away from Paris. A rapid forward movement, he felt, would hasten the disintegration of the French army. Some of his officers warned him, however, of the great risks involved in this advance, yet he rejected their objections as being "imaginations of pessimistic minds." He saw the situation of the enemy through the lens of his own wishes and refused to be disturbed by the "Ghost of Paris" until he had seen it in flesh and blood.

So the singular situation arose that the governor of Paris was lying in wait for his game and spotted all the movements of the Germans. Galliéni could deliberately choose the right moment, because the Germans had concentrated their attention to the south and ignored the dangers from Paris. They continued to march southward thereby more and more uncovering their flank, against which a lurking enemy was about to strike a hard blow.

As it was, the French attack on September 5 from Paris took the German First Army completely by surprise. On that day, the disposition of the German units was particularly unfavorable[4]. The danger for the whole German flank was extreme. The numerical weakness of the French attacking forces was solely responsible for the limited French success, although the German leaders at last became equal to their responsibilities and, together with their troops, showed themselves able to master a particularly difficult situation. Had the French attacked with stronger forces, a disaster for the German army would have been unavoidable. Had the French attacked with double or triple the strength of Galliéni's force, and had they encountered an opponent of lesser military qualities, their attack would possibly have decided the whole war[4].

In the Battle of the Marne, the French commander certainly sinned against the principle of concentration. His mistake was repeated by the German chief-of-staff when in November, 1914, he sought not only to smash by a counter-attack the right flank of the Russian army, but by pressing against their rear to force the Russians to accept battle on a reversed front. If General von Falkenhayn with twelve German corps had adhered to his original plan of making a surprise attack in the region of Thorn, a great victory would have been won and the war in the east would perhaps have been triumphantly ended.

Victories Bred Crisis

The German Eastern Army was to weak for such an ambitious undertaking. Big victories require big means. The offensive of Lodz, attempted with insufficient forces, came quickly to a standstill and despite brilliant victories led to a serious crisis for the Germans. It miscarried because it proved to be impossible to maintain numerical superiority throughout the battle.

The Germans started their offensive under particularly favorable circumstances. The German commander knew all the details of the Russian strength, disposition and organization. In the last minute, he learned beyond any doubt that the Russians had ceased to advance farther to the south. Hence he was

Baltic Sea

O KOINGSBERG

GUMBINNEN

DANZIG O

Eastern Prussia 8TH

Western Prussia

German Army

O STETTIN

Bobr

TANNENBERG

Netze

BERLIN

KUSTRIN

HOHENSALZA

THORN

Warthe

O FRANKFURT

POSEN

Oder

Vistula

Narew

NOWOGEORGIEWSK

O WARSAW

Posen

Polen

O LODZ

Piliza

O IWANGOROD

WJELUN

BRESLAU

NOW. RADOMSK

CZENSTOCHAU

K JELZY

San

Silesia

9TH

German Army

KATTOWITZ

CRACOW

1ST Austro Hungarian Army

Bohemia

PRZEMYSL

Galicia

Moravia

Carpathian Mountains.

WIEN

Hungary

Danube

GERMANS

AUSTRIANS AND HUNGARIANS

RUSSIANS

BUDAPEST

November 3, 1914

able to take strong forces away from the southern front and to organize an offensive center of gravity in the area of Thorn. The reports of German air reconnaissance and of the German land forces were confirmed by lengthy Russian radio messages which the Germans deciphered without difficulty. Thus, the enemy facilitated the German preparations for a battle of annihilation. It was only necessary to hide from the Russians the transport of German shock-troops from southern Poland and East Prussia to Thorn. Extensive precautions were taken to keep the German troop movements secret. *The weaker one's own force, the more is surprise essential.*

The successful surprise of the Russians was facilitated by a set of favorable conditions. The Russians did not yet possess modern air reconnaissance. The brevity and relative darkness of November days made the screening of marches and railway transports comparatively simple. The concentration of the German offensive force could be covered by German cavalry because the Russians remained passive and were not at all eager to learn about developments behind the German lines. The Russians ignored the fact that some German formations had been diverted from southern Poland to another front; the Russian cavalry had failed to push on with its pursuit behind the retreating German Eighth Army. There is little doubt, therefore, that the Germans were favored by luck when preparing the maneuver of Lodz.

If motorized reconnaissance units had existed at that time, heavy railroad traffic almost under the noses of the Russians could hardly have remained unnoticed. Besides, the speed of the German maneuver contributed to the success of the surprise operation. The decision to attack the northern Russian flank was made on November 3. On November 4, the assembly of the German attack formation began. On November 10, the German concentration was terminated and the German cavalry began its forward movement. On November 11, the offensive started in full.

The Russians unwittingly and carelessly continued to inform the Germans about their dispositions by transmitting inter-army orders and intelligence in clear by radio. Like General Galliéni before the Battle of the Marne, General von Mackensen prior to the offensive of Lodz knew everything about the Russian situation. In addition, the Russians failed to discover the

German concentration near Thorn and learned of the impending storm only a short while before the Germans actually began to move.

Fruits of Surprise Lost

This surprise concentration of the German Ninth Army was an excellent performance and had been recognized as such by the Russians themselves. General Danilov writes: "Our slowness and incapacity for gaining information of the opponent must be contrasted with the German speed and with their accomplished art of maintaining secrecy. Therefore, their blow caught us entirely by surprise."

Neither German efficiency nor the luck by which the Germans were favored, nor finally the information which unconsciously the Russians vouchsafed to the Germans were, however, sufficient for gaining a really decisive success. The surprise which had so brilliantly been accomplished was not exploited by the Germans who failed to achieve numerical superiority at the decisive point. They did not succeed in concentrating more troops than the enemy expected. Obviously, surprise alone can never be effective, it is only a *condition* of success, not the success itself. *Surprise must be supplemented by numerical superiority which, under all conditions, remains the most important objective of the strategical art and the most general principle of victory. (Clausewitz).*

The offensive of Lodz, it is true, was begun on the German side with a small margin of superiority, but this margin was speedily lost. Eleven German infantry and five cavalry divisions marched on November 11 against four Russian infantry and five cavalry divisions. Up to November 25, when the offensive finally stopped, the Germans had been reinforced by five weak Landsturm brigades, that is to say, by a second-rate reserve force, hardly suitable for active warfare. During the same period, Russian infantry had grown to 26½ divisions. Altogether about 123 German battalions with about 800 guns fought against 204 Russian battalions with 750 guns in the region of Lodz. In the area of Lovitch, the situation was still more unfavorable for the Germans. Here, 34 German battalions with 100 guns were opposed by 160 Russian battalions and 384 guns.

In a modern battle, even the highest heroism cannot compensate for such inferiority. The overwhelming importance of numerical superiority did not diminish in the least with the improvement of modern matériel, regardless of whether it is absolute or merely a relative superiority achieved by good generalship. The failure to concentrate sufficient forces for the Lodz offensive was largely due to the fact that Germany had to wage war on two separate fronts.

Before World War I, Count von Schlieffen had often discussed the strategic implications of a simultaneous war against France and Russia. He repeatedly pondered situations which necessitated the shifting of the main effort from one front to the other. Schlieffen emphatically warned against dividing the German Army so that it would be numerically weaker on both fronts. According to him, the minimum force for large-scale strategic operations against Russia was an army of nine to eleven corps.

To conclude this chapter, we desire to discuss several examples of successful strategic counter-attacks. The Serbian campaign of autumn 1914 is one of the most impressive examples of that kind. The Serbian commander-in-chief, Voyvod Putnik, evaded the Austrian-Hungarian offensive until the Austrian army had over-extended its communication lines and slowed down its movements. The Serbian leader had strong enough nerves to wait for a long time for striking back, though the Serbian army had suffered severely under the strain of the continuous retreat and though the commanders of the Serbian armies urged an early counter-offensive.

Concentration and Surprise Won

The Serbian counter-offensive was launched after the Serbian wing had been strongly reinforced. The Serbs had concentrated their main striking power at the point where they wished to make their main effort. The Serbian counter-offensive proved to be highly successful, particularly because the Austrian commander, General Potiorek, did not believe that the Serbs were still able to attack. He thought that after long weeks of retreat the Serbs were at the end of their rope. Thus, Putnik held both trump cards, surprise and concentration, in his hands and achieved with his little army a brilliant victory against two entire Austro-Hungarian armies.

The most impressive example of a surprise-counter-attack is

the Battle of Warsaw which decided the Russian-Polish war. On the night of August 7-8, 1920, the Polish northern front continued its retreat from the line Biala-Janov, north of Siedlce-Sokolov-Rozan. During the retreat, the Polish army was to be re-grouped for the counter-offensive ordered by Marshal Pilsudski on August 6. This offensive was based upon the fundamental idea that the Poles should hold a line along the Orzyc-Narev rivers and along the Vistula as far down as Ivangorod. They should also try to retain the strongly fortified bridge-heads of Modlin and Warsaw. The main Polish attack was to be launched from the positions along the Wieprz river to the north and northeast against the southern flank of the advancing Russians. The Polish striking force was to comprise two infantry divisions and one cavalry brigade of the Polish southern front and three and one-half infantry divisions of the Polish northern front. During the evening of August 7, the Polish Fourteenth, Sixteenth and Twenty-First infantry divisions held positions southwest and west of the Bug river, as it is shown on the map. In the following nights, these divisions retreated due west to the line Siedlce-Lucov-Kock. During the night of August 11-12, they turned around and moved southward to the Wieprz river.

This perpendicular march across the axis of the enemy's advance resembles somewhat. the German deployment for the Battle of Tannenberg. The Russian Army of the Niemen in 1914 ignored the frontal march of two German corps. Similarly in 1920, the Russian Sixteenth Army and the Russian High Command failed to discover the departure of three Polish divisions to the southwest and south. Tuchatchevsky, the commander of the Russian western front made the *a priori* assumption that the Polés would continue to retreat behind the Vistula. He was therefore also convinced that the three Polish divisions which had disappeared were continuing their retreat to the west.

Tuchatchevsky was firmly resolved not to change his opinions concerning his opponent's attitude. He had the "strong conviction" that the Poles would never accept a decisive battle east of the Vistula with the river in their rear, but would use the Vistula as a military obstacle. Hence they would concentrate their forces west of the river and so protect their capital and their vital supply line with the port of Dantzig.

Poles Surprised Russians

Tuchatchevsky planned to concentrate his main strength on his northern flank in order to envelop the Polish left wing north of Warsaw. His own left wing had to deliver a frontal attack on the bridgehead of Warsaw. For the protection of the Russian left wing itself, Tuchatchevsky had earmarked only a small force. To protect himself in that zone he counted entirely upon the early arrival of the Russian Twelfth Army and of a large cavalry force which was still held up near Lemberg. His plan, however, was purely wishful thinking, for the expected reinforcements for the Russian left flank failed to appear.

In conclusion, three Russian armies moved northward while the Russian Sixteenth Army operated directly towards Warsaw, with its main concentration in the northern sector of the battlefield. The protection of the Russian left flank became the mission of the small Mosyr group, some four thousand men, which was ordered to move forward towards Parczev-Ivangorod. This strange disposition of the Russian army certainly facilitated the execution of Marshal Pilsudski's plan. The three Polish divisions which marched southward to take up their positions on the Wieprz disengaged themselves from the enemy and marched along his front without great difficulties. They were only in intermittent contact with the Mosyr group and could calmly prepare for their counter-attack.

Not even once did Tuchatchevsky consider the possibility that Polish units would be diverted from the northern to the southern front. This is the more astonishing, as the Russian High Command for a long time had already expected a Polish counteroffensive from the area of Ivangorod and repeatedly drew Tuchatchevsky's attention to this danger. The Russian commander did not even become doubtful when the southern flank of his Sixteenth Army failed to encounter any Polish resistance. Where were the Poles? Had they retreated from this front?

Tuchatchevsky did not doubt for one moment that the Poles had retreated to the west. When some days before the start of Pilsudski's offensive an army order was found on a dead Polish officer revealing the concentration of a new Polish army south of Warsaw, Tuchatchevsky considered this as a ruse to mislead him. Like many other generals, he fancied a situation based on personal wishes, not on reality.

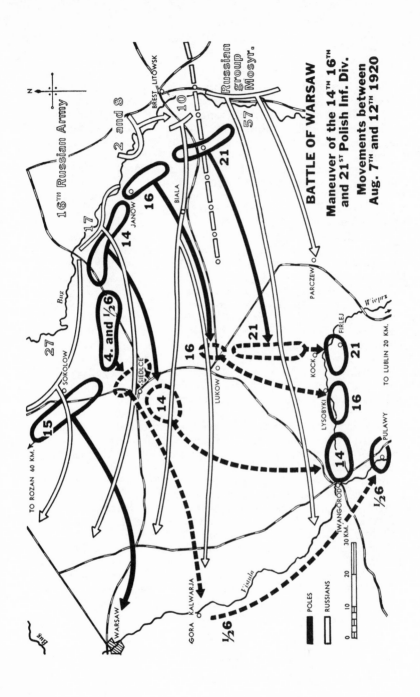

BATTLE OF WARSAW

Maneuver of the 14TH 16TH
and 21ST Polish Inf. Div.

Movements between
Aug. 7TH and 12TH 1920

16TH Russian Army

Russian group Mosyr.

BREST LITOWSK

JANOW

BIALA

2 and 8

10

17

57

27

Bug

SOKOLOW

SIEDLCE

4. and 1/26

15

14

16

21

16

16

21

LUKOW

PARCZEW

Wieprz

FIRLEJ

KOCK

21

LYSOBYKI

16

PULAWY

14

TO LUBLIN 20 KM.

IWANGOROD

1/26

TO ROZAN 60 KM.

GORA KALWARJA

1/26

Wisla

Bug

WARSAW

POLES

RUSSIANS

0   10   20   30 KM.

As a consequence of these errors, which occurred despite repeated warnings, the Soviet leaders were fully surprised by the Polish counter-offensive of August 16 against the Russian southern flank from the Wieprz. The success of this strategic *retour offensif* was beyond expectation. The numerical weakness of the Polish offensive-group was more than compensated by the exhaustion of the Russian troops which were tired by forced marches of five weeks. The Poles achieved numerical superiority at their point of attack and inflicted a crushing defeat on the Mosyr group. The Russian Sixteenth Army was unfavorably deployed at the time of the Polish attack and was quickly over-run. The Poles continued their northward advance and attacked the flanks of the Russian Third and Fifteenth Army. These armies tried hard to stop the Polish offensive and to keep open a line of retreat for the Russian Fourth Army which had advanced far to the west. But their efforts were in vain. The Third and Fifteenth Army suffered extreme losses and the Fourth Army could not be salvaged. It was pushed back to the frontier of East Prussia and finally forced to save itself by passing the German frontier. "Thus our magnificent operation which made the capitals of almost every European country tremble came to an end," wrote Tuchatchevsky.

Nevertheless, the Battle of Warsaw did not become a Cannae, for the simple reason that the forces of Marshal Pilsudski were too weak. Moreover there were no speedy units on the right Polish flank to overtake the Russians and to cut off their retreat. The entire Russian western army group could have been encircled or pushed against the German frontier if the Polish right wing had possessed greater mobility and speed than it actually had. But even so, the Polish victory was decisive. The Russian troops which escaped the Polish pursuit according to Tuchatchevsky himself, reached the line Grodno-Volkovysk "in a lamentable state." The Russo-Polish War was decided on the Vistula. The Battle of the Niemen which took place at a later date was nothing but an aftermath of the victorious Polish counter-offensive.

Basic Principle Inapplicable

Our survey of recent wars revealed the singular fact that, in the period of mass-armies, it was rarely possible to apply the basic principle of warfare and to concentrate superior masses at the decisive point. That the concentration of vast numbers in one sector should be particularly difficult, in spite of our modern transport facilities, is certainly a paradox. There is hardly any doubt that World War I could have been decided on several occasions if the principle of concentration had been applied. The failure to exploit strategic opportunities by quick concentrations must be attributed to many and different causes.

Many promising opportunities were lost as a consequence of errors of judgment, such as those on the German side in the Battle of Mons and Namur. Sometimes the surprise could not be accomplished because the attacked party prematurely detected the intentions of its opponent and was able to take timely precautions, as did the Russians late in 1914 when they frustrated the Austro-German advance to the middle Vistula. It is true that errors of judgment and unsuccessful surprise moves happen in any war and are by no means typical only of World War I. It is, however, characteristic of that war that decisive results were not even accomplished in those instances where the opponent was surprised and had himself contributed to the surpriser's victory. In such cases, full success was not achieved because the surprise was not utilized for developing numerical superiority at the decisive point, as happened in the Battle of the Marne in September, 1914, and during the offensive of Lodz in the autumn of the same year.

What is the reason for these repeated failures to utilize succesful surprise for strategic concentration? The military leaders of World War I realized of course, the necessity of forming a center of gravity at the point of attack. Most of their actions certainly served the idea of strategic concentration. Yet in practice, they were unable to concentrate sufficient masses at the decisive point. It appears thus that under modern conditions concentration of large forces is much more difficult than in previous wars. Before World War I, doubts had been expressed whether operations with an army of millions would be as easy as with the typical nineteenth century army of one hundred thousand men.

To many soldiers, the conduct of an army of several millions appeared as an insoluble problem. This view was strongly opposed by Count von Schlieffen. "It is true," he wrote, "that the command of an army was always an extremely difficult enterprise, whether the army was small or big. But it will be hard to prove that the difficulties of military leadership increase in the same proportion as the numbers of armies.[6]"

Schlieffen repeatedly discussed the question of how the enemy's flank should be attacked. His answer was: "Not with one or two corps, *but with one or several armies. The attack of these armies should not be directed against the enemy's wing, but against his line of retreat.*" He admitted, however, that only a military genius would dare take the risk of moving all, or the largest part, of his forces against the enemy's flank, let alone operate in the enemy's rear. His own war plan against France is an example for such a risk.

Defense Acquires Strength

The principle of concentration is more important in our time than it ever was before, for the simple reason that defense has acquired a technical strength unknown in previous periods and that, moreover, defense quickly increases its power during battle, while the power of attack diminishes. Consequently, only the commander has a chance of winning a decisive victory who, *by surprise,* is able to concentrate an almost *incredible* numerical superiority at the center of the battle. This superiority must be so overwhelming that the organization of the enemy army is immediately crushed.

Moreover, the numerical superiority must be maintained throughout the entire operation without ever giving the opponent a chance to re-establish quantitative equilibrium. Schlieffen proposed to carry out attacks on the enemy flanks with some twenty corps. This figure is certainly not a fantastic exaggeration. A striking force of that size is an absolute necessity if a victory of annihilation shall be won against a modern mass-army[7].

Such thoughts clearly oppose many uses of modern linear strategy which, on the whole, is the result rather of technical progress than of the numerical increase of armies. The armies of the Russo-Polish War in 1920 were not larger than those of the last century, yet linear strategy was applied in this war still more than in World War I.

The importance of terrain is being rated more highly since 1914 than by the classical writers of the last century. The maxim "hold whatever you have and never abandon a foot of ground which you won," was regarded by General von

Falkenhayn as a new truth "beyond any doubt." Certainly, this doctrine would not have found the approval of Napoleon, Lee, Moltke, nor of Schlieffen who had taught the exact opposite: "It is better to abandon a whole province than to divide an army."

Schlieffen clearly recognized that especially in the period of mass-armies, *strategy of annihilation is only possible by continuous movement.* Only by movement can rigid fronts be avoided. It is possible that Falkenhayn spoke more as a politician than as a soldier and a strategist. He who does not abandon terrain, usually obeys political pressure, but rarely follows strategic consideration[8].

The tendency to fill large spaces with a limited number of troops in linear deployment, a tendency which made its appearance in World War I, certainly does not correspond to the opinions of the military classics.

Modern equipment makes it possible to protect vast expanses by weak forces. This fact may be used as a favorable argument for the division and dispersion of force which in former times would have invited disaster. Unfortunately, technical progress strengthened the old inclination to divide military forces according to unconscious sentiments and "traditional manners without knowing why." (Clausewitz). Such habits are dangerous because they may prevent the concentration of sufficient numbers.

Since it is impossible to attack everywhere on a broad front, the forms of fighting must differ on various sectors. Attack requires incomparably more force than defense. Therefore strictest economy of force must prevail on all sectors where no attacks take place. Schlieffen propounded the rule of diverting to all secondary fronts "as much French forces as possible by as few German forces as possible."

Sacrifices Must Be Made

This rule still holds good today; the unimportant fronts, or at least those fronts where the decisive battle is not being fought, must make sacrifices for the sake of the decisive front. Consequently, the maxim "never abandon any ground" is not valid with respect to secondary fronts. If one wishes to win a conclusive victory, one should not scatter one's forces in order to hold unimportant terrain, nor protect areas of lesser importance.

The annihilation of the enemy army is the only objective, not the defense of localities or regions. Also today, in the period of mass-armies, there is "no higher and simpler strategic law than: Hold together all your forces." (Clausewitz). This sounds easy, indeed. Yet the history of war proves that only a Titan is able to apply this seemingly simple principle. He who will win everything, must dare staking everything on one single card. By doing so, a military genius does not act like a gambler. He acts rather as a serenely self-confident and bold personality who is inspired by the "sacred fire" of the will to win and who aspires to the highest success.

To concentrate overwhelmingly superior numbers at the decisive points is impossible without strategic surprise. The assembly of the shock-group must therefore be done as quickly as possible in such a way that all units can attack at one and the same time. "The more the concentration can be compressed into one act and one moment, the more perfect are its results." (Clausewitz). To use one's forces "in driblets," as for instance during the *course à la mer* or during the offensive of Lodz, must be avoided by all means. Only a complete and quick concentration makes possible an attack which, like a mighty avalanche, overwhelms the surprised opponent and everything that is put in its path.

There is little reason to doubt the possibility of a modern battle of annihilation according to the model of Cannae, provided all necessary conditions are fulfilled. This opinion cannot be invalidated by the fact that in recent wars only one perfect Cannae, the Battle of Tannenberg and only one near-Cannae, the Battle of Warsaw, were won. For also in former times an entirely successful battle of annihilation was extremely rare. Two thousand years passed after the Battle of Cannae until at Sedan in 1940 a new Cannae was won.

In the lengthy period between these two battles numerous incomplete battles of annihilation were fought and they usually occurred at historic turning points. If in a future war, a commander will appear with all the qualities of Hannibal, then a perfect masterpiece in the art of war, that is to say a battle of Cannae, may again succeed. It would be preposterous and dangerous to deny such a possibility. The essence and nature of war are best understood if one supposes that war always tends to reach its extreme. This happens when "the idea of war is realized by an efficient army and an independent will." (Clausewitz).

NOTES, CHAPTER VI

1. Difficulties of pursuit: During the Battle of France pursuit was most effectively undertaken by the German army. The reason was that the German army had overwhelming fire power and that, due to mechanization and motorization, its average speed was superior to the speed of the French army. This superiority was however exceptional. General Erfurth's arguments are still valid in the case of more or less equal armament and motorization on both sides. The war in Russia and North Africa has shown that effective pursuit soon comes on a standstill and that it is extremely difficult to overtake a beaten enemy.

2. Indecisive orders: In war one should never wait to get the best possible plan. On account of the scarcity of reliable information, *the* best plan is unobtainable. The most important thing is to have *one* plan and to adhere strictly to it, so far as possible. The function of the commander-in-chief is perhaps less to be a genius than to force his subordinates to obey the one plan which he has adopted. There is some truth in the old rule that, in war, the simplest plan is the best. "In war so much is always unknown that it frequently happens that even the simplest actions rapidly become exceedingly complex. As from the simple to the complex is the rule in war, therefore the simpler, more direct and clearer the beginning the less likely is action to get out of hand". (Major General Fuller.)

3. Schlieffen's Idea: It must again be pointed out that such an operation with "everything one has," or with more than 20 corps as Schlieffen textually said, is not a practical, but a fantastic idea. There will be rarely enough space, or sufficient transportation for moving such a force. Nor will it be possible to move more than 20 corps around the enemy's flank secretly and speedily. Consequently no surprise will be possible if a flanking effort with such a force is attempted. The German General, Wetzell, Ludendorff's chief-of-operations, asserts that such a strategy would not have been possible during World War I, even against the Russians, let alone against the western powers.

4. French position: This statement must be taken with several grains of salt. It is undoubtedly true that the French could have attacked with stronger forces and therefore won the Battle of the Marne much

more conclusively. Yet they would have been unable to use a force two or three times stronger, as Erfurth suggests. To begin with, they did not have the means of transporting such a force to the battlefield. Galliéni's army may have been small, but it appeared suddenly on the battlefield and, for this very reason, achieved a surprise which perhaps was more important for the outcome of the battle than anything else. With greater forces, Galliéni would have attacked later and in all likelihood would have been unable to surprise the Germans.

On the other hand, the concentration of 30 to 45 divisions in the region of Paris would have dangerously weakened the French between Verdun and Belfort. The French might have won an important battle north of Paris, but they would have lost an equally important battle east of their capital. Nevertheless, the Allies on the Marne did lose an opportunity for shortening the war. In addition to stronger French forces which could have been used, there was also the theoretical possibility of having on the battlefield those English troops which still remained in Great Britain, not to mention the possibility that the British might have entered the war with a few divisons more.

5. Possibilities of Deciding World War I Earlier: The attack on the Dardanelles was one of the best chances of the Allies to win the war at an early date because, if successful, it would have made possible the supplying of Russia and moreover strong Allied operations in the Balkans against Austria. As it is well known, the attack against the Dardanelles failed because: (a.) no surprise was achieved and (b.) no strong forces were used. This example is therefore one of the best arguments for General Erfurth's doctrine of surprise. Incidentally, is must be noted that the Dardanelles enterprise was opposed by the British General Staff as a violation of the principle of concentration. The Allied victory in the war was certainly delayed by the refusal of orthodox soldiers to use available military strength against secondary enemies so long as the Allied armies were not strong enough to tackle Germany herself.

6. Leadership Complex: This opinion is, however, questionable. It may be difficult to decide whether military leadership has become more "difficult", yet there is no doubt at all that it has become more complex. A modern commander has to concern himself with numerous complicated problems of which his forerunners had no idea, and there is not a single instance to show that his task has become easier. A modern general must have an encyclopedic knowledge of modern industry, transportation, economics, sociology, etc. which in former times was certainly not required. To the end of the 18th century, a military commander did not even need a general staff and could issue orders "on sight". At present, he relies on a whole academy of scientifically

trained officers and the general staff has still a tendency to grow. The complexity of modern warfare has given rise to a strong military bureaucracy which, though indispensable, in turn increases the difficulties of command. The "decline" of generalship must partly be attributed to the complexity of modern war.

7. Fantastic Figures: It must again be pointed out that this figure *is* fantastic. There will be available rarely enough means of transport for the concentration of such a force. Neither can such a force be moved secretly, nor with appropriate speed, so that "concentration of 20 corps" and "surprise" are incompatible notions. For all practical purposes, the rule should read as follows: Attack with the maximum of force which you can quickly and secretly transport. There is an optimum size for an attacking force which is a product of, or a compromise between, transport capacity, maneuvering space, fire power, mobility and secrecy. Fire superiority is a relative term and dependent upon the enemy's fire power at the point of attack.

8. Value of Terrain: This statement certainly requires qualification. The value of terrain is not equal everywhere; on the contrary, there is terrain, the conquest of which has decisive importance. Erfurth's opinion is entirely justified in the case of, comparatively speaking, useless terrain. Falkenhayn could indeed have abandoned parts of conquered Belgium terrain and thereby have improved his position. The Russians, repeatedly in their history, relinquished vast territory without impairing their situation, while retreats in the desert usually even improve the situation of the retreating army (shortening of supply lines).

Yet it is entirely different with other kinds of terrain. The French in 1914, abandoned the iron ore mines of Briey and Longwy and this turned out to be one of the major causes why Germany could maintain her military strength for four years, while France had difficulties in equipping her army. It is also obvious that the loss of Paris, of the use of the Suez Canal and the Caucaus was of a decisive nature for France, Great Britain and Russia respectively, but not the loss of Arras, of El Alamein or of Odessa. To be sure, the main goal in war is the destruction of the enemy army and not the conquest of territory. Yet the strength of the enemy army is dependent upon some parts of territory, the loss of which may have the same effect as the defeat of the enemy in open battle.

VII

Surprise, War of Position; Attack

$\blacksquare$URING World War I, both sides
tried to overcome the war of position and to restore the war of
movement. In the first years of this struggle, the importance
of terrain was overstressed. Consequently, it was never attempted to regain liberty of movement by voluntary retreats.
The resumption of the war of movement was chiefly attempted
by a break-through of enemy fronts. The break-through, in
turn, required tactical victory. In the course of this war tactical
victories were often won and appropriate methods had been
developed to master the intricate tactical problems of modern
war. Yet this was only the first step. The second step, by
far the more important, was to find a method of developing
tactical into strategic success. This proved to be an extremely
difficult task which was accomplished only under exceptionally
favorable conditions.

Imposed by particular conditions of the war of position,
preparations for attack were frequently prematurely discovered
by the opponent; attacks seldom came unexpectedly. The selection of the point of attack was usually conditioned by the
situation in general and by the shape of the front in particular.
This is especially true of the offensive projects of the Entente
which usually could be deduced beforehand. The Central
Powers had the advantage of inner lines and were therefore
in a better position to surprise their opponents since they had
a certain liberty of choice where to strike. A central position
may be an advantage at the beginning of a war because it facilitates the formation of a center of gravity; in a war of
position, it also facilitates strategic surprise.

In the first years of World War I, the Central Powers took

full advantage of inner lines and attacked on various fronts. They lost the advantage of the central position during the last year of that conflict. After fighting had ceased on the eastern front, Germany and Austria were left only with the alternate choice of attacking either in France or in Italy. The conditions of the Italian front were not altogether favorable for large scale operations. Consequently, the big German offensive during the first part of 1918 was not unexpected by the French and British. The Germans could therefore accomplish only tactical surprise, and tried to keep secret the strength of their offensive, the exact point of attack and the time of its start.

To screen the preparations for a big offensive is much more difficult in a war of position than in a war of movement. The front lines are very close together and the intelligence service finds many indications which reveal any kind of unusual activity, however well hidden. Since the secrecy of offensive preparations is a dubious affair, surprise should have been attempted by speeding up the execution of the offensive plan. But speed was made very difficult by the fact that frontal attacks against a modern defensive system which is equipped with most powerful and numerous defensive weapons, requires an immense amount of military strength. Numerous units and immense quantities of weapons must be brought to the point of attack and be deployed before the operation. This preparation lasts, of course, for a considerable period. Thorough preparation and speed exclude each other.

Surprise Important in Break-throughs

We shall discuss a few examples from World War I and examine the importance of surprise for break-through operations in a war of position. We shall also examine whether Clausewitz's principle to utilize surprise for gaining relative superiority at the decisive point was followed as it should have been.

The offensive methods employed by the French during the winter battle in the Champagne (February to March, 1915) show many deficiencies which are characteristic of World War I methods. The greatest deficiency was the complete lack of any kind of surprise. Already at the end of December, 1914, the German Third Army reported that a French offensive in the

Champagne was imminent. These reports were confirmed by secret agents. The French were as yet unexperienced in the subtle art of camouflaging military preparations. They were extremely active in the sectors where they intended to attack and openly built up their assault positions. Their intentions were betrayed to the Germans by visible lively activity in the French trenches. Moreover, the French General Staff hoped by several partial attacks to exhaust the Germans before the beginning of the main operation. This tactic, of course, only warned the Germans who finally knew everything about the French plan, including the date of attack. The result of the offensive was necessarily disappointing for the military leaders of the Entente. After the failure of the first onslaught, the battle degenerated into protracted and inconclusive fighting. The French maintained a heavy artillery fire against the German positions and launched many smaller attacks by day as well as by night in the vain hope of achieving a break-through.

The course of this offensive suggested that any offensive should be concentrated into one main effort and that the success of an offensive operation is dependent upon speed and the power of the first blow. Frontal attacks require a very substantial superiority on the part of the attacker. If numerical superiority cannot be established, the offensive peters out into successive blows which become increasingly weaker without yielding any appreciable result. Victory at the decisive point alone is important and compensates for any losses which may occur on secondary fronts. Conseqently, the fronts where no decisions are being sought, should be manned with a minimum of force[1]. Everything has to be subordinated to the intention of bringing "the maximum of force into battle" at the decisive point. It is a law that heavy blows must be concentrated in space and time. All the advantages of surprise are sacrificed if one attempts to reach victory not by one big blow, but by several simultaneous and successive actions. An insufficient effort not only leads to failure, but usually to damage (Clausewitz). An offensive which has been stopped can rarely be started again.

Attack! Attack! Attack!

The French generalissimo took these lessons into account, when he launched his next offensive (spring battle in Artois, 1915). He prescribed that the attack should be continued without respite until the objective was reached. Reinforcements were to be continuously brought up to the first lines. In the battle of Artois, the Entente used superior forces at the decisive point at the same time and for one single operation. But the question must be asked whether they also brought the maximum of numerical force into battle. The answer is a clear negative. Clausewitz's "first principle of strategy" was not adhered to by the High Command of the Allies.

Between May 9 and June 18, 33 infantry divisions of the British First Army and the French Tenth Army tried in vain to drive 20 German infantry divisions from their positions. Looking at the relation of total infantry strength on the entire western theatre of war, it appears that the Allies in June 1915, had altogether a superiority of around 600 battalions. They were therefore much stronger than the German army. If they had complied with the doctrine of Clausewitz, they would have concentrated far greater forces for their offensive in Artois. In this case, the Germans probably would have been unable to prevent a break-through of their lines because even with, comparatively speaking, the small forces which the Allies actually led into combat, the Allies succeeded in opening a gap of four miles in the German front. They also took a large part of the Loretto Hill. The Germans were thus confronted by a serious crisis.

These initial successes of the Entente were largely due to the surprise which this time the French had been able to accomplish. Their troops had been drawn up so skillfully that the Germans did not realize the impending danger. Fire-preparation had been compressed into a few hours. Repeated intervals in the heavy artillery fire deceived the Germans about the time of the assault. When the operation finally started, the German command and troops were caught by surprise.

On the contrary, the preparations of the British did not remain hidden from the Germans. They deployed so openly that the "German flyers had almost an exact blue-print of the offensive the British were preparing" (Krafft von Dellmensingen.) No wonder that the British attack failed on the entire line.

Envelopment Should Have Been Easy

On the whole, the Allied offensive was a failure, although the Allies had many advantages on their side and the shape of the German line would have made an envelopment comparatively easy. Surprise and superiority made initial successes possible. But the battle did not develop into a decisive victory, chiefly because coordination and cooperation between the separate units of the Allied forces were deficient. To overcome the tenacious defense of the German troops, who continued to resist even in the most desperate situations, a greater numerical superiority than the Allies actually mustered at the beginning of the battle would have been necessary.

But the military leaders of the Entente still were far from grasping the essential problem. In their next big offensive (autumn battle in Artois and in the Champagne) they attempted to break the German lines by an artillery preparation of unprecedented intensity. The French High Command hoped to break German resistance by a mass-fire of many days for which immense quantities of ammunition had been made ready. They did not bother about surprise. In the offensive sector, the French had brought up their first trenches as near to the German lines as possible. The assault trenches were considerably lengthened and increased. Precautions were taken for the assembly of large forces. All these preparations were, of course, easily discovered by German flyers. Their reports enabled the German Command to forecast correctly the details of the French offensive.

The British, on the other hand, had in the meantime learned the rudiments of the art of camouflage. Though their preparations in Artois were similar to those of the French in the Champagne, it was much more difficult to deduce their true intentions.

The double offensive of the Entente aimed at a strategic break-through. It was undertaken on a sufficiently broad front and with strong force. In addition, the conditions on the side of the defender favored the plans of the Allies, for the German High Command was not prepared for the Franco-British offensive. Up to the last moment, General von Falkenhayn refused to believe in a serious attempt at a break-through, although the Allies had not at all concealed their intentions and while the commanders of the threatened German armies had repeatedly asked for reinforcements in order to forestall the imminent danger. Falkenhayn was convinced that the enemy was merely feinting. Even the intense Allied artillery preparation and the increase of air activity could not shake his belief. Falkenhayn rated the moral power of the Allies, and particularly of the French, as poor and did not consider them capable of a strong military effort. His attitude is an impressive example of the frequent incredulity of senior commanders with respect to justified warnings of subordinate officers.

Risk in Denying the Obvious

As a result, the enemy achieved a surprise which he had taken no trouble to prepare. The preparatory artillery fire started on September 22. But only on September 25, when the German Third and Sixth Army had reported the launching of an enemy offensive, did General von Falkenhayn cease to deny the obvious. The seriousness of the situation was no longer doubtful. Few reserves were available and they were far from the menaced fronts. It was therefore highly questionable whether the enemy offensive could be stopped. Falkenhayn, however, was lucky because some German forces returning from the eastern front arrived in Belgium in time to bolster the weak German defenses. But even with these reinforcements, there was a considerable danger not only that the German defenders would be pushed back for some miles, but that their lines would be completely crushed. The numerical superiority of the attacker should have sufficed for an important victory.

Although the importance of the surprise factor was considerable in all Allied offensives in 1915, the Allies, astonishingly enough, neglected it in their operations during 1916 and 1917. The French generalissimo thought that the maximum of material force, in particular that of artillery fire, applied on a front as broad as possible was the surest way to victory. In addition, the importance of neutralizing or destroying the enemy's reserves was recognized. The Allies no longer believed in the possibility of achieving a break-through by one single operation, but thought that it required several successive offensives. With painful efforts and an immense amount of work and material, the western powers through many months systematically prepared the Battle of the Somme. They staked everything on an overwhelming artillery assault and entirely disregarded the element of surprise. Consequently, the Germans had sufficient advance knowledge of the coming Franco-British attack.

By May 26, 1916, the commander of the German Second Army had gained the impression that the British were preparing an offensive north of the Somme. On June 2 the same Army reported the aggravation of the situation on its right flank. A big British offensive seemed to be impending. During the course of June it became apparent that the French were preparing to participate with considerable force in the British offensive, despite the still raging Battle of Verdun which tied up strong French forces. By the middle of June it was definitely established that the French had taken over a part of the British front north of the Somme.

It is hard to explain why General von Falkenhayn did not sufficiently reinforce the threatened front, especially since enough reserves were available for strengthening the Second Army. General van Falkenhayn made a very economical use of the German reserves before and during the Battle of the Somme, possibly because he planned to decide the war in the west by a German counter-offensive after the British had exhausted themselves by the Somme offensive. He was also thrifty, because the German reserves had been reduced by the Battle of Verdun and by General Brussilov's offensive on the Russian front. This scarcity of reserves may be the main reason why the German High Command did not take appropriate measures to transform the Battle of the Somme into a German victory.

Better Fighting Than Leadership

The Allies began their offensive with a preparatory artillery assault of seven days. This effort dispelled any doubts about the violence of the impending storm, but it did not change Falkenhayn's dispositions. When on July 1 the Franco-British attack broke only seven German divisions, already reduced by the Allied artillery assault, faced fourteen British and five French divisions. The Allied offensive was thus undertaken under particularly favorable circumstances, chiefly because the

German defenders had failed to take the necessary precautionary measures and to reinforce the menaced sector of their front in time. Nevertheless, the western powers did not achieve the coveted break-through. But this result must be ascribed less to the skill of the German leadership than to the fighting qualities of the German troops.

Every subsequent Allied offensive in 1917 was planned according to the pattern of the Battle of the Somme which was the first battle of matériel in history. Summarizing the lessons of the Battle of the Somme, the French *Grand Quartier General* acknowledged the importance of surprising the enemy by the first blows of an offensive. This sound principle was, however, not utilized when the offensives of 1917 were being planned. Perhaps, the French did not properly understand the conditions necessary for strategic surprise. They did not believe in the chances of an offensive without an artillery preparation of several days, though obviously the artillery assault served as a warning signal for the opponent and precluded any real surprise.

Shortly before the start of the French offensive in the spring of 1917, General Nivelle became French generalissimo. He was little favored by luck. First of all, the weather upset his calculations. His artillery preparations of seven days had to be prolonged, because storm, rain and snow made exact fire impossible. The French infantry attack did not begin on April 12, as originally intended, but on April 14.

The Germans had known of the impending French offensive since the middle of February. In the course of March, photographic reconnaissance showed many changes in the French positions in front of the German Third and Seventh Army which indicated offensive intentions on the part of the French. Prisoners confirmed these suspicions. On April 4, during an attack northwest of Heims, important documents were captured which contained exact information of the preparations for an offensive on the Aisne. Some months previous, on December 16, 1916, a new French regulation on offensive tactics had also been captured by the Germans who therefore knew everything about the French methods. Thus, the Germans had enough time and opportunity to make thorough defensive preparations.

Nivelle's offensive ended in a serious French defeat. Many

reasons have been advanced for Nivelle's failure. But all critics are agreed that its essential cause was the complete lack of surprise.

The British offensive around Arras which took place almost at the same time was not more successful. Also in this case, the Germans had advance knowledge of the British intentions. They rightly deduced the exact location of the British attack and could consequently take all necessary precautions.

Matériel as a Factor

The concept of the battle of matériel is to defeat the opponent by crushing material superiority without relying on generalship. It found its extreme expression in the British offensive in Flanders in the summer and fall of 1917. The war industries of the western powers and the United States had mobilized to their full capacity to crush German resistance. In the second half of June, 1917, the German command expected a big British offensive in Flanders. The Germans also knew against which sector of their positions the onslaught would be directed. They lacked only knowledge of the date of the British attack, but the British artillery preparations did not fail to provide them with this bit of important information. The British bombardment lasted from July 22 to 31. The subsequent British attack yielded only moderate results which, despite continuous and repeated efforts and attacks of the majority of the engaged British formations, could not be improved. By August 25 the first round of the gigantic struggle came to a standstill.

Altogether the great Battle of Flanders raged more than one hundred days. It only confirmed the former experience that a break-through either succeeds quickly or never.

After the failure of these offensives, the Allies adopted a new theory, according to which a gigantic single blow was to be replaced by continuous partial attacks with limited objectives. It should have been clear, however, that such technique could not yield important results. The new doctrine was in flagrant contradiction of Clausewitz's principle that all forces which are earmarked and available for one strategic purpose, should be used simultaneously. The idea of a continuous battle of attrition in Flanders and on the Somme did not provide a solution for the tactical difficulties of the break-through.

The numerous Allied offensives until the Battle of Flanders conclusively proved the indispensability of surprise. Surprise and concentration are, and remain, the main conditions for any tactical and strategical success. The break-through in the war of position is undoubtedly the most difficult form of attack. It cannot be accomplished without surprise, the purpose of which is to prevent the defender from organizing his defenses and bringing up his reserves. If the offensive fails in its initial phases, its continuation against an alert and warned enemy has not the slightest chance. Up to the Battle of Flanders in 1917 the western powers had found no solution for the difficult task of breaking through a front defended with modern weapons.

The German military leaders merit the credit of having developed an efficient method of attack in the war of position. For them, surprise was the starting point of all their planning.

Surprise in Offensive Technique

In a small engagement near Vailly on October 31, 1914, and on November 2 near Soupir, both of which had only local importance, the Germans made their first experiments for developing appropriate offensive methods. The same technique was later employed in the Battle of Soissons during January, 1915. The methods of Vailly, Soupir and Soissons were improved by the Germans and became the basis of all their later break-through operations. The essential idea was to surprise the enemy. The German technique was always effective, provided the enemy had been surprised. On the contrary, it always failed when surprise could not be accomplished and when the enemy had been able to take timely precautions. Surprise, it cannot longer be doubted, is the condition *sine qua non* of any offensive technique.

The Russians by April 12, 1915, had already rather accurate information about the Austro-German preparations for an attack in the area of Gorlice. They believed the Germans would bring up strong reinforcements to counter the Russian offensive in the Carpathians. They had also gathered indications of a coming German attack against the center of the Russian Third Army which, if successful, would hit the right flank of those Russian units which had advanced beyond the ridge of the Carpathians. The attack of Gorlice-Tarnov was therefore not a complete surprise, although the Russians ignored one essential point: the participation of German units in the operation. Curiously enough, the Russians despite their knowledge and the increasing amount of incoming information, did nothing to strengthen their menaced front.

Already in 1914, the Russian secret service functioned poorly. For instance, the shifting of an entire German army from southern Poland to the vicinity of Thorn remained unnoticed. But in the spring of 1915 the performance of the Russian secret service was even worse. The Russian High Command failed to learn to which sector of the eastern front the German forces had been transported from the west. They received many contradictory reports of the location of these German units and were therefore unable to gain a reliable picture.

The Germans, of course, had spared no efforts to confuse the Russians. They circulated false information of strong German concentrations in East Prussia. In addition, they skillfully screened their railway transports from the west. The three railroads to Eastern Prussia were crowded with numerous trains. The troops which were to go to eastern Galicia were first transported on the railroads leading to East Prussia; their trains were re-directed to Galicia only from the most advanced railroad junctions. The assembly on the Galician front was made in such a way that Russian air reconnaissance did not gather any information. German officers who reconnoitered the enemy positions wore Austrian uniforms.

In contrast to the technique of the western powers, the German artillery preparation was compressed within a few hours. The leader of the Russian Third Army realized the imminence of a strong attack on his forces only a very short time before the attack actually began. (May 1, 1915). On the morning of the next day, he received some reinforcements. They were not sufficient to prevent the collapse of his front. Part. of the reinforcements arrived too late.

Verdun Attack Belated

The German attack on Verdun in February, 1916, was strangely influenced by the element of surprise. For the first time during the war, multiple preparations for a difficult offensive had been concealed from the enemy; in particular the concentration of large artillery forces and of an immense quantity of ammunition. The importance of secrecy had been strongly emphasized by the German High Command and every detail was carried out as secretly as possible. In order to deceive the enemy, the Germans prepared sham attacks on several other sectors of the western front.

These precautions were effective. If the Germans had really attacked on February 12, as it was originally intended, they would have encountered an incompletely prepared opponent. The French on the afternoon of February 10 received a report from a "very reliable source" announcing the German offensive. Within two days the menaced front of Verdun could not be reinforced. On February 12, the positions around Verdun were held only by five French divisions. One of the most important sectors of this front was defended by a wholly insufficient force; one division approached the front, but was still lagging far behind. Against this weakly defended sector alone, the Germans had concentrated seven and one-half infantry divisions, six of which had just arrived at the front.

All conditions seemed to be favorable for the German offensive against Verdun. Yet the weather came to the assistance of the French. Visibility was impaired by torrential rains and thick fog. The offensive, at first planned as a lightning attack, was postponed for one day. The weather did not improve and the offensive finally started on February 21. In this period, the French were able to make up for all the deficiencies of their defense organization. Moreover, they received additional information of the German plan and could therefore take all necessary measures. The defenders of Verdun on February 21 were ready for the German attack.

The postponement of the German offensive against Verdun proved to be fatal. The question has often been discussed whether this postponement was really unavoidable. Opinions are divided. But even assuming that as a consequence of bad weather effective artillery preparation was out of question, it is certainly hard to approve the decision to wait passively for ten long days and then to launch the offensive in rigorously the same disposition, with the same strength and according to the same plan as that upon which it was to be started ten days before.

Surprise cannot be accomplished after so long a delay. Yet

the success of the Verdun offensive was dependent upon initial surprise and extreme speed. The German High Command could not expect that the French would remain inactive during ten long days and do nothing to strengthen their defense[2]. Consequently, the attacker had to do everything possible to increase the power of his own attack. If this was not practical, there remained no other alternative but to renounce the whole enterprise. To be sure, this would have been an extremely difficult decision, but it was preferable to the useless expenditure of valuable strength upon an impossible task. The long battle of Verdun only confirmed the old experience that a break-through operation which fails at the start, might better be discontinued.

From their own and from the experience of the Allies the German leaders had concluded that the time of artillery preparation of an offensive should be still further shortened, if surprise was to be accomplished. The preparation for the Battle of Verdun began only a few hours before the attack was launched. The Central Powers steadily improved their artillery technique. Their later offensives were characterized by artillery preparation in minimum time which was supplemented by many tricks to deceive the enemy. This improved technique led to the victories in the fall of 1917 in Italy and in the first half of 1918 in France.

Cadorna's Theory of Caporetto

The question whether the Italian defeat at Karfeit (Caporetto) was the result of successful surprise has been widely discussed. It is controversial whether the Austro-German offensive on the Isonzo in 1917 began with strategic or only a tactical surprise. General Cadorna, then Italian generalissimo, ascribes the collapse of his army less to the efficiency of the attacker than to the poor morale of the Italians. There is little doubt that the Italians themselves contributed to their defeat, quite in accordance with Schlieffen's doctrine relating to the necessary conditions for a battle of annihilation. It is also true that many special circumstances favored the success on the Isonzo. The German attack began at the worst possible moment for the Italians. Besides, the Germans counted upon the fact that the fog which at that season prevails in the higher altitudes would prevent the Italians from observing the activity in the valleys. This assumption proved to be correct. Merit and luck on the part of the attacker paralleled weakness on the part of the defender.

The Battle of Karfreit is a classical example of Clausewitz's assertion that surprise may have independent intellectual effects beyond its purely military consequences. Many Italian units fought with great bravery. Nevertheless, confusion and lack of courage quickly infected the bulk of the Italian army and caused its virtual disintegration[3]. This twelfth battle of the Isonzo also proved Clausewitz's tenet: "Only he can surprise who imposes his law on the enemy." The Austro-German armies possessed the initiative throughout the entire battle. The Italians were unable to liberate themselves from their intellectual subjection to the enemy's measures and to regain their physical liberty of movement and decision.

In the preparation of the German offensive in March, 1918, the experiences of the Battle of Karfreit and of the tank battle of Cambrai in November and December, 1917, were taken into account. The German counter-attack of November 30, 1917, near Cambrai had been successful chiefly because the Germans were forced to compress their preparations within five to six days. Hence the preparations for the great offensive in March, 1918, were reduced to the extreme minimum. In the meantime the German Captain, Pulkowski, had invented an artillery technique which made it possible to begin directly with destruction-fire without previous range testing. This invention seemed to be the "lacking keystone for an effective system of surprise" (General von Kuhl). In addition, every precaution was taken to conceal from the enemy preparations for the offensive. Confusion and deception were systematically applied in most minute detail. Still the enemy was not entirely fooled. After the Russian collapse, the military and political leaders of the Entente counted firmly upon an energetic German attempt to win the war before the American army could intervene on the European battlefields. During the winter months, the tension in Paris grew constantly. The French press conjectured upon the direction and strength of the expected German attack.

Haig Expected Attack

The German High Command did everything possible to screen its projects. A plan of deception was drawn up for the entire western front in order to make the Allies believe in a German offensive between Rheims and the Argonne, or in the vicinity of Verdun and to reassure them of the safety of the British sector[4]. Nevertheless, Field Marshal Haig realized soon enough that the main German effort would be directed against his own front. As early as March 2, he expressed this opinion to the commanders of the different British armies. The presence in front of the British lines of the German Generals von Hutier and von Bulow, both reputed to be offensive specialists, confirmed Haig. On the other hand, extensive preparation behind the German lines in the Champagne suggested an offensive in that area. General Pétain steadfastedly believed that the Germans would concentrate their main blow against the French lines. However, shortly before the German offensive, the British came into possession of reliable information. Their secret service and their air reconnaissance did good work. The depositions of prisoners, and deserters of Alastian and Polish origin, removed the last doubts. It only remained dubious whether the German attack on the British lines would not be supplemented by another operation, possibly in the Champagne.

British military historians bared many different reasons for the severe British defeat in March, 1918, such as insufficient numerical strength of the British positions. The commander of the British Fifth Army also lacked reserves. One British corps had retreated without any apparent reason because its commander had interpreted his orders erroneously. Indeed, there is little doubt that British generalship assisted the German army and made many precious contributions to the German victory[5].

Yet the surprise which was successfully effected by the Germans must be considered as the essential factor of that victory. Since October-November, 1914, that is to say, after the first Battle of Ypres, the British had fought no defensive battle. They still clung to their outmoded rigid linear-defense system and were being thoroughly taken aback by the newly developed efficient German offensive technique. Churchill was entirely right when he pointed out that the British were being surprised by the violence, the extent and the strength of the German attack. This explains the enormous intellectual consequences which followed the German blow and which almost paralyzed the resistance of the British Fifth Army. But chance also intervened to the disadvantage of the British. The morning of March 21, 1918, was particularly foggy. The British troops were practically blindfolded for a long time and were unable to use the most important defensive weapon in their possession, the machine gun. Chance thus made the German assault technique much more effective than could ever have been foreseen.

The German March offensive had, however, one particular weakness: the Germans attacked at only one sector. Deceptive information, sham movements and other ruses could not divert the Allied reserves, let alone neutralize them. In order to prevent the enemy reserves from intervening in the battle, they had to be pinned down by strong secondary attacks on distant fronts. Whether forces could have been made available for such a purpose, is another question. Yet the previous offensives of the Entente showed that even a successful break-through cannot strategically be exploited unless the enemy-reserves are neutralized. A break-through attempt against the center of a broad front is the most difficult of all attacks, since the defender can bring up his reserves from both sides and thus compensate for the numerical superiority of the attacker before the decision has fallen. Only a very heavy numerical superiority can counterbalance this advantage for the defender. The German offensive gained considerable initial successes, but its strong power was prematurely exhausted.

Allies' Initial Surprise

The Allies accomplished their first surprise in November 1917, when the British unexpectedly attacked on a quiet front. A new technique of attack was the main feature of the British success near Cambrai. For the first time, the infantry assault was not prepared by artillery, but by tanks, which also for the first time were used in considerable quantity. The attack broke with a suddenness hitherto unknown. The technique of Cambrai was refined and used in all later offensive and counter-offensive operations of the Entente. The tank provided the western powers with an offensive weapon superior to anything the Germans had developed up to the end of the war.

The Franco-American counter-offensive of July 18, 1918,

and the Franco-British attack of August 8, 1918, did not surprise the German soldiers on the battlefield, but the German High Command. This must be emphasized if the right conclusions are to be drawn from these operations. Before July 1918, the Germans already had been told by reliable agents and deserters of the presence of strong enemy concentrations in the forest of Villers-Cotterets. They were specifically warned that an enemy-attack between the Aisne and the Marne was imminent. The German troops did everything to improve their defenses. The High Command expected an Allied offensive by July 15. When this offensive failed to materialize it was assumed that, as a consequence of the then proceeding German offensive on both sides of Rheims, the Allies had no force available for this operation. This optimism was not shared by the troops of the menaced front who were ready for the enemy when he attacked on July 18; as ready as was possible in the weak German positions and with the insufficient strength of their garrisons.

Again the German troops reported about enemy offensive preparations at the beginning of August, 1918. On August 3 pronounced sound of motors in movement were noticed which disclosed the imminence of an enemy tank attack from the region of Villers-Bretonneux. These reports were laid to imagination and nerves. Nothing was done to improve the German tank defenses in that sector.

A German flyer on August 6 discovered about one hundred tanks in front of the German Second Army. The commander of this army received this information from his superior authorities, although, characteristically, without comment. The German High Command, the commander of the army group and even the commander of the Second Army did not believe in the possibility of a strong enemy offensive until on August 8 a gigantic blow smashed the front of the Second Army[6].

This strategic surprise was in part due to the enemy's mastery of the air. Nevertheless, the German High Command lacked perspicacity. They should have become suspicious after one hundred tanks had been reported near the flank of the Second Army and after two Canadian divisions had disappeared without trace from a position where they had fought for only a very short time.

The troops themselves were surprised by the Allied offensive technique. Strangely enough, the troops of the Second Army had never been informed of the experience resulting from the Battle of Cambrai and the recent battle of July 18, 1918 west of Soissons. The German High Command had not taken pains to tell the troops what to do in case the enemy attacked with tanks and without artillery preparation. It must be admitted, however, that they could not provide the troops with efficient means of counter-technique. It was impossible to furnish effective anti-tank weapons to the troops. And no other expedient would have been effective.

NOTES, CHAPTER VII

1. Fronts and Force: This statement is correct in case there is no doubt which front is to be considered as the main front. One should not forget, however, that the earth is round and that "every road leads to Rome". It is quite possible that the enemy takes advantage of the subtle destinction between primary and secondary fronts and considers a front which we fancy to be of secondary importance as a primary front. Napoleon considered Spain as a secondary front; the collapse of Germany in 1918 began in Palestine.

In a great war, there are many decisive points, hence many primary and only few secondary fronts. The difficulty of applying the principle of concentration is caused just by this fact: It is almost impossible to make a neat distinction between primary and secondary fronts. One has to cover all decisive points and that may practically mean dispersion of force. It is strange that Erfurth does not realize that strategic surprise is very often the result of choosing that front which the enemy considers as secondary as one's primary front of attack. Throughout history, British strategy excelled in this kind of surprise strategy, while the continental armies usually had very rigid and narrow notions about the location of the primary front. In World War I, for instance, the Germans as well as the Entente would have had good possibilities for striking decisive blows in and through Italy. Yet neither side did, despite Caporetto which had demonstrated the strategic potentialities of the Italian front.

2. Verdun: The idea of launching a surprise attack against one of the strongest fortifications in the world sounds strange indeed. Such an attack may have been possible if the Germans, as in 1940 at Eben Emael had used new tactics and techniques. But at Verdun, the German attack, even under the most favorable circumstances, would have lasted a considerable period of time, so that the French probably would have been able to bring up their reserves at any rate. Erfurth fails to point out that the main purpose of the Verdun offensive was to bleed the French army white, and that therefore the Germans had

a certain interest in prolonging the battle. This example shows that surprise should not be limited to the purely strategic field, but that in principle every strategic surprise should be combined with tactical and technical surprises. The enemy must be surprised not only by the "where?" and "when?" but also by the "how?".

3. Surprise at Caporetto: The Battle of Caporetto is a remarkable example of surprise operations. The Italian army had suffered heavy losses in their previous offensive on the Isonzo. Therefore, their units comprised many young and unexperienced recruits. In addition, the hazard of the previous battle had left the Italians in rather unfavorable and vulnerable positions. The Austro-German armies launched their attack against the weakest parts of the Italian front. The Italians were not prepared for an attack by the best German shock troops and had expected merely an attack from the Austrians. Moreover, the attacker employed new tactics. The main blows were delivered is the valleys, instead of across the mountains, as it was the tradition of mountain warfare. A very effective kind of artillery preparation (gas-shells) was applied, a surprise on the Italian front. Besides, the attacker was favored by fog.

Of course, the Italians themselves contributed to their own defeat. One of the principal Italian commanders had been ill for several days and was therefore unable to supervise the defense preparations. Due to a misunderstanding, the Italian artillery held back its fire until it was too late. The numerous Italian recruits became panicky when, unexpectedly, they were attacked by gas. Had the Italians not spent a large part of their striking power in a dozen unsuccessful offensives on the Isonzo, the moral resistance of their troops would have been considerably stronger.

Of equal importance was the panic which seized the Italian High Command when they learned that one of the positions which they considered as vital (Monte Maggiore) had fallen. When General Cadorna received news of the fall of Monte Maggiore, he immediately ordered the retreat behind the Tagliamento and even began to make preparations for a retreat across the Piave. There is little doubt that he attached too great an importance to Monte Maggiore. The Italians could have fought on in their positions without this little fort.

Thus the most important effect of successful surprise is the disorganization of the enemy command. The High Command loses its control; it ignores the true situation. Orders are no longer transmitted, hence every division or even regiment makes its own decision. Besides, the general tension prevents clear and sober thinking. The degree of the defeat is overestimated and a retreat is ordered, for fear that parts of the army may be cut off and annihilated. The fall of the weak positions sweeps away the strong ones; the strong positions failed to bolster the weak.

4. Von Hutier: The British deduced the location of the German attack from an obituary in a provincial German newspaper which was signed by General von Hutier. The date-line of the obituary also indicated the place of Hutier's command. Since Hutier was the foremost German expert for offensive operations, the British had no difficulty in drawing correct conclusions as to the sector of the German offensive.

5. Uncoordinated Command: The main reason for the German success was the uncoordinated command of the British and French Armies. Pétain and Haig had different strategic conceptions and apprehensions, hence each placed his reserves where he thought he needed them most. The result was that the weakest spot of the entire Allied front—the joint between the French and British—remained virtually unprotected and without reserves.

6. August 8th: The surprise of August 8, 1918 was much more important and far-reaching than would appear from Erfurth's text. As a matter of fact, the German High Command believed that as a consequence of the German spring and summer offensives, the offensive power of the Allies was broken and that for a long time to come they would be unable to resume active warfare.

This dream was definitely shattered on August 8, 1918, the day which Ludendorff christened the "black day of the German Army". He realized that he himself had broken the offensive power of his own army, but not of his enemy. This intellectual surprise was at the bottom of the German capitulation. The surprised Ludendorff had lost his faculty of sober reasoning and was unable to understand how Germany could fight on on the defensive. The top became panicky, and the panic spread all over the country and infected the army.

Erfurth, for reasons of loyalty, cannot write openly and objectively on these events. Had he done so, he could have made clear that surprise has a still greater military importance than his text conveys. The successful surprise of August 8, 1918, spared the Allies at least one further year of war. Space prevents further elaboration on this point. It suffices to emphasize that the general impression, created by numerous incorrect historical accounts, according to which Germany, in November, 1918, was "finished", does not correspond to the facts. The German food supply was improving, the German submarine strength was again increasing, while the Allies were approaching a serious transport crisis. There was no *material* necessity for the Germans to capitulate. With their army and with their munition and food supply, they would have been able to continue the war, at least on the defensive. The main causes of the German collapse were of a psychological nature and the main psychological cause was the surprise bred by a realization that the Allies were not beaten and therefore never could be beaten.

VIII

Surprise, War of Position; Defense

THE possibility of surprising the attacker after he has made his plan clear by his actions is one of the most important advantages of defense, according to Clausewitz. Defensive surprise requires not only a very mobile but an active defense wherever possible. After the beginning of positional warfare in the World War I, defensive battles were conducted in a different form. The defender did not fight, as he should have done, for victory and for the annihilation of the opponent, but merely for his positions.

Defense was rigid and passive. By renouncing mobile and active tactics in defense one did, by the same token, renounce the advantages of surprise. For a long time the Germans clung to the peace time principle that a single line should be occupied and defended. Only gradually and slowly did they overcome this doctrine of rigid defense. After the Battle of the Somme the idea of linear defense was definitely abandoned. Hence forward defense was organized in depth and conducted in a mobile and active way. Defensive tactics again took advantage of the element of surprise.

Yet, as has been pointed out by Liddell Hart, strategic surprise in the defensive was re-discovered only at the end of the war. The main elements of classical strategy, maneuver and movement, were replaced by trench warfare. According to Marshal Pilsudski, a special "trench-psychology" had developed which exercised a strong influence on almost all military leaders in both camps. It is indeed astonishing to see how long a time it took before the strategical concepts of the World War leaders were divested of such errors and reconciled with old and experienced truths. The strange dogma that every position, however unnecessary or unfavorable, should be defended to the very last caused many unnecessary losses and led to many belated evacuations. Heavy fighting for a locality often degenerated into a contest for mere prestige. In this case, sentiment interferes with reason and prevents arriving at appropriate decisions. World War I witnessed numerous examples of this unfortunate strategy. We may only refer to the refusal of the German High Command to evacuate the undefendable arc of Wytschaete in June, 1917. The result was a successful British surprise-attack and bloody as well as useless fighting.

Immobility of the troops and clumsiness of the leaders were the almost natural consequence of the long positional war. The easy expedient of forestalling a strong blow by a timely retreat to rear positions was rarely executed, although by such a surprise move even a thoroughly prepared offensive could have been frustrated. To evade a heavy artillery assault by withdrawing the first lines to positions farther behind seems today a fairly simple device. Yet it was invented only rather recently. In March, 1917, the Germans retreated before an impending strong French offensive which, as a consequence, became a blow at a vacuum. It required a great deal of courage to break with General von Falkenhayn's principle "not to relinquish a single foot of conquered ground." Indeed, the German High Command could not carry out this strategic retreat without encountering very serious objections of a politico-military nature.

Public Opinion Feared

The Italian High Command lacked the necessary boldness for a similar decision, although long before the Austro-German offensive on the Isonzo in October, 1917, in case of attack they intended to abandon their unfavorable positions and to fight the opponent from a stronger defense line. For a long time the Italians hesitated to put their plan into effect. At last it was too late to retreat successfully.

It is today hardly comprehensible why the British did not evade the extremely strong German offensive of March, 1918. When on May 26, 1918, through the deposition of two prisoners, the French were informed of the German offensive against the Chemin des Dames which was to begin two days later, they also considered a voluntary retreat because they were by no means prepared for that battle. This expedient however, was rejected under the pretext that it would endanger near-by positions.

In reality, the French generals were afraid of public opinion, believing that the people would not understand the abandonment without a fight of a position for which the French had made so many bloody sacrifices.[1]

The Poles, at the end of June, 1920, followed this disastrous French example. After Marshal Pilsudski had recognized that the Polish army would not be able to resist the Russian offensive, he recommended a timely and orderly retreat. General Szeptycki, one of Pilsudski's advisors, believed that a defense from prepared Polish positions would be more promising than a retreat into the open rear. Pilsudski finally agreed with him. Like the French at the Chemin des Dames, the Poles remained in their positions although they knew well what they were facing. In both cases this kind of passive defense enabled the attacker to win a considerable victory.

One of Clausewitz's main principles was never to assume a passive attitude, but to attack the front and the flank, even of an offensive enemy. According to Clausewitz, the "offensive defense" should start at the very moment the enemy launches his offensive. In Clausewitz's opinion, it may sometimes be practical to retreat in order to lure the enemy into unfamiliar terrain and then to strike back from every side. Clausewitz would probably have considered the German strategic retreat of March, 1917, as incomplete, since it lacked a strong surprise counterblow against the pursuing enemy.

As a matter of fact, such an operation had been discussed by the German High Command. It was rejected with reasons which certainly are not convincing. The Germans did not propose to destroy the French Army. Their intention was merely "to reach as quickly as possible new positions, to re-group and to make strong reserves available." Gain of valuable time and the evasion of the enemy offensive were thus the main results of this operation. The voluntary retreat of the German army therefore did not serve as a means to render the western front more mobile and active. It must be emphasized that the Germans had effectively camouflaged the preparations for their retreat, although they lasted several weeks. At the last moment, the enemy captured several German orders revealing most important details. For unknown reasons these orders had been forgotten in a German dug-out. But they were found when it was too late to attack the retreating German formations and to interfere with their plan.

No German Counter-Offense

During World War I, the Germans were unable to launch a large scale counter-offensive on the western front. When a big counter-offensive would have been practical, as for instance after the Allied offensives in 1915 and after the Battle of the Somme, sufficient German forces were not available and only a weak counterblow would have been possible. The situation was, however, somewhat different after the failure of Nivelle's spring offensive in 1917 and after the battles of Flanders in the summer and fall of the same year.

After the collapse of Nivelle's offensive, the great moral crisis of the French army would have strongly favored a German counter-stroke. Painlevé, the French Minister of War, observed that the situation would have become extremely critical, had the Germans energetically attacked. The French army was discouraged; its morale was seriously affected. Yet the German intelligence service reported these important facts only after the French High Command had already overcome the moral crisis of its army.[2] It is as yet unknown whether the German High Command had ever envisaged a counter-offensive and, if so, for what reasons this offensive was rejected.

The Germans soon discovered the preparations for the British offensive in Flanders (summer 1917). The General Staff of the army group under the command of Field Marshal Crown Prince Rupprecht discussed the question of a voluntary retreat to new positions prepared in advance. But at the end of June the resolution was taken to accept battle and not to retreat. "With respect to the particular conditions on the Flanders front, a retreat could not offer many advantages. The positions farther back were not yet ready. On the other hand, the German commander considered his present positions strong enough to resist any attack. It appeared, therefore, that the evacuation of the German positions in Flanders would have offered more disadvantages than advantages." It is almost a law that local commanders, particularly in a protracted war of position, object to the evacuation of a well equipped and effectively organized defensive system in exchange for positions farther back, especially if they have reason to believe that these "positions" exist only in theory.

A very strong will on the part of the High Command is necessary to transform passive into active defense. To be sure, the Germans in the summer and autumn of 1917 won a considerable defensive victory in Flanders. But immense German forces were necessary to stop the British offensive, namely 86 divisions, 22 of which were used twice during this battle, and, moreover, the bulk of the German medium and heavy artillery. The question might well be asked whether with the same forces the Germans could not have attained more than the mere passive holding of their lines. If a timely voluntary retreat had been followed up by a strong counter-offensive with the firm intention to crush the enemy, the Germans would have won a much greater success. Only in the last year of the war were similar solutions adopted, in particular by the French and Americans during the Battle of Soissons in July, 1918.

Brussilov's Counter-Offensive

On the eastern front the Germans made frequent use of counter-offensives. Yet it never became necessary to precede counter-offensives by voluntary retreats. Provided the counter-offensive was undertaken with sufficient strength and it began with an effective surprise, it usually led to success. The only exception was the counter-offensive after Brussilov's big offensive in 1916.

The Russian leader in due time recognized the danger of a German counterblow and brought up strong reinforcements to bolster his menaced flank. Besides, the German divisions were prematurely thrown into the battle, in some cases even before their assembly was finished. The Germans were compelled to do so, because the Austrian divisions began to give way. The Austro-German units lacked striking power and hence could not neutralize the Russian reserves. Conditions did not favor this particular counter-attack, which was commanded by General Linsingen.

It was different in the case of Kerensky's offensive in 1917. General Hoffmann, the German commander of the eastern front had foreseen the Russian move, a counter-offensive in the general direction of Lemberg-Tarnopol. At first, things did not develop quite according to plan, since the Russians achieved considerable successes and in the area of Stanislau broke into the Austrian lines. Three German divisions which just arrived from the western front for the counter-offensive against Tarnopol hurried to the assistance of the Austrian army. Finally, Kerensky's offensive was stopped and the Germans launched their long premeditated counter-offensive. The right flank of the Russian offensive formation on July 19, 1917, was broken on a front of thirteen miles. As a result, the entire Russian front collapsed. The German attack on Tarnopol is one of the most brilliant examples of successful counter-offensive. It liberated almost two Austrian provinces from the enemy.

Rewards of Counter-Offensive

Clausewitz's doctrine of active defense maintains its value in the war of position. An effective defense requires continuous movement and repeated surprise. It is never profitable to assume passive attitudes. On the contrary, one should strike surprise blows against the enemy even during defensive operations. A strong counter-offensive is undoubtedly the defender's most efficient means of thwarting the plans of the attacker. Under favorable circumstances, a counter-offensive may lead to a major victory and perhaps to the destruction of the enemy army, a result which passive defense can never attain.

It is therefore not astonishing that Hans Delbrueck considers the counter-offensive or the "defensive-offensive" as the strongest form of modern war. Liddell Hart praises the advantages of a "baited offensive," that is to say, of a combination of offensive operations with defensive tactics. In World War I the "baited offensive" was a very effective method indeed. Its advantages increased in the same degree as the emergence of modern matériel makes other methods more difficult. Its success, however, is dependent upon effectively accomplished initial surprise.[3]

We may be permitted to mention briefly the importance of surprise for virtually all kinds of special operations. The crossing of a river, for instance, will be possible only after the opponent has been surprised, or rather fooled. The larger the river and the more difficult the terrain (steep banks, etc.), the more necessary it is to surprise the enemy. If the opponent realizes our intention to cross the river, severe losses will be the consequence and the crossing may fail. Similarly, crossing of, or attack across, mountains is not practical unless the defender can be surprised or deceived. Since the time of Leonidas, attempts to cross reputedly impassable terrain to get at the enemy's rear are characteristic for mountain warfare. Change of weather, fog, rain and snow often favor attacks in the mountains and may favor the defender to cope with many unexpected situations.[4]

Darkness was always a precious ally of surprise. Night attacks are usually launched for the sake of surprise, but on the whole the difficulties of night operations permit only local engagements. Large scale attacks occur rarely during the night. They are possible, however, if the attacker has already gained a strong moral ascendancy. In a war of position, night operations may be practical on a larger scale. But in a war of movement, darkness should only be utilized for marches and for the approach to the battlefield, while the actual attack should not be launched before dawn. *The German soldier traditionally is not a great admirer of night fighting.* Yet it may safely be predicted that in future night operations will occur more frequently, for darkness is sometimes the only effective protection against modern weapons. Increased night activity would automatically lead to a higher frequency of surprise.[5]

NOTES, CHAPTER VIII

1. Chemin des Dames: The French generals were certainly afraid of public opinion, but the main reason why they did not abandon the Chemin des Dames was the hope that the enemy could be held. Indeed, the Germans would have had difficulties with their offensive, if the French commanding general had not stubbornly stuck to antiquated tactics and refused to adopt modern, more appropriate tactics which, months before had been worked out by the French General Staff and which were most successfully applied six weeks later by the French troops under General Gouraud.

2. Morale: Ancient writers like Frontinus, who have written of surprises and ruses of war, devote much space to ways and means of restoring morale. Pétain's main achievement as French commander-in-chief was that he succeeded in repairing the shaken morale of the French Army. He applied three methods: 1. He remedied abuses, particularly with respect to food, and leave. 2. He made it clear to the troops that he did not intend to sacrifice them in costly and useless offensives, and that he was eager to save as much blood as possible.

3. He restored the self-confidence of the troops by organizing offensives with limited objectives which were bound to be successful, using at the same time these offensives for experimenting with new fighting techniques. It can be seen from this example that an offensive must not always necessarily aim at the total destruction of the enemy. Operations with too ambitious goals very often contribute to one's own weakness rather than to the weakening of the enemy.

3. "Baited Offensive:" One of the few advantages of combined operations is the possibility of staging a "baited offensive". If the attacker makes a successful landing, he can then remain on the defensive. That is to say, he undertakes a strategic offensive, but has a chance to fight, tactically speaking, on the defensive.

4. Natural Obstacles: Natural obstacles of all kinds have offered many promising possibilities for surprise attacks. It is a habit among second-rate soldiers to overrate the difficulties of natural obstacles, while a military genius is usually characterized by his conviction that natural obstacles can be overcome, however difficult and costly it may be. For a military genius there are no "insurmountable" mountains, nor "impassable" rivers. On the contrary, most great captains won impressive victories by attacking at places where their enemies thought that they could never attack.

In modern times, there are few natural obstacles left that an enemy cannot overcome, Disregarding a few exceptions, one can say that military operations have become possible *everywhere*.

However, the former problem of the natural obstacle still exists under the term "transport difficulties". Rivers or deserts are today no longer limiting factors in warfare, yet transport facilities, or rather their lack, are. A modern military operation is considered feasible or not according to the available means of transport. It is obvious that surprise may play a big role with respect to the transport problem. The military genius will find unexpected solutions of difficult transport problems and attack at a place where the enemy does not expect him, or at least not with sufficient force, while the second rate soldier will be hypnotized by transport difficulties and undertake only operations for which he has abundant means of transport.

5. Night operations: At that place, General Erfurth discusses the importance of surprise in "combined operations." He refers to an article by Captain Sorge in "Militaerwissenschaftliche Rundschau," 1938 in which the German attack on the Baltic island of Oesel in 1917 is analyzed. The opinions of both Erfurth and Sorge with respect to combined operations, however, are out of date. It is obvious that surprise is a most important element in any combined operation, as incidentally evidenced by the Battle of Dieppe.

An attack which comes from the sea is by necessity much weaker than defense on the shore, because the defender has stronger fire-power, superior mobility and also usually the mastery of the air. The problem, therefore, is to hit the defender either when he is unprepared or when and where he cannot bring his superiority into play. In addition, the attacker must operate unexpectedly, so that the defender is unable to use the strength he possesses. And finally, the attacker must concentrate a greater military force than the defender is prepared to meet. On the whole, combined operations on a large scale will only be successful if the defender of the attacked coast has been successfully deceived as to the point of attack. It must be added that the emergence of air-borne troops may change the characteristic of combined operations and possibly facilitate them. (Crete. This example is not typical because the British had inferior fire-power). At any rate, it can be said that the traditional opinion, according to which combined operations against strong opposition have little chance of success, is no longer entirely correct.

IX

Surprise Value of New Weapons and Combat Techniques

THERE is one important military principle of almost eternal validity: if, at the beginning of a war, absolute numerical superiority is not obtainable, one should try to be superior at least in *one* important weapon. The immense importance of superiority in modern equipment, aircraft, tanks and, in particular, artillery has been demonstrated by all recent hostilities. It would not be reasonable to expect great differences between the armaments of the major powers. Yet special progress in technical inventions is always possible. During the last war, science offered many assets to the German High Command. Still, the mere existence of new implements of war does not solve all military problems. The art of waiting and using new weapons at the right moment is particularly difficult. A new weapon must be put in use suddenly and in great quantity, nay, in maximum quantity. Otherwise, the surprise of the opponent is neither complete nor decisive. Consequently, one must wait until the new weapon is available in large numbers. But even in this case, its effects will depend upon the absence of any offsetting factors on the enemy side.

Poison gas was used by the Germans as a surprise, although the first gas attack of April, 1915, in the salient of Ypres, served only a modest purpose. On the whole, it was nothing more than an experiment for testing the new weapon. In vain Professor Haber, who is credited with being the inventor of poison-gas, pleaded with the General Staff to hold large forces in reserve for the exploitation of the success which, in his opinion, was sure to come. The commander of the German Fourth Army in whose sector the experiment was to be carried out, also asked General von Falkenhayn for reserves, but only for one division. Even this modest request was flatly rejected. Thus, an especially good chance to achieve a decisive success on the western front was lost, although the opponent had done his share to facilitate German victory. Prisoners and deserters, as well as secret agents who were stationed in Belgium, had informed the Allies of the German preparations. Even the Allied troops in the trenches had acquired similar knowledge. None of these warnings was taken seriously by the Allied general staffs. Hence surprise was accomplished in spite of the betrayal of the German intentions.

The material effects of the German gas-attack were extraordinary. However, its moral effects were still greater, chiefly because the Allied troops lacked anti-gas equipment. In the evening of April 22 a wide gap had been opened in the Allied front. Yet the Germans missed their chance because no German forces were ready for immediate action. Consequently, the German success developed into a conspicuous failure. The Allies gained enough knowledge of the new weapon to organize quickly efficient protective measures. A new weapon can surprise but once. If it is used for the second time the opponent is already more or less ready for it.

The German air raids on England failed similarly. The Germans several times failed to profit from excellent chances which arose as a consequence of German technical progress in the development of aeronautical weapons. In the first two years of World War I British air defenses were poor; Britain was more or less defenseless against German Zeppelin attacks. The German air ships in 1917 were able to fly at an altitude far beyond the reach of British antiaircraft defense. In the fall of 1917, when Britain did not yet have trained night-fighters, the Germans initiated night-bombing. All these different possibilities were not exploited as they could, or should, have been.

Submarines Could Have Won War

The submarine was a weapon which, if correctly used, could have won the war for Germany. At the outbreak of the war, German submarines were the most modern of their kind and the only ones which could be used strategically and as an independent force. Germany's opponents had virtually no anti-submarine defenses. It can hardly longer be doubted that the submarine would have decided the war, had it not been used prematurely. Before a large number of submarines was available, the blockade of Great Britain should not have been started. Having assembled a considerable submarine fleet, every single German submarine should have been thrown into battle at one stroke and with maximum energy. Of course, no political restrictions should have hampered this submarine offensive. In this case, the insufficient British anti-submarine organization would scarcely have been able to prevent an effective, and possibly decisive, blockade of the British Isles.

These theoretical principles sound simple and convincing. They are, however, seldom applied in practice. All new weapons which were invented during World War I were used prematurely and in small quantity. Perhaps human imagination is incapable of forecasting correctly the effects of a new weapon. Usually these effects are exaggerated by those introducing it. One likes to be optimistic.

In a long war, timely changes and incessant improvement of fighting techniques are of extreme importance. The opponent can be fundamentally surprised by new techniques. Novel methods can basically change the course of the war. Consequently, the science of war should never be suppressed; even, or rather particularly in time of war, it should supplement and direct the practice of the battlefield. It is the task of the theorist to understand quickly every novelty and to advise on• their adoption. We have pointed out how long a time it took for the Entente to find an effective defense against German artillery assault. Only by the summer of 1918, had the Italians on the Piave and the French on the Marne abandoned passive for mobile defense.

To the end of the war the Germans were unable to devise an efficient antitank method, though the Entente had committed the error of warning them beforehand of the tank. For the Allies did not wait until they had a sufficient number of tanks available. The famous tank battle of Cambrai, November 20, 1917, had been preceded by many tank-operations; for instance, during the Battle of the Somme in the fall of 1916, later near Arras and on the Aisne in April, 1917, and in October of the same year near Laffaux. The number of tanks employed in the attack increased each time. But at Cambrai the Allies used new technique and replaced their traditional lengthy artillery preparation by a concentrated mass-attack of tanks. This new technique made possible a high degree of surprise and was used for all later Allied offensives after July 18, 1918.

Had the Allies used their new technique with a sufficient number of tanks and supporting troops and not tried it out beforehand with small tank formations and virtually no support from other weapons, they possibly would have been able to win a decisive success at the first stroke. In this case it would have been necessary to postpone the big tank offensive until enough tanks were ready. However this may be, the German High Command had received ample warning of the new weapon and its tactical potentialities. When the first enemy tank appeared on the battlefield, the German High Command was confronted with the alternative of either building tanks in great numbers in order to catch up with the enemy's lead or, if this was not practical, to develop efficient antitank defenses. There was no other possible solution.

Every new weapon is immediately imitated in time of peace by the neighbor; in time of war by the enemy. No country has a monopoly of any weapon. This is a law. No technical advantage lasts for a long period of time.

X

Results and Conclusions

MODERN strategy does not differ fundamentally from the strategy of former times. Count von Schlieffen was justified when he wrote: "The conditions and structure of battle do not change. A battle of annihilation can be fought today according to the same pattern that had been thought out by Hannibal." On the whole, the entire strategical art can be summarized in the old law, that numerical superiority must be concentrated at the decisive point. The only difference in comparison to former periods is that as a consequence of the increased power of defense, a three-fold numerical superiority at the decisive point is by no means too much.

On the contrary, many experts will consider such a superiority as a minimum and all of them will agree that it is better to launch an attack with still heavier odds. The best method is to attack at the decisive point with "everything one has." This advice of Schlieffen's certainly amounts to the rejection of linear strategy. And let there be no doubt: A modern battle must be fought in depth!

The concentration of three-fold superiority at the decisive point is possible only if the enemy is surprised. If the enemy learns of our intentions, or if he is able to make a correct guess, he will take counter-measures and frustrate our plan for battle. The experience of recent wars shows that the chances of attack depend chiefly upon successful surprise. In some way or other the accomplished surprise must paralyze the defender's resistance. Surprise is today more indispensable than ever before. *Every military plan and its execution should be conceived in view of the necessity of surprise.*

Surprise thus appears as the primary objective of military planning. The importance of surprise has often been overlooked.

It was sometimes supposed that surprise could not be prepared but was simply a welcome by-product of other military measures. This opinion has already been refuted by Clausewitz, who particularly opposed the "dark idea" that a surprise attack can be improvised. In reality, strategic surprise is an extremely difficult performance. Secrecy requires painful planning and careful thinking, if all possible leaks are to be closed. If in spite of all endeavours, secrecy is impossible to maintain, speed must be increased to the extreme limit.

The commander who concentrates strong forces for quick and annihilating blows must possess a very strong will. In addition, he must be able to maintain high mobility, A military leader about to surprise his opponent must be able to adapt himself quickly to changing conditions. He also must find new solutions if the operation develops in an unexpected manner. If surprise cannot be accomplished, it is altogether preferable to call off the offensive. A leader who aims at mobility should not be afraid to strain his troops to the limit in order that they may reach the battlefield in time. Many victories were made possible by forced marches. Mobility equals increase in numbers.

Axioms of Martial Operations

Surprise is a necessary element of all military operations, not only of attack but also of defense.

Only a mobile defender can surprise. Schlieffen's doctrine that the defender must constantly move and maneuver if he aims to surprise the attacker was fully confirmed in all recent wars. All great commanders of the past fought their defensive battles actively.

Inversely, success in war depends upon the commander's ability to prevent the enemy from accomplishing his own surprise. Good commanders usually have a particular talent for foreseeing the actions of the enemy. They are good psychologists who can put themselves into the position of their opponent and guess his decisions. A military leader should always carefully inquire whether his acts favor the intentions of the enemy or facilitate their execution.

In peacetime military training the factor of surprise should also gain the attention it actually deserves. Military operations are only too often represented as a mechanical development which is neither materially nor intellectually influenced by surprise. Mobile maneuver-strategy frequently interferes with the intentions of the officers in charge of the maneuver. If the maneuver is planned beforehand, the commanders of the different parties have no liberty left. Of course, the conduct of maneuvers is made considerably more difficult if the commanders are free to do whatever they like and, in particular, to attempt surprises.

Questions to Be Decided

On principle, however, the element of surprise should be taken into account in every maneuver and also in the discussions which usually conclude them. These discussions should clarify the lessons of the maneuver. Therefore, it is pertinent to ask constantly the following questions: Was one party able to effect surprise? How did surprise actually affect the operations of the surprised party? What expedients have been adopted?

As night is usually an element indispensable to surprise, training in marches and deployment must be repeatedly given during the dark hours. *The troops must become accustomed to night operations.* Disengaging and re-grouping of large forces during the night in order to launch an attack at an unexpected point, is a very difficult undertaking which requires much exercise. The German maneuvers before World War I provided for adequate drill for night operations. There is little doubt that an army capable of executing large scale night operations will possess a distinct military advantage and will often surprise its enemies.

It is not enough to pay mere lip-service to surprise. Strong emphasis should be laid upon new tactics, for these offer the best way of achieving surprise. Novel ideas should constantly be tested, and old ideas not always repeated. Theory and practice must cooperate to find fresh ways and means of war.

Ruses As Essentials

Ruses form an essential, if sometimes minor, part of any surprise. This has always been stressed by Clausewitz. Ruses are by no means a weapon exclusively for a weak army. They can also be used to the advantage of the stronger. Nor did they lose their value in the period of mass-armies. A modern war is not like a tourney. The code of honor of feudal times is no longer valid. Every means is permitted which deceives the enemy and induces him to take wrong steps. The lion's bravery and the fox's cleverness must combine to wrest the victory from the enemy.

In mass-warfare, systematic deception and camouflage require a considerable amount of time and strength. Weak means, so-called demonstrations, will make little impression on the enemy. The sham concentrations of strong German formations before the offensive in March, 1918, in France and of the Austro-German troops before the offensive on the Isonzo in the autumn of 1917, are illustrative examples of how the enemy can be deceived.

During World War I many offensives were prematurely betrayed by deserters and prisoners. Important orders and maps showing the dispositions of the troops were frequently captured by the enemy. The frequency of such incidents makes it necessary to adopt preventive remedies. The troops must be educated for secrecy and they must learn to guard important documents very carefully. Every private should know that success in war is dependent upon the maintenance of secrecy. He must know how to behave if, unfortunately, he is taken prisoner. Never should he allow himself to be intimidated and he should know that after the war he will be held responsible if he betrayed military secrets to the enemy.

Recent wars showed that radio sometimes may be the means of betraying important secrets. During World War I, when radio was used for the first time, all belligerents used to broadcast falsified orders in order to deceive the enemy. Before the offensive on the Isonzo a whole net of radio-stations was built in Tyrol to detract the attention of the Italians from the Isonzo to the Tyrolean front. On the eastern front, as we already related, the German army profited from the amateurish way in which the Russians used their radio. The French were also clever at deciphering German orders and actually detected German movements before the Battle of the Marne by radio listening. According to the French Minister of War, Messimy, the chief of the French radio and cipher bureau was a kind of sorcerer who, within the shortest time, discovered some of the deepest German secrets. He was helped in his task by the Germans themselves. Once two German codes fell into the hands of the French, while at another time some German staffs simultaneously broadcast the same text *en clair* and enciphered. Messimy asserts that the services rendered by the French cipher bureau were "*éclatant.*"

Also the British excelled in the art of deciphering. A professor from Edinburgh, A. Ewing, was in charge of this important work for the British Admiralty and became famous in his country. By the end of August, 1914, Russian divers removed the German naval code from the stranded and abandoned cruiser Magdeburg. The code was quickly dispatched to the British Admiralty which profited largely from it.

In the Russo-Polish War radio listening played an important role and often revealed the intentions of the enemy to the last details. The Poles deciphered the Russian orders for the Russian counter-offensive in the Ukraine in May, 1920. In Abyssinia only the Italians profited from the radio messages of the opponent. Marshal Badoglio revealed that the few Abyssinian transmitters were actually more helpful to the Italians than to the Abyssinians. It goes without saying that precautions must be taken against such occurrences. The army whose radio-messages are read by the opponent renounces all chances of surprise, while it offers vast strategic possibilities to the enemy.

It is to be hoped that in future wars, and as a consequence of new weapons, complete and decisive victories will again be possible. New arms and new techniques will certainly give excellent opportunities for good generalship. But the main condition of future victories lies in the restoration of the art of maneuver. Movement makes surprise possible and surprise opens the way for new movements. Surprise is dependent upon secrecy and speed.

Secrecy, speed, movement and surprise are thus the prerequisites of victory. Luck and art must combine to catch the enemy by surprise. In war, the unexpected is the most successful. Thus, surprise is the key to victory.[1]

NOTE, CHAPTER X

1. Five Principles: Fuller mentions five "prerequisites of victory:" security, surprise, mobility, concentration of force and cooperation which, according to him, result in economy of force. "The more force is

economized, the more can be held in reserve and in consequence the higher will be the staying power of the attack". These different principles should be integrated in the simplest way. Fuller thus believes that simplicity is the highest principle of war. Foch's famous *"de quoi s'agit-il??"* is nothing but a different form of the same idea. The principle of surprise closely tallies with this general idea. For this principle essentially says only this: Strike at the enemy where, when and how he does not expect you; strike at weak and unprotected points. War has become a form of gigantic collective jiu-jitsu.